Programming Microsoft Office 365

Covers Microsoft Graph, Office 365 applications, SharePoint Add-ins, Office 365 Groups, and more

Paolo Pialorsi

PUBLISHED BY
Microsoft Press
A division of Microsoft Corporation
One Microsoft Way
Redmond, Washington 98052-6399

Library of Congress Control Number: 2015938171
ISBN: 978-1-5093-0091-4

Printed and bound in the United States of America.

First Printing

Microsoft Press books are available through booksellers and distributors worldwide. If you need support related to this book, email Microsoft Press Support at *mspinput@microsoft.com*. Please tell us what you think of this book at *http://aka.ms/tellpress*.

Acquisitions Editor: Devon Musgrave
Developmental Editor: Devon Musgrave
Editorial Production: Cohesion
Technical Reviewer: Steve Caravajal; Technical Review services provided by Content Master, a member of CM Group, Ltd.
Copyeditor: Ann Weaver
Indexer: Jack Lewis
Cover: Twist Creative • Seattle

This book is dedicated to my family: Paola, Andrea, and Marta. I love you!

—PAOLO PIALORSI

Contents at a glance

Table of Contents

What do you think of this book? We want to hear from you!

Microsoft is interested in hearing your feedback so we can continually improve our books and learning resources for you. To participate in a brief online survey, please visit:

microsoft.com/learning/booksurvey

PART II   OFFICE 365 PROGRAMMING MODEL

PART III   CONSUMING OFFICE 365

Chapter 12 Publishing your applications and add-ins   351

What do you think of this book? We want to hear from you!

Microsoft is interested in hearing your feedback so we can continually improve our books and learning resources for you. To participate in a brief online survey, please visit:

microsoft.com/learning/booksurvey

Introduction

M icrosoft Office 365 is a cloud-based software solution that Microsoft offers as a service, targeting the customers who want to externalize the main services they use to run their businesses, like email, collaboration, video conferencing, file sharing, and so on. From a developer perspective, the Microsoft Office 365 offering is a great opportunity to build smart, mobile-aware, and fully integrated solutions that potentially can be sold to millions of users through the public Office Store, leveraging the Office 365 ecosystem and embracing the new add-in development model.

Programming Microsoft Office 365 provides a clear and practical overview of the architectural aspects of Microsoft Office 365 and of the services included in the platform. Moreover, by reading this book, you can learn about the Microsoft Graph API and the Microsoft Graph SDK and about how to create and distribute Office 365 applications, SharePoint Add-ins, and Office Add-ins that fully leverage the Office 365 ecosystem.

Who should read this book

This book is intended to help existing SharePoint and Office developers target the new Office 365 offering, upgrading their skills and knowledge related to the new cloud-based development model. Although it is not fundamental to know about SharePoint and Office 365, this book is really useful for developers who come from the old server-side or full trust code development world. Nevertheless, the book can be useful for developers working with any kind of platform, as long as they can make HTTP requests against the Microsoft Graph API.

Assumptions

This book expects that you have at least a minimal understanding of web development, especially of HTTP, REST, and JSON. Moreover, if you are a .NET developer and you know about ASP.NET, you will find it easier to follow and understand some of the code samples shared within the book. Although the Microsoft Graph API is available to any development platform that supports HTTP and JSON, most of the samples in this book are based on ASP.NET, C#, and PowerShell.

With a heavy focus on the Microsoft Graph API, Azure Active Directory, and the architectural patterns for creating real business-level solutions, this book assumes that you have a basic understanding of the most common collaboration needs.

This book might not be for you if . . .

This book might not be for you if you are not developing solutions for Office 365 or for SharePoint. Moreover, if you don't know anything about C# and ASP.NET, you could find it difficult to understand some of the code samples related to the book.

In contrast, if you are an experienced Office 365 developer using the latest tools and techniques like those illustrated in the Office 365 Developer Patterns & Practices community project, you may already know some of the information shared through this book.

Organization of this book

This book is divided into four sections, each of which focuses on a different aspect or technology related to developing Office 365 solutions. Part I, "Getting started," provides a quick overview of Microsoft Office 365 and the offered services as well as an overview of the extensibility points available and suitable for creating real business-level solutions built on top of Office 365. Part II, "Office 365 programming model," gives you fundamental knowledge about the Microsoft Graph API, from a REST and JSON viewpoint. Moreover, there is a solid introduction to Azure Active Directory (Azure AD) and how to configure authentication and authorization in custom developed solutions that leverage Azure AD. Part III, "Consuming Office 365," provides concrete and practical examples of how to use the Microsoft Graph API in .NET, leveraging Mail, Calendar, Contacts, Users and Groups, and File services. Furthermore, in Part III you can learn about the Microsoft Graph SDK for .NET and about the SharePoint REST API. Finally, Part IV, "SharePoint & Office Add-ins," provides you information about how to architect and create real business-level Office 365 applications and gives some overview information about how to create Office Add-ins. The last chapter of the book gives instructions on how to publish your custom development solutions, whether you are releasing an Office 365 application, a SharePoint Add-in, or an Office Add-in.

Finding your best starting point in this book

The sections of *Programming Microsoft Office 365* cover a wide range of technologies associated with the services Office 365 offers. Depending on your needs and your existing understanding of Office 365, you may wish to focus on specific areas of the book. Use the following table to determine how best to proceed through the book.

If you are	Follow these steps
New to Office 365 in general	Start from Chapter 1 and read the entire book in sequence.
New to Office 365 development or an existing SharePoint 2013 (or earlier) developer, but aware of Office 365 architecture and services	Briefly skim Part I if you need a refresh on the core concepts. Read from Part II through Part IV.
New to the Microsoft Graph API	Read Part II and Part III. Read Part IV if you need to create Office 365 applications or Office Add-ins.
Experienced Microsoft Graph API developer	Briefly skim Part II if you need a refresh on the main topics. Read Part IV to understand how to create real solutions that leverage the Microsoft Graph API.

Most of the book's chapters include code samples that let you try out the concepts you just learned. No matter which sections you choose to focus on, be sure to download and install the sample applications on your system.

Conventions and features in this book

This book presents information using conventions designed to make the information readable and easy to follow.

- In most cases, the book provides step-by-step code samples that you can follow on your own development machine. It is suggested that you download the code samples related to the book to follow the samples more easily.

- Boxed elements with labels such as "Note" provide additional information or alternative methods for completing a step.

- Text that you type (apart from code blocks) appears in bold.

- A vertical bar between two or more menu items (for example, File | Close), means that you should select the first menu or menu item, then the next, and so on.

System requirements

You will need the following hardware and software to complete the practice exercises in this book:

- Any Windows version that can run Microsoft Visual Studio 2015 Update 2 or later or any Mac operating system that can run Visual Studio Code

- Microsoft Visual Studio 2015 Update 2 or Visual Studio Code

- Computer that has a 1.6 GHz or faster processor (2 GHz recommended)

- 1 GB (32-bit) or 2 GB (64-bit) RAM

- 10 GB of available hard disk space

- 5400 RPM hard disk drive

- DirectX 9 capable video card running at 1024 × 768 or higher resolution display

- DVD-ROM drive (if installing Visual Studio from DVD)

- Internet connection to download software or chapter examples and to connect to Microsoft Office 365 and Microsoft Azure

- A Microsoft Office 365 subscription and access to the Office 365 admin portal

- A Microsoft Azure subscription and access to the Azure portal

- Telerik Fiddler 4 (*http://www.telerik.com/fiddler*)

Depending on your Windows configuration, you might require local administrator rights to install or configure Visual Studio 2015.

If you don't have an Office 365 subscription, you can sign up to join the Office 365 Developer Program, and you will get a one-year FREE Office 365 Developer subscription at the following URL: *http://dev.office.com/*.

Downloads

Most of the chapters in this book include exercises that let you interactively try out new material learned in the main text. All sample projects can be downloaded from the following page:

https://aka.ms/ProgOffice365/downloads

Follow the instructions on the target page to download the code sample files.

 Note In addition to the code samples, your system should have Visual Studio 2015 or Visual Studio Code installed. If available, install the latest service packs for each product.

Installing the code samples

Follow these steps to install the code samples on your computer so that you can use them with the exercises in this book.

1. Unzip the ProgOffice365.ZIP file that you downloaded from the book's website.

2. If prompted, review the displayed end user license agreement. If you accept the terms, select the Accept option, and then click Next.

Using the code samples

All the code samples are stored within a unique .ZIP file, which can be downloaded and installed following the instructions provided in the previous paragraphs.

- Samples of Chapter 3, "Microsoft Graph API reference," are made of a .SAZ file for Fiddler 4 (*http://www.telerik.com/fiddler*). Install Fiddler 4 and open the file, which is included in the .ZIP file related to the book. Browse the HTTP requests and responses and inspect the related JSON messages, following the flow of the chapter.

- Samples of Part III, "Consuming Office 365" are included in folder MicrosoftGraph.Office365.Generic of the .ZIP file.

- Samples of Chapter 8, "Microsoft Graph SDK for .NET," are included in folder MicrosoftGraph.Office365.DotNetSDK of the .ZIP file.

- Samples of Chapter 9, "SharePoint REST API," are included in folder SharePoint.RESTAPI of the .ZIP file.

- Samples of Chapter 10, "Creating Office 365 applications," are included in folder BusinessApps.O365ProjectsApp of the .ZIP file.

- Samples of Chapter 11, "Overview of Office Add-ins," are included in folder Outlook.ConsumeGraphAPI of the .ZIP file.

Current Book Service

This book is part of our new Current Book Service, which provides content updates for major technology changes and improvements related to programming Office 365. As significant updates are made, sections of this book will be updated or new sections will be added to address the changes. The updates will be delivered to you via a free Web Edition of this book, which can be accessed with any Internet connection at *MicrosoftPressStore.com*.

Register this book at *MicrosoftPressStore.com* to receive access to the latest content as an online Web Edition. If you bought this book through *MicrosoftPressStore.com*, you do not need to register; this book and any updates are already in your account.

How to register your book

If you have not registered your book, follow these steps:

1. Go to *www.MicrosoftPressStore.com/register*.

2. Sign in or create a new account.

3. Enter the ISBN found on the copyright page of this book.

4. Answer the questions as proof of purchase.

5. The Web Edition will appear under the Digital Purchases tab on your Account page. Click "Launch" to access your product.

Find out about updates

Sign up for the What's New newsletter at *www.MicrosoftPressStore.com/newsletters* to receive an email alerting you of the changes each time this book's Web Edition has been updated. The email address you use to sign up for the newsletter must be the same email address used for your *MicrosoftPressStore.com* account in order to receive the email alerts. If you choose not to sign up, you can periodically check your account at *MicrosoftPressStore.com* to find out if updates have been made to the Web Edition.

This book will receive periodic updates to address significant software changes for 12 to 18 months following first publication date. After the update period has ended, no more changes will be made to the book, but the final update to the Web Edition will remain available in your account at *MicrosoftPressStore.com*.

The Web Edition can be used on tablets that use current web browsers. Simply log into your *MicrosoftPressStore.com* account and access the Web Edition from the Digital Purchases tab.

For more information about the Current Book Service, visit *www.MicrosoftPressStore .com/CBS*.

Acknowledgments

This book has been the most complex and challenging manuscript I ever wrote. Usually, writing a book is a well-defined and time-scoped process, which can be accomplished following a clear schedule.

However, this book covers a topic (Microsoft Office 365) that is continuously changing and growing, almost on a monthly basis, and what you write now should be slightly different within the next few months. Luckily, and thanks to Microsoft Press, I had the opportunity to embrace the Current Book Service model, which allows me to keep the book updated in electronic format and allows you—the reader—to read a continuously updated book that will follow the evolution of the target product. In fact, we will ship three updates within the next 18 months after the first release of the book, and you will be able to stay on track, refreshing and updating your knowledge according to the growth of Microsoft Office 365.

First of all, I would like to thank Microsoft Press and all the publishing people who contributed to this book project. Mainly, I'd like to thank Devon Musgrave, who trusted me and allowed me to write this book and made it possible for this book to be part of the Current Book Service model. Devon helped me during the production process of this book, and without him and his contribution this book wouldn't be possible.

In addition, my colleagues in the Core Team of the Office 365 Dev and SharePoint Patterns & Practices (PnP: *http://aka.ms/OfficeDevPnP*) deserve special thanks because they greatly helped me create the content of this book, helping me find the right ideas and samples and sharing with me their vision, their time, and their minds. In particular, I would like to thank Vesa Juvonen, Bert Jansen, Erwin van Hunen, and Patrick Rodgers. PnP really rocks, and you guys rock even more! "Sharing is caring," and this book is clear proof of that.

Furthermore, I'd like to thank the people from Microsoft who helped me during the definition of the outline of this book. In particular, I want to thank Jeremy Thake, Luca Bandinelli, Yina Arenas, and Vittorio Bertocci.

Last but not least, there are special people who deserve a huge thank you. They are my wife, Paola, my son, Andrea, and my daughter, Marta. I need to thank them for their support, patience, and understanding during the last 12 months. We know that whenever daddy writes a book, it will be a very busy time. However, having you guys counting with me the chapters and the pages lasting to the end of the book and having your unconditioned support to achieve my goals helps me a lot. We are a team, and I'm really thankful for your fundamental and unique contribution.

Errata, updates, & book support

We've made every effort to ensure the accuracy of this book and its companion content. You can access updates to this book—in the form of a list of submitted errata and their related corrections—at:

> *https://aka.ms/ProgOffice365/errata*

If you discover an error that is not already listed, please submit it to us at the same page.

If you need additional support, email Microsoft Press Book Support at *mspinput@microsoft.com*.

Please note that product support for Microsoft software and hardware is not offered through the previous addresses. For help with Microsoft software or hardware, go to *http://support.microsoft.com*.

Free ebooks from Microsoft Press

From technical overviews to in-depth information on special topics, the free ebooks from Microsoft Press cover a wide range of topics. These ebooks are available in PDF, EPUB, and Mobi for Kindle formats, ready for you to download at:

> *http://aka.ms/mspressfree*

Check back often to see what is new!

We want to hear from you

At Microsoft Press, your satisfaction is our top priority, and your feedback our most valuable asset. Please tell us what you think of this book at:

> *http://aka.ms/tellpress*

We know you're busy, so we've kept it short with just a few questions. Your answers go directly to the editors at Microsoft Press. (No personal information will be requested.) Thanks in advance for your input!

Stay in touch

Let's keep the conversation going! We're on Twitter: *http://twitter.com/MicrosoftPress*

PART I

Getting started

This first part of this book introduces the Microsoft Office 365 ecosystem from both a functional and a developer perspective. The overall goal of this part is to give you an understanding of the fundamental services that power the Office 365 offering. Moreover, this part offers an overview of the development tools and techniques for creating software solutions to extend Office 365.

Chapter 1, "Microsoft Office 365: A quick tour," provides a quick overview of Office 365, bringing you through the main services and capabilities of Microsoft's main Software as a Service (SaaS) offering. It explains the role of Azure Active Directory and introduces Exchange Online, SharePoint Online, and Skype for Business. It also discusses Office Delve, Office 365 Video, Office 365 Groups, and other NextGen Portals. If you already know about Office 365 in general, maybe you can skip this chapter.

Chapter 2, "Overview of Office 365 development," provides robust information about what a developer can do to extend the native set of services Office 365 offers. The chapter also covers the tools and techniques that are available for developing Office 365 applications, Office Add-ins, and SharePoint Add-ins. Moreover, the chapter instructs you about how to set up a development environment to develop this kind of solution.

## CHAPTER 1

Microsoft Office 365: A quick tour

Microsoft Office 365 is one of the most innovative sets of services Microsoft has offered in the last decade, together with Microsoft Azure. In this chapter, you will learn what Office 365 is and the fundamental services on which the Office 365 offering is built.

What is Microsoft Office 365?

Microsoft Office 365 is the most important Software as a Service offering Microsoft currently provides. Software as a Service (SaaS) provides a software solution with a licensing model based on a subscription and delivered through a centrally hosted infrastructure that typically is on the cloud. In Figure 1-1, you can see a graphical representation of the main software hosting models and business models that are available now.

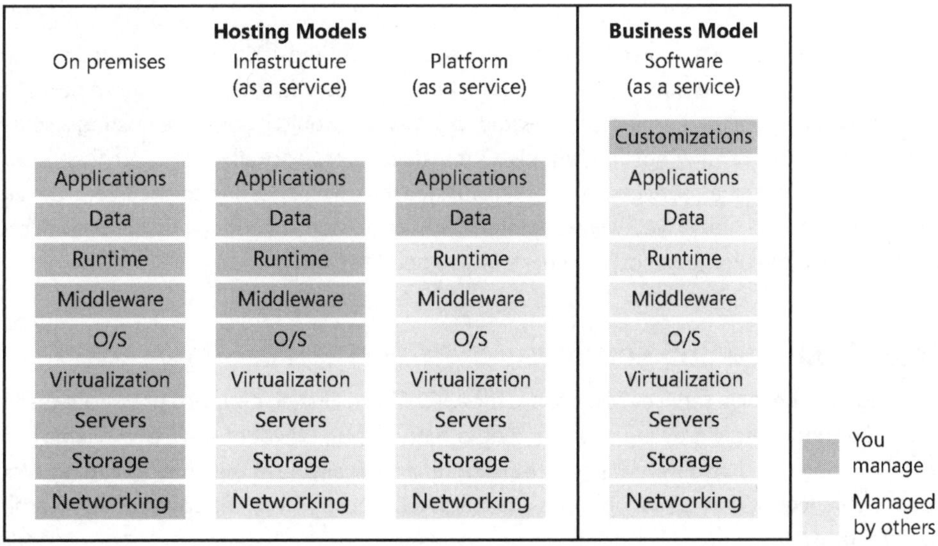

FIGURE 1-1 The main software hosting models and business models available on the market

There are four main offerings available:

- **On-premises**   Everything is based on hardware and software that is installed within the building (the premises) of the company or person using the software. All the key aspects of a software solution, like availability, scalability, and security, are the responsibility of the company or person who runs that software.

- **Infrastructure as a Service (IaaS)**   The software is installed on one or more virtual machines that are hosted by a third party, abstracting the subject that uses that software from taking care of all the physical infrastructural topics like networking, storage, physical servers, and virtualization.

- **Platform as a Service (PaaS)**   The software is hosted and executed in a platform that allows developers to focus on data and custom application development. The resources used to host the software solution can be shared across multiple subjects. In that case, PaaS guarantees isolation and data partitioning.

- **Software as a Service (SaaS)**   The software solution is provided on a subscription basis and is delivered through a centrally hosted infrastructure. Typically, the software solution can be improved by creating customizations and/or embracing an extensibility model that keeps the SaaS offering safe and isolated from any third-party customization.

Office 365 fits into the SaaS category. Following the guidance in this book, you—as a developer—will be able to build customizations and extensions according to the extensibility model of a SaaS offering.

One fundamental concept that you need to understand about the various hosting models is that developing solutions for SaaS allows you to focus on your business requirements without having to take care of any infrastructural or platform-related tasks, as you would if you were hosting a solution running in any of the other hosting models. Often, developers waste their time architecting and configuring virtual machines, services, and servers just for the sake of hosting their custom-developed solutions. With the SaaS model, you will completely focus on customizing the software provided as a service by realizing the business requirements that you need to satisfy.

Microsoft Office 365 services

Let's now dig into the main services Microsoft Office 365 offers. First, it is important to note that Office 365 is a continuously growing and changing offering. Thus, the list of services available at the time of this writing could be different from the list of services available at the time of reading. From a developer's perspective, this is awesome and challenging because you will be continuously learning as the platform grows.

The basis of Office 365 is Microsoft Azure Active Directory (Azure AD), which will be covered in detail in Chapter 4, "Azure Active Directory and security." Azure AD is the directory system on the cloud that sits under the cover of every Office 365 tenant. Azure AD is used to store users' identities, to authenticate them, and to federate tenants with third-party identity providers on-premises. All the licensed users of an Office 365 tenant are first users in the Azure AD tenant related to the Office 365 tenant.

Once you assign a license to a user stored in Azure AD, that user will be able to consume the assigned services. Azure AD is almost unknown to the end users, but you cannot have an Office 365 tenant without Azure AD. Every time an end user authenticates to access a tenant, she interacts with the authentication process of Azure AD. However, this is often fluent and transparent to the user.

From an administrative perspective, the Azure AD service that supports an Office 365 tenant is available and can be reached through the Office 365 admin portal within the list of services that can be administered.

Aside from Azure AD, all the other services available for an end user are accessible through the Office 365 app launcher. The app launcher is accessible by clicking the command button shown in Figure 1-2 in the upper-left corner of the screen when using Office 365 from a desktop PC within a browser. As you can see, the number of apps that you can utilize is quite large, and it is growing continually. Every user will see the apps for which he has been granted access in the Office 365 app launcher.

The first fundamental set of provided capabilities are those related to Microsoft Exchange Online (also known as EXO), which is the cloud-based SaaS version of Microsoft Exchange. Through Exchange Online, you can leverage and provide to your users services like Mail, Calendar, People, and Tasks. From a technical perspective, Exchange Online is just an Exchange Server hosted on the cloud, and the above services are provided either through the web browser or by using any compliant client like Microsoft Outlook or any mobile software available to consume the Exchange Online services. For example, if you have an Android or an iOS mobile phone or tablet, you will be able to consume Exchange Online even without installing or having Office or Outlook. Often, Exchange Online is the first service that enterprises move to the cloud to reduce their total cost of mailbox ownership and to improve their mobile users' experience.

In many cases, the second service that makes companies move to Office 365 is Skype for Business (also known as S4B). By using Skype for Business, you can enable powerful real-time collaboration and teamwork. To give a few examples: you can make one-to-one or one-to-many conference calls; you can share a presenter's screen, even providing remote control of a PC; you can share a whiteboard or a notes file; you can present a slide deck; and you can make a poll. You can also register a conference call for your own reference or for sharing an .mp4 file with people who were not present on the call. Furthermore, by using S4B you can make a call between an Office 365 user who uses S4B and an external user who uses Skype personal. Moreover, you can leverage the service called PSTN Conferencing, which enables you to make conference calls with people who do not have a PC or any other kind of modern device—just a legacy telephone. By leveraging S4B, you can even use the Cloud PBX service, which allows your PC or device running S4B to become a replacement for a classic telephone. Your S4B account will be associated with a legacy telephone number, and anyone using a telephone will be able to make a phone call to you. You will answer the call by using S4B instead of the classic telephone. Depending on your business requirements and geographical location, these last two capabilities (PSTN Conferencing and Cloud PBX) can require some on-premises infrastructural servers and services to make it possible to connect your on-premises telephone infrastructure to S4B.

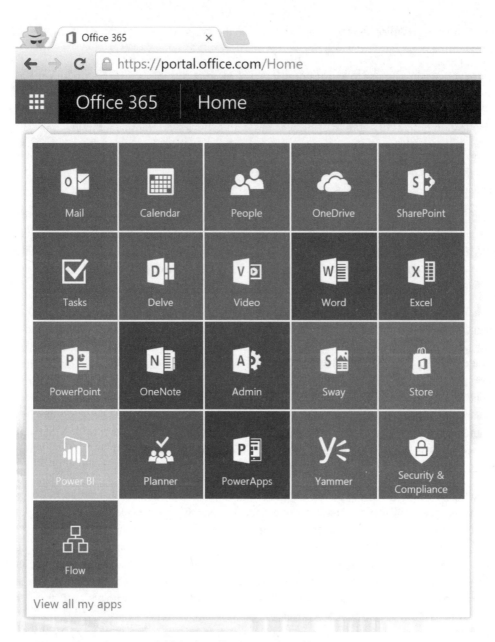

FIGURE 1-2 The main apps available in the Office 365 app launcher

Moreover, in 2015 Microsoft introduced a service called Skype Meeting Broadcast, which enables you to produce, host, and broadcast live online meetings to large online audiences, which can reach up to 10,000 concurrent users/viewers. The attendees of the meeting will just need to have a web browser, while the presenter/producer will have to use S4B. This powerful service enables you to make broad presentations to a set of defined and authorized users, to all the users who have a company-related account in a specific Office 365 tenant, or even publicly to any anonymous users. You can also configure the meeting to be integrated with a Yammer network for social discussion about the presented content. Furthermore, you can measure the mood of the people attending the meeting by using Bing Pulse, which can be integrated in the UI of the meeting broadcast.

OneDrive for Business (also known as OD4B) is another outstanding feature of Office 365 that allows users—typically employees—to store, sync, and share their personal and work documents in a cloud-based repository that they can access securely from everywhere and from any device just by providing the proper set of user credentials. At the time of this writing, every user who owns a OneDrive for Business license can store up to 1 terabytes (TB) of data in her personal repository. There is also the capability to keep an offline copy of the personal document on your desktop PC, which can be synchronized with the cloud whenever there is network connectivity. Due to high demand, the synchronization client of OneDrive for Business is subject to improvements and the introduction of new capabilities. Often, the OneDrive for Business service name is also used to embrace the capability to keep an offline copy of the SharePoint Online libraries that you have in Office 365 or even in SharePoint on-premises. In the past, the same synchronization client was used to synchronize both the personal storage in OneDrive for Business and the business-related document libraries stored in the intranet. However, at the time of this writing, there are two different clients: the old one, which can still be used to synchronize document libraries, and the new one (called NextGen Synchronization Client) just for OneDrive for Business and OneDrive Personal.

We just talked about document libraries stored in SharePoint Online because SharePoint Online (also known as SPO) is another fundamental service Office 365 offers and is filed under the SharePoint icon in the app launcher. Like Exchange Online, SharePoint Online is a cloud-hosted version of the well-known Microsoft SharePoint Server product. Although SharePoint Online shares the main architectural pillars with the on-premises version of SharePoint 2016, on the cloud there are some services, capabilities, and architectural choices that make the SPO offering unique and not 100 percent comparable with SharePoint on-premises. For example, there are services or capabilities of SharePoint 2016 that are available on-premises only (for example, some Business Intelligence capabilities), and there are other services that are available on the cloud only (for example, the external sharing capability of SPO that allows users to share sites and documents with people outside the company if company policies allow it). Many other capabilities and functionalities can be mentioned when comparing SharePoint 2016 on-premises and SharePoint Online, but they are outside the scope of this book.

When you click the SharePoint app in the app launcher, you get access to the new SharePoint home page, which was introduced by Jeff Teper (Corporate Vice President for SharePoint and OneDrive in Microsoft Corporation) together with other new user interface enhancements on May 4, 2016, during an online conference called "The Future of SharePoint." In the new SharePoint home page, users will find a list of companywide promoted sites, a list of followed sites, some useful companywide links, and a direct link to the most frequently accessed sites. This page is the entry point, from a SharePoint Online perspective, to the entire set of sites (site collections in SharePoint) of interest to the current user.

When you work with documents stored in SharePoint Online or in OneDrive for Business, if those files are Office documents you can leverage the Office Online services, which allow you to read and write/modify those documents just by using a web browser. This is a powerful capability that makes it possible to realize mobile working and to have a digital workplace that requires nothing more than a web browser. Every Office 365 user with a web browser such as Microsoft Edge, Internet Explorer, Google Chrome, or Firefox can be productive, read documents, or write/modify/create documents using Word Online, Excel Online, PowerPoint Online, or OneNote Online. This service makes it possible to work everywhere with almost any device.

Another powerful capability Office 365 provides that integrates some of the services we have just seen is Office 365 Groups. Office 365 Groups are a service mainly built on top of Azure AD, Exchange Online, SharePoint Online, and OneDrive for Business. Office 365 Groups enable people using Office 365 to create work groups, which can be considered modern digital workplaces, where they can share conversations, a mailbox that behaves like a distribution list, files, a OneNote notebook, a calendar, a directory of people contributing to the group, and direct Skype for Business integration. Office 365 Groups provide a self-service experience for users, who can create both public and private groups and can invite people to contribute to the groups. At the time of this writing, Office 365 Groups are available for tenant internal users only. However, the public roadmap for the service includes upcoming support for external users. Another key feature of Office 365 Groups is the capability for tenant admins to manage groups from the Office 365 admin portal, to enforce naming policies for self-service created groups, and to orchestrate groups' creation by allowing or denying group creation permissions to users. Later in this chapter, you will learn about what is available for tenant admins to accomplish administrative, management, and governance tasks. In Figure 1-3, you can see a graphical representation of the architecture of Office 365 Groups.

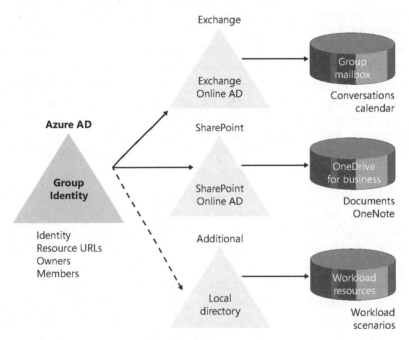

FIGURE 1-3 The architectural schema of Office 365 Groups

From an end user perspective, Office 365 Groups can be consumed by using the web browser on any device, by using Microsoft Outlook 2016, and soon even by using Microsoft Outlook for Mac.

From a developer perspective, Office 365 Groups can be managed through a set of REST-based APIs, which are part of the Microsoft Graph API. In Section II, "Office 365 programming model," and in Section III, "Consuming Office 365," you will learn how to use the Microsoft Graph API to consume and manage Office 365 Groups. Moreover, as a developer, you can connect custom applications with Office 365 Groups, providing support for getting useful information and content from external services or applications into groups. For example, there are already connectors for BingNews, GitHub, BitBucket, JIRA, and many other services. You can even create your own custom connectors, and in Chapter 10, "Creating Office 365 applications," you will learn how to do that.

The Planner app is a new service that Microsoft released in early June 2016 that offers a visual tool to organize teamwork. By using Planner, you can create and organize plans, assign and monitor tasks that are part of a plan, organize tasks in buckets, and attach files or links to any specific task. In general, Planner is a tool to manage time, resources, and tasks with a visual board and a set of graphical charts to better understand the overall progress of a plan. In Figure 1-4, you can see a sample set of charts taken from a plan in Planner.

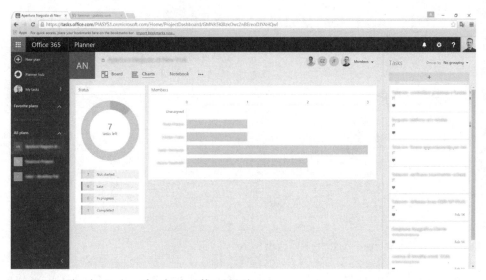

FIGURE 1-4 The charts view of a plan in Office 365 Planner

One key feature of plans in Planner is that—internally and from an architectural perspective— they are based on and leverage Office 365 Groups. Thus, whenever you create a new plan in Planner, you will also have a related Office 365 Group, which implies having conversations, a calendar, files, a OneNote notebook, and the Skype for Business integration.

From a developer perspective, Planner can be consumed by using a specific set of REST APIs, which are in beta/preview version at the time of this writing but are scheduled for release in 2016. Thus, you can think about creating custom software solutions that integrate emails (EXO), files (OD4B and SPO), and groups and plans, orchestrating real business-level solutions.

Microsoft Power BI is an important service to visualize data that is integrated to Office 365. By using Power BI, you can import or consume datasets, presenting data through reports that can visualize charts and graphs and can be organized into dashboards that present data and information through tiles coming from different reports. Power BI is an extensible platform that can be consumed and embedded without an Office 365 subscription. It provides additional features such as automatic refresh of data models based on data stored on OneDrive for Business. This platform also provides features that help users navigate data, such as Power BI Q&A, which allows users to ask for data using natural language questions, and Quick Insights, which automatically finds valuable relationships in a data model. In Figure 1-5, you can see a dashboard built with Power BI.

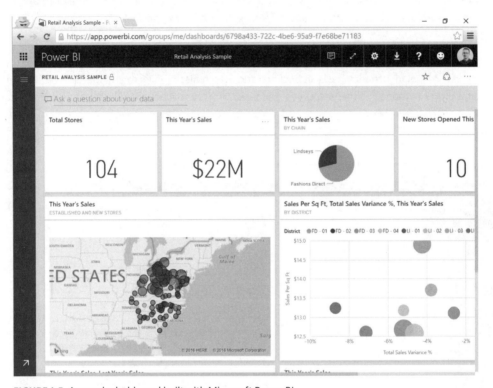

FIGURE 1-5 A sample dashboard built with Microsoft Power BI

Yammer is another service that can be consumed as part of the Office 365 offering. Yammer is a cloud-based SaaS solution that provides the capability to create a private enterprise social network for a company. By using Yammer, employees can collaborate; exchange messages; chat; and share content across departments, locations, and business apps. Yammer's overall goal is to provide a social network to improve productivity, connect people, and freely share ideas and content without the common and reasonable constraints of a classic intranet or collaboration portal. Through Yammer, you can also involve partners, customers, and vendors in external networks that can go beyond the limits of your company network. Within a network, whether it is private and company-related or external and open to third parties, users can freely create public or private groups, discuss and share documents and videos, make polls, give prizes to other members, and in general enjoy being part of an enterprise social network, working from anywhere and using any client device.

Another interesting service is Office Delve, which is one of the most innovative emerging technologies available in Office 365. It is one of the new services Microsoft introduced in 2015 in the category of NextGen Portals. NextGen Portals are services typically based on SharePoint Online, from a user interface perspective, that leverage the Office 365 ecosystem and the Office Graph to provide high-level services and tools to improve quality of work—and quality of life—for Office 365 users. Office Delve is a service based on Microsoft SharePoint Online that provides users the most relevant content based on what they are working on and whom they are working with.

The basic idea of Office Delve is to leverage the Office Graph, going beyond the common information silos that exist across the applications available in the Office 365 ecosystem. Instead of thinking in terms of emails in Exchange Online, attachments to emails, documents stored in SharePoint Online, documents stored in OneDrive for Business, video files, and so on, you need to consider the most useful and/or recently updated content with which you should work, regardless of where it is. Delve will take care of highlighting for you exactly what really matters for your daily job.

The Office Graph is an intelligent mapping among people, content, and interactions that happen in Office 365. Office Delve uses the insights and the relationships stored within the Office Graph to proactively and actively suggest content to the users, providing each user with a dashboard of cards that refers to what should be most relevant to that user. In Figure 1-6, you can see a screenshot of the Office Delve dashboard of Popular Documents in action.

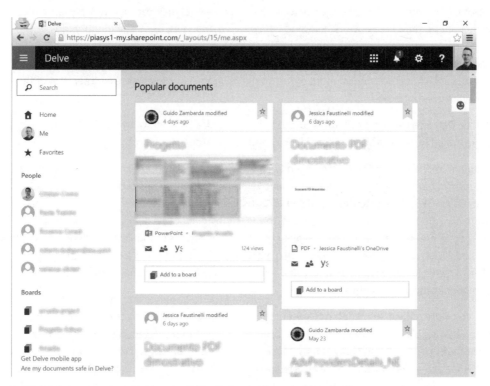

FIGURE 1-6 A screenshot showing the Office Delve dashboard of Popular Documents in action

By using Office Delve, users can organize cards in boards, grouping items that share the same goal, project, or group of people working on it. Boards can be used to tag content and to retrieve personalized/grouped views of popular documents and contents that share a tag.

The key benefit of Office Delve is that users don't have to search for what they seek. They just need to access Office Delve and—regardless of the source of the content—they will be able to find and consume the content if it is relevant for them. Users can also organize content and boards into a list of favorites to keep track of what matters most to them.

Moreover, through Office Delve all users have a personal profile page called "Me" that they can use to keep track of their personal activity and content, filtered by file type. Through the personal page, a user can consume and customize his personal profile data, which includes all the information that is stored in Azure AD and that defines the user profile in Office 365, including the company organizational chart if applicable. Every user has a personal page in Office Delve, and every user can browse the personal pages of the other users, consuming only public, nonsensitive data, browsing and searching the Office Graph based on users' profile properties, information, and expertise.

Additionally, through the Office Delve interface a user can create and maintain an enterprise blog that can be indexed by the search index of SharePoint Online and becomes discoverable by the other people working within the same company.

Another noteable feature of Office Delve is Office Delve Analytics, through which users can measure how they spend their time at work. By using Office Delve Analytics, users can identify the people and activities that represent their priorities and their most time-consuming targets. This can help them determine how to spend a workday in an effective and productive way. They can also set goals and track their progress toward accomplishment of the goals. In Figure 1-7, you can see a screenshot of the Office Delve Analytics dashboard.

Office Delve can even be consumed using a mobile device by leveraging the Android and iOS clients that are available, respectively, on Google Play and on the Apple App Store.

Another interesting and useful NextGen Portal is Office 365 Video, which enables enterprises—and companies in general—to post, share, and discover video content that is organized in channels. The goal of Office 365 Video is to provide a beautiful, usable, socially aware user interface for consuming multimedia video content, either from a desktop PC or from a mobile device. Through the Office 365 Video portal, enterprises can create training channels, repositories of marketing videos, and companywide libraries of videos. Office 365 Video also makes it possible to discuss a specific video on Yammer, to share a direct link to a video by email, and to embed the video into a SharePoint Online site or within the companywide infrastructure.

Furthermore, Office 365 Video has a set of management and administrative tools for administrators and is available only to the users of the target tenant, without the capability to share video content outside the current company boundaries. Maybe in the near future, based on a publicly declared roadmap, Office 365 Video will become available for sharing videos with people outside the current tenant.

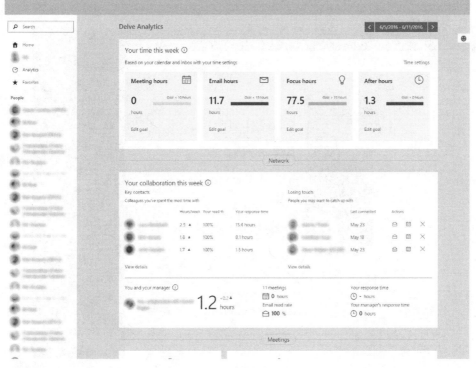

FIGURE 1-7 The Office Delve Analytics dashboard in action

Office 365 Video leverages the well-known and solid Azure Media Services for encoding and streaming the video content. Azure Media Services leverages a smooth streaming technology to adapt the video quality to the consuming device and the available bandwidth. Moreover, Office 365 Video uses a set of SharePoint Online site collections for storing all the original video files. As a result of this architectural choice, the same technical boundaries that apply to SharePoint Online apply to Office 365 Video. For example, you cannot upload files larger than 10 gigabytes (GB), and you cannot have a channel bigger than 1 terabyte (TB), which is the upper size limit for a single site collection in SharePoint Online.

One relatively new product that is part of the Office 365 ecosystem is Office Sway, which is a new tool to visualize and share ideas, news, projects, or whatever else is on your mind that you want to express to others. A Sway is a canvas that renders its content as a sequence, adapating the rendering to the target device. For example, by using Sway you can render a presentation of a new project, mixing text, technical drawings, pictures, and whatever else you want to express within a sequence of views. You can organize content coming from multiple sources like OneDrive for Business, Twitter, YouTube, and Flickr. You can also use your mobile smartphone or tablet to take pictures and present them in Sway. In general, Sway is a fresh new tool to create dynamic presentations that you can build on the go and share with other people in your company. In Figure 1-8, you can see Sway in action.

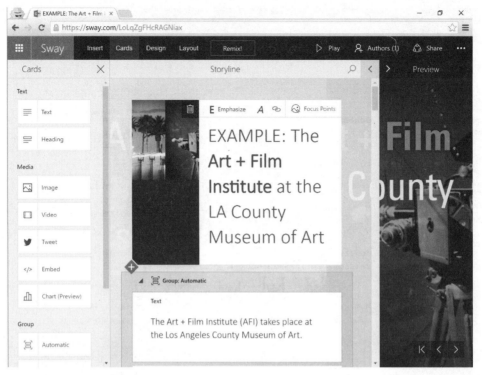

FIGURE 1-8 A screenshot showing Office Sway in action

The final application that can be part of the Office 365 offering is Microsoft PowerApps, which is in preview at the time of this writing. By using PowerApps, you can create mobile-aware software apps that consume data from multiple data sources, providing customizable and responsive UI forms and integrating data in logic flows that can behave like enterprise-level workflows. The power of applications built with PowerApps is their capability to consume data securely through an open connector model and to connect with external REST-based services to execute actions. By using this approach, you can design an app that can be used to integrate different software and technologies, and you can consume that app from any place and using any device. Microsoft PowerApps is available as a web-based application for building and consuming apps, but there are also client apps for Windows and iOS.

Microsoft PowerApps natively provide connectors for: Office 365 (including Exchange Online, SharePoint Online, and OneDrive for Business), Dropbox, Twitter, Salesforce, Microsoft CRM, Google Drive, SQL Database on Microsoft Azure, and any HTTP/HTTPS service in general. Based on the data consumed from the above data connections, you can define logic flows and wait for approvals, send email notifications, invoke commands, and so on. For example, the logic flows can be built by using Microsoft Flow, which is another new service provided by Microsoft as part of the Office 365 offering.

Overall, the idea of PowerApps is to make it possible for power users to easily design multidevice and multistep forms and logic flows that can be shared with others without needing to be developers. In Figure 1-9, you can see a screenshot of the PowerApps app for Windows.

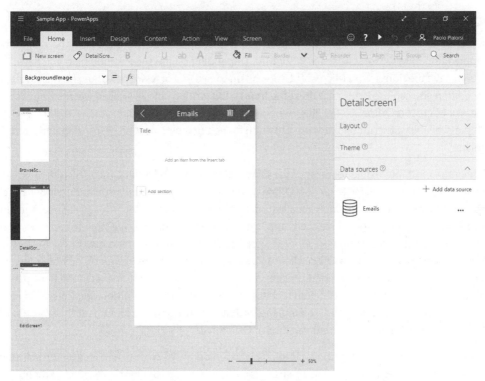

FIGURE 1-9 A screenshot showing the PowerApps app for Windows

If there is anything you are looking for that is not yet available out of the box in the Office 365 offering, you can search for it in the Office Store, where you can find thousands of business-level SharePoint Add-ins and Office 365 applications provided for free or sold by third parties that you can download, install, and use in your tenant. You should also keep an eye on the Office 365 Public Roadmap, which is available at the following URL: *http://roadmap.office.com/*. There, you will find a list of all the launched new features, the features that are currently rolling out, those that are under development, and those that have been cancelled. By periodically checking the Office 365 Public Roadmap, you can have a quick look at the status of the ecosystem, and you can plan adoption of upcoming technologies and services.

One last component that is available in the app launcher if you are an administrator of your Office 365 tenant is the *Admin* command, which brings you to the Office 365 admin portal. From there, you can administer the entire tenant and every service for which you have been designated as an administrator. For example, if you are a tenant global admin user, you will have access to all the settings and services. However, if you have been assigned only the SharePoint Online administrative rights, you will still have access to the Office 365 admin portal, but from there you will only have access to the SharePoint Online Admin Center and a subset of tenant settings that are available to SharePoint administrators. In the upcoming section, "Administration in Office 365," you will dig into more details about the administrative UI and common tasks in Office 365.

Microsoft Office on PC/Mac and Click-to-Run

Aside from the online services, the Office 365 offering can also include licenses to use the well-known desktop edition of Microsoft Office for PC or Mac. Depending on the subscription plan you have, you could have the right to run Microsoft Office on up to five PCs or Macs per user. The Microsoft Office edition you can use is Office 2016 at the time of this writing, and it is called Microsoft Office 365 Business or Microsoft Office 365 ProPlus, depending on the subscription plan you have. Further details about the available subscription plans are provided in the upcoming section, "Licensing and subscription plans."

One of the most interesting features of the Office client provided within Office 365 is the Click-to-Run installation. You can install Microsoft Office through a completely new installation model, which is based on a Microsoft streaming and virtualization technology. This new technology reduces the time required to install and run the Office client applications, which are usually available to run in a matter of seconds or minutes, depending on your network bandwidth. The streaming part of the Click-to-Run technology allows you to run the Office client software before the entire product is downloaded. In the meantime, an asynchronous download process will download all the components in the background. The virtualization part of the Click-to-Run technology allows you to run multiple versions of Office on the same computer by providing an isolated and virtualized environment for Office. This is just to allow a smooth transition between different versions of Office; it is not a long-term solution.

Under the cover, the virtualization technology is based on the Microsoft Application Virtualization (App-V) technology and runs Office in a self-contained, virtual environment on the local computer. The isolated environment provides a separate location for each version of the Office product files and settings so that they don't change other applications that are already installed on the computer. Additionally, this prevents any conflict between different versions of Office, which can be installed and executed on the same machine. The only constraint is that all the concurrently installed Office versions have to be the same edition. For example, they can be all 32-bit editions or 64-bit editions, but you cannot mix 32-bit and 64-bit editions on the same machine.

Click-to-Run is a setup process completely different from the Windows Installer (MSI) technique that was used in the past. When using the old approach based on MSI setup processes, you had to wait for the entire product to be installed before being able to use it. In contrast, the streaming technology first downloads all the fundamental components to run the Office client, followed by all the other components, which will be downloaded in the background. If you try to use a feature that is not yet downloaded and installed, Click-to-Run immediately downloads and installs that feature. The streaming process ends when all the products and features are completely downloaded and installed. Another interesting difference between the MSI installation and the new Click-to-Run setup process is that in the former you were able to select the components to install, while with the latter you always install the whole product. You cannot install a subset of the components unless you manually customize a configuration file that defines the installation rules. By default, you will always end up having the full Office client components included in your license subscription.

This new installation technique always provides you the most recent version of Office, so you don't have to install the product and all the related patches and service packs before being able to use it, like you did with the MSI installation. By default, the product version installed with Click-to-Run will be the latest one. Furthermore, whenever a new Office patch or update comes out, updating an already installed Office client that has been installed using Click-to-Run is an automatic process that can be handled in a matter of seconds or minutes, based on the download time of the update.

Once you have installed the Office client and the product is completely downloaded and installed, you don't need to be connected to the network or the Internet to use Office. From a licensing perspective, the Office client will need to check that your Office 365 subscription is active and valid at least once a month (specifically, at least once every 30 days). Thus, you need to be sure that your users can connect to the Office Licensing Service via the Internet at least once every 30 days. The licensing service will double-check that the users still have valid Office 365 subscription licenses and that they don't use a number of Office client installations over the licensed number. For example, as you will see in the following section, "Licensing and subscription plans," in the Office 365 E3 plan every user can run Office client on up to five devices. The monthly license check will verify not only the subscription license, but also that the total number of installed copies of Office client does not exceed the licensed limit. If the computer goes offline for more than 30 days, Office client commutes to the reduced functionality mode until the next time a connection can be made and the license can be verified. In reduced functionality mode, Office client remains installed on the computer, but users can only view and print their documents. All features for editing or creating new documents are disabled.

In the previous paragraphs, you saw that you need to be connected to the network or the Internet to install or update your Office client. This means that the Click-to-Run technology can be used even without a permanent Internet connection. Another key feature of Click-to-Run is that you are not required to be connected to the Internet to set up Office client. For example, you can distribute Office client via Click-to-Run using a software distribution network share. This approach reduces the Internet bandwidth needed to download and install Office client on multiple devices and improves the download speed, making it possible to download the Click-to-Run packages once and make them available to all the users through an internal network share. Moreover, the capability to download the Click-to-Run packages locally enables you to leverage any software distribution tool and technique you like and to test patches and updates on some pre-defined devices, distributing the updates across the company based on your own schedule. Otherwise, and by default, if your client computers installed Office client via Click-to-Run using the public Internet distribution point, they will get updates automatically as soon as Microsoft releases them.

In big, enterprise-level companies, the capability to leverage the new Click-to-Run installation technology without losing control over devices, users, and updates is important. Fortunately, the Click-to-Run technology is totally compliant with common enterprise-level software distribution techniques and rules.

Licensing and subscription plans

In the previous section, you learned about the services available in Office 365. However, not all services are available to all users or customers. The set of available services depends on the purchased subscriptions and licenses. Table 1-1 is a list of the most common subscription plans available for purchase.

TABLE 1-1 The main Office 365 subscription plans available for purchase

Subscription Plan	Description and Included Services
Office 365 Business Essentials	Online versions of Office with email and video conferencing. Included services: Office Online, Exchange Online, SharePoint Online, OneDrive for Business, Skype for Business, Sway, Yammer. Maximum number of users: 300.
Office 365 Business	Full Office on PC/Mac with apps for tablets and phones, without email. Included services: Office 2016 for PC/Mac, SharePoint Online, OneDrive for Business, Sway. Maximum number of users: 300.
Office 365 Business Premium	All the features of Business Essentials and Business in one integrated plan. Included services: Exchange Online, SharePoint Online, OneDrive for Business, Skype for Business, Sway, Yammer, Office 2016 for PC/Mac. Maximum number of users: 300.
Office 365 ProPlus	Full Office on PC/Mac with apps for tablets and phones. Included services: Office 2016 for PC/Mac, OneDrive for Business, Sway. Unlimited number of users.
Office 365 Enterprise E1	Online versions of Office with email and video conferencing. Included services: Office Online, Exchange Online (50 GB inbox), SharePoint Online, OneDrive for Business, Skype for Business, Yammer, Video, Skype Meeting Broadcast, Sway. Unlimited number of users.
Office 365 Enterprise E3	Full Office on PC/Mac with apps for tablets and phones. Included services: Office 2016 for PC/Mac, Exchange Online (unlimited inbox), SharePoint Online, OneDrive for Business, Skype for Business, Yammer, Video, Skype Meeting Broadcast, Sway. Unlimited number of users.
Office 365 Enterprise E5	Full Office on PC/Mac with apps for tablets and phones. Included services: Office 2016 for PC/Mac, Exchange Online (unlimited inbox), SharePoint Online, OneDrive for Business, Skype for Business, Yammer, Video, Skype Meeting Broadcast, Sway, PSTN conferencing, Cloud PBX. Unlimited number of users.
Office 365 Education	Online versions of Office with email and video conferencing. Included services: Office Online, Exchange Online (50 GB inbox), SharePoint Online, OneDrive for Business, Skype for Business, Yammer, Video, Skype Meeting Broadcast, Sway. Unlimited number of users, education edition.
Office 365 Government E1	Like Office 365 Enterprise E1, but for government.
Office 365 Government E3	Like Office 365 Enterprise E3, but for government.
Office 365 Government E4	Like Office 365 Enterprise E5, but for government.
Office 365 Nonprofit Business Essentials	Like Office 365 Business Essentials, but for nonprofit.
Office 365 Nonprofit Business Premium	Like Office 365 Business Premium, but for nonprofit.
Office 365 Nonprofit E1	Like Office 365 Enterprise E1, but for nonprofit.
Office 365 Nonprofit E3	Like Office 365 Enterprise E3, but for nonprofit.
Office 365 Home	Full Office on PC/Mac with apps for tablets and phones. Included services: Office 2016 for PC/Mac, 1 TB of storage in OneDrive Personal, Skype Personal. Valid for home use only, up to five users.
Office 365 Personal	Full Office on PC/Mac with apps for tablets and phones. Included services: Office 2016 for PC/Mac, 1 TB of storage in OneDrive Personal, Skype Personal. Valid for home use only, one user only.

As you can see, there are a wide variety of offerings—and this list is not complete and could be even longer. For the sake of simplicity, we focused on the main options. Nevertheless, it is important to keep in mind that you can mix some of the plans based on your needs, which makes it possible to tailor the best solution for every business.

For example, imagine that you have an enterprise company with 8,000 employees, 1,500 external consultants, 500 resellers, 20,000 customers, and 2,000 suppliers. In this situation, you can buy 8,000 subscriptions of Office 365 Enterprise E5 for the employees so that they will have Office 365 ProPlus on their client devices and the Cloud PBX and the PSTN Conferencing capability. This way, your employees will be able to do their work from wherever they want (office, home, or traveling) and will always be available and reachable, even by phone. Furthermore, you can buy 1,500 subscriptions of Office 365 Enterprise E1 for the external consultants so that they will have almost the same services as the employees, except the Office 365 ProPlus license and the telephony capabilities. Then, you can buy 500 subscriptions of Office 365 E3 for the resellers so that they will be almost like employees, without the Cloud PBX capabilities but including Office 365 ProPlus on their mobile devices. Last, to share documents and sites with customers and suppliers, you will just need to leverage the external sharing capabilities of Office 365, which are available for free and for an unlimited number of external users.

Administration in Office 365

Having such a big landscape of services and tools, like those offered by Office 365, requires having some effective and productive tools for administration and governance of the entire platform. In this section, you will see some of the available out-of-box administrative tools that are useful to keep control of your tenant and services.

To administer one or more of the services offered by the Office 365 ecosystem, a user should belong to one of the following roles:

- **Global administrator**   This is the highest administrative role. It implies access to all the administrative features of all the services and administrative rights on the Azure AD under the cover of the Office 365 tenant. Users in the global administrator role are the only ones who can assign other administrative roles. There could be multiple global administrator users, and for safety and recovery reasons you should have at least two users with this role. The person who signs up the tenant subscription is assigned to this role automatically.

- **Billing administrator**   This is the role for users who can purchase new licenses, manage subscriptions, manage support tickets, and monitor the health of services. Moreover, users in this role can download the invoices for billed services.

- **Exchange administrator**   This is the role for users administering Exchange Online. Users who belong to this role have access to the Exchange Admin Center (EAC).

- **Password administrator**   Users in this role can reset other users' passwords, manage service requests, and monitor the health of services.

- **Skype for Business administrator**   This is the role for users administering Skype for Business. Users who belong to this role have access to the Skype for Business Admin Center.

- **Service administrator**   Users in this role manage service requests and monitor the health of services. This role requires users to have administrative permission for any specific service that has to be managed.

- **SharePoint administrator**   This is the role for users administering SharePoint Online. Users who belong to this role have access to the SharePoint Online Admin Center.

- **User management administrator**   Users in this role can reset users' passwords; monitor the health of services; and manage users' accounts, groups, and service requests. Users in this role can't delete a global admin, create other admin roles, or reset passwords for billing, global, and service administrators.

The global administrator role is an all-or-nothing role, while all the other roles can be assigned selectively based on the effective permissions that you want to provide. In the following sections, you will see the main tools available for administrators in Office 365.

Notice that whenever you define an administrative role for a target user, you will have to provide an alternative email address for any further account recovery action. You should also consider enabling multifactor authentication for the administrative users to have a better level of security and privacy. Moreover, it is common to have administrative users who just accomplish their administrative roles and are not associated with any specific license. It is up to you to define whether you want to assign a subscription license to an administrative account, but it is not mandatory to have a subscription license to administer a specific service. Thus, you don't need to pay any license fee to have any of the administrative accounts.

The new Office 365 Admin Center

Every user belonging to an administrative role can access the Office 365 Admin Center, which is a site dedicated to administrators of one or more of the available services and of the whole tenant. The Admin Center has been renewed in early 2016 and provides a nice web UI, which can be consumed from almost any device and in any place. There is also a mobile app available for the main mobile platforms (iOS, Android, and Windows Phone) if you prefer to use a native app. In Figure 1-10, you can see a screenshot of the home page of the new Admin Center.

The screenshot has been taken using a global administrative account. Thus, all the services are available. As you can see, the home page provides a dashboard with a first look at the health status of the farm and of the services. In case of any issue, including services with reduced functionalities even if they are still running, you will be informed and will have access to detailed information about the issue and a roadmap for the resolution of the issue. Moreover, through the welcome dashboard, you can access the most common and frequently used actions, like those related to managing users, the activity reports, the billing information, and the message center.

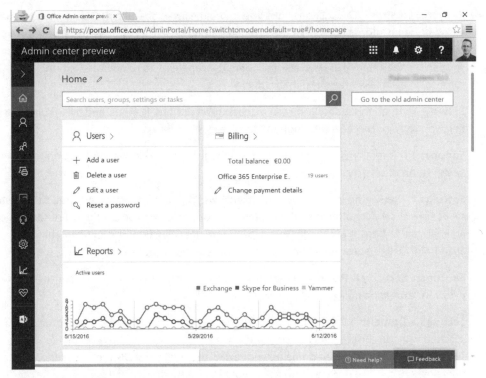

FIGURE 1-10 The home page of the Office 365 Admin Center

On the left side of the screen, you can access all the tenant-wide settings as long as you have proper permissions to access them. The following list explains the main sections of the new administrative user interface.

- **Home**   This is the home page of the Office 365 Admin Center.

- **Users**   Within this section, you can manage active users, restore deleted users, and manage email migration. The latest capability allows you to import mailbox content from external services or repositories like Gmail, Outlook.com, Hotmail, Yahoo, a PST file, and any other mail service that is accessible through the IMAP protocol.

- **Groups**   This section can be used to administer distribution lists, security groups, or Office 365 Groups.

- **Groups > Shared Mailboxes**   This section provides the user interface for administering any shared mailbox in Exchange Online. Keep in mind that shared mailboxes do not require any additional license for Exchange Online.

- **Resources > Rooms & Equipment**   This section allows you to manage company assets like meeting rooms or cars, which can be allocated and booked for meetings or for any shared usage. This list of resources will be available to all users in the tenant.

- **Resources > Sites**   This section allows you to see the list of SharePoint Online site collections, including some information about the external sharing settings. From this page, you can also enable/disable and configure the external sharing settings for any specific site collection, and you can see the external users, if any, including the capability to remove any external user. You can also create a new site collection from scratch.

- **Billing**   Through this section, you can manage subscriptions, licenses, and bills. From this section, you can also buy new subscriptions and licenses, if needed.

- **Support**   This section is used to create and manage support requests and to monitor the health status of services.

- **Settings > Apps**   This is a wide section that allows you to define settings related to the whole set of apps or services offered within the tenant. From here, you can configure antispam and antimalware settings in Exchange Online, configure site collections and external sharing in SharePoint Online, software updates, user software settings, and so on.

- **Settings > Security & Privacy**   From this section, you can define general security rules like password expiration policies.

- **Settings > Domains**   This section provides the user interface to manage DNS domains associated with the current tenant. From here, you can register new DNS domains, configure DNS settings of already registered domains, and review the suggested DNS settings for configured domains. You can also make a live check of your DNS settings, if needed.

- **Settings > Organization Profile**   This section allows you to define general information about your organization and the physical location of your business in Bing Places for Business. Within this section, you can also enable the First Release capability, which allows you to test upcoming new features for a subset of test users before they are released. Moreover, here you can define a custom theme for your tenant and you can define any custom tile for the Office 365 app launcher.

- **Settings > Partner Relationship**   This section allows you to manage delegated partners, which are external Microsoft partners that can perform delegated administration for you on your tenant. For example, a delegated partner could be the partner who sold you the Office 365 subscription. To access and manage your tenant, a delegated partner has to be authorized by a global administrator of your tenant. The delegation process starts with the partner sending an email to ask if you want to give him permission to act as a partner on your tenant.

- **Reports > Usage**   From this section, you can see reports about the services used. Here, you can find reports like users' email activity, Office license activations, and so on.

- **Reports > Security & Compliance**   From this section, you can configure any rule about auditing, protection, security, and data loss prevention (DLP).

- **Health > Service Health**   Through this section, you can check the history of issues, double-check any future maintenance plan, and check the current status of the services running your Office 365 tenant.

- **Health > Message Center**   This section gives you access to the latest messages about the health status of your tenant and its related services.

- **Health > Recently Added**   This section gives you a quick overview, with links to detailed information, of the newly released capabilities and features and the upcoming news based on the current Office 365 public roadmap.

- **Health > Directory Sync Status**   This section provides a useful user interface to review, monitor, and manage the DNS domains configured for directory synchronization and federation. It will show up just in case the current tenant has directory synchronization in place.

- **Admin Centers > Exchange**   From this section, you can access the Exchange Online Admin Center.

- **Admin Centers > Skype for Business**   From this section, you can access the Skype for Business Admin Center.

- **Admin Centers > SharePoint**   From this section, you can access the SharePoint Online Admin Center.

- **Admin Centers > Yammer**   From this section, you can access the administrative settings of the Yammer network related to the current Office 365 tenant, if any.

- **Admin Centers > Security & Compliance**   From this section, you can access the Office 365 Compliance Center.

- **Admin Centers > Azure AD**   By following this link, you can access the Azure management portal to manage the Azure AD tenant that is under the cover of the current Office 365 tenant.

At the time of this writing, the new Office 365 Admin Center is still under public preview, even if fully functional and code complete.

The classic Office 365 Admin Center

If you prefer to use the previous edition of the Office 365 Admin Center, which is still available for backward compatibility, you can select the Go to the old Admin Center button in the upper-right corner of the home page of the new Admin Center, and you will be brought to the old, or "classic," UI. From there, you will find almost the same actions and commands available through a different UI.

For your own reference, here you can find the settings and menu items as they are organized in the previous edition of the Office 365 Admin Center.

- **Dashboard**   The home page of the old Office 365 Admin Center.

- **Setup**   From here, you can follow a multistep setup wizard that will enable you to set up your tenant, including any related DNS domain; define the users; copy data into mailboxes; and start delivering email messages. It usually takes between 20 and 30 minutes to be ready with a properly set up tenant.

- **Users**   Within this section, you can manage active users, restore deleted users, and manage delegated partners (external Microsoft Partners that can perform delegated administration for you on your tenant). You already read information about delegated partners in the previous section about the new Office 365 Admin Center.

- **Company Profile**   Through this section, you can define companywide information like the company profile, any custom theme for the whole tenant, custom tiles in the app launcher, and custom help desk services.

- **Import**   This section provides the capability to import large amounts of data, like PST mailboxes or large files and folders, into Exchange Online or SharePoint Online. You can upload those files using the Internet network, or you can ship hard drives to Microsoft. You can find further details about importing PST files in the article "Import PST files to Office 365," which is available on Microsoft TechNet at the following URL: *https://technet.microsoft.com/library/ms.o365 .cc.IngestionHelp.aspx*. You can also find more details about importing large numbers of files to SharePoint Online in the article "Import data to Office 365," which is available on Microsoft TechNet at the following URL: *https://technet.microsoft.com/library/mt210445.aspx*.

- **Contacts**   This section allows you to manage an All Contacts address list for the tenant. Contacts recorded in this list will be available to all users in the tenant.

- **Shared Mailboxes**   This section provides the user interface for administering any shared mailbox in Exchange Online. Keep in mind that shared mailboxes do not require any additional license for Exchange Online.

- **Meeting Rooms**   This section allows you to manage company assets like meeting rooms, which can be allocated and booked for meetings. This list of resources will be available to all users in the tenant.

- **Groups**   These can be used to administer distribution lists or Office 365 Groups.

- **Domains**   This section provides the user interface to manage DNS domains associated with the current tenant. From here, you can register new DNS domains and configure DNS settings of already registered domains.

- **Public Website**   This is an informative page that explains how to create a public website for your company by leveraging any of the third-party services available. For some old tenants, it is still possible to create or manage a public website hosted in SharePoint Online, but it is an old and retired capability that you should no longer use and on which you should no longer rely.

- **Billing**   Through this section, you can manage subscriptions, licenses, and bills. You can also buy new subscriptions and licenses. Moreover, you can define the users who will receive billing notifications.

- **External Sharing**   This section allows you to define at the tenant level if you want to enable external sharing for SharePoint Online sites, calendars, Skype for Business, or Integrated Apps. You can also see some reporting that allows you to understand what is shared with whom, keeping your data under control.

- **Mobile Management**   This section provides the capability to manage mobile devices, like smartphones and tablets, remotely by applying settings and restrictions, controlling mobile access, and being able to do remote wipe of corporate data.

- **Service Settings**   This is a wide section that allows you to define settings related to the entire set of services offered within the tenant. From here, you can configure antispam and antimalware settings in Exchange Online; create site collections in SharePoint Online; define general rules like password expiration rules, software updates, and user software settings; and so on. Within this section, you can also enable the First Release capability, which allows you to test upcoming new features for a subset of test users before they are released.

- **Reports**   From this section, you can see reports about the services used. Here, you can find reports like users' resources and licenses usage, Skype for Business activities, SharePoint Online storage metrics and statistics, OneDrive for Business storage metrics, auditing of security critical events, data loss prevention (DLP) reports, and so on.

- **Service Health**   Through this section, you can check the history of issues and double-check any future maintenance plan.

- **Support**   This section is used to create and manage support requests and to monitor the health status of services.

- **Purchase Services**   This section provides access to the store, from which you can buy additional services and licenses.

- **Message Center**   This section gives you access to the latest messages about the health status of your tenant and its related services.

- **Tools**   This is the main entry point for a set of useful tools for checking the overall tenant configuration, the Exchange Server on-premises configuration with the Office 365 Best Practices Analyzer, the network connectivity and bandwidth with the Microsoft Connectivity Analyzer, and the Office 365 Client Performance Analyzer.

- **Admin**   This section provides access to the administrative interface of all the services available at the tenant level, like Exchange Online, Skype for Business, SharePoint Online, Yammer, the Compliance Center, Azure AD, Bing Places for Business, and so on.

However, because this book targets developers, in this chapter you will not see many more details about the available administrative sections, except for a couple of areas that are of interest to a developer.

Two sections in particular really matter from a developer perspective, and the following sections will dig into them.

Organization Profile

The section related to the Organization Profile allows admins to manage a custom theme for the whole tenant and custom tiles for the app launcher or a custom help desk.

The Organization Profile page provides access to some descriptive information about your company. This information includes the organization name, the address, the telephone number, and the main technical reference email addresses. The most interesting sections of the Organization Profile, from a developer perspective, are the Custom Theming and the Custom Tiles.

A custom theme for the tenant applies to the Office 365 suite bar and in particular to the top navigation bar. In Figure 1-11, you can see these elements.

FIGURE 1-11 The main Office 365 suite bar and the top navigation bar

A custom theme is made of the following elements:

- **Customo logo**   This is an image with a fixed size of 200 × 30 pixels, not larger than 10 KB, which can be a JPG, PNG, or GIF. It will be shown in the middle of the top navigation bar.

- **URL for a clickable logo**   If you want to make the custom logo clickable, here you can provide the target URL that will be loaded by clicking the logo. Provide full URL, including http:// or https://.

- **Background image**   Defines a background image with a fixed size of 1366 × 50 pixels or fewer, not larger than 15 KB, which can be a JPG, PNG, or GIF. It will be shown as the background for the top navigation bar.

- **Accent color**   The color that is used for the app launcher button, for mouse over, and for other accents.

- **Nav bar background color**   Defines the background color for the top navigation bar.

- **Text and icons**   Defines the color used for text and icons in the top navigation bar.

- **App launcher icon**   Allows you to select the color for the app launcher icon.

Through the Custom Theming page, you have the option to remove any applied custom theming or custom colors, and you can prevent users from overriding the custom theming with their own theme.

In Figure 1-12, you can see the UI of the page that allows you to define a custom theme.

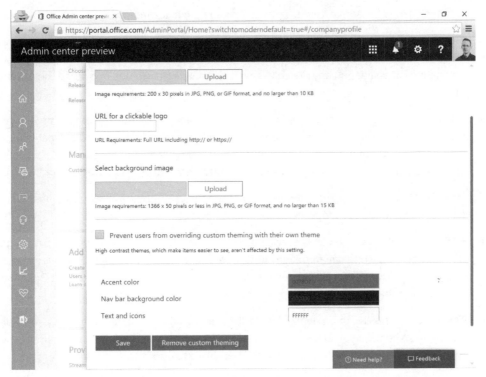

FIGURE 1-12 The page to define a custom theme available in the Office 365 Admin Center

Custom Tiles is another useful section that allows you to define custom items that will be available to the end users for pinning in the app launcher. Every tile is made of a Title, a URL that can target a link inside or outside the tenant, a Description, and an Image URL for the image that will be shown inside the tile. At the time of this writing, any custom tile will be available to the end users, but they will have to pin the tile in their app launcher manually. Otherwise, that tile will be visible only by clicking the My Apps link in the lower area of the app launcher. Soon it likely will be possible to force the pinning of a tile in the app launcher for all the users in the tenant, improving the governance experience for tenant administrators.

You can also extend the app launcher with custom tiles by creating and registering applications in Azure AD. This topic will be covered in upcoming chapters, particularly Chapter 4 and Chapter 10.

SharePoint Admin Center

Another useful administrative tool, not only from an IT professional perspective but also from a developer perspective, is the SharePoint Admin Center. In fact, most of the development done around Office 365 includes or at least leverages the SharePoint Online service. You could do any custom development solution that does not relate to SharePoint Online, but most of the developers who were working in SharePoint on-premises are moving to SharePoint Online and to the cloud development model, so they will need to manage SharePoint Online through the SharePoint Admin Center.

Through the SharePoint Admin Center, you can manage the following sections:

- **Site Collections**   This section allows you to create and manage all the site collections defined in the current tenant. From this section, you can also enable and configure or disable the external sharing capabilities on any site collection and manage the storage quota and the resource quota.

- **InfoPath**   This section is available for managing the settings of the InfoPath Forms Services. However, InfoPath is a discontinued technology, only available for backward compatibility, and you should avoid using it. In the following chapters, particularly those in Section 4, "SharePoint and Office Add-ins," you will see some suitable alternatives to and remediations for InfoPath.

- **User Profiles**   From this section, you can manage the users' user profiles, including their capability to manage custom properties, audiences, and so on.

- **BCS**   The Business Connectivity Services (BCS) section allows you to configure and manage BCS connections, which can target any REST-based service. This capability becomes interesting when you have hybrid topologies and you want to consume within SharePoint Online some business data that are available on-premises.

- **Term Store**   This is a fundamental section for defining and managing term groups, term sets, and terms. Whenever you are working in real-world enterprise-level projects, you usually need to define taxonomies, and this section is the best place to go.

- **Records Management**   This section allows you to define "send to" connections for submitting content to sites with configured Content Organizer.

- **Search**   This section provides the main entry point for configuring the Search service at the tenant level. It includes the capability to configure the search schema, the query rules, the result sources, and many other search-related settings.

- **Secure Store**   This section can be used to define Secure Store applications for accessing external services by providing a specific set of credentials.

- **Apps**   This section can be used to set up the tenant-level app catalog, if any. It also allows you to configure the settings related to the SharePoint Add-ins in general, like add-in settings, licenses, store settings, and so on.

- **Settings**   This section allows you to make some tenant-level configuration settings like showing or hiding OneDrive for Business to the users, allowing or deying access to the Microsoft Graph, chosing between having Yammer or the old newsfeeds enabled by default, configuring services like Information Rights Management (IRM), enabling or disabling the new SharePoint UI experience, and so on.

- **Configure Hybrid**   This section provides an easy-to-use wizard to set up a hybrid topology between Office 365 and SharePoint on-premises.

If you like, you can also administer SharePoint Online by using Microsoft PowerShell scripting. You can leverage both the SharePoint Online Management Shell, which is available at the following URL (*https://technet.microsoft.com/en-us/library/fp161362.aspx*), and the OfficeDev PnP PowerShell extensions, which are available for free as an open source project at the following URL: *http://aka.ms/ OfficeDevPnPPowerShell*. Further details about the OfficeDev PnP project will be provided in Chapter 2, "Overview of Office 365 development."

Summary

In this chapter, you studied the overall architecture of Office 365, and you learned that it is one of Microsoft's main SaaS offerings. You examined the main services the Office 365 ecosystem offers, and you learned about the new Office client offering, which is installed through the Click-to-Run setup model. You saw the main subscriptions available on the market and the services included in each subscription.

Moreover, you explored the main administrative roles of an Office 365 tenant and the administrative tools available to manage, monitor, and maintain the services included. In particular, you saw the administrative tools for customizing the UI and branding of an Office 365 tenant and for administering the Microsoft SharePoint Online service.

In Chapter 2, you will learn how to leverage Office 365 from a developer perspective, and you will explore the main extensibility areas and tools to build business-level solutions to improve your users' and customers' productivity.

Overview of Office 365 development

I n Chapter 1, "Microsoft Office 365: A quick tour," you got a general overview of Microsoft Office 365 and of all the services that enrich it. Because this book targets developers, this chapter will give you an overview of the main areas of development and customization of Office 365. Moreover, you will see some of the most useful tools available on the market, most of them made by the community of Office 365 developers, to realize the potential of the platform.

Setting up your development environment

First of all, to develop solutions for Office 365, you need to set up your development environment. One piece of great news in the Office 365 development world is that you don't need to install any server-side components. You just need to have a client machine that is connected to the Internet to consume the chonline services of Office 365.

Setting up an Office 365 developer tenant

To develop solutions for Office 365 and practice with the samples that are illustrated in this book, you need to have an Office 365 subscription, which can be used for development and testing purposes only.

Office 365 is a service Microsoft provides through a subscription model, but if you are new to Office 365 development you can register to have a free one-year subscription and a dedicated developer tenant. Open your browser and navigate to the URL: *http://dev.office.com/*. Follow the instructions to join the Office 365 Developer Program and sign up. By joining the Developer Program, you will get a free subscription to Office 365 valid for one year and some other content and free licenses of third-party tools that can help you develop your solutions.

You should think about having a dedicated development and testing environment for the full cycle of development, not only for the first year. Most likely, you will also need a Microsoft Azure subscription for publishing some of the developments you will make.

If you have a valid MSDN subscription, you should be able to activate a corresponding Microsoft Azure subscription with some prepaid credits. If you do not, you should register for a new Azure subscription, providing a credit card as a guarantee.

Configuring your development machine

Once you have defined the Office 365 and Azure subscriptions, you are ready to set up your development machine.

Nowdays, a common development environment is made of Microsoft Visual Studio Code or Microsoft Visual Studio 2015 and some other useful development tools. Note that for most of the development tasks that we will cover in this book, the free license of Visual Studio Code will suffice. However, if you are a professional developer, you probably will find it beneficial to have a professional tool like Microsoft Visual Studio 2015, updated with Update 2 and enriched with the latest version of Office development tools for Visual Studio, which you can download from the following URL: *http://aka.ms/getlatestofficedevtools*. For example, if you are using Microsoft Visual Studio 2015, you can find some ready-to-go project templates that are helpful when developing SharePoint Add-ins or Office Add-ins.

In fact—as you can see in Figure 2-1—in Visual Studio 2015 there are a bunch of project templates for creating Office Add-ins and SharePoint Add-ins. In Visual Studio 2015, you can find many more project templates targeting Office VSTO and SharePoint solutions, but they all target the old development model for on-premises only (SharePoint 2010 and SharePoint 2013) or the old extensibility model of Office client. Thus, when working in Visual Studio 2015 and targeting Office 365, you should focus your attention on the group of project templates highlighted in Figure 2-1.

However, as you will learn by reading this book, programming for Office 365 doesn't mean developing solutions for SharePoint Online and Office client only. In general, you will learn how to write web applications, or native applications, that leverage the entire Office 365 ecosystem.

In contrast, if you are using Visual Studio Code, you will have to write almost everything from scratch, even though there are some useful open source tools about which you will learn in the upcoming pages. In addition to the main development tools, you probably will need some additional tools and SDKs to develop a whole set of Office 365 solutions.

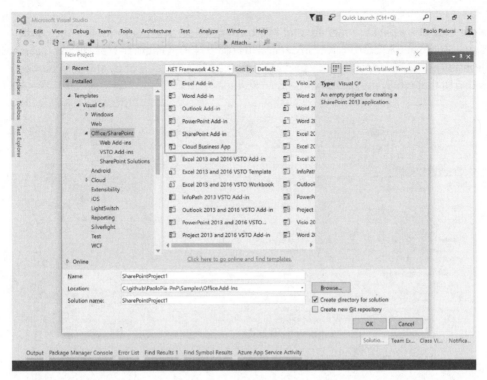

FIGURE 2-1 The project templates available in Microsoft Visual Studio 2015 for developing SharePoint and Office solutions

Office 365 Developer Patterns & Practices tools

First, there is a community project called Office 365 Developer Patterns & Practices (PnP), which is an initiative originally made by some Microsoft internal people and today held by a core team of a few Microsoft internals and external community members like MCSMs (Microsoft Certified Solution Masters for SharePoint) and MVPs (Microsoft Most Valuable Professionals). You can find more information about PnP at the following URL: *http://aka.ms/OfficeDevPnP*. The focus of PnP is to provide training, guidance articles, samples, solutions, and more to support the community of Office 365 developers.

One of the key elements of the PnP offering is a library of helper types, extension methods, and frameworks to make it easy to develop Office 365 solutions. The library is called SharePoint PnP Core library, and it is an open source library that is available for free on GitHub (*https://github.com/OfficeDev /PnP-Sites-Core/*). It can be installed in any Visual Studio project by searching for "SharePointPnP" on NuGet, as shown in Figure 2-2.

Note NuGet is a package manager for Microsoft development platforms like Microsoft Visual Studio and Microsoft .NET in general. By using NuGet Package Manager, you can easily install and keep up to date any package provided by Microsoft or by any third parties, with a UI that is fully integrated with Visual Studio.

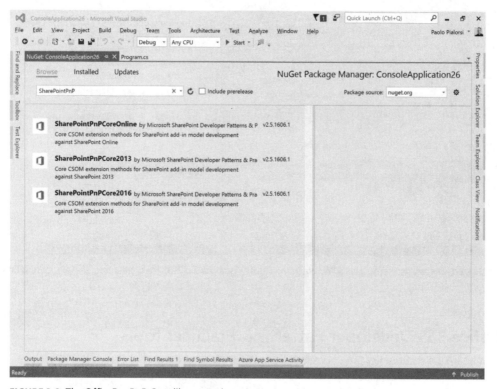

FIGURE 2-2 The OfficeDevPnP Core library package in NuGet within Microsoft Visual Studio 2015

As you can see in Figure 2-2, there are three flavors available for the library.

- **SharePointPnPCore2013** Targets SharePoint 2013 on-premises and uses the CSOM (client-side object model) library for SharePoint 2013 on-premises

- **SharePointPnPCore2016** Targets SharePoint 2016 on-premises

- **SharePointPnPCoreOnline** Targets SharePoint Online and leverages the latest CSOM library for SharePoint Online

Depending on your target platform, you will have to download the proper package. All the packages provide almost the same set of capabilities except for the functionalities that are available only on the cloud or only on SharePoint 2016.

Because the PnP Core library is so powerful, you probably will find it useful to reference it in every Office 365 solution.

Another amazing feature included in the PnP Core library is the PnP Remote Provisioning Engine, which targets provisioning on SharePoint 2013, SharePoint 2016, or SharePoint Online. If you are a SharePoint developer for on-premises, and you are used to developing solutions using the old FTC (Full Trust Code) development model, you probably know that in SharePoint on-premises—since SharePoint 2007—it is possible to provision artifacts (lists, libraries, content types, site columns, and so on) by using the feature framework. The feature framework uses CAML (Collaborative Application Markup Language) and XML-based files to define the artifacts to provision. However, the FTC development model and the feature framework are not available in the new world of SharePoint Online and Office 365.

Nevertheless, you can do remote provisioning. This means using SharePoint CSOM to provision artifacts instead of using the CAML/XML-based feature framework. While transforming FTC solutions, WSP (Windows SharePoint Services) packages, and Sandboxed solutions into the new add-in model, you should also approach provisioning artifacts and settings in a more maintainable manner. Using pure CSOM enables you to control by code the provisioning and the versioning of artifacts. This is the option Microsoft engineering officially recommends because CAML/XML-based provisioning will cause maintenance challenges with the evolving templates or definitions. Nevertheless, doing all the provisioning manually and by writing CSOM-based code could be a long and painful task.

Luckily, the PnP Core team and the entire OfficeDev PnP community have built an engine that is part of the PnP Core library. It leverages the PnP Core library extensions, enabling you to provision artifacts easily. Moreover, the PnP Remote Provisioning Engine enables you to model your artifacts within the web browser by using a prototype or a model site and to extract the designed artifacts into a template file, which can then be applied to any target site.

The overall goal of the PnP Remote Provisioning Engine is to make it simple to accomplish useful and common tasks while provisioning sites and artifacts. The provisioning template can be created in memory by using a domain model that is defined within the PnP Core library, or, as already stated, it can be persisted as a file. In the latter scenario, out of the box the file can be an XML file based on a community-defined XML Schema (*https://github.com/OfficeDev/PnP-Provisioning-Schema/*), or it can be a JSON file. Since June 2016, there is also support for an OpenXML file format, which includes all of the information for provisioning artifacts within a unique ZIP file that adheres to the OPC (Open Packaging Conventions) specification. By default, a template can be read from or written to a file system folder, a document library in SharePoint, or a container in Azure Blob storage, which is a cloud-based repository for binary blobs (that is, files) available on Microsoft Azure. However, from an architectural perspective, you can implement your own template formatter and your custom persistence provider to save or load a template with whatever format and persistence storage you like.[1]

Built on top of the PnP Core library and the PnP Remote Provisioning Engine is the PnP Partner Pack, which can be considered a starter kit for customers and partners. The PnP Partner Pack provides most of the patterns described by PnP within a unique and articulated solution that can be installed on any Office 365 tenant. The solution enables you to provide a high-level user interface for managing self-service site collections and site creation based on stored PnP provisioning templates and gives you the

---

[1] If you want further information about the PnP Remote Provisioning Engine, you can watch the following video on Channel 9: *https://channel9.msdn.com/blogs/OfficeDevPnP/Getting-Started-with-PnP-Provisioning-Engine*.

capability to save and manage a companywide catalog of provisioning templates. Moreover, the PnP Partner Pack includes other interesting samples and tools in the fields of governance and maintenance of SharePoint Online site collections.

Another powerful component of the PnP offering is the PnP PowerShell cmdlets. On GitHub (*https://github.com/OfficeDev/PnP-PowerShell*)—thanks to the efforts of Erwin van Hunen (*https://twitter.com/erwinvanhunen*)—you can find about a hundred open source custom cmdlets that make it possible to consume SharePoint on-premises (2013/2016) and SharePoint Online from PowerShell. You can accomplish tasks like creating site collections and sites, lists, content types, site columns, and so on. As an Office 365 developer, you will need to have this set of cmdlets on your environment.

To install the PnP PowerShell cmdlets, you can download a .MSI setup package from GitHub by browsing to the following URL: *https://github.com/OfficeDev/PnP-PowerShell/tree/master/Binaries*.

There, you will find three flavors, which pair the same options as the PnP Core library:

- **SharePointPnPPowerShell2013.msi**   Targets SharePoint 2013 on-premises

- **SharePointPnPPowerShell2016.msi**   Targets SharePoint 2016 on-premises

- **SharePointPnPPowerShellOnline.msi**   Targets SharePoint Online

Another option you have, if your main operating system is Windows 10 or if you have at least PowerShell 3.0 and PowerShell Package Management, is to install the PnP PowerShell package directly within PowerShell by using the Install-Module cmdlet, using any of the following statements, based on the version of cmdlets that you want to install:

```
Install-Module SharePointPnPPowerShellOnline
```

```
Install-Module SharePointPnPPowerShell2016
```

```
Install-Module SharePointPnPPowerShell2013
```

Once you have installed the PnP PowerShell cmdlets on your machine and the PnP Core library in your development projects, you will have a rich set of tools for developing Office 365 solutions.

Preparing for the SharePoint Framework

Another interesting option available for developing SharePoint Online and general Office 365 solutions is to leverage development languages like JavaScript, TypeScript, and Node.js.

The REST API offered by SharePoint 2013/2016 and SharePoint Online, which will be covered in Chapter 9, "SharePoint REST API," and the emerging Microsoft Graph API, which will be covered in the next section of this chapter and in Chapter 3, "Microsoft Graph API reference," provide the capability to create powerful solutions written with JavaScript or any other script language that can consume REST endpoints. Moreover, the evolution announced on May 4, 2016, about the SharePoint Framework will involve developing client-side web parts and applications using JavaScript.

Thus, it's worth spending some time setting up your development environment to support these modern development techniques, which will be the future for developing the UI of SharePoint.

First of all, it is fundamental to say that to develop with the SharePoint Framework, you can use either a Windows or a Mac development machine. Thus, you are no longer forced to have a specific Microsoft operating system to develop. The tools needed to develop modern solutions are, as for SharePoint Add-ins and Office Add-ins, any of the Visual Studio flavors like Visual Studio Code or Visual Studio 2015. Nevertheless, you can use any text or code editor you like, as long as you can use it to write JavaScript or TypeScript code.

 Note TypeScript is a typed superset of JavaScript that compiles to plain JavaScript. It is useful whenever you need to create large JavaScript development projects because it allows you to write fully typed code, with syntax check and compile time check, but produce plain JavaScript files as a result. Microsoft has introduced TypeScript, but most enterprise companies worldwide use it. You can find samples, documentation, and further details about TypeScript on the language's official website: *https://www.typescriptlang.org/*.

You will also need to install the latest version of a Node.js runtime, which can be downloaded from the official Node.js site: *https://nodejs.org/en/*. With Node.js you will also use NPM, which is a package manager similar to NuGet for .NET. It is suggested that you update the NPM package manager to the latest version, which can be accomplished by using NPM by itself with a command like the following:

```
npm install -g npm
```

The solutions that you create with Node.js can be easily hosted on the cloud—for example, using Microsoft Azure. This realizes the potential of any Node.js solution for Office 365 or SharePoint Framework.

Moreover, it is useful to have a console emulator to play with Node.js and some other tools that you will install later. Thus, it is suggested that you install Curl for Windows (*http://www.confusedbycode.com/curl/*) and Cmder for Windows (*http://cmder.net/*), which is a console emulator for Windows.

There are two more useful tools for automating scaffolding of solutions and compilation tasks. The first tool is Yeoman (*http://yeoman.io/*), which can be installed through NPM while in the Cmder console, for example. The second tool is Gulp (*http://gulpjs.com/*), which automates the compilation and release of code through a set of customizable workflows. Gulp can also be installed using NPM from the console emulator.

In Section IV of this book, "SharePoint & Office Add-ins," you will see some of these tools in action.

Office 365 applications development

Now that you have your development environment set up and ready to go, let's start thinking about the various kinds of solutions that you can develop in Office 365.

First of all, you should know that every kind of project that interacts with Office 365 by consuming its services can be considered an Office 365 application. Later in this book, in Chapter 10, "Creating Office 365 applications," you will learn about development techniques and see a real business solution in practice. In this section, you will get an overview of the main architectural patterns and the most common scenarios that developing a custom Office 365 application can satisfy. The following list is far from complete, but it provides a good set of common types of applications and solutions that you probably will need to create or at least consider in your real-life projects.

Web applications

The first flavor of applications for Office 365 is applications with a web-based user interface. You can develop such applications with whatever development environment you like. However, if you usually develop with Microsoft technologies, you probably will use Microsoft ASP.NET.

Nowdays, one of the most common techniques for developing ASP.NET applications is to leverage the Model-View-Controller (MVC) pattern and to create an ASP.NET MVC application. However, from a technological perspective, you are free to create an ASP.NET WebForm application. That said, in the field of Office 365 development, you should consider that there are many more samples on the network for MVC than for WebForm.

Moreover, if you are not a .NET developer and, for example, prefer to develop web applications using PHP or Java, you can still realize almost the same potentials that you could by using Microsoft .NET.

Full-page web applications

When you create a web application that extends Office 365, you have to face multiple architectural patterns and hosting options. One option is to create an application that will be hosted externally from Office 365—for example, using an Azure website within an Azure App Service.

> **Note** An Azure App Service is a cloud Platform as a Service (PaaS) offering provided by Microsoft Azure that enables you to build and host websites and REST services for mobile applications, connecting to data services and consuming data available on the cloud or on-premises.

Generally, these kinds of solutions are called provider-hosted applications (PHAs). This option is interesting when your application has an autonomous and independent UX (user experience) that can be integrated with the UX of the Office 365 ecosystem. In such a scenario, you typically can leverage toolkits like Office UI Fabric (*http://dev.office.com/fabric*) to brand the UI of your application with controls and building blocks that will make your application behave like the standard Office 365 UX but will keep a lot of control over the entire UI/UX of the solution. The end users will have a dedicated experience in which the custom Office 365 application will be provided as a full-screen, full-browser solution. In this kind of solution, you should try to preserve the common UI of Office 365, including the Office 365 suite bar. In Figure 2-3, you can see a screenshot of the PnP Partner Pack, which is built by leveraging this hosting model and keeping the UI of Office 365.

This solution can be applied to any kind of application, whatever Office 365 services it consumes or extends. In fact, the application will provide the entire UI, and the Office 365 services will be consumed through the Microsoft Graph. You will have to register the application in Microsoft Azure Active Directory (AD), and in Chapter 4, "Azure Active Directory and security," you will learn how to accomplish this task.

The end users will be brought to the custom application by clicking a tile in the Office 365 app launcher, by following a direct link in a SharePoint site page, or by activating an add-in in the UI of Office client, among other methods. The application will communicate with Office 365 by using REST over HTTPS and the Microsoft Graph or the SharePoint REST API. If the application has to execute some background and/or long-running processes, you can apply some decoupling and asynchronous patterns that will be discussed in more detail in Chapter 10.

FIGURE 2-3 A sample Office 365 application hosted externally from Office 365

A typical use case for this kind of application is a scenario in which you have to coordinate multiple services, like Exchange Online, SharePoint Online, the Office 365 Groups, and so on, and you need to provide a unique and common UI/UX to the end users, working in the background with the back-end services.

From an implementation cost perspective, these solutions guarantee a very convenient cost of development because they are basically simple web applications that consume Office 365 through a set of documented APIs.

These kinds of solutions are also cost-effective from a knowledge and learning perspective. They have a very low total cost of development and maintenance because the developers can be general ASP.NET developers—you don't need to have dedicated developers with deep vertical expertise on every involved service of the Office 365 ecosystem. Of course, knowing a little bit about Office 365 development could be useful.

Web API applications

Another option that you have is to create a web application that just hosts a set of custom REST APIs. These REST APIs can consume the Office 365 ecosystem in the back end, providing a richer set of services as custom endpoints. From a security (authentication and authorization) perspective, you can fully leverage Azure AD for users' authentication and authorization. In fact, in Azure AD you can register not only applications that will consume third-party services like those offered by the Microsoft Graph, but also your own services, providing authorization rules that Azure AD will enforce during the consumption of those services.

A typical use case for hosting a web API application for Office 365 is when you want to enrich the native services, integrating custom data repositories or third-party applications. This kind of solution becomes particularly interesting when the consumer of the REST API is another web application or a native application.

You can mix the two solutions to create a web-based application that provides a set of UI elements and pages together with some custom REST API endpoints.

Single-page applications

A third option for developing an Office 365 application is to create a single-page application (SPA). An SPA is basically a web application that provides the UX through a unique page with some client-side JavaScript code. These kinds of solutions typically are based on one of the JavaScript toolkits available on the market and in the community like KnockoutJS, AngularJS, and many others.

The key point of an SPA is to provide the end users with an immersive UX based on a single page that mimics the experience of a classic desktop solution, avoiding the need to reload the whole page or change the current page. An SPA typically leverages AJAX and WebSockets to communicate with the server, dynamically updating the UI by leveraging HTML5, CSS3, JavaScript/jQuery, and/or any other toolkit for creating dynamic pages in JavaScript. A common scenario in these use cases is to have a set of custom Web APIs in the back end hosted, for example, on Azure and invoked by the client-side code in the SPA.

Such applications are usually hosted within SharePoint Online in dedicated pages, even if theorically you can host them wherever you like. Hosting them within the domain that provides SharePoint Online content makes it simple to solve any cross-domain or cross-origin resource sharing (CORS) issue—in particular, if those applications just need to consume resources hosted in SharePoint Online, which is often the case.

Typical examples of native SPAs are Office 365 Video and most of the NextGen Portals that Microsoft is releasing. The upcoming SharePoint Framework can also leverage the same development model.

Native applications

Another common use case is related to native applications, which are custom applications targeting specific devices and/or client operating systems. Typically, they are mobile applications or desktop applications. They could be apps for smartphones, for tablets, or for any other devices. The key point is that the UI/UX is built using device-specific frameworks and programming languages, while the back-end information and services could be directly provided by the Microsoft Graph and Office 365 or could be a set of custom REST API hosted in a web API application. Regardless of the kind of REST API the native application consumes, from an architectural perspective the application will leverage Azure AD and OpenID Connect for users' authentication and the Open Authorization protocol (OAuth) for users' authorization.

In the Microsoft technology landscape, you can use toolkits like Visual Studio 2015 and Xamarin to create multidevice applications for iOS, Android, and Windows Phone and for creating Universal Windows Platform (UWP) apps. From an architectural perspective, having a common set of APIs in the back end and a common UI/UX framework that targets all the potential platforms makes the overall solution promising.

These kinds of applications are completely integrated with the out-of-box Office 365 and Microsoft Azure offerings, and through them you can realize great potential.

Office 365 Connectors

One last flavor of Office 365 custom development solutions that deserves a section in this chapter is the capability to create Office 365 Connectors, which are custom extensions that can be plugged into Office 365 Groups.

As you saw in Chapter 1, Office 365 Groups are a new and emerging capability of Office 365 that allow people using Office 365 to self-create modern digital workplaces that are completely integrated with Outlook 2016 client and with the web-based UI of Outlook Web Access. Office 365 Groups provide a unique and modern place where people can keep track of documents, notes, emails, calendars, Skype calls, and so on. However, nowdays most people also use third-party tools and cloud-based applications like Twitter, Trello, Asana, Slack, GitHub, Zendesk, Salesforce, and many others.

The Office 365 Connectors are a new technology that enables you to deliver relevant content and events from external applications into the shared inbox of an Office 365 Group. The content and events are delivered as cards into the shared inbox so that everybody belonging to the target Office 365 Group can see them by using Outlook 2016 Client, Outlook Web Access, or even the native mobile applications for Office 365 Groups available for iOS, Android, and Windows Phone.

At the time of this writing, there are already more than 50 connectors available, and many more will come in the near future. For example, you can set up a connection between an Office 365 Group focused on marketing a specific product and Twitter to get a notification card whenever there is a new tweet referring to any specific hashtag or account in Twitter. Or you can connect that Office 365 Group to Asana to manage tasks, and so on.

From a developer perspective, you can create custom connectors, which have to be registered in Office 365 to be able to communicate with Office 365 Groups. The communication protocol between your custom connectors and the Office 365 Groups leverages a webhook that the connector has to invoke by providing a JSON message via an HTTP POST request over SSL. In Figure 2-4, you can see a sample card for a custom event provided by a custom connector.

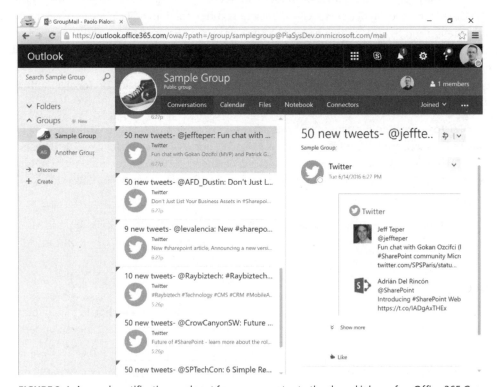

FIGURE 2-4 A sample notification card sent from a connector to the shared inbox of an Office 365 Group

If you like, you can also publish your connectors on the Office 365 Connectors catalog to make them available to others via the Office Store. A connector published on the public catalog will have to pass an approval process held by Microsoft.

An even easier way of providing custom events and messages is to register a webhook for a specific Office 365 Group manually. This option is only for one-shot scenarios in which you don't need to reuse the same connector on multiple groups, and it requires an IT buddy to register the webhook manually in the group and to fire JSON messages to deliver cards to the target group.

In Chapter 10, you will see an example of how to use Office 365 Connectors, and you will learn how to create a custom connector.

SharePoint online development

When developing solutions for Office 365, SharePoint Online often plays a big role. In fact, most of the solutions leverage SharePoint Online for storing documents, providing the basic UI elements, handling lists of tasks and calendars, and so on.

Thus, in this section you will learn about the most common development scenarios that you can satisfy with SharePoint Online and some of the tools that you installed on your development machine.

SharePoint Add-ins

The first and main scope of custom development in SharePoint Online is the development of SharePoint Add-ins. To be fair, all topics related to developing SharePoint Add-ins for SharePoint Online also target SharePoint on-premises. The environments share the same development and extensibility model, so despite the need to learn a new development model—especially if you come from the FTC (Full Trust Code) development model—the return on investment is worth it. This is an excellent feature of the SharePoint Add-in model because you write once and use twice (online and on-premises).

> **Note** If you are migrating from existing solutions for SharePoint on-premises, you can also have a look at the PnP (*http://aka.ms/OfficeDevPnP*) guidance articles about transformation from the FTC model to the cloud model.

Nowadays, you can develop a custom SharePoint Add-in whenever you need to create a custom solution that mainly targets SharePoint Online. As you saw in the previous section, "Office 365 applications develpoment," the capability to develop an Office 365 application that can target SharePoint Online and all the other services of the Office 365 ecosystem makes this last option more interesting.

The main difference between a SharePoint Add-in and an Office 365 application is that the SharePoint Add-in is registered in Microsoft Azure ACS (Access Control Service) through the add-in registration UI provided by SharePoint Online and can consume SharePoint Online only. In contrast, an Office 365 application is registered in Azure AD and can consume any service provided by Office 365 as long as it has proper permissions.

However, there are use cases in which you will need to create a SharePoint Add-in to achieve your results. Here is a short list of the most common scenarios in which you probably will create a SharePoint Add-in instead of an Office 365 application:

- **Custom overriding of SharePoint UI through JavaScript embedding** Customize the out-of-box UI and behavior of SharePoint by embedding custom JavaScript files—for example, through a user's custom actions—and by changing the HTML DOM (Document Object Model) of the pages or the behavior of some of the out-of-box commands. You can achieve the same result by creating an Office 365 application, but the investment of having a superset of capabilities just to provision a user's custom action is not worth the time required.

- **Custom SharePoint workflow solutions developed in Visual Studio 2015** Create SharePoint hosted workflow applications that can be executed in integrated mode to provide custom workflows through the standard UI of SharePoint and by extending lists and libraries within a host site. This cannot be achieved by creating an Office 365 application because the workflow manager component is available only within a SharePoint Add-in. Moreover, a workflow-integrated application can only be created through a SharePoint Add-in.

- **Custom list and library forms** Override the out-of-box add/display/edit forms of lists or libraries by replacing them with custom pages hosted in a provider-hosted SharePoint Add-in (PHA). Like UI overriding via JavaScript, this can be done by using an Office 365 application, but it is easier to create a SharePoint Add-in.

- **Remote event receivers** Create and register remote event receivers based on a WCF (Windows Communication Foundation) channel to handle events related to sites, lists, libraries, and so on. This is another typical SharePoint-oriented development scenario in which an Office 365 application does not fit. You will see more details about this topic in the upcoming section "Remote event receivers" of this chapter.

- **Any SharePoint on-premises custom development solution** You cannot customize a SharePoint on-premises farm with an Office 365 application, and unless you are in a hybrid topology, generally you cannot consume SharePoint on-premises from Office 365. A custom solution that has to target both SharePoint Online and SharePoint on-premises falls into this category. Because this book is about programming Office 365 and not about SharePoint on-premises, this last bullet can be considered an edge case.

In this book, you will not dig into development of SharePoint Add-ins because the focus is the entire Office 365 development. Nevertheless, it is important to know real use cases that require you to create a customization solution tied to SharePoint Online.

> **Note** If you want to read more about developing SharePoint Add-ins, you can read the book *Microsoft SharePoint 2013 Developer Reference* from Microsoft Press (ISBN: 0735670714), most of which is still valid for SharePoint 2016 in the field of SharePoint Add-ins development.

Remote timer jobs for SharePoint

Another common use case in which you can create a solution for SharePoint Online is the creation of a remote timer job. Aside from the word *remote* in the name, a timer job is a piece of code, typically executed based on a schedule, that interacts with SharePoint and executes some kind of maintenance task like synchronizing list items with external line of business systems, updating or uploading documents from external file repositories, checking governance rules, and so on.

In SharePoint on-premises, there were the FTC timer jobs. On the cloud—in SharePoint Online—you can replace them with remote timer jobs. *Remote* means that the job interacts with SharePoint Online using the client-side object model (CSOM) instead of running on the server and using the server object model of SharePoint, as it did for on-premises and FTC timer jobs. You can and should create jobs as remote timer jobs, even if your target is SharePoint on-premises, to be ready to migrate to SharePoint Online if and when you need to.

Moreover, if you are targeting SharePoint Online, a common architectural pattern is to use an Azure WebJob within an Azure App Service for running the batch software. An Azure WebJob is a portion of code that can be executed on demand or based on a schedule and that consumes compute resources of the Azure App Service in which it is deployed. From a developer's perspective, an Azure WebJob can be a console application written in C#, a PowerShell script, a Node.js program, and so on.

A key point to keep in mind while developing a remote timer job is that usually it interacts with SharePoint Online using an App-Only OAuth token. You will dig into details of OAuth in Chapter 4, but basically it means that one option is to register the job application as a SharePoint Add-in and to provide App-Only permissions to it. Thus, from a technical perspective, the remote timer job will be similar to any other SharePoint Add-in, giving you the same development experience.

A remote timer job can also be created as an Office 365 application, registering it in Azure AD instead of using Azure ACS. The benefit of creating a remote timer job for SharePoint Online as an Office 365 application is that you can target the entire Office 365 ecosystem and easily consume the Microsoft Graph instead of targeting SharePoint Online only.

Remote timer jobs are useful in most real enterprise-level solutions because you can decouple the execution of business tasks, which will happen in the background within the job, from the user interface that the end users will use to provide input for and to schedule those tasks.

One common architectural pattern that will be discussed in detail in Chapter 10 uses an Azure Blob storage queue to enqueue messages (that is, tasks), having a continuously running remote timer job that will dequeue the tasks and execute them. Indeed, whenever you provide a web-based UI to end users, like when you create a SharePoint Add-in or an Office 365 application, you shouldn't execute long-running and/or business-critical tasks within the process that is servicing web requests. Any issue, any request timeout, or any application pool recycle in the front end could compromise the running processes. Decoupling the UI from the real business processes allows you to run, monitor, and recover/repeat the business processes without any dependency from the UI layer. Furthermore, having an asynchronous pattern based on a queue allows you to scale more and be resilient in case of any sudden increase in user requests.

In the Office 365 Dev PnP Core library, you can find the remote timer job framework, which is useful for creating a remote timer job for SharePoint. In the remote timer job framework, you have all the base types and plumbing available for creating your jobs. You can find further details about this framework and about the Office 365 Dev PnP Core library in general in the PnP Core Training videos, which are available at the following URL: *http://aka.ms/OfficeDevPnPCoreTraining*.

Remote event receivers

One more use case that deserves custom development for SharePoint Online is remote event receivers (RERs). As in the previous section, the word *remote* just means that the event receiver will not be an FTC event receiver running on a SharePoint server and leveraging the server object model. It will be a bunch of code, typically C# and wrapped into a WCF service, which will be invoked by SharePoint Online (or on-premises) upon one or more events to which the RER subscribed. SharePoint Online will fire a SOAP request against the WCF service whenever any of the subscribed events happens.

The architectural model of the RERs makes them suitable for SharePoint only. Nowdays, the solutions based on REST webhooks are much more interesting and open because having a WCF service wrapper to make the RER endpoint available is a tight requirement.

Nevertheless, you might have to create a RER for SharePoint Online or for SharePoint on-premises, and in that case you will leverage almost the same syntax, tools, and knowledge that you need to create a SharePoint Add-in.

Remote provisioning

One last scenario in which you probably will create a solution specific for SharePoint Online is the remote provisioning of artifacts and settings onto a target SharePoint Online site, site collection, or tenant.

Earlier in this chapter, you saw the concept of remote provisioning in SharePoint Online as the capability to set up configuration settings and to create artifacts like lists, libraries, content types, site columns, and so on by using CSOM. To do that, you will need a custom SharePoint Add-in or a remote timer job that will execute the CSOM requests against the target SharePoint Online.

If you just need to provision a site based on a template and you want to leverage the PnP Remote Provisioning Engine, it will suffice to use the PnP PowerShell cmdlets to get a template from a model site and save it as an OpenXML, XML, or JSON file. For example, by using the PnP PowerShell extensions you can export a site as a template into an OpenXML .pnp file, including all the taxonomy terms and persisting any branding file, by using the following syntax:

```
Connect-SPOnline "https://[tenant-name].sharepoint.com/sites/[template-site]"

Get-SPOProvisioningTemplate -Out template.pnp -IncludeAllTermGroups -PersistBrandingFiles
```

where *[tenant-name]* and *[template-site]* have to be replaced with real values coming from your environment. Later, you can apply that template to a target site by using the following syntax, still in PowerShell:

```
Connect-SPOnline "https://[tenant-name].sharepoint.com/sites/[target-site]"

Apply-SPOProvisioningTemplate -Path .\template.pnp
```

However, if you want to do more, like dynamically creating lists, libraries, or sites based on the current user inputs or any specific event that could happen in SharePoint Online, you will need to do remote provisioning programmatically. You can still leverage the PnP Core library and the Provisioning Engine to accomplish this task, but you will have to write some custom code. In Chapter 10, you will see a sample code excerpt about how to provision artifacts in code by using the PnP Provisioning Engine.

Once again, if the provisioning of artifacts is part of a bigger solution that includes provisioning and something else not directly related to SharePoint Online, you can consider creating an Office 365 application registered in Azure AD instead.

Office client development

So far, you have seen some common use cases and custom development scenarios for solutions that target the online services the Office 365 ecosystem offers. Another fundamental set of customization projects are those for extending the Office client offering.

Since Office 2013, the extensibility model of Office client, whether it is the desktop version or the web-based version offered through Office Online services, is possible through a new development model called Office Add-ins.

The Office Add-ins model enables you to extend Office applications like Word, Excel, Outlook, and PowerPoint by using a set of well-know web technologies like HTML, CSS, and JavaScript together with the capability to consume a set of REST services. Furthermore, you can create custom add-ins for Microsoft Access Web Apps, which are the web version of Access that is hosted in SharePoint Online. This book will not cover the add-ins for Access Web Apps.

At the time of this writing, Microsoft has greatly improved the capabilities and the potential of Office Add-ins, making it possible to create add-ins that can be executed on a PC (Office 2013 or Office 2016), on a Mac (Office 2016 for Mac), in Office Online, or even on an iPad (Office for iPad). Moreover, Microsoft is currently working on making it possible to leverage the same development model to extend Office for iPhone, Office for Android, and Office Mobile for Windows 10.

Office Add-ins can be used to add new functionalities to applications and documents or to embed complex and interactive objects into documents. For example, you could have an Office Add-in for Word that binds external data into a document. Or, you could have an Office Add-in for Excel that embeds a dynamic map or a graph into a spreadsheet.

An Office Add-in is basically made of an XML manifest file and a web application made of a bunch of HTML, CSS, and JavaScript files, which represent the real add-in implementation. In Figure 2-5, you can see an architectural overview of the Office Add-ins.

The manifest file defines some general information about the add-in and the integration points of the add-in with the Office client applications, like the buttons or commands that extend the native UI and the URL of the pages that will be embedded in the target client application. Within the manifest, you can define permissions and data access requirements for the add-in.

The very basic web application could be a single, simple HTML page, hosted somewhere like a private web server or any other hosting infrastructure. However, usually the web application under the cover of an Office Add-in is built using both client-side and server-side technologies like JavaScript, Node.js, ASP.NET, PHP, and so on, and it can be hosted within an Azure App Service.

Usually, an Office Add-in interacts with the Office client environment by leveraging a JavaScript API for Office clients, provided by Microsoft. Moreover, Word and Excel have a dedicated set of host-specific object models for JavaScript to provide more contextual objects for interacting with the Office client hosting environment. Often, you will also need to consume third-party services or REST APIs within the Office Add-in. For example, you can consume the Microsoft Graph or even a custom set of REST APIs. In case you want to consume third-party services from the HTML code of the Office Add-in and avoid any CORS or same-origin policy issues, you can just leverage some server-side code published by the web host that publishes the add-in, or you can leverage the JSON-P protocol. Further details about the entire development model of the Office Add-ins, including an explanation of the available APIs and the techniques to work around CORS and same-origin policies, will be provided in Chapter 11, "Creating Office Add-ins." This section gives only a general overview of the Office Add-ins development model.

XML manifest   Web application   Office add-in

FIGURE 2-5 An architectural overview of the Office Add-ins

When you think about the Office Add-ins, you should consider some different flavors of add-ins, which are described in the following list:

- **Task Pane** The user interface is based on panels that are usually docked on the UI of the Office client application. The add-in will enhance the overall user experience, and it will not be tight to a specific document, but generally available in the UI of the Office clients. Users can drag the task pane around the UI of the Office client, having a user experience similar to the out-of-box task panes provided by Office. A Task Pane add-in targets almost any Office client application like Word, Excel, Outlook, PowerPoint, and even Project.

- **Content** This kind of add-in is useful to extend the content of a document. The overall user experience from an end user's perspective is to embed an external object into the content of a document. A Content add-in targets only Excel, PowerPoint, or browser-based Access.

- **Outlook** These add-ins target the mail or calendar appointment reading/composing experience and are usually activated based on a trigger like a specific word in the subject or body of a message, a particular sender of a received email message, and so on. An Outlook add-in targets Outlook client, Outlook Web App, and Outlook Web Access (OWA) for devices.

- **Command** This kind of add-in can add buttons on the Office ribbon or on selected contextual menus. The overall goal is to provide the end users with the same user experience they have for consuming out-of-box capabilities when they consume Office Add-ins. A Command add-in can be used to open a Task Pane add-in, to execute a command, or to insert custom content into a document. At the time of this writing, the App Command add-ins are supported in Outlook and are in preview for Excel, Word, and PowerPoint.

In Table 2-1, you can see the current status (at the time of this writing) of the support for the various Office Add-in flavors in the Office offering.

TABLE 2-1 Availability of Office Add-ins in the Microsoft Office offering

Office Version	Excel	Outlook	Word	PowerPoint
Office Online	Task Pane, Content, App Commands (Preview)	Mail Read, Mail Compose, App Commands	Task Pane	Content, Task Pane, App Commands (Preview)
Office 2013 for Windows	Task Pane, Content	Mail Read, Mail Compose, App Commands	Task Pane	Content, Task Pane
Office 2016 for Windows	Task Pane, Content, App Commands (Preview)	Mail Read, Mail Compose, App Commands	Task Pane	Content, Task Pane, App Commands (Preview)
Office for iPad	Taskpane, Content	-	Task Pane	Content, Task Pane
Office 2016 for Mac	Task Pane (Preview), Content (Preview)	Mail Read	Task Pane	Content, Task Pane
Office for iPhone	-	-	-	-
Office for Android	-	-	-	-
Office for Windows Phone 10	-	-	-	-

To develop Office Add-ins, you can use almost any text editor because you just need to write the XML manifest file and the HTML/CSS/JS files. However, by using Visual Studio Code or Visual Studio 2015 you can improve your quality of life because you will have some tooling for generating the XML manifest file for you and some autogenerated HTML and JavaScript code to speed up the overall add-in development process.

If you are using Visual Studio Code, you can consider leveraging a Yeoman Office Add-in generator, which will create all the scaffolding for you, and you will be able to implement the core functionalities of your Office Add-in without taking care of all the plumbing and details. In Chapter 11, you will see how to use this generator with Visual Studio Code. In the meantime, you can find further details here: *https://code.visualstudio.com/Docs/runtimes/office*.

If you are using Visual Studio 2015 and the latest Office development tools for Visual Studio, you will be able to develop add-ins using all the professional tools available in Visual Studio 2015. Again, in Chapter 11 you will see further details about how to use Visual Studio 2015 to develop Office Add-ins.

Nevertheless, it is fundamental to understand that to create Office Add-ins, you can use whatever development tool you like and whatever development platform you like, including ASP.NET, PHP, Node.js, and so on.

Once you have created an Office Add-in, you probably will want to install it on a testing environment, as you will learn by reading Chapter 11. You can do this by leveraging the sideloading capabilities of Office Online. You can find further details about sideloading add-ins for Word, Excel, and

PowerPoint at the following URL: *https://msdn.microsoft.com/en-us/library/office/mt657708.aspx*. You can find further information about sideloading Outlook add-ins at the following URL: *https://msdn. microsoft.com/en-us/library/office/mt657707.aspx*.

After proper testing, you will be able to release the add-in at the corporate level by using the add-in corporate catalog or even worldwide on the public marketplace by leveraging the Office Store. In Chapter 12, "Publishing your application and add-ins," you will learn more about how to publish an Office Add-in, a SharePoint Add-in, or an Office 365 application either on the corporate catalog or in the Office Store.

Summary

In this chapter, you had an overview of the most common and useful development techniques for extending and customizing Office 365. First, you learned about how to set up your development environment properly, not only installing the most common tools like Visual Studio Code or Visual Studio 2015, but also installing and leveraging third-parties' SDKs, libraries, and community projects to improve your code and your quality of life.

Then, you discovered Office 365 applications and the various flavors of projects like web applications, including full-page web applications, web API applications, single-page applications, and native applications. You also learned about the new Office 365 Connectors.

From a SharePoint perspective, you were introduced to SharePoint Add-ins, remote timer jobs, and remote event receivers, and you saw that you can use them to extend the SharePoint Online and SharePoint on-premises experiences. You also had an overview of the remote provisioning techniques, which enable you to provision artifacts and configurations settings on both SharePoint Online and SharePoint on-premises.

Last, you had a sneak preview of the Office client development model. You saw the Office Add-in flavors available at the time of this writing and the support matrix related to the various versions of Office Online, Office 2013 or 2016 for Windows, and Office 2016 for Mac or iPad.

All the concepts you learned in this chapter will be covered in detail in the upcoming sections, so by reading the remaining chapters of this book you will learn how to create real solutions leveraging all the potentials of the Office 365 ecosystem as a complete platform for developing custom solutions.

Office 365 programming model

This part introduces the Microsoft Office 365 programming model from a developer's perspective. The overall goal of Part II is to provide you a solid foundation for understanding the following parts and for mastering the Office 365 programming model.

Chapter 3, "Microsoft Graph API reference," provides a brief introduction and a reference about the Microsoft Graph API. The chapter illustrates the Microsoft Graph API, the main endpoints available, and how to invoke them using bare HTTP requests from whatever platform you like. The chapter targets any device or development framework, as long as it supports making HTTP requests.

Chapter 4, "Azure Active Directory and security," introduces and explains the security infrastructure that sits under the cover of the Microsoft Graph API. The chapter covers the architecture of Microsoft Azure Active Directory (Azure AD) and its main capabilities. Moreover, the chapter shows you how to configure an app in Azure AD to authenticate users against an online tenant and explains how to consume the Microsoft Graph API.

Microsoft Graph API reference

This chapter introduces the Microsoft Graph API and provides a practical reference about how to consume it from any device and any development framework. To better understand this chapter, you should have a good knowledge about the HTTP protocol, the REST (Representational State Transfer) protocol, and JSON (JavaScript Object Notation).

What is the Microsoft Graph API?

The Microsoft Graph API is a set of services, published through a unique and consolidated REST endpoint, that allow users to consume the main functionalities and the most useful capabilities of the services offered by Microsoft Office 365. As you have seen in Chapter 1, "Microsoft Office 365: A quick tour," some of the main services offered by Office 365 are:

- Microsoft Exchange Online

- Microsoft SharePoint Online

- Microsoft Skype for Business

- Microsoft OneDrive for Business

- Microsoft Video Portal

- Microsoft Power BI

- Microsoft Azure Active Directory

Many other services will become available in the near future, leveraging a common model of consumption and a shared set of development patterns that make it easier for developers to consume the entire Office 365 platform and provide business-level solutions fully integrated with Office 365.

From a low-level perspective, those services can be consumed from any development platform such as Microsoft .NET Framework, Java, PHP, JavaScript/jQuery, Node.js, and so on. The only requirement is the capability to make HTTP requests and to handle the JSON serialization to encode requests and decode responses.

From a high-level perspective, the Microsoft Graph API is a way to consume all the services that were already available as a separate set of REST endpoints, through a unique set of rules and using a consolidated endpoint address. Chapter 4, "Azure Active Directory and security," further explains why having a unique endpoint for the REST-based API makes the overall consumption easier and faster. For now, just consider that consolidation improves the code quality, performance, and usability of Microsoft Graph.

In Figure 3-1, you can see a schema of the overall architecture of the Microsoft Graph API.

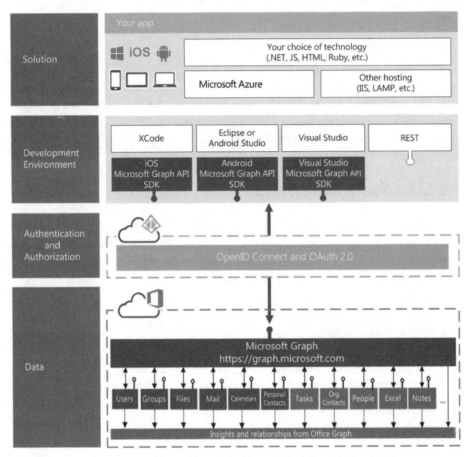

FIGURE 3-1 A representation of the architectural schema of the Microsoft Graph API

As you can see, the Microsoft Graph endpoint is a kind of wrapper on top of the APIs that were already available in Office 365 through the disparate Office 365 REST API, with the addition of some new API and the Office Graph insights and relationships. So far, the main services offered by the Microsoft Graph API are:

- Users and Groups, which are services related to users' information, groups' definitions, and groups' membership. These services will be covered in depth in Chapter 6, "Users and Groups services."

- Files, which target the OneDrive for Business service and will be explained in Chapter 7, "File services."

- Mail, calendar, and contacts, which are services related to the Exchange Online service and will be covered in depth in Chapter 5, "Mail, calendar and contact services."

The authentication and authorization layer is provided by Microsoft Azure Active Directory (Azure AD), and from a development perspective you will be able to implement a client wrapper within whatever development platform you choose, including Microsoft .NET, iOS, and Android.

From a URL perspective, the unified approach the Microsoft Graph API supports and sponsors allows you to consume all the services from a basic unique URL, which is *https://graph.microsoft.com.* To consume a specific API or service, you will have to append to the base URL the version number of the API that you want to consume and the name of the target API. For example, if you want to consume version 1.0 of the Microsoft Graph, the URL will be like the following:

http://graph.microsoft.com/v1.0/<service-specific-endpoint>

If you want to consume the beta version of the Microsoft Graph, you can substitute the v1.0 version number with the *beta* keyword, using a URL like the following:

http://graph.microsoft.com/beta/<service-specific-endpoint>

In general, for any existing or future version of the API, the URL to consume it will be like the following:

http://graph.microsoft.com/<version>/<service-specific-endpoint>

Microsoft is also working on some open source SDK projects hosted on GitHub that allow you to consume the Microsoft Graph easily from custom developed solutions. These open source SDK projects can be accessed through the following URL:

http://graph.microsoft.io/code-samples-and-sdks

In particular, if you want to consume the Microsoft Graph API from a Microsoft .NET software solution, you can leverage the Microsoft Graph SDK library for .NET, which is available as a NuGet package in Microsoft Visual Studio. The name of the NuGet package is Microsoft.Graph. In Chapter 8, "Microsoft Graph SDK for .NET," you will learn how to use this SDK in your solutions.

On GitHub, under the MicrosoftGraph main organization that is available at the URL *https://github .com/MicrosoftGraph/,* there are samples of how to use the Microsoft Graph API within iOS (*https:// github.com/microsoftgraph/msgraph-sdk-ios*) and Android (*https://github.com/microsoftgraph /msgraph-sdk-android*).

In general, if you want to leverage the Microsoft Graph API from any platform, you can always use the REST API directly via HTTP. You can also consider using the VIPR tool (*https://github.com/microsoft /vipr*), which is a toolkit for generating client libraries for any OData service. The VIPR tool supports C#, Objective-C, and Java. Internally, the Microsoft Graph SDKs use the VIPR tool.

You can even use the Office 365 REST API; however, is not unified under a unique and common endpoint URL. The old development model already has client libraries targeting the main and most-adopted development platforms like Microsoft .NET, JavaScript, and some Open Source SDKs for Android and iOS. In particular, there is a .NET client library that is still available on NuGet to consume the Office 365 REST API easily with Microsoft Visual Studio and the Microsoft Office development tools for Visual Studio. This client library allows you to leverage the Office 365 REST API within a wide range of Microsoft .NET custom software solutions. The supported flavors of .NET software solutions that can leverage the .NET client library for the Office 365 REST API are:

- .NET Windows Store apps

- Windows Forms applications

- WPF applications

- ASP.NET MVC web applications

- ASP.NET Web Forms applications

- Xamarin Android and iOS applications

- Multidevice hybrid apps

In this chapter, you will focus on the Microsoft Graph API, and in the following chapters, you will see how to leverage it within Microsoft .NET Framework. From a technology choice perspective, you should use the new Microsoft Graph API as much as you can and avoid using the per-service REST API.

In the following sections, you will find many more details about the main and most relevant Microsoft Graph services. To properly consume them, you will have to leverage an HTTP and REST client tool. Microsoft, for testing and development purposes, provides a tool with a web-based UI that is called Graph Explorer. It is available at the following URL:

https://graph.microsoft.io/en-us/graph-explorer

In Figure 3-2, you can see a screenshot of the UI of the Graph Explorer application. To use the Graph Explorer, you have to sign in, clicking the button in the upper-right corner of the welcome screen and providing your Office 365 tenant credentials. Then, you will be able to query (HTTP GET/POST/PATCH/DELETE) the services using a friendly web-based UI. The Graph Explorer will handle all the security plumbing required to query the target tenant via REST API.

Another useful tool for testing any REST API is Fiddler, which is a free tool made available by Telerik. It can be downloaded from the following URL:

http://www.telerik.com/fiddler

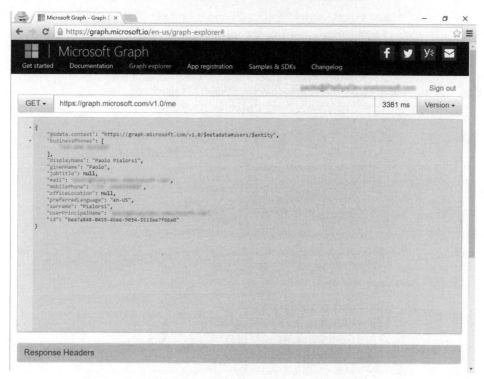

FIGURE 3-2 The sample Graph Explorer app in action

Microsoft Graph API metadata

Before diving into some of the available flavors of the provided API, it is useful to note that the Microsoft Graph API adheres to the OData 4.0 protocol specification. Thus, the first thing you can do to discover the entire set of available entities, actions, and services is to query the metadata of the OData service. You just need to make an HTTP GET request for the following URL:

https://graph.microsoft.com/v1.0/$metadata

This URL is freely available and does not require any kind of authentication. Thus, you can plan to periodically query for that URL in an unattended process to refresh the metadata of the provided services and rebuild any autogenerated client library—for example, one built using the VIPR tool that you saw in the previous section. If you use any of the SDK provided by Microsoft, you can just keep the SDK package updated.

The result of such an HTTP request will be an XML-based representation of the Microsoft Graph API metadata, leveraging the EDMX namespace (*http://docs.oasis-open.org/odata/ns/edmx*). It is out of the scope of this chapter to comment in detail on the resulting metadata XML. However, it is useful to examine the structure of the *EntityContainer* element, which is unique for each metadata document and defines the entity sets, singletons, function, and action imports exposed by the OData service. In Table 3-1, you can see the main entity sets exposed by the Microsoft Graph API endpoint v 1.0. To invoke them, you just need to make an HTTP request using the proper HTTP verb (GET, POST, PUT, PATCH, DELETE, and so on) targeting a URL with the following template:

https://graph.microsoft.com/<version>/<targetEntitySet|singleton|function|action>

TABLE 3-1 The main entity sets exposed by the Microsoft Graph API endpoint

Entity Set Relative URL	Description
directoryObjects	Entity pool that enables random access to any DirectoryObject based on the objectId property. You can use this collection to start querying any specific DirectoryObject instance.
devices	List of devices registered within the current tenant.
groups	List of security groups created in the current tenant.
directoryRoles	List of directory roles for the current tenant.
directoryRoleTemplates	List of directory role templates for the current tenant.
organization	Details of the configuration of the current tenant (assigned and provisioned plans, verified DNS domain names, customer's information, DirSync information, and so on).
subscribedSkus	List of service plans subscribed for the current tenant.
users	List of users for the current tenant.
drives	List of file drives in the current tenant.
subscriptions	Available for registering a webhook listener for events related to changes in data available through the Microsft Graph, like email messages, contacts, calendars, and conversations.
me	Singleton that represents the current user.
drive	Singleton that represents the entry point for the OneDrive for Business of the current user.

Each of the previous entity sets or singletons returns a definition based on a single *EntityType* XML element, which is detailed in the metadata schema. For example, for the *users* collection, each user element is of type *Microsoft.Graph.User*, which is defined in a specific *EntityType* element. The *Microsoft.Graph.User* definition declares the properties available for every user object, like *displayName*, *givenName*, and so on. Moreover, every user object provides a set of navigation properties, like *messages*, *calendars*, *events*, and *drive*, and each navigation property leads to another collection of objects. This makes it possible to navigate the directory as an object hierarchy with a fluent approach.

Note that the behavior described for the *Microsoft.Graph.User* type can be applied to any other *EntityType* defined in the metadata schema.

In the following sections, you will see some of these entities in more detail, working with direct HTTP requests, to better understand how to consume the Microsoft Graph API from any device or platform capable of using the HTTP protocol.

Consuming users and security groups

Let's start consuming some services related to the current user, other users, and groups. As you saw in Figure 3-1, the main endpoint of the Microsoft Graph API is based on the URL *https://graph.microsoft .com/*, and you have to append the protocol version and the target service to this base URL. Notice that the Microsoft Graph API URLs are not case-sensitive.

All the sample HTTP requests and responses illustrated from here to the end of this chapter can be simulated by using the Microsoft Graph Explorer or Fiddler. For the sake of completeness, included in the code samples of this book you will find a file (Microsoft-Graph-Samples.saz) that represents a trace saved from Fiddler that reproduces all of the requests illustrated.

Yourself and other users

Accessing the current user's profile, the user's properties, and the assigned Office 365 licenses is a well-known use case. In fact, whenever you create an app or an external tool that leverages the Office 365 services, you probably will have to define the current user's context.

To access the current user, the entry point is *https://graph.microsoft.com/v1.0/me/*. You can consume that URL with an HTTP GET request, providing the proper authentication information, which will be explained in Chapter 4. In response, you will get a JSON object that will define a bunch of useful information. Depending on the Accept HTTP header for controlling OData, you can request an object with three different behaviors:

- ■ **Accept: application/json;odata.metadata=none; =>** The service should omit any metadata information. The only OData metadata attribute provided, if any, will be the *@odata.nextLink* to provide the link to the next page of objects when browsing for an entity set.

- ■ **Accept: application/json;odata.metadata=minimal; =>** The service should remove computable control information from the response payload. Only the attributes *@odata.context*, *@ odata.nextLink* (if any), *@odata.id*, and a few others will be provided in the response payload.

- ■ **Accept: application/json;odata.metadata=full; =>** The service must include all the control information explicitly in the response payload.

Based on the *odata.metadata* attribute that you provide, the payload size can be very different. By default, if you omit the *odata.metadata* attribute, the Microsoft Graph API applies a *minimal* behavior for OData metadata.

In Listing 3-1, you can see an excerpt of such a JSON response, based on minimal metadata.

LISTING 3-1 An excerpt of a JSON response for the *https://graph.microsoft.com/v1.0/me/* API request

```
{
  "@odata.context": "https://graph.microsoft.com/v1.0/$metadata#users/$entity",
  "@odata.type": "#microsoft.graph.user",
  "@odata.id": "users/bea7a848-0459-4bee-9034-5513ee7f66e0",
```

```
  "businessPhones": [
    "030-22446688"
  ],
  "displayName": "Paolo Pialorsi",
  "givenName": "Paolo",
  "jobTitle": null,
  "mail": "paolo@PiaSysDev.onmicrosoft.com",
  "mobilePhone": "+391234567890",
  "officeLocation": null,
  "preferredLanguage": "en-US",
  "surname": "Pialorsi",
  "userPrincipalName": "paolo@PiaSysDev.onmicrosoft.com",
  "id": "bea7a848-0459-4bee-9034-5513ee7f66e0"
}
```

As you can see, there is information about the JSON object itself, which is an instance of a *Microsoft. Graph.User* type. There is information about the current user such as address, display name, telephone, email, and so on. Another set of information that deserves attention is the list of properties related to on-premises directory synchronization, if it is configured. For example, you can see the on-premises user's SID (*onPremisesImmutableId*), when the last synchronization happened (*onPremisesLastSync-DateTime*), and so on. Last, you will find the proxy address and the fundamental UPN (User Principal Name), which will be a unique identifier for the current user.

You can use the UPN to access any specific user profile as long as you have the permissions to consume the user's directory in Azure AD. Let's say that you want to access the entire list of users for a specific tenant. You can make an HTTP GET request for the following URL: *https://graph.microsoft .com/v1.0/users*. In this case, the result will be a JSON representation of an array of *Microsoft.Graph.User* objects.

If you want to access the profile properties of a specific user, you can make an HTTP GET request for the following URL: *https://graph.microsoft.com/v1.0/users/UPN*. For example, when the current user has a UPN value like *name@domain.com*, the following URL defines a direct entry point to the user's profile: *https://graph.microsoft.com/v1.0/users/name@domain.com*.

It is also possible to read the values of single properties instead of getting the entire JSON object. Moreover, there are complex properties like the user's photo that can be accessed only through a direct request. To access a single property, you can append the property name to the URL path of the user's profile URL. You can see such a request in Listing 3-2, in which the HTTP request headers include the authentication information (the OAuth bearer token), which will be explained in Chapter 4.

LISTING 3-2 The HTTP GET request for the *userPrincipalName* property of the current user

```
GET /v1.0/me/userPrincipalName HTTP/1.1

Authorization: Bearer eyJ0...
Host: graph.microsoft.com
Content-Length: 0
```

In Listing 3-3, you can see the response that you should get back.

LISTING 3-3 The HTTP response for the current user's *userPrincipalName* property

```
HTTP/1.1 200 OK

Cache-Control: private
Content-Type: application/json;odata.metadata=minimal;odata.streaming=true;IEEE754Compatib
le=false;charset=utf-8
Server: Microsoft-IIS/8.5
request-id: 0c2f199c-782e-4918-8bd0-91b0c246a9c8
client-request-id: 0c2f199c-782e-4918-8bd0-91b0c246a9c8
OData-Version: 4.0
OutBoundDuration: 71.2145
Duration: 113.3553
X-Powered-By: ASP.NET
Date: Sat, 05 Sep 2015 08:54:52 GMT
Content-Length: 192

{"@odata.context":"https://graph.microsoft.com/v1.0/$metadata#users('<UserID>')/userPrinci
palName","value":"paolo@<tenant>.onmicrosoft.com"}
```

Notice that the response contains a bunch of useful information like the ID of the request, the target server version and engine, and the overall duration of the request processing. The response is in JSON format, and you should deserialize it. However, you can also directly access the bare property value as text by appending the *$value* path to the property URL. The final URL will look like the following:

https://graph.microsoft.com/v1.0/me/userPrincipalName/$value

This technique becomes increasingly useful when you want to retrieve binary properties like the user's photo. By providing the *$value* path at the end of the user's photo property, you will get back the binary image file directly, which is useful for creating great user experiences in your applications. In Listing 3-4, you can see the user's photo request.

LISTING 3-4 The HTTP GET request for the photo binary property value of the current user

```
GET /v1.0/me/photo/$value HTTP/1.1

Authorization: Bearer eyJ0...
Host: graph.microsoft.com
Content-Length: 0
```

In Listing 3-5, you can see the response from an HTTP perspective.

LISTING 3-5 The HTTP response for the binary value of the current user's photo property

```
HTTP/1.1 200 OK

Cache-Control: private
Content-Type: image/jpeg
Server: Microsoft-IIS/8.5
request-id: 528841c7-eda8-4eb7-99f7-b241be2b66f9
client-request-id: 528841c7-eda8-4eb7-99f7-b241be2b66f9
OutBoundDuration: 1080.2745
Duration: 1268.9802
X-Powered-By: ASP.NET
Date: Sat, 05 Sep 2015 08:26:09 GMT
Content-Length: 31194
```

You can read information about yourself or other users, and you can update that information if you have proper permissions. To change data or execute operations, you will have to switch from HTTP GET requests to other HTTP verbs like POST, PATCH, and so on.

For example, to update your current mobile phone number, you can make an HTTP PATCH request against your profile URL (*https://graph.microsoft.com/v1.0/me*). You will have to provide a JSON object that defines the profile properties that you want to patch. It is fundamental in this case to set the Content Type header of the request according to the JSON. For example, in Listing 3-6, you can see the sample request for updating your mobile phone number.

LISTING 3-6 The HTTP PATCH request to update the mobile phone number of the current user

```
PATCH /v1.0/me HTTP/1.1

Authorization: Bearer eyJ0...
Host: graph.microsoft.com
Content-Type: application/json;
Content-Length: 31

{ "mobilePhone":"+39-123456789" }
```

In Listing 3-7, you can see the response that you should get back.

LISTING 3-7 The HTTP response for the current user's profile update request

```
HTTP/1.1 204 No Content

Cache-Control: private
Transfer-Encoding: chunked
Content-Type: text/plain
Server: Microsoft-IIS/8.5
request-id: fbb823c4-0de9-40e1-bba1-eb5b9101baac
client-request-id: fbb823c4-0de9-40e1-bba1-eb5b9101baac
```

```
OutBoundDuration: 491.0361
Duration: 494.4198
X-Powered-By: ASP.NET
Date: Sat, 05 Sep 2015 07:07:27 GMT
```

From a content perspective, the response just confirms that the operation was successful (HTTP Status 204).

Security groups

Through the Microsoft Graph API, you can also access groups, including both security groups, synchronized across premises using directory synchronization tools, and the new Office 365 Groups, which are also called Unified Groups from an Office 365 perspective. The new Office 365 Groups are covered later in this chapter in the section "Working with Office 365 Groups." The security groups are accessible as objects of type *Microsoft.Graph.Group* through the following URL:

> *https://graph.microsoft.com/v1.0/groups*

The URL returns the entire list of groups, regardless of whether they are security groups or Office 365 Groups. However, you can play with the *groupTypes* property, which has a null value for security groups and a value of *Unified* for any Office 365 Group.

You can also access any specific group by providing the group's ID in the URL. For example:

> *https://graph.microsoft.com/v1.0/ groups/<Group_ObjectId>*

To access the members of a specific group, you can add the *members* keyword at the end of the single group endpoint URL.

Consuming mail, contacts, and calendars

Now that you have learned how to consume users, security groups, and licenses, you are ready to leverage the other APIs—for example, those for Microsoft Exchange Online, which is another common and useful scenario.

Thanks to the unified API model, the base URL remains the same; you just have to change the relative URL of the service endpoint. The personal emails of the current user are available through the following base URL:

> *https://graph.microsoft.com/v1.0/me/Messages*

Mail messages

As already stated, to access the current user's mailbox, you can query the *https://graph.microsoft.com /v1.0/me/Messages* URL. The result will be an array of JSON objects of type *Microsoft.Graph.Message* or of type *Microsoft.Graph.EventMessage*, which are the email messages and the event-related messages in the current user's mailbox, regardless of the folder in which they are stored. In Listing 3-8, you can see an excerpt of the JSON result.

LISTING 3-8 An excerpt of a JSON response for the *https://graph.microsoft.com/v1.0/me/Messages* API request

```
{
  "@odata.context": "https://graph.microsoft.com/v1.0/$metadata#users('paolo.
pialorsi%40sharepoint-camp.com')
/messages",
  "@odata.nextLink": "https://graph.microsoft.com/v1.0/me/Messages?$skip=10",
  "value": [
    {
      "@odata.type": "#Microsoft.Graph.Message",
      "@odata.id":
"users/paolo.pialorsi%40sharepoint-camp.com/Messages/AAMkADU4Zjk3ZTQzLWFjMDctNDM5Mi04NzAwL
WFkZGExY2M5NDR1ZQBGAAAAAACIOUtE7VENSpDAypZBE6ONBwBrFd4C2tvVRa8oaXCdn19HAAAAAAENAABrFd4C2tv
VRa8oaXCdn19HAAIQUEEDAAA%3D",
      "Id":
"AAMkADU4Zjk3ZTQzLWFjMDctNDM5Mi04NzAwLWFkZGExY2M5NDR1ZQBGAAAAAACIOUtE7VENSpDAypZBE6ONBwBrF
d4C2tvVRa8oaXCdn19HAAAAAAENAABrFd4C2tvVRa8oaXCdn19HAAIQUEEDAAA=",
      "ChangeKey": "CQAAABYAAABrFd4C2tvVRa8oaXCdn19HAAIQVSNq",
      "Categories": [],
      "DateTimeCreated": "2015-09-03T03:22:23Z",
      "DateTimeLastModified": "2015-09-03T03:22:23Z",
      "Subject": "Sample message!",
      "BodyPreview": "Hello from Office 365!",
      "Body": {
        "ContentType": "HTML",
        "Content": " ... ",
    },
      "Importance": "Normal",
      "HasAttachments": false,
      "ParentFolderId":
"AAMkADU4Zjk3ZTQzLWFjMDctNDM5Mi04NzAwLWFkZGExY2M5NDR1ZQAuAAAAAACIOUtE7VENSpDAypZBE6ONAQBrF
d4C2tvVRa8oaXCdn19HAAAAAAENAAA=",
      "From": {
        "EmailAddress": {
          "Address": "someone@contoso.com",
          "Name": "Contoso Team"
        }
      },
      "Sender": {
        "EmailAddress": {
          "Address": "someone@contoso.com",
          "Name": "Contoso Team"
        }
      },
      "ToRecipients": [
        {
```

```
        "EmailAddress": {
          "Address": "paolo.pialorsi@sharepoint-camp.com",
          "Name": "Paolo Pialorsi"
        }
      }
    ],
    "CcRecipients": [],
    "BccRecipients": [],
    "ReplyTo": [
      {
        "EmailAddress": {
          "Address": "someone@contoso.com",
          "Name": "someone@contoso.com"
        }
      }
    ],
    "ConversationId":
"AAQkADU4Zjk3ZTQzLWFjMDctNDM5Mi04NzAwLWFkZGExY2M5NDR1ZQAQAH2etUG4dspGkfBsjAGHi4M=",
    "DateTimeReceived": "2015-09-03T03:22:23Z",
    "DateTimeSent": "2015-09-03T03:22:13Z",
    "IsDeliveryReceiptRequested": null,
    "IsReadReceiptRequested": false,
    "IsDraft": false,
    "IsRead": false,
    "WebLink": "https://outlook.office365.com/owa/?ItemID=AAMkADU4Zjk3ZTQzLWFjMDctNDM5Mi
04NzAwLWFkZGExY2M
5NDR1ZQBGAAAAAACIOUtE7VENSpDAypZBE6ONBwBrFd4C2tvVRa8oaXCdn19HAAAAAAENAABrFd4C2tvVRa8oaXCdn
19HAAIQUEEDAAA%3D&exvsurl=1&viewmodel=ReadMessageItem"
  },
...
 ]
}
```

It is interesting to notice that by default, the mail service will do output paging and, unless you specify something different in the OData query sent to the service, the default page size will be 10 items per page. At the beginning of the JSON answer, you will find a property with name *@odata. nexLink* that contains the URL to access the next page of results, and this kind of "next page" link will be available in any requested page. As a result, developers are obliged to do paging, which is a good habit but unfortunately is not always a common practice.

Moreover, you can see that each message provides well-known information like subject, sender, recipients, content, parent folder Id, and so on. One fundamental piece of information for each message is the *Id* property. By appending a specific message *Id* at the end of the messages path, you can access that specific message item directly. The HTTP GET request will look like the following, where the message *Id* has been truncated for typographic needs:

https://graph.microsoft.com/v1.0/me/messages/AAMk...AA=

The response will be a JSON object of type *Microsoft.Graph.Message* with the same properties that were available for each message within the list of messages.

Because we are using the OData protocol to query the Microsoft Graph API, we can also use the standard protocol's syntax to project a subset of properties or to partition the results. For example, imagine that you want to retrieve just the *Id*, *Subject*, *From*, and *ToRecipients* properties of the current message. In Listing 3-9, you can see the HTTP GET request to achieve this result, which will target the following URL:

https://graph.microsoft.com/v1.0/me/messages/AAMk...AA=?$select=Id,Subject,From ,ToRecipients

LISTING 3-9 The HTTP GET request for a subset of properties for a specific email message

```
GET /v1.0/me/messages/AAMk...AA=?$select=Id,Subject,From,ToRecipients HTTP/1.1

Authorization: Bearer eyJ0...
Host: graph.microsoft.com
Content-Type: application/json
Content-Length: 31
```

In Listing 3-10, you can see the response that you should get back.

LISTING 3-10 The JSON response for a projection of properties of a specific email message

```
{
  "@odata.context": "https://graph.microsoft.com/v1.0/<tenant>/$metadata#users('paolo.
pialorsi%40sharepoint
-camp.com')/Messages/$entity",
  "@odata.type": "#Microsoft.Graph.Message",
  "@odata.id": "users/paolo.pialorsi%40sharepoint-camp.com/Messages/
AAMkADU4Zjk3ZTQzLWFjMDctNDM5Mi04NzAwL
WFkZGExY2M5NDR1ZQBGAAAAAACIOUtE7VENSpDAypZBE6ONBwBrFd4C2tvVRa8oaXCdnl9HAAAAAAENAABrFd4C2tv
VRa8oaXCdnl9HAAIQ3Vk_AAA%3D",
  "@odata.etag": "W/\"CQAAABYAAABrFd4C2tvVRa8oaXCdnl9HAAJVc9Lf\"",
  "Id":
"AAMkADU4Zjk3ZTQzLWFjMDctNDM5Mi04NzAwLWFkZGExY2M5NDR1ZQBGAAAAAACIOUtE7VENSpDAypZBE6ONBwBrF
d4C2tvVRa8oaXCdnl9HAAAAAAENAABrFd4C2tvVRa8oaXCdnl9HAAIQ3Vk_AAA=",
  "Subject": "This is a sample message!",
  "From": {
    "EmailAddress": {
      "Address": "someone@contoso.com",
      "Name": "someone@contoso.com"
    }
  },
  "ToRecipients": [
    {
      "EmailAddress": {
        "Address": "paolo.pialorsi@sharepoint-camp.com",
        "Name": "Paolo Pialorsi"
      }
    }
  ]
}
```

If you want to filter all the messages in the current user's inbox based on a specific subject value, here is the corresponding OData query URL:

https://graph.microsoft.com/v1.0/me/messages?$filter=Subject%20eq%20'Office%20365%20 Book'

Sending an email message by using the Microsoft Graph API is also a simple task. You just need to make an HTTP POST request with the JSON object representing the message to send and targeting the URL of the list of messages to store the message as a draft. In Listing 3-11, you can see the HTTP POST request to achieve this result.

LISTING 3-11 The HTTP POST request to save a draft of a new email message

```
POST /v1.0/me/messages HTTP/1.1

Authorization: Bearer eyJ0...
Host: graph.microsoft.com
Content-Length: 383
Content-Type: application/json

{
    "Subject": "Sample email from Microsoft Graph API",
    "Body": {
        "ContentType": "HTML",
        "Content": "Hey! This email comes to you from the <b>Microsoft Graph API</b>!"
    },
    "Importance": "High",
    "ToRecipients": [
        {
            "EmailAddress": {
                "Address": "paolo@pialorsi.com"
            }
        }
    ]
}
```

The HTTP response that you will get back will be the JSON representation of the just-saved draft message. In the message object, you will see the *IsDraft* property with a value of *true*. To send that message, you will need to invoke the *send* action, which can be addressed by appending the *send* keyword at the end of the URL of the message and using an HTTP POST method. In Listing 3-12, you can see a sample request to send a message.

LISTING 3-12 The HTTP POST request to send a draft email message

```
POST /v1.0/me/messages/AAMk...AA=/send HTTP/1.1

Authorization: Bearer eyJ0...
Host: graph.microsoft.com
Content-Length: 0
Content-Type: application/json
```

The HTTP response will confirm that the message has been sent by providing an HTTP Status Code with a value of 202 (Accepted). Note that if you have sent a message draft and you try to send it again, the REST API call will fail because the engine will not find that draft (HTTP Status 404 Not Found). If you try to retrieve the just-sent message, it will no longer be available. The message draft has been sent and moved to the Sent Items folder, where you will find the message with the *IsDraft* property with a value of *false*, which means that the message has been sent.

To access a specific mail folder, you can use the *mailFolders* navigation property of any *Microsoft. Graph.User* object for which the current user has the rights to access the mailbox. For example, the following URL retrieves the list of available mail folders:

https://graph.microsoft.com/v1.0/me/mailFolders

As with the mail messages, you can access any specific folder by *Id*, and you can browse the messages of that specific folder by appending the *messages* keyword to the URL of the folder.

Another option for sending an email message quickly is to directly leverage the *sendMail* action, which is available for any object of type *Microsoft.Graph.User*. In Listing 3-13, you can see the HTTP POST request to invoke the action, which is available as *microsoft.graph.sendMail* or just *sendMail*.

LISTING 3-13 The HTTP POST request to send an email message

```
POST /v1.0/me/sendMail HTTP/1.1

Authorization: Bearer eyJ0...
Host: graph.microsoft.com
Content-Length: 383
Content-Type: application/json

{
  "Message": {
    "Subject": "Sample email from Microsoft Graph API",
    "Body": {
        "ContentType": "HTML",
        "Content": "Hey! This email comes to you from the <b>Microsoft Graph API"
    },
    "ToRecipients": [
        {
            "EmailAddress": {
                "Address": "paolo@pialorsi.com"
            }
        }
    ]
  },
  "SaveToSentItems": "true"
}
```

Again, the HTTP response will confirm that the message has been sent by providing an HTTP Status Code with a value of 202 (Accepted).

If you want to reply to a received message, you can leverage the *reply* action provided by each message instance. You just need to make an HTTP POST request targeting the message to which you want to reply and appending the *reply* path to the URL of the message. Within the HTTP POST request body message, you provide a JSON response made of a comment property, which will be the response to the received message. In Listing 3-14, you can see a sample reply to a message.

LISTING 3-14 The HTTP POST request to reply to a specific email message

```
POST /v1.0/me/messages/AAMk...AA=/reply HTTP/1.1

Authorization: Bearer eyJ0...
Host: graph.microsoft.com
Content-Type: application/json
Content-Length: 59

{
  "Comment": "Wow! This message is really amazing!"
}
```

The response will be empty with an HTTP Status Code with a value of 202 (Accepted).

To reply to all the recipients of a message, there is the replyAll action that has to be invoked like the *reply* action. To forward the message to someone, you can use the *forward* action, which accepts in the HTTP POST request a list of recipients who will receive the forwarded message and an optional comment that will be included in the forwarded message. In Listing 3-15, you can see a message forwarding example.

LISTING 3-15 The HTTP request to forward a message to someone, including a comment

```
POST /v1.0/me/messages/AAMk...AA=/forward HTTP/1.1

Authorization: Bearer eyJ0...
Host: graph.microsoft.com
Content-Type: application/json
Content-Length: 237

{
  "Comment": "Please read and give me a feedback...",
  "ToRecipients": [
    {
      "EmailAddress": {
        "Address": "someone@contoso.com"
      }
    },
    {
      "EmailAddress": {
        "Address": "paolo.pialorsi@sharepoint-camp.com"
      }
    }
  ]
}
```

Some other interesting actions are *move*, which moves an email from one folder to another, and *copy*, which copies a message from one folder to another. Both the *move* and *copy* actions accept a JSON object that declares where to move or copy the message.

One more common use case is the deletion of a message, which can be accomplished by making an HTTP DELETE request targeting the URL of the email message. In Listing 3-16, you can see the sample request syntax.

LISTING 3-16 The HTTP request to delete an email message

```
DELETE /v1.0/me/messages/AAMk...AA= HTTP/1.1

Authorization: Bearer eyJ0...
Host: graph.microsoft.com
Content-Type: application/json
Content-Length: 0
```

The response will be empty with an HTTP Status Code with a value of 204 (No Content).

The last use case related to messages and emails is the handling of attachments. To enumerate the attachments of an email, if any, you need to make an HTTP GET request targeting the email's direct URL and appending the *attachments* keyword at the end of the URL. This will give you access to the collection of attachments. In Listing 3-17, you can see a sample request.

LISTING 3-17 The HTTP request to access the collection of attachments of an email message

```
GET /v1.0/me/messages/AAMk...AA=/attachments HTTP/1.1

Authorization: Bearer eyJ0...
Host: graph.microsoft.com
Content-Type: application/json
Content-Length: 0
```

In Listing 3-18, you can see an excerpt of the JSON response that enumerates the attachments of an email message.

LISTING 3-18 An excerpt of the HTTP response that enumerates the attachments of an email message

```
HTTP/1.1 200 OK

Cache-Control: private
Content-Type: application/json;odata.metadata=minimal;odata.streaming=true
;IEEE754Compatible
=false;charset=utf-8
Server: Microsoft-IIS/8.5
request-id: a3c1cd57-f2a0-4c0b-8a76-409c7f848fea
client-request-id: a3c1cd57-f2a0-4c0b-8a76-409c7f848fea
```

```
OData-Version: 4.0
OutBoundDuration: 165.8664
Duration: 175.4871
X-Powered-By: ASP.NET
Date: Sat, 05 Sep 2015 14:15:39 GMT
Content-Length: 720

{
  "@odata.context": "https://graph.microsoft.com/v1.0/$metadata#users('paolo.
pialorsi%40sharepoint-camp.com')
/Messages('AAMkADU4Zjk3ZTQzLWFjMDctNDM5Mi04NzAwLWFkZGExY2M5NDR1ZQBGAAAAAACIOUtE7VENSpDAypZ
BE6ONBwBrFd4C2tvVRa8oaXCdnl9HAAAAAAENAABrFd4C2tvVRa8oaXCdnl9HAAIQ3Vk3AAA%3D')/Attachments"
,
  "value": [
    {
      "@odata.type": "#Microsoft.Graph.fileAttachment",
      "@odata.id": "users/paolo.pialorsi%40sharepoint-camp.com/Messages/
AAMkADU4Zjk3ZTQzLWFjMDctNDM5Mi04NzAwL
WFkZGExY2M5NDR1ZQBGAAAAAACIOUtE7VENSpDAypZBE6ONBwBrFd4C2tvVRa8oaXCdnl9HAAAAAAENAABrFd4C2tv
VRa8oaXCdnl9HAAIQ3Vk3AAA%3D/Attachments/AAMkADU4Zjk3ZTQzLWFjMDctNDM5Mi04NzAwLWFkZGExY2M5ND
R1ZQBGAAAAAACIOUtE7VENSpDAypZBE6ONBwBrFd4C2tvVRa8oaXCdnl9HAAAAAAENAABrFd4C2tvVRa8oaXCdnl9H
AAIQ3Vk3AAABEgAQAElsx9CtSZdKkGk_UhYBJDQ%3D",
      "Id":
"AAMkADU4Zjk3ZTQzLWFjMDctNDM5Mi04NzAwLWFkZGExY2M5NDR1ZQBGAAAAAACIOUtE7VENSpDAypZBE6ONBwBrF
d4C2tvVRa8oaXCdnl9HAAAAAAENAABrFd4C2tvVRa8oaXCdnl9HAAIQ3Vk3AAABEgAQAElsx9CtSZdKkGk_UhYBJDQ
=",
      "Name": "CEM41wGUUAEjpHH.jpg",
      "ContentType": "image/jpeg",
      "Size": 110796,
      "IsInline": false,
      "DateTimeLastModified": "2015-05-06T03:45:26Z",
      "ContentId": "A4216D1F77482F49B2765EBDD1788161@eurprd01.prod.exchangelabs.com",
      "ContentLocation": null,
      "IsContactPhoto": false,
      "ContentBytes": "LzlqLzRBQVFTa1pKUmdBQkFRUFBUUUFCUFELzJ..."
    }
  ]
}
```

As you can see, the result is a JSON array of objects of type *Microsoft.Graph.FileAttachment*, in which each item is identified by a unique *Id* property. Moreover, you can see there are fundamental properties like the *ContentType* and the *ContentBytes* that allow you to access the real file attachment properly typed from a content-type perspective. If you want to access a specific attachment file, you can append the value of the related *Id* to the URL of the collection of attachments.

Contacts

The current user's contacts are another useful capability that is available through the new Microsoft Graph API. To consume the contacts, you have to make an HTTP GET request against the following URL:

https://graph.microsoft.com/v1.0/<user>/contacts

In Listing 3-19, you can see an excerpt of the resulting JSON response, which represents an array of objects of type *Microsoft.Graph.Contact*.

LISTING 3-19 An excerpt of the HTTP response that enumerates the organizational or personal contacts in a tenant

```
{
    "@odata.context":
"https://graph.microsoft.com/v1.0/$metadata#users('paolo.pialorsi%40sharepoint-camp.com')
/contacts",
    "value": [
        {
            "@odata.etag": "W/\"EQAAABYAAABrFd4C2tvVRa8oaXCdnl9HAAIQ4ll9\"",
            "id":
"AAMkADU4Zjk3ZTQzLWFjMDctNDM5MiO4NzAwLWFkZGExY2M5NDRlZQBGAAAAAACIOUtE7VENSpDAypZBE6ONBwBrF
d4C2tvVRa8oaXCdnl9HAAAAAAEPAABrFd4C2tvVRa8oaXCdnl9HAAIQ3XCjAAA=",
            "createdDateTime": "2015-09-06T08:41:30Z",
            "lastModifiedDateTime": "2015-09-06T08:41:30Z",
            "changeKey": "EQAAABYAAABrFd4C2tvVRa8oaXCdnl9HAAIQ4ll9",
            "categories": [],
            "parentFolderId":
"AAMkADU4Zjk3ZTQzLWFjMDctNDM5MiO4NzAwLWFkZGExY2M5NDRlZQAuAAAAAACIOUtE7VENSpDAypZBE6ONAQBrF
d4C2tvVRa8oaXCdnl9HAAAAAAEPAAA=",
            "birthday": null,
            "fileAs": "Green, Mike",
            "displayName": "Mike Green",
            "givenName": "Mike",
            "initials": null,
            "middleName": null,
            "nickName": null,
            "surname": "Green",
            "title": null,
            "yomiGivenName": null,
            "yomiSurname": null,
            "yomiCompanyName": null,
            "generation": null,
            "emailAddresses": [
                {
                    "name": "Mike Green",
                    "address": "mike.green@contoso.com"
                }
            ],
            "imAddresses": [],
            "jobTitle": null,
            "companyName": null,
            "department": null,
            "officeLocation": null,
            "profession": null,
            "businessHomePage": null,
            "assistantName": null,
            "manager": null,
            "homePhones": [],
            "businessPhones": [],
            "homeAddress": {},
            "businessAddress": {},
            "otherAddress": {},
```

```
            "spouseName": null,
            "personalNotes": null,
            "children": []
        },
        ...
    ]
}
```

The structure of a contact is defined in the metadata XML document for the Microsoft Graph API. You can see there is an *Id* property, which can be used to retrieve a specific contact instance directly. Moreover, there are all the common properties for a contact, like *displayName*, *emailAddresses*, *companyName*, and so on.

You can also browse users' various contact folders by querying the *contactFolders* navigation property of an object of type *Microsoft.Graph.User*. Every contact folder can be accessed by *Id*, and you can browse its contacts through the *contacts* navigation property. You can even add contacts or contact folders by making an HTTP POST request against the target collection and providing the JSON representation of the object to create.

Calendars and events

Another common use case is the consumption of calendars and events, which are available through a user-oriented set of URLs. In Table 3-2, you can see the main entry points available.

TABLE 3-2 These are the main URL entry points for consuming calendars and events.

Entry Point Relative URL	Description
/me/Calendar	Represents the default calendar for the current user.
/me/Calendars	List of all the calendars that belong to the current user.
/me/Events	List of all events defined in calendars of the current user.
/users/<UPN>/Calendar	Represents the default calendar for the specified user. You can access it as long as you have delegation permissions for the target user's mailbox.
/users/<UPN>/Calendars	List of all the calendars that belong to the specified user. You can access it as long as you have delegation permissions for the target user's mailbox.
/users/<UPN>/Events	List of all events defined in calendars of the specified user. You can access it as long as you have delegation permissions for the target user's mailbox.

All the entry point relative URLs illustrated in Table 3-2 are relative to the *https://graph.microsoft.com/v1.0/* base URL. For example, in Listing 3-20, you can see the JSON representation of the default calendar for the current user.

LISTING 3-20 An excerpt of the HTTP response that represents the default calendar of the current user

```json
{
    "@odata.context": "https://graph.microsoft.com/v1.0/<tenant>/$metadata#users('paolo.
pialorsi%40sharepoint
    "@odata.type": "#Microsoft.Graph.Calendar",
    "@odata.id": "users/paolo.pialorsi%40sharepoint-camp.com/Calendar",
    "Id":
"AAMkADU4Zjk3ZTQzLWFjMDctNDM5Mi04NzAwLWFkZGExY2M5NDR1ZQBGAAAAAACIOUtE7VENSpDAypZBE6ONBwBrF
d4C2tvVRa8oaXCdnl9HAAAAAAEGAABrFd4C2tvVRa8oaXCdnl9HAAAAAAUSAAA=",
    "Name": "Calendar",
    "ChangeKey": "axXeAtrb1UWvKGlwnZ5fRwACEOJhrw==",
    "Color": "LightGreen"
}
```

The object is a JSON serialization of type *Microsoft.Graph.Calendar*, which is made of a few properties like *Name*, *Color*, and *Id*. If you invoke the *calendars* entry point, you will get back an array of objects of type *Microsoft.Graph.Calendar*.

Once you have a calendar, regardless of whether it is the default calendar or a secondary calendar, you can access the events of a specific time and date interval by invoking the *calendarView* navigation property through an HTTP GET request and providing a couple of query string arguments to declare the *startDateTime* and the *endDateTime* in UTC time format. In Listing 3-21, you can see a sample request.

LISTING 3-21 The HTTP request to get a calendar view on the current user's default calendar

```
GET /v1.0/me/calendar/calendarView?
startDateTime=2015-09-01T12:00:00Z&endDateTime=2015-09-30T12:00:00Z HTTP/1.1

Authorization: Bearer eyJ0...
Host: graph.microsoft.com
Content-Length: 0
Content-Type: application/json
```

In Listing 3-22, you can see an excerpt of the JSON response, which is an array of objects of type *Microsoft.Graph.Event*.

LISTING 3-22 An excerpt of the JSON response for a calendar view on the current user's default calendar

```json
{
    "@odata.context":
"https://graph.microsoft.com/v1.0/$metadata#users('paolo.pialorsi%40sharepoint-camp.com')
/calendar/calendarView",
    "value": [
        {
            "@odata.type": "#microsoft.graph.event",
            "@odata.id":
```

```
"users/paolo.pialorsi%40sharepoint-camp.com/calendar/calendarView/AAMkADU4Zjk3ZTQzLWFjMDct
NDM5Mi04NzAwLWFkZGExY2M5NDRlZQBGAAAAAACIOUtE7VENSpDAypZBE6ONBwBrFd4C2tvVRa8oaXCdnl9HAAAAAA
EOAABrFd4C2tvVRa8oaXCdnl9HAAIQ3XhyAAA%3D",
                "@odata.etag": "W/\"axXeAtrb1UWvKGlwnZ5fRwACEOJdvQ==\"",
                "@odata.editLink":
"users/paolo.pialorsi%40sharepoint-camp.com/calendar/calendarView/AAMkADU4Zjk3ZTQzLWFjMDct
NDM5Mi04NzAwLWFkZGExY2M5NDRlZQBGAAAAAACIOUtE7VENSpDAypZBE6ONBwBrFd4C2tvVRa8oaXCdnl9HAAAAAA
EOAABrFd4C2tvVRa8oaXCdnl9HAAIQ3XhyAAA%3D",
                "id":
"AAMkADU4Zjk3ZTQzLWFjMDctNDM5Mi04NzAwLWFkZGExY2M5NDRlZQBGAAAAAACIOUtE7VENSpDAypZBE6ONBwBrF
d4C2tvVRa8oaXCdnl9HAAAAAAEOAABrFd4C2tvVRa8oaXCdnl9HAAIQ3XhyAAA=",
                "createdDateTime@odata.type": "#DateTimeOffset",
                "createdDateTime": "2015-09-06T16:15:13.6997343Z",
                "lastModifiedDateTime@odata.type": "#DateTimeOffset",
                "lastModifiedDateTime": "2015-09-06T16:16:00.310226Z",
                "changeKey": "axXeAtrb1UWvKGlwnZ5fRwACEOJdvQ==",
                "categories@odata.type": "#Collection(String)",
                "categories": [],
                "originalStartTimeZone": "W. Europe Standard Time",
                "originalEndTimeZone": "W. Europe Standard Time",
                "responseStatus": {
                    "@odata.type": "#microsoft.graph.responseStatus",
                    "response": "organizer",
                    "time@odata.type": "#DateTimeOffset",
                    "time": "0001-01-01T00:00:00Z"
                },
                "iCalUId":
"040000008200E00074C5B7101A82E008000000009B481236BFE8D00100000000000000000001000000097E769044
41F7F408C5AFB6669E97439",
                "reminderMinutesBeforeStart": 15,
                "isReminderOn": false,
                "hasAttachments": false,
                "subject": "Sample Meeting",
                "body": {
                    "@odata.type": "#microsoft.graph.itemBody",
                    "contentType": "html",
                    "content": "<html>...</html>\r\n"
                },
                "bodyPreview": "This is the description of a sample meeting!",
                "importance": "normal",
                "sensitivity": "normal",
                "start": {
                    "@odata.type": "#microsoft.graph.dateTimeTimeZone",
                    "dateTime": "2015-09-06T16:30:00.0000000",
                    "timeZone": "UTC"
                },
                "end": {
                    "@odata.type": "#microsoft.graph.dateTimeTimeZone",
                    "dateTime": "2015-09-06T17:00:00.0000000",
                    "timeZone": "UTC"
                },
                "location": {
                    "@odata.type": "#microsoft.graph.location",
                    "displayName": "Main Office"
                },
```

```
            "isAllDay": false,
            "isCancelled": false,
            "isOrganizer": true,
            "recurrence": null,
            "responseRequested": true,
            "seriesMasterId": null,
            "showAs": "busy",
            "type": "singleInstance",
            "attendees@odata.type": "#Collection(microsoft.graph.attendee)",
            "attendees": [],
            "organizer": {
                "@odata.type": "#microsoft.graph.recipient",
                "emailAddress": {
                    "@odata.type": "#microsoft.graph.emailAddress",
                    "name": "Paolo Pialorsi",
                    "address": "paolo.pialorsi@sharepoint-camp.com"
                }
            },
            "webLink": "https://outlook.office365.com/owa/?ItemID=AAMkADU4Zjk3ZTQzLWFjMDct
NDM5Mi04NzAwLWFkZGExY2M
5NDR1ZQBGAAAAAACIOUtE7VENSpDAypZBE6ONBwBrFd4C2tvVRa8oaXCdnl9HAAAAAAEOAABrFd4C2tvVRa8oaXCdn
l9HAAIQ3XhyAAA%3D&exvsurl=1&viewmodel=ICalendarItemDetailsViewModelFactory",
        },
        ...
    ]
}
```

As you can see, the response includes all the typical information for an event, like *Subject*, *Body*, *Start* and *End* dates (including their time zone), *ShowAs*, *Attendees*, *Responses*, *Organizer*, and so on.

You can also access the entire list of events for the current user by invoking the *events* navigation property of the current calendar or of the current user through an HTTP GET request. The *events* navigation property will give you back a JSON array of *Microsoft.Graph.Event* objects.

As with email messages, discussed in the previous section, you can add, update, or delete calendar events by leveraging the various HTTP verbs. For example, in Listing 3-23, you can see an HTTP request to create a new event in the current user's default calendar.

LISTING 3-23 The HTTP request to add a new event to the current user's default calendar

```
POST /v1.0/me/calendar/events HTTP/1.1

Authorization: Bearer eyJO...
Host: graph.microsoft.com
Content-Length: 599
Content-Type: application/json

{
  "Subject": "Sample meeting create via Microsoft Graph API",
  "Body": {
    "ContentType": "HTML",
```

```
      "Content": "The <b>Microsoft Graph API</b> really rock!"
    },
    "start": {
      "@odata.type": "#microsoft.graph.dateTimeTimeZone",
      "dateTime": "2015-12-22T16:30:00.0000000",
      "timeZone": "UTC"
    },
    "end": {
      "@odata.type": "#microsoft.graph.dateTimeTimeZone",
      "dateTime": "2015-12-22T17:00:00.0000000",
      "timeZone": "UTC"
    },
    "Attendees": [
      {
        "EmailAddress": {
          "Address": "someone@contoso.com",
          "Name": "Paolo Pialorsi"
        },
        "Type": "Required"
      }
    ],
    "Location": {
      "DisplayName": "Headquarters"
    },
    "ShowAs": "Busy",
}
```

The HTTP response will confirm that the event has been created by providing an HTTP Status Code with a value of 201 (Created). If you want to update an existing event, you can make an HTTP PATCH request, targeting that event by *Id* and sending the updated properties as a JSON object. For example, in Listing 3-24, you can see how to update the *Subject* property of the just-created event.

LISTING 3-24 The HTTP request to update an existing event in the current user's default calendar

```
PATCH /v1.0/me/calendar/events/AAMkADU... HTTP/1.1

Authorization: Bearer eyJO...
Host: graph.microsoft.com
Content-Length: 79
Content-Type: application/json

{
  "Subject": "Sample meeting create via Microsoft Graph AP - Updated!"
}
```

The HTTP response will confirm the successful update by providing an HTTP Status Code with a value of 200 (OK) and providing the JSON serialization of the updated event in the response body. Last, if you want to delete an event from a calendar, you can use the HTTP DELETE method, targeting the event URL. The response will be an HTTP Status Code 204 (No Content), meaning that the event has been deleted. Under the cover, Microsoft Exchange Online will handle all the email notifications like sending invitations, updates, and event cancellations.

It is interesting to note that the same REST-based techniques used for managing single events can be used to manage calendars. For example, you can create, update, or delete a secondary calendar by targeting the collection:

https://graph.microsoft.com/v1.0/me/calendars

This is a powerful capability that enables you to create custom software solutions that can completely handle messages, contacts, calendars, and events via REST.

Event invitations

Another common scenario is to manage invitations for events sent to the current user by third parties. In Microsoft Exchange Online, any meeting invitation will automatically be placed in the target user's default calendar, as happens on-premises. Thus, to access an invitation, you just need to target the specific calendar event object that you want to manage by providing the *Id* of the object. In Listing 3-25, you can see an excerpt of a meeting request the current user has received.

LISTING 3-25 An excerpt of the JSON object representing a meeting request the current user has received

```
{
  "@odata.context":
"https://graph.microsoft.com/v1.0/$metadata#users('paolo.pialorsi%40sharepoint-camp.com')
/Calendar/Events/$entity",
  "@odata.type": "#Microsoft.Graph.Event",
  "@odata.id":
"users/paolo%40PiaSysDev.onmicrosoft.com/Calendar/Events/AAMkADU4Zjk3ZTQzLWFjMDctNDM5MiO4N
zAwLWFkZGExY2M5NDR1ZQBGAAAAAACIOUtE7VENSpDAypZBE6ONBwBrFd4C2tvVRa8oaXCdn19HAAAAAAEOAABrFd4
C2tvVRa8oaXCdn19HAAIQ3Xh2AAA%3D",
  "Id":
"AAMkADU4Zjk3ZTQzLWFjMDctNDM5MiO4NzAwLWFkZGExY2M5NDR1ZQBGAAAAAACIOUtE7VENSpDAypZBE6ONBwBrF
d4C2tvVRa8oaXCdn19HAAAAAAEOAABrFd4C2tvVRa8oaXCdn19HAAIQ3Xh2AAA=",
  ...
  "Importance": "Normal",
  "HasAttachments": false,
  "start": {    "@odata.type": "#microsoft.graph.dateTimeTimeZone",
    "dateTime": "2015-12-22T16:30:00.0000000",
    "timeZone": "UTC"
  },  "end": {
    "@odata.type": "#microsoft.graph.dateTimeTimeZone",
    "dateTime": "2015-12-22T17:00:00.0000000",
    "timeZone": "UTC"
  },
  ...
  "ResponseStatus": {
    "Response": "NotResponded",
    "Time": "0001-01-01T00:00:00Z"
  },
  ...
}
```

As you can see highlighted in bold text, there are *Id* and *ResponseStatus* properties, together with the rich set of properties defining the event. If the *ResponseStatus* property has a value of *NotResponded* for the property with name *Response*, it means that the meeting request is pending response.

To accept the meeting request, you can make an HTTP POST request targeting the event URL and appending the accept operation to the URL. The *ResponseStatus* property of the target event will assume a value of *Accepted* for the property with name *Response*, and the *Time* property will assume the value of the date and time when you accepted the meeting request. To decline a meeting request, the operation to append to the URL of the event is decline. To give a tentative answer, you can append the tentativelyAccept operation to the URL of the event.

Regardless of whether you accept, decline, or tentatively accept the meeting request, you will have the option to provide to the meeting organizer a response message that will be provided to the REST API as a JSON object in the body of the request. In Listing 3-26, you can see a sample HTTP request to accept a meeting request.

LISTING 3-26 The HTTP request to accept a meeting request, providing a comment to the meeting organizer

```
POST /v1.0/me/calendar/events/AAMkADU.../accept HTTP/1.1

Authorization: Bearer eyJO...
Host: graph.microsoft.com
Content-Length: 59
Content-Type: application/json;charset=utf-8;odata=minimalmetadata

{
  "Comment": "Sure, I'm looking forward to meet you!"
}
```

The HTTP response will confirm the successful response by providing an HTTP Status Code with a value of 202 (Accepted).

Consuming OneDrive for Business

Another useful set of operations and services is related to OneDrive for Business. To access the files for the current user, you need to target the HTTP endpoint available at the URL *https://graph.microsoft.com/v1.0/me/drive*.

Through the OneDrive URL, you can read information about the owner of the drive and about the storage quota and available storage space. By browsing the navigation properties of the drive, you can access all of its contents.

Querying files and folders

The first step to access the files of a OneDrive for Business drive instance is to query the *root* navigation property of the *drive* by using a URL like the following:

https://graph.microsoft.com/v1.0/me/drive/root

By making an HTTP GET request for the *items* URL, you will get back a JSON array of objects of type *Microsoft.Graph.driveItem*, which can be a folder item or a single file item.

By default, the query for the *children* of the root URL will return only those files and folders defined in the root folder of the current user's OneDrive for Business. If you want to browse the available folders, you have to do it manually, accessing every folder by *Id*. For example, in Listing 3-27, you can see a sample HTTP GET request for the root folder.

LISTING 3-27 The HTTP GET request for the OneDrive for Business root folder for the current user

```
GET /v1.0/me/drive/root/children HTTP/1.1

Authorization: Bearer eyJ0...
Host: graph.microsoft.com
Content-Length: 0
Content-Type: application/json
```

In Listing 3-28, you can see an excerpt of the corresponding JSON response. Note that every item of the array has a unique *id* property, which you can use to access that item directly.

LISTING 3-28 An excerpt of the JSON response for the OneDrive for Business root folder for the current user

```
{
    "@odata.context":
"https://graph.microsoft.com/v1.0/$metadata#users('paolo.pialorsi%40sharepoint-camp.com')
/drive/root/children",
    "value": [
        {
            "@odata.type": "#microsoft.graph.driveItem",
            "@odata.id":
"users/paolo.pialorsi%40sharepoint-camp.com/drive/root/children/01MDKYG3F4IHNFZ6ZQCVCIKPZ4
KVAHJDCH",
            "@odata.etag": "\"{5CDA41BC-30FB-4415-853F-3C5540748C47},2\"",
            "@odata.editLink": "users/paolo.pialorsi%40sharepoint-camp.com/drive/root/chil
dren/01MDKYG3G3MLQJYQ7CUZG3GQRA
7MBBY57D",
            "createdBy": {
                "@odata.type": "#microsoft.graph.identitySet",
                "user": {
                    "@odata.type": "#microsoft.graph.identity",
                    "id": "bea7a848-0459-4bee-9034-5513ee7f66e0",
                    "displayName": "Paolo Pialorsi"
                }
            }
```

```json
        },
        "createdDateTime@odata.type": "#DateTimeOffset",
        "createdDateTime": "2013-06-17T14:52:51Z",
        "eTag": "\"{5CDA41BC-30FB-4415-853F-3C5540748C47},2\"",
        "folder": {
            "@odata.type": "#microsoft.graph.folder",
            "childCount": 5
        },
        "id": "01MDKYG3G3MLQJYQ7CUZG3GQRA7MBBY57D",
        "lastModifiedBy": {
            "@odata.type": "#microsoft.graph.identitySet",
            "user": {
                "@odata.type": "#microsoft.graph.identity",
                "id": "bea7a848-0459-4bee-9034-5513ee7f66e0",
                "displayName": "Paolo Pialorsi"
            }
        },
        "lastModifiedDateTime@odata.type": "#DateTimeOffset",
        "lastModifiedDateTime": "2015-11-11T13:50:58Z",
        "name": "Sample Share",
        "parentReference": {
            "@odata.type": "#microsoft.graph.itemReference",
            "driveId": "b!CznMej4oZOKJYE8EtyeZy0qsx1HxNyJDoP4k_dtjPcx_
OZIUemtpSLqU6V6ZwmfE",
            "id": "01MDKYG3F6Y2GOVW7725BZO354PWSELRRZ",
            "path": "/drive/root:"
        },
        "size@odata.type": "#Int64",
        "size": 0,
        "webUrl": "https://piasysdev-my.sharepoint.com/personal/paolo_pialorsi_
sharepoint-camp_com/Documents
/Sample%20Share",
        },
    ...
    {
        "@odata.type": "#microsoft.graph.driveItem",
        "@odata.id":
"users/paolo.pialorsi%40sharepoint-camp.com/drive/root/children/01MDKYG3HEDOLKC33SVREYSJKG
IHLCBRIC",
        "@odata.etag": "\"{A1961BE4-726F-49AC-8925-4641D620C502},1\"",
        "@odata.editLink": "users/paolo.pialorsi%40sharepoint-camp.com/drive/root/chil
dren/01MDKYG3HEDOLKC33SVREYSJKG
IHLCBRIC",
        "createdBy": {
            "@odata.type": "#microsoft.graph.identitySet",
            "user": {
                "@odata.type": "#microsoft.graph.identity",
                "id": "bea7a848-0459-4bee-9034-5513ee7f66e0",
                "displayName": "Paolo Pialorsi"
            }
        },
        "createdDateTime@odata.type": "#DateTimeOffset",
        "createdDateTime": "2015-02-15T09:33:04Z",
        "cTag": "\"c:{A1961BE4-726F-49AC-8925-4641D620C502},2\"",
        "eTag": "\"{A1961BE4-726F-49AC-8925-4641D620C502},1\"",
```

```
            "file": {
                "@odata.type": "#microsoft.graph.file"
            },
            "id": "01MDKYG3HEDOLKC33SVREYSJKGIHLCBRIC",
            "lastModifiedBy": {
                "@odata.type": "#microsoft.graph.identitySet",
                "user": {
                    "@odata.type": "#microsoft.graph.identity",
                    "id": "bea7a848-0459-4bee-9034-5513ee7f66e0",
                    "displayName": "Paolo Pialorsi"
                }
            },
            "lastModifiedDateTime@odata.type": "#DateTimeOffset",
            "lastModifiedDateTime": "2015-02-15T09:33:04Z",
            "name": "contract.docx",
            "parentReference": {
                "@odata.type": "#microsoft.graph.itemReference",
                "driveId": "b!CznMej4oZOKJYE8EtyeZy0qsx1HxNyJDoP4k_dtjPcx_
OZIUemtpSLqU6V6ZwmfE",
                "id": "01MDKYG3F6Y2GOVW7725BZO354PWSELRRZ",
                "path": "/drive/root:"
            },
            "size@odata.type": "#Int64",
            "size": 18698,
            "webUrl":
"https://piasysdev-my.sharepoint.com/personal/paolo_pialorsi_sharepoint-camp_com/Documents
/contract.docx",
        },
    ...
    }
    ]
}
```

There is also a useful set of item properties like *name*, *createdBy*, *lastModifiedBy*, *createdDateTime*, *lastModifiedDateTime*, *webUrl*, and so on. The *webUrl* property for a file allows direct access to the file content through a direct URL, which is a useful capability. Moreover, when the resulting item is a folder, you will also find the *childCount* property that indicates whether there are child items (subfolders or files) within that folder.

Let's say that you want to access the Sample Share folder defined in the result presented in Listing 3-28. You will just need to make an HTTP GET request for the following URL:

*https://graph.microsoft.com/v1.0/me/drive/items
/01MDKYG3G3MLQJYQ7CUZG3GQRA7MBBY57D*

where the value at the end of the URL is the unique Id of the folder. If you prefer to access the folder by name instead of by using the unique Id, you can use a URL like the following:

https://graph.microsoft.com/v1.0/me/drive/root/children/Sample%20Share

However, by doing this you will not access the files—just the folder object and its properties. To access any child files or folders, you can query the *children* navigation property of the *Microsoft.Graph. driveItem* type. In Listing 3-29, you can see a sample of this kind of request.

LISTING 3-29 The HTTP GET request for the children of a folder in OneDrive for Business for the current user

```
GET /v1.0/me/drive/items/01MDKYG3G3MLQJYQ7CUZG3GQRA7MBBY57D/children HTTP/1.1

Authorization: Bearer eyJO...
Host: graph.microsoft.com
Content-Length: 0
Content-Type: application/json
```

The result will be an array of objects of type *Microsoft.Graph.driveItem* and will look like the excerpt in Listing 3-28. Using this approach, you can navigate through the hierarchy of folders in OneDrive for Business.

Other interesting capabilities that are available for folders and files are the navigation properties to access the *createdByUser* and the *lastModifiedByUser* objects. Through these navigation properties, you can access the object of type *Microsoft.Graph.User* that represents the user who created the item and the user who last modified the item. This is another way to traverse the graph and to access the objects described in the previous section, "Consuming users and security groups."

You can also empower the OData querying capabilities, like you did with the email messages, to retrieve just a subset of files or folders, to select a subset of properties, or to customize the order of results. For example, in Listing 3-30, you can see an HTTP GET request for all the files in a folder, sorted by name, selecting only the file name, size, and dates of creation and last modification.

LISTING 3-30 The HTTP GET request to project some properties of files in a folder of OneDrive for Business

```
GET /v1.0/me/drive/items/01MDKYG3G3MLQJYQ7CUZG3GQRA7MBBY57D/children?$select=name,
dateTimeCreated,dateTimeLastModified&$orderby=name HTTP/1.1

Authorization: Bearer eyJO...
Host: graph.microsoft.com
Content-Length: 0
Content-Type: application/json
```

The result will be like the excerpt illustrated in Listing 3-31.

LISTING 3-31 An excerpt of the result for the query described in Listing 3-30

```
{
    "@odata.context":
"https://graph.microsoft.com/v1.0/$metadata#users('paolo.pialorsi%40sharepoint-camp.com')
/drive/items('01MDKYG3G3MLQJYQ7CUZG3GQRA7MBBY57D')/children(name,dateTimeCreated,
```

```
dateTimeLastModified)",
    "value": [
        {
            "@odata.type": "#microsoft.graph.driveItem",
            "@odata.id":
"users/paolo.pialorsi%40sharepoint.camp.com/drive/items/01MDKYG3G3MLQJYQ7CUZG3GQRA7MBBY57D
/children/01MDKYG3HAJD7AK4IMLVFIEPWGF4SJCTBX",
            "@odata.etag": "\"{05FE48E0-0C71-4A5D-823E-C62F24914C37},2\"",
            "@odata.editLink":
"users/paolo.pialorsi%40sharepoint-camp.com/drive/items/01MDKYG3G3MLQJYQ7CUZG3GQRA7MBBY57D
/children/01MDKYG3HAJD7AK4IMLVFIEPWGF4SJCTBX",
            "id": "01MDKYG3HAJD7AK4IMLVFIEPWGF4SJCTBX",
            "name": "Child Folder"
        },
        ...
        {
            "@odata.type": "#microsoft.graph.driveItem",
            "@odata.id":
"users/paolo.pialorsi%40sharepoint.camp.com/drive/items/01MDKYG3G3MLQJYQ7CUZG3GQRA7MBBY57D
/children/01MDKYG3EIHAILISRHVBDJQVXKTI3LGHVA",
            "@odata.etag": "\"{B4103888-274A-46A8-9856-EA9A36B31EA0},1\"",
            "@odata.editLink":
"users/paolo.pialorsi%40sharepoint.camp.com/drive/items/01MDKYG3G3MLQJYQ7CUZG3GQRA7MBBY57D
/children/01MDKYG3EIHAILISRHVBDJQVXKTI3LGHVA",
            "id": "01MDKYG3EIHAILISRHVBDJQVXKTI3LGHVA",
            "name": "Office 365 Sample File.pdf"
        },
        ...
    ]
}
```

One last use case to consider is downloading a file. To retrieve the raw content of a file, you can make a direct HTTP GET request for the URL of the *Microsoft.Graph.driveItem* object instance, appending the *content* function name just after the file URL. The URL will look like the following:

> *https://graph.microsoft.com/v1.0/me/drive/items/01MDKYG3EIHAILISRHVBDJQVXKTI3LGHVA /Content*

The result will be an HTTP Status Code with a value of 302 (Redirect), which will redirect the HTTP request to the real URL of the file in OneDrive for Business, providing a temporary guest access token that will be valid for a small amount of time (approximately two hours).

It is interesting to notice that you can also leverage the *webUrl* property, which will open the file in the web browser instead of providing the content for download. This capability is useful to access Microsoft Office files within the browser to leverage the document rendering and editing capabilities of Office web applications.

Managing files and folders

In the previous section, you learned how to query folders and files, traverse the folder hierarchy, and download files directly. In this section, you will see how to create new folders and files, update the properties and content of files, and move or delete a file.

Let's start by creating a folder. You just need to make an HTTP POST request against the *children* collection of items of the parent folder in which you would like to create the new folder. For example, imagine that you want to create a new folder called "Child Folder" in the existing folder named "Sample Folder" that you saw in previous examples. In Listing 3-32, you can see such a request.

LISTING 3-32 The HTTP POST request to create a new folder in OneDrive for Business

```
POST /v1.0/me/drive/items/01MDKYG3G3MLQJYQ7CUZG3GQRA7MBBY57D/children HTTP/1.1

Authorization: Bearer eyJ0...
Host: graph.microsoft.com
Content-Length: 51
Content-Type: application/json

{
  "folder": {},
  "name": "Child Folder - 2"
}
```

As you can see, the request is straightforward, and the response will be an HTTP Status Code with a value of 201 (Created). In the body of the response, you will find a JSON object that represents the just-created folder. If you plan to use the newly created folder—for example, to upload some files into it—you can grab the *Id* property for subsequent requests.

Once you have created a new folder and grabbed its *Id* property, to create a file in that folder you can make an HTTP POST request against the collection of children of the new folder. In Listing 3-33, you can see an example.

LISTING 3-33 The HTTP POST request to upload a new file into a target folder in OneDrive for Business

```
POST /v1.0/me/drive/items/01MDKYG3G3MLQJYQ7CUZG3GQRA7MBBY57D/children HTTP/1.1

Authorization: Bearer eyJ0...
Host: graph.microsoft.com
Content-Length: 219
Content-Type: application/json

{
  "file": {},
  "name": "SampleImage.png"
}
```

After you have created the *Microsoft.Graph.driveItem* object, you will have to provide the real content of the file. For example, if the file is an image in JPEG format, you will have to upload the binary content of the image.

To upload or update the content of a file, you have to make an HTTP PUT request for the URL of the file, appending the *content* operation name, setting the proper content type for the request, and putting the file content in the body of the request. In Listing 3-34, you can see a sample request to upload the content of the text file created in Listing 3-33.

LISTING 3-34 The HTTP POST request to upload content into a file created in OneDrive for Business

```
PUT /v1.0/me/drive/items/01MDKYG3GK3HVL5QVCGFELA4Z7NECG2PON/content HTTP/1.1

Authorization: Bearer eyJ0...
Host: graph.microsoft.com
Content-Length: 51
Content-Type: image/png

<Here goes the binary content of the image file>
```

Copying a file around the OneDrive for Business repository is another common requirement that can be accomplished by invoking the *microsoft.graph.copy* (or *copy*) method exposed by every instance of type *Microsoft.Graph.driveItem*, whether it is a file or a folder. In Listing 3-35, you can see a sample request to copy the just-created file from the current folder to another folder.

LISTING 3-35 The HTTP POST request to copy a file from the current folder to another folder in OneDrive for Business

```
POST /v1.0/me/drive/items/01MDKYG3G3MLQJYQ7CUZG3GQRA7MBBY57D/copy HTTP/1.1

Authorization: Bearer eyJ0...
Host: graph.microsoft.com
Content-Length: 60
Content-Type: application/json

{
    "parentReference": {
        "id": "01MDKYG3G3MLQJYQ7CUZG3GQRA7MBBY57D",
    },
  "name": "SampleImageCopied.png"
}
```

Again, the result will be an HTTP Status Code with a value of 202 (Accepted).

If you want to update the properties of the just-created or copied file, you can use the HTTP PATCH method, targeting the URL of the file for which you want to update the properties. In Listing 3-36, you can see a sample update request that renames a file by patching the *name* property.

LISTING 3-36 The HTTP PATCH request to update the properties of a file in OneDrive for Business

```
PATCH /v1.0/me/drive/items/01MDKYG3G3MLQJYQ7CUZG3GQRA7MBBY57D HTTP/1.1

Authorization: Bearer eyJ0...
Host: graph.microsoft.com
Content-Length: 45
Content-Type: application/json
IF-MATCH: "{BD6935D3-C45B-40E6-9251-2BCB3EDA7881},2"

{
  "name": "SampleImage-Renamed.png"
}
```

Notice the IF-MATCH header in the HTTP request, which is required to update an object of type *Microsoft.Graph.Item*. You can get the value of the *eTag* property from the JSON serialization of any item (file or folder). If the eTag value you provide in the header is not equal to the eTag value existing on the service side, it means that someone else already updated the target item. You will get back a concurrency exception with a message like the following excerpt:

```
{"error": {"code": "notAllowed","message": "ETag does not match current item's value",
"innerError": {"request-id": "4367386f-d3a3-4d93-ac4b-cf4662a028ac","date": "2016-06-
15T14:51:24"}}
}
```

If you want to force your update, regardless any other concurrent update, you can provide a value of "*" (without quotes) for the IF-MATCH header, or—at your own risk—you can even skip the IF-MATCH header.

Aside from any concurrency issue, the result of a successful update will be the JSON serialization of the updated *Microsoft.Graph.driveItem* object.

Last, to delete a file or a folder, you can leverage the HTTP DELETE method, targeting the unique *Id* of the item to delete. Listing 3-37 shows how to make such a request.

LISTING 3-37 The HTTP DELETE request to delete a file in OneDrive for Business

```
DELETE /v1.0/me/drive/items/01MDKYG3G3MLQJYQ7CUZG3GQRA7MBBY57D HTTP/1.1

Authorization: Bearer eyJ0...
Host: graph.microsoft.com
Content-Length: 0
Content-Type: application/json
```

The response will be an HTTP Status Code with a value of 204 (No Content), which implies a successful deletion of the target file or folder.

Searching within a drive

In real-life scenarios, users have a lot of files in their OneDrive for Business, especially considering the huge amount of data that every user is allowed to store there. Thus, browsing the folders and files is not always the best way to find content. Luckily, OneDrive for Business is based on Microsoft SharePoint Online, which provides a powerful search engine that can be used to search OneDrive for Business.

Searching for content, whether files or folders, is straightforward. You just need to target an object of type *Microsoft.Graph.driveItem*, which can be the root folder or any subfolder, and invoke the *microsoft.graph.search* (or *search*) function providing a search query text. In Listing 3-38, you can see a sample search request that looks for any file or folder containing the word "sample."

LISTING 3-38 The HTTP GET request to search for files or folders containing the word "sample"

```
GET /v1.0/me/drive/root/microsoft.graph.search(q='sample') HTTP/1.1

Authorization: Bearer eyJ0...
Host: graph.microsoft.com
Content-Length: 0
Content-Type: application/json
```

The response will look like the excerpt in Listing 3-39 and will include both files and folders matching the search criteria.

LISTING 3-39 An excerpt of the JSON array returned by invoking the *search* operation for the root folder of the OneDrive for Business of the current user

```
{
    "@odata.context": "https://graph.microsoft.com/v1.0/$metadata#driveItem",
    "value": [
        {
            "@odata.type": "#microsoft.graph.driveItem",
            "createdBy": {
                "user": {
                    "displayName": "Paolo Pialorsi"
                }
            },
            "createdDateTime": "2015-07-10T17:13:04Z",
            "folder": {
                "childCount": 0
            },
            "id": "01MDKYG3G3MLQJYQ7CUZG3GQRA7MBBY57D",
            "lastModifiedBy": {
                "user": {
                    "displayName": "Paolo Pialorsi"
                }
            },
            "lastModifiedDateTime": "2015-07-10T17:13:04Z",
            "name": "Sample Share",
```

```
            "searchResult": {},
            "size": 0,
            "webUrl": "https://piasysdev-my.sharepoint.com/personal/paolo_pialorsi_
sharepoint-camp_com/Documents
/Sample%20Share"
        },
        {
            "@odata.type": "#microsoft.graph.driveItem",
            "createdBy": {
                "user": {
                    "displayName": "Paolo Pialorsi"
                }
            },
            "createdDateTime": "2015-09-09T04:25:26Z",
            "file": {},
            "id": "01MDKYG3EIHAILISRHVBDJQVXKTI3LGHVA",
            "lastModifiedBy": {
                "user": {
                    "displayName": "Paolo Pialorsi"
                }
            },
            "lastModifiedDateTime": "2013-07-11T00:23:31Z",
            "name": "Office 365 Sample File.pdf",
            "searchResult": {},
            "size": 426620,
            "webUrl": "https://piasysdev-my.sharepoint.com/personal/paolo_pialorsi_
sharepoint-camp_com/Documents
/Sample%20Share/Office%20365%20Sample%20File.pdf"
        },
        ...
    ]
}
```

Note that the search engine will not only search for files and folders with matching names, but also will search the content inside files, as happens with the classic Microsoft SharePoint search engine.

Sharing files and folders

Sharing a file or a folder is another useful capability that is available through the Microsoft Graph API. Whenever you want to share an object of type *Microsoft.Graph.driveItem*, you can invoke the *microsoft. graph.createLink* (or *createLink*) action using an HTTP POST method. The *createLink* action accepts two input parameters:

- **type** A string parameter that defines whether the item will be shared for *view*, which means read-only; for *edit*, which means read and write; or for *embed*, which creates an embeddable link

- **scope** Defines the scope of the action link and can have a value of *organization*, which means that the target users will have to access the resource with an organizational account; or *anonymous*, which means that the link will be accessible anonymously

These parameters have to be provided through a JSON serialized object. In Listing 3-40, you can see a sample file sharing request.

LISTING 3-40 The HTTP POST request to share a file for anonymous viewing

```
POST /v1.0/me/drive/items/01MDKYG3AUTHKROIRYDVHIHLBSZQU7ZNUE/microsoft.graph.createLink
HTTP/1.1

Authorization: Bearer eyJ0...
Host: graph.microsoft.com
Content-Length: 0
Content-Type: application/json


{
  "type": "view",
  "scope": "anonymous"
}
```

The response is illustrated in Listing 3-41 and represents an instance of an object of type *Microsoft. Graph.Permission*.

LISTING 3-41 An excerpt of the JSON returned by invoking the *microsoft.graph.createLink* operation for a *driveItem*

```
{
    "@odata.context": "https://graph.microsoft.com/v1.0/$metadata#permission",
    "@odata.type": "#microsoft.graph.permission",
    "id": "NOJCQTQ2MzItRTAxQi00RD1BLUFEMkEtNEZCMTZDRkFDODM3",
    "roles": [
        "read"
    ],
    "link": {
        "type": "view",
        "webUrl":
"https://piasysdev-my.sharepoint.com/_layouts/15/guestaccess.aspx?guestaccesstoken=0Q7bQd8
WRvu00Txu2%2fuKi6KoHB%2bidQgE6tZVGnoC35c%3d&docid=2_0e34e1f4b0e5640388180ae9a6e49f703"
    }
}
```

The sharing link will be available in the *webUrl* property of the *link* object.

Working with Office 365 Groups

Office 365 Groups are a new feature of Office 365, as you have seen in Chapter 1. The Microsoft Graph API provides a way to interact with the Office 365 Groups and to browse all the capabilities of each group.

As stated in the section "Consuming users and security groups" earlier in this chapter, to access the Office 365 Groups you can browse the *groups* entity set of the current tenant to get a list of objects of type *Microsoft.Graph.Group*, where the *groupTypes* property contains the value *Unified*. Here, you can see the corresponding URL, which leverages OData filtering capabilities:

https://graph.microsoft.com/v1.0/groups?$filter=groupTypes/any(g:%20g%20eq%20'Unified')

Notice the *any* operator applied on the collection property named *groupTypes* and the OData syntax to represent a kind of predicate. In Listing 3-42, you can see an excerpt of the result for the query defined above.

LISTING 3-42 An excerpt of the JSON array providing the groups of type Office 365 Group

```
{
  "value": [
  {
    "id": "c748625f-ece2-4951-bab7-6e89ad8b6f10",
    "description": "Sample Group",
    "displayName": "Sample Group",
    "groupTypes": [
      "Unified"
    ],
    "mail": "samplegroup@PiaSysDev.onmicrosoft.com",
    "mailEnabled": true,
    "mailNickname": "samplegroup",
    "onPremisesLastSyncDateTime": null,
    "onPremisesSecurityIdentifier": null,
    "onPremisesSyncEnabled": null,
    "proxyAddresses": [
      "SMTP:samplegroup@PiaSysDev.onmicrosoft.com"
    ],
    "securityEnabled": false,
    "visibility": "Public"
  }]
}
```

The result of such a URL query will be a JSON object that represents a collection of Office 365 Groups. You can see the main properties of the Office 365 Group instance, including the *id*, *displayName*, *mail* address, *visibility*, and so on.

As with any group, you can access a specific group by appending the *id* value after the *groups* collection URL. For example, to retrieve a direct reference to the Sample Group that is illustrated in Listing 3-42, you can make an HTTP GET request for the following URL:

https://graph.microsoft.com/v1.0/groups/c748625f-ece2-4951-bab7-6e89ad8b6f10

Moreover, every Office 365 Group provides a set of navigation properties to browse the photo for the group, the calendar, the conversations, the files, and the group's members. For example, if you want to access the photo of the group, here is the sample URL to use:

https://graph.microsoft.com/v1.0/groups/<group-id>/photo/$value

To access the calendar of a group, you just need to make an HTTP GET request for a URL like the following:

https://graph.microsoft.com/v1.0/groups/<group-id>/calendar

You will get back an object of type *Microsoft.Graph.Calendar*, which can be used exactly like any other calendar in the Microsoft Graph. You can refer to the section "Consuming mail, contacts, and calendars" earlier in this chapter for further details about how to manage calendars, events, and meetings.

To access a group's conversations, there is a straightforward navigation property called *conversations*, which can be used to get a list of all the conversations or to access a specific conversation by *id*. In Listing 3-43, you can see the JSON representation of a conversation.

LISTING 3-43 An excerpt of the JSON representation of a conversation within an Office 365 Group

```
{
    "id":
"AAQkADdkNjZjMDUwLTA1ZmItNGRiNSO4ZWI5LTdjOTQwZTk1MDZiNAAQABzdWzBNd3VKtWsenlfeLcw=",
    "topic": "The new group Sample Group is ready",
    "hasAttachments": true,
    "lastDeliveredDateTime": "2015-12-03T12:01:30Z",
    "uniqueSenders": [
        "Sample Group"
    ],
    "preview": "Welcome to the group Sample Group."
}
```

The group's members can be queried by invoking the *members* navigation property, like in the following URL:

https://graph.microsoft.com/v1.0/groups/<group-id>/members

You can subscribe to or unsubscribe from email notifications by using the *subscribeByMail* and the *unsubscribeByMail* actions, and you can manage the group as a favorite by using the *addFavorite* and *removeFavorite* methods.

Last, you can access the OneDrive for Business storage dedicated to a specific Office 365 Group just by requesting, via HTTP GET, the *drive* entry point with a URL like the following:

https://graph.microsoft.com/v1.0/groups/<group-id>/drive

The result will be an object of type *Microsoft.Graph.drive*, which behaves exactly as the users' OneDrive for Business file storage. Refer to the section "Consuming OneDrive for Business" earlier in this chapter for further details.

Summary

In this chapter, you learned about the Microsoft Graph API: its architecture and the overall goal of having a unified set of API. Moreover, you learned how to consume services related to users and groups in the Office Graph. You explored how to consume Exchange Online–related services to browse email messages, send a new message, and reply to a received message. You also saw how to query and manage calendars and contacts. You learned how to query, update, and manage files and folders in OneDrive for Business. Last, you explored how to browse the new Office 365 Groups and their content.

In Chapter 4, you will learn how to authenticate against Azure AD and how to leverage the OAuth 2.0 authorization protocol to consume the Microsoft Graph API securely.

The information provided in this and the following chapter enables you to consume the Microsoft Graph API from any device and using any development platform as long as it supports the capability to fire HTTP requests and to serialize/deserialize JSON objects.

## CHAPTER 4

Azure Active Directory and security

This chapter explains the architecture and the capabilities of Microsoft Azure Active Directory. You will learn how the authentication and authorization engine of the Microsoft Graph API works and how to provision custom applications and services that consume the Microsoft Graph API securely.

Introducing Azure Active Directory

To understand how the Microsoft Graph API works, you need to figure out the security architecture of the provided services. All the services available through the Microsoft Graph API share a common underlying security infrastructure, which is based on Microsoft Azure Active Directory (Azure AD) that uses OpenID Connect and OAuth 2.0 protocols for authentication and authorization.

The Azure AD services are offered on a per-Office 365 tenant basis, and there is a direct mapping and relationship between an Azure AD service instance and the identities managed within a specific tenant and with a Microsoft Office 365 tenant. Azure AD is a cloud-based directory service that sits under the cover of any Office 365 tenant. Azure AD is used to store users' identities, authenticate them, and federate tenants with third-party identity providers like Microsoft Active Directory Federation Services (ADFS) on-premises. Moreover, in the business-to-consumer offering (known as Azure AD B2C) it is an open identity provider that can be configured as an intermediary for authenticating users through external identity providers like Facebook, Google, Microsoft Account, LinkedIn, Amazon, and any other provider that is compliant with Open ID Connect, OAuth 2.0, or WS-Federation. One more option is Azure AD Business-to-Business (known as Azure AD B2B), which allows companies to share applications and data with business partners by allowing those partners to use their self-managed identities. Internally, Azure AD supports all of these authentication or authorization protocols and provides a rich set of endpoints to consume them.

Moreover, Azure AD allows you to configure custom apps and services that can leverage its authentication and authorization infrastructure to securely provide services and capabilities to users' identities stored in Azure AD. The beauty of Azure AD is the capability to consume it through a set of REST API, which are secured via OAuth 2.0 and Azure AD, as with third-party services and apps that Azure AD supports. As discussed in Chapter 3, "Microsoft Graph API reference," there is a rich REST-based Graph API that allows browsing the objects defined in the directory and creating, updating, or deleting objects, services, and security-related objects.

In Figure 4-1, you can see a diagram that illustrates the overall architecture of Azure AD.

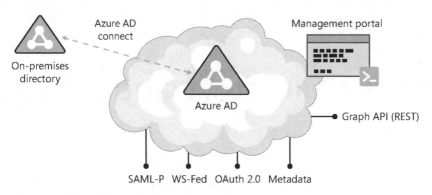

FIGURE 4-1 The architectural schema of Azure AD

Azure AD is available for free in its entry-level offering and is always included in every Office 365 tenant. If you like, you can pay for Azure AD to have access to more advanced features like multifactor authentication, more advanced users and passwords management tools, group-based access management, and many more capabilities. For further details about the capabilities and services Azure AD offers based on the available offerings, you can read the online documentation, which is available at the following URL: *http://azure.microsoft.com/en-us/services/active-directory/*. In Table 4-1, you can compare the main features of the available Azure AD offerings, which are FREE, BASIC, and PREMIUM.

TABLE 4-1 Features comparison for Azure AD offerings

Feature/Capability	Free	Basic	Premium
Directory as a Service	✓	✓	✓
User and Group Management	✓	✓	✓
Device registration	✓	✓	✓
Directory Objects	500K	Unlimited	Unlimited
End User Access Panel	✓	✓	✓
SSO for SaaS Apps	10 Apps / User	10 Apps / User	Unlimited
Directory Synchronization	✓	✓	✓
User-based Access Management and Provisioning	✓	✓	✓
Logon/Access Panel Branding Customization		✓	✓
Group-based Access Management and Provisioning		✓	✓
Self-Service Password Reset for Cloud Users		✓	✓
Self-Service Password Reset for Users with writeback to on-premises directories			✓
Self-service group management for cloud users			✓
Multifactor Authentication (for cloud and on-premises applications)			✓

Feature/Capability	Free	Basic	Premium
Cloud App Discovery			✓
Microsoft Identity Manager User CAL			✓
Service Level Agreement		99.9%	99.9%

Identities in Azure AD

Whenever you deploy an Azure AD tenant, whether manually or automatically within the creation of a new Office 365 tenant, you can manage users' identities. From an architectural perspective, there are three flavors of identities:

- **Cloud identities**   These are cloud-only identities that are created, managed, and handled completely by Azure AD. This is the best option for small businesses or widely geographically distributed companies that don't want to have an on-premises directory system or don't have an on-premises infrastructure at all. It is also a good option for applications that want to support OpenID Connect, OAuth, or SAML through a cloud-based offering.

- **Synchronized identities**   These are identities that get synchronized between on-premises and the cloud. Microsoft provides tools that enable you to synchronize objects between an on-premises directory system and an Azure AD tenant. This is a suitable solution for businesses that have an on-premises infrastructure, including a directory system—for example, Microsoft Windows Active Directory—and are willing to share users' identities across on-premises and the cloud, including the authentication credentials (user names and hashes of passwords). In this scenario, end users will consume cloud services—for example, Office 365—using a completely cloud-based security infrastructure, which under the cover is synchronized with the on-premises environment. Users will authenticate against the Azure AD authentication infrastructure, providing credentials that can be a replica of those defined on-premises and having the Same Sign-On experience, which allows them to access the cloud services by using the same credentials they have on-premises. From a management perspective, some policies or password rules can vary between on-premises and the copied synchronized identities on the cloud. Moreover, it is fundamental to highlight that the synchronization process does not copy users' passwords to the cloud. Rather, it stores a hash of their passwords in the cloud.

- **Federated identities**   This is a more advanced scenario, in which you can federate Azure AD with your on-premises infrastructure. In an on-premises Microsoft Windows Active Directory infrastructure, you will leverage the Microsoft ADFS feature of Microsoft Windows Server to federate your local Active Directory with Azure AD. In this scenario, end users will be able to leverage a Single Sign-On (SSO) logon approach, which will improve their overall experience. This is often the best option for large businesses that want to have a centralized identity management system and provide a consistent end user experience. From a management perspective, the on-premises directory system is the unique repository of policies and password rules, providing a more consistent management experience. The users' authentication process will involve services and workloads hosted on-premises instead of using the classic Azure AD authentication form.

These three options can be mixed within the same Azure AD tenant according to your needs. You can also start with one identity management model and transition to another one almost transparently from your end users' perspective.

In Figure 4-2, you can see a schema of the available identity management options.

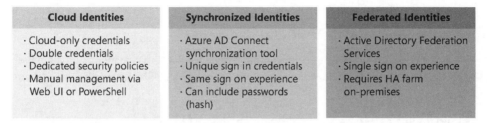

Cloud Identities	Synchronized Identities	Federated Identities

· Cloud-only credentials
· Double credentials
· Dedicated security policies
· Manual management via
  Web UI or PowerShell
	· Azure AD Connect
	  synchronization tool
	· Unique sign in credentials
	· Same sign on experience
	· Can include passwords
	  (hash)
		· Active Directory Federation
		  Services
		· Single sign on experience
		· Requires HA farm
		  on-premises

FIGURE 4-2 The identity management options available in Azure AD

Managing Office 365 identities

From an Office 365 perspective, you can manage your users' identities from the admin portal, which is available at the URL *https://portal.office.com/* under the Admin Center application, by selecting the *Users > Active Users* menu item in the left command tree, as you can see in Figure 4-3.

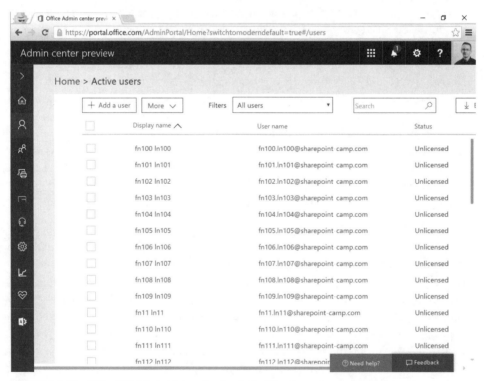

FIGURE 4-3 The Office 365 Admin UI showing the Active Users management panel

There, you will be able to add, update, or delete users and map them with Office 365 licenses. Under the cover, that management UI will store users' information in the related Azure AD tenant. To see that, you can click the Azure AD link, which is available in the left command tree of the Admin Center in the group of menu items called Admin Centers. When you click the Azure AD menu, your web browser will be redirected to the Azure management portal. There, you will be able to completely manage the Azure AD tenant related to your Office 365 tenant.

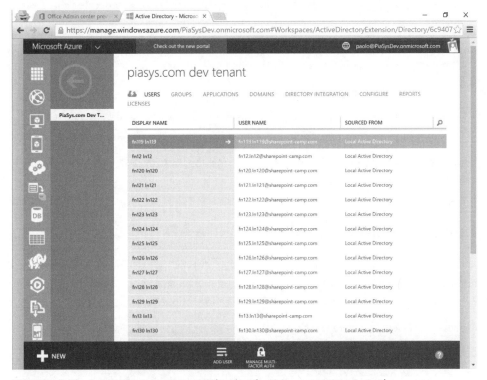

FIGURE 4-4 The Azure AD management UI showing the Users management panel

As you can see in Figure 4-4, after selecting the Active Directory section and choosing your target Azure AD tenant, in the Azure AD management UI there is a tab called Users. From this tab, you can manage the same users' identities as in the admin portal of Office 365, but you can do even more. If you click any user's identity, you can see and manage the user's profile information, including the work information and the devices used to log on (only if you purchase and enable the Premium features), and you can read a log of the user's recent activities and logons.

In general, within the Azure AD administrative UI provided by the Azure management portal, you have the following sections:

- **Users** Manage all the users' information and configuration.

- **Groups** Configure users' groups.

- **Applications**   Define applications and services, which will rely on the current tenant for users' authentication and authorization.

- **Domains**   Configure the list of Internet domains associated with the current tenant.

- **Directory Integration**   Provision directory integration between the current tenant and one or more on-premises directory services. For instance, from this section you can configure Microsoft Windows Active Directory domains synchronized or even federated with the current tenant.

- **Configure**   Allows configuring the tenant name, branding the login page, users' password reset rules, users' and devices access rules, and much more.

- **Reports**   Monitor the tenant activities through advanced reports.

- **Licenses**   Through this section, you can upgrade to Azure AD Premium or buy the Enterprise Mobility Suite, which includes tools like Microsoft Intune and Azure Rights Management.

In the following sections, you will learn how to manage apps in Azure AD, which is the main focus of this chapter.

Configuring apps and services in Azure AD

To leverage the capabilities of Azure AD within your apps and services, you need to register those apps and services in the target tenant. Any apps or services relying on an Azure AD tenant for authentication and authorization services will need an issued Client ID and, optionally, a shared secret.

To achieve this result, you have two options:

- Registering the app manually through the web management UI of Azure AD

- Provisioning the app automatically by leveraging the capabilities offered by Microsoft Visual Studio 2015

In the following sections, you will learn how to leverage both of the above scenarios.

Manual configuration

To manually configure an app or service to rely on Azure AD, you have to access the Azure AD management portal and click the Applications tab. From there, you will be able to browse the already registered apps, or you can add other custom apps or services.

Before adding a new app, let's browse the directory to see what is available out of the box, as shown in Figure 4-5.

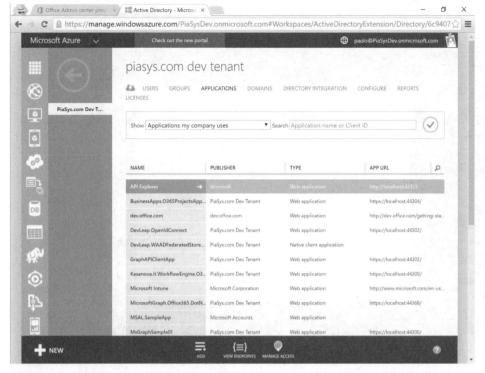

FIGURE 4-5 The UI to manage applications registered in Azure AD

As you can see in Figure 4-5, if your Azure AD tenant is associated with an Office 365 tenant, you will have some apps already registered:

- Office 365 Exchange Online

- Office 365 Management APIs

- Office 365 SharePoint Online

- Office 365 Yammer

Those are the native apps registered by Office 365 to provide the Office 365 services. You cannot manage or delete them; you can only see that they are registered.

Now, let's click the Add button in the lower-middle area of the Azure AD management UI. An app registration wizard, shown in Figure 4-6, will prompt you to select whether you want to "Add An Application My Organization is Developing" or "Add An Application From The Gallery." The first option is the one in which you are interested because it will allow you to register a custom application. The second option will allow you to browse the Application Gallery and add an app from the online market-place. At the time of this writing, there are more than 2,500 apps available in the gallery.

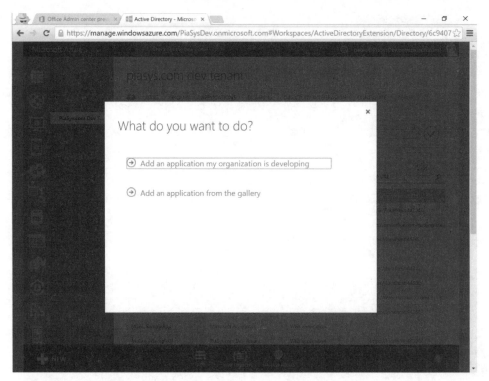

FIGURE 4-6 The wizard for adding a new application to an Azure AD tenant

Select the first option (Add An Application My Organization Is Developing), and you will have to provide a name for your app and choose between a Web Application And/Or Web API or a Native Client Application. The former defines an application that will have a web-based UI. The latter defines any native platform application—for example, those for desktops, tablets, or smartphones. For instance, name the app Programming.Office365.SampleApp, select Web Application And/Or Web API, and make a step forward by clicking the arrows in the bottom-right corner of the page. You will have to provide a Sign-On URL for the app, which is the URL that the end users will use to access your app. You can also provide an App ID URI, which has to be a valid unique URI.

Now, you are almost done. The wizard will register the app in Azure AD and generate a unique Client ID (a GUID) for that app. As you can see in Figure 4-7, just after the registration phase you will be able to access the configuration panels of the app.

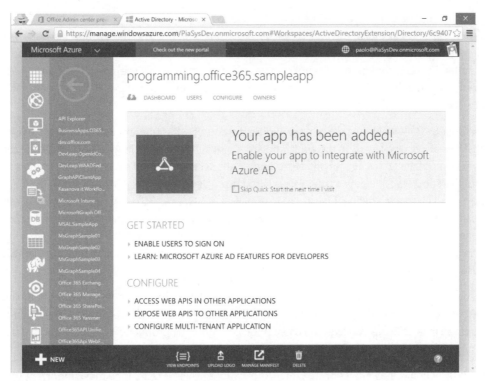

FIGURE 4-7 The Azure AD management UI just after registering a new app

The following is a brief explanation of the available tabs.

- **Dashboard**   Here, you can see a recap of the configuration parameters. You can see all the available endpoints (Metadata, WS-Federation, SAML-P, OAuth 2.0, Azure AD Graph) available to access the app through the current Azure AD tenant. You can upload a custom logo for your app, and you can manage the app manifest, which will be covered in more detail later in this chapter. You can delete the app if you don't want to use it anymore.

- **Users**   Through this tab, you can assign or remove the right to access the app to the users of the current Azure AD tenant.

- **Configure**   This tab includes the most useful options and configuration parameters, including the Sign-On URL, the ClientID, the shared secret (if any), the Reply URL, and so on. The Reply URL is the list of URLs to which the application can redirect users after the authentication phase. Moreover, you will find the permissions for the app. This tab will be explored in more detail later in this section.

- **Owners**   This tab allows you to define the users within your directory who will be owners of the current app. It is a functionality that is under preview at the time of this writing.

Let's focus on the Configure tab. The first information you can view or edit within that tab is the name and the Sign-On URL of the app. Moreover, you can configure whether the app will behave as a multitenant app, which is a concept that will be explained in much more detail in the next section of this chapter. For now, configure the sample app as multitenant; you will leverage this capability later. Then, you have the Client ID, which is fundamental from an OAuth perspective. It is read-only and can only be copied to the clipboard.

Just after the ClientID, you can see or configure the flag User Assignment Required To Access App, which if *true* allows you to assign the application to a specific set of users in Azure AD instead of targeting every user of the Office 365 tenant. Next, there is the section through which you can create security keys for the app. You can create as many keys (also known as Client Secret) as you want, and when you create a new key you can define if it will expire after one or two years. The key value will be available after saving the configuration tab. Be careful that the key value of a newly generated key will be visible only one time, just after its creation. Store it in a safe place just after creation. If you lose the key value, you will have to generate a new one. If you want to follow the flow of this chapter, save the Client Secret because you will use it soon.

Following the keys, there is the Single Sign-On section where you can define the App ID URI and the URLs to which Azure AD will consent to redirect the end users after authentication. Here, you can configure as many URLs as you like, and usually you configure the production URL of the app and any development, testing, or staging URL.

The last section is the Permission To Other Applications, which is one of the most important sections. From here, you can configure what services and applications will be accessible by the current app and the related custom permissions for the current app against every other accessible app. To configure a permission, click the Add Application button and search for the application that you want to configure. By default, every app will be configured to access the Azure AD services to sign in users and read their profile.

For example, to configure the just-created app to access Microsoft SharePoint Online, you can click the Add Application button, select the Office 365 SharePoint Online application, and click the Complete button in the lower-right corner of the dialog (see Figure 4-8). To access the Microsoft Graph API, click the Add Application button and select the Microsoft Graph application. You can also add third-party applications, not only those released by Microsoft. Moreover, you can add your own applications if you want to consume a custom set of API that you have developed and provisioned on Azure AD.

Notice that the list of applications available in Figure 4-8 can vary based on the current user and the current tenant status.

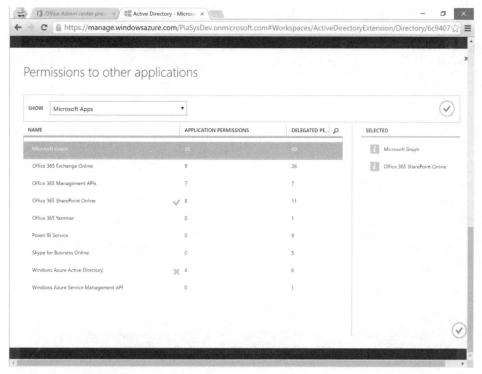

FIGURE 4-8 The Azure AD management UI while configuring an app to consume another app

You can now configure two groups of permissions for the application that you added:

- **Application permissions**   These are the permissions that pertain to the app by itself, and they apply whenever the custom app accesses the other app with an app-only token (on behalf of the app only).

- **Delegated permissions**   These are the permissions that are granted to the app when delegating an end user, and they apply whenever the custom app accesses the other app on behalf of a specific user. In this case, the final set of permissions granted to the app will be the intersection of these permissions and those of the user.

The permissions that can be granted to any app are customizable based on the app, and you can also configure your own custom permissions for your custom apps. In Figure 4-9, you can see a sample of the available delegated permissions for the Microsoft Graph.

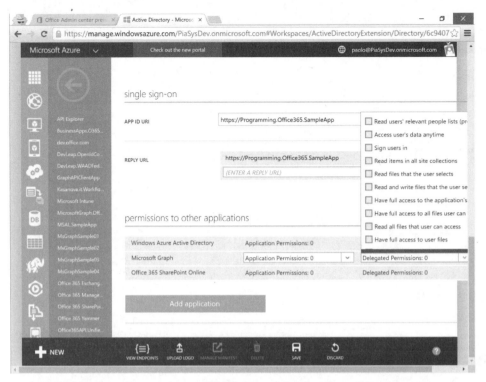

FIGURE 4-9 The delegated permissions available for consuming the Microsoft Graph

As you can see, there are permissions for reading, writing, and managing resources like files, sites, mail, contacts, groups, and so on.

Multitenancy

Whenever you register an app in Azure AD, you are in a specific tenant. If you want to provide your app to multiple customers who will have different Azure AD tenants, you can configure your app as a multitenant app.

As you have seen in the previous section, there is a switch in the Configure tab of any app that you can use to configure multitenancy support. The result of this action will be the capability to support multiple tenants with a unique app registration. From your customers' perspective, they will have to sign up their tenant to be able to leverage your app. For further details about how to define the code for an app sign-up process, see Chapter 10, "Creating Office 365 applications." To follow the flow of this chapter, you should enable multitenancy for the test app you are registering in your tenant. This choice will become useful in the upcoming sections. Whenever you register an app as multitenant, you have to pay attention on the value of the AppID URI, which has to be unique and should identify the domain name of the main tenant in which you are registering the app.

The sign-up process will require your customers to trust your app and to consent for it to have those rights—against their domains and/or users' accounts—that you declared in the permissions setting. Usually, the sign-up process has to be handled by a user who has administrative rights on the target Azure AD tenant. This way, the application will be available to all the users of the target tenant. However, even a single user can sign up for personal use of a specific application.

By signing up a tenant, your multitenant app will be configured automatically in that target tenant and, just after that, the tenant administrators will be able to manage, and even remove, your app from their tenant.

Using Microsoft Visual Studio

Another suitable option for registering an app in Azure AD is to use Microsoft Visual Studio 2015 or Microsoft Visual Studio 2013 Update 2 or later. If you create a new Visual Studio project, which could be a native app (like Windows Forms, WPF, or Universal Windows App) or a web app (ASP.NET 4.x or ASP. NET 5.0), you easily can configure that app as an application in Azure AD.

To follow this process, let's create a new ASP.NET MVC website in Microsoft Visual Studio 2015. In the New ASP.NET Project creation wizard, select to configure users' authentication by clicking the Change Authentication button. You will see a wizard (see Figure 4-10) that allows you to choose from four available users' authentication options.

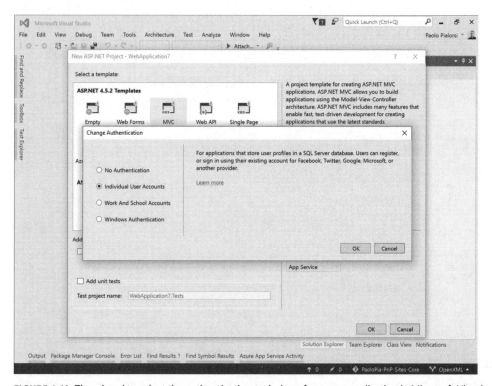

FIGURE 4-10 The wizard to select the authentication technique for a new application in Microsoft Visual Studio 2015

The available options are:

- **No Authentication**   The name should be clear, but it means that your web app will be accessible to anonymous users and there will not be any authentication technique configured.

- **Individual User Accounts**   Allows you to manage identities that are related only to the current application. Users can register and sign in with the app, or they can sign in using their existing Facebook, Twitter, Google, or Microsoft account or any other provider's account.

- **Work And School Accounts**   Leverages Azure AD or ADFS through OWIN for ASP.NET.

- **Windows Authentication**   Relies on an on-premises Active Directory domain for users' authentication via Windows integrated security.

To leverage the Azure AD service for authenticating your users, you will have to choose the Work And School Accounts option. Moreover, you will have to properly configure the tenant name and the application unique name for your app. You can also choose whether to use Azure AD single tenant, which is presented as Cloud – Single Organization; Azure AD multitenant, which is the Cloud – Multiple Organizations option; or an on-premises ADFS server, which is presented as On-Premises. In Figure 4-11, you can see an example of how to configure such an authentication method.

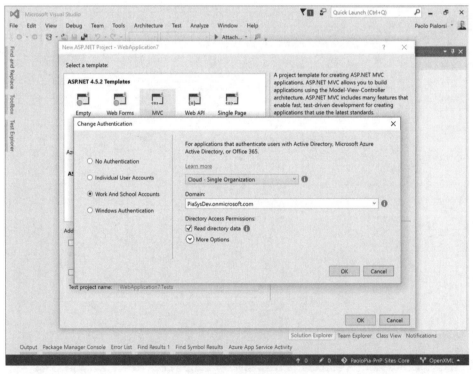

FIGURE 4-11 The user interface available in Microsoft Visual Studio 2015 to configure the authentication provider

In this example, select Cloud – Single Organization to use Azure AD with a single-tenant application. After configuring the Work And School Accounts option and creating the Visual Studio project, the project creation wizard will automatically register your project in Azure AD as a new application, which will have the right to access Azure AD for authentication purposes and read users' information from Azure AD. The project creation wizard will also add some configuration items to the .config file of your project. In the following code excerpt, you can see those configuration items.

```
<appSettings>
  <!-- Here there will be the custom configuration sample, as soon as VS2015 will be RTM ...
-->
    <add key="ida:ClientId" value="07974dc3-ae70-4f56-80eb-1feac570e15d" />
    <add key="ida:AADInstance" value="https://login.windows.net/" />
    <add key="ida:ClientSecret" value="****************************************" />
    <add key="ida:Domain" value="tenant.onmicrosoft.com" />
    <add key="ida:TenantId" value="6c94075a-da0a-4c6a-8411-badf652e8b53" />
    <add key="ida:PostLogoutRedirectUri" value="https://localhost:44300/" />
</appSettings>
```

Here is a brief explanation of the configuration items:

- **ida:ClientId**   Represents the ClientId from an OAuth 2.0 perspective

- **ida:AADInstance**   Defines the base URL of the authorization server, which is always *https:// login.windows.net/* in Azure AD

- **ida:ClientSecret**   The shared secret of the app registered in Microsoft Azure AD

- **ida:Domain**   Represents the Azure AD reference domain name

- **ida:TenantId**   Defines the tenant ID, which can be concatenated to the ida:AADInstance argument

- **ida:PostLogoutRedirectUri**   The URL to which the browsers will be redirected in case of logout

If you now start the web application that you have just created, before accessing the home page you will be asked to log in using your Office 365 tenant credentials. After a successful login, you will have to grant (consent) the permissions to the app, as illustrated in Figure 4-12. After the authentication phase and after having granted permissions, you will be able to use the just-created web application.

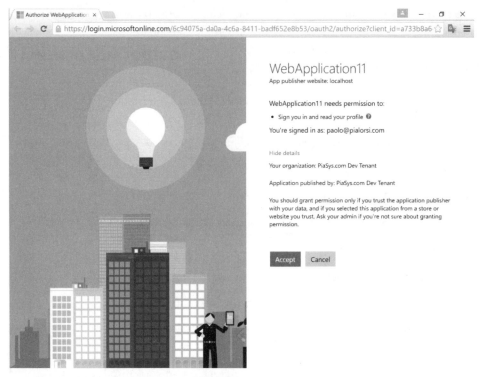

FIGURE 4-12 The Azure AD consent user interface

Just after the authentication and after accepting to grant those rights to the app, you will be back to your web application with an authenticated session for the user's account you used.

Understanding OpenID Connect and OAuth 2.0

Before leveraging the Azure AD service for consuming the Microsoft Graph API, it is useful to understand the protocols involved and how they work, aside from any specific programming language or development environment. If you don't like to learn about the inner workings of the involved protocols, you can skip this section or you can read it later, when you need to satisfy some geeky curiosity.

First of all, the suggested protocol for users' authentication against Office 365 is OpenID Connect, which is an identity layer on top of the OAuth 2.0 protocol, as stated on the OpenID Connect site (*http://openid.net/connect/*). The OpenID Connect protocol allows authenticating users across websites and native apps in a flexible and technology/platform independent manner that leverages REST/JSON messages flows. The goal is to allow developers to authenticate end users to let them consume specific services without having to manage or own their credentials (mainly user names and passwords).

The SAML (Security Assertion Markup Language) token format and the WS-Federation protocol have been—and continue to be—available to authenticate users. However, those technologies mainly target web-based applications and manage XML-based tokens, which are not very mobile friendly and flexible. In contrast, OAuth 2.0 and OpenID Connect were created with cross-platform, interoperability, multidevice, and flexibility in mind.

You may be wondering why there is another protocol on top of OAuth 2.0 and why we cannot use OAuth 2.0 directly for authentication. First, you need to keep in mind that OAuth is an authorization framework, not an authentication protocol. Moreover, the goal of OAuth 2.0 is to grant access to resources through an access-granting protocol, not to authenticate subjects.

Since February 26, 2014, the OpenID Connect specification is a released standard, and companies like Google, Microsoft, PayPal, and others are releasing technologies that are self-certified to be compliant with the specification.

As already stated, under the cover of OpenID Connect there is OAuth 2.0, which can be understood by reading its definition on the IETF (Internet Engineering Task Force) site. If you browse to the OAuth 2.0 specification URL (*http://tools.ietf.org/html/rfc6749*), you will find the following sentence:

> *The OAuth 2.0 authorization framework enables a third-party application to obtain limited access to an HTTP service, either on behalf of a resource owner by orchestrating an approval interaction between the resource owner and the HTTP service, or by allowing the third-party application to obtain access on its own behalf.*

From an Office 365 perspective, the third-party application is any Office application or SharePoint Add-in or any other software that will consume the Microsoft Graph API. The Microsoft Graph API by themselves are the HTTP service to which the previous sentence refers. The limited access defined in the above description is an OAuth 2.0 granted access token, which can be used to act on behalf of a specific user who is the resource owner or on behalf of the add-in or software by itself when OAuth 2.0 grants an app-only OAuth token. Thus, in the Office 365 world, we can rephrase the previous sentence like this:

> *The OAuth 2.0 authorization framework enables any add-in or software solution to obtain a limited access token to access the Microsoft Graph API, either on behalf of a user by orchestrating an approval interaction between the user and the Microsoft Graph API, or by allowing the add-in or software solution to obtain an app-only access token to act on its own behalf.*

Just after a user authenticates through OpenID Connect within an add-in or a software solution, the security infrastructure of Office 365 will engage the OAuth 2.0 protocol to grant an access token to consume the Microsoft Graph API.

The OpenID Connect communication flow

To better understand how the OpenID Connect specification works, you need to consider the communication flow built on top of OAuth 2.0 as an extension of its authorization process. As you can read in the OpenID Connect Core Specification 1.0,[1] the authentication flow is based on five fundamental steps. In Figure 4-13, you can see a graphical representation of the flow.

---

[1] For further details about the OpenID Connect Core Specification 1.0, you can read the online documentation available at the following URL: *http://openid.net/specs/openid-connect-core-1_0.html*.

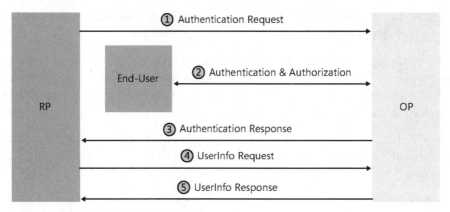

FIGURE 4-13 The OpenID authentication flow

In that schema, the RP stands for Relying Party and represents the Client node, and the OP stands for OpenID Provider and corresponds to the authentication server/infrastructure. In OpenID Connect Core Specification 1.0, the OP can also provide a UserInfo Endpoint.

At the beginning of the flow, the RP sends an authentication request to the OP. After that, the OP authenticates the end user and obtains an authorization to consume a specific resource. Then, the OP answers the authentication request by providing an ID token, which is represented as JWT (JSON Web Token) token, and usually there is also an access token. Then, the RP can send a request, including the access token, to the OP to retrieve the UserInfo, which are claims about the current user. At the end, the OP sends the UserInfo back to the RP.

From a Microsoft Azure AD and Office 365 viewpoint, the flow you have just seen can be represented like in Figure 4-14.

First, the application—whether it is a SharePoint Add-in, an Office Add-in, an Office 365 application, or something else—will contact an Azure AD authorization endpoint to authenticate the end user and to request an authorization code. The Azure AD authorization endpoint is the webpage that authenticates the end user and asks to grant (consent) the application to access a user's resources on his own behalf, if any authorization is needed. After a successful authentication and authorization/consent, the application will get back an authorization code. At this time, the application will be able to send a token request to the Azure AD token endpoint, providing a reference to the resource to access and the just-assigned authorization code. The Azure AD token endpoint will send back an ID token (it is a JWT token) together with an access token and a refresh token. If the application just needs to authenticate the end user, the process is completed and the ID token will suffice. If the application also needs to consume any further API/service/resource, like the Microsoft Graph API, then it will be able to use the access token to invoke the target service or API.

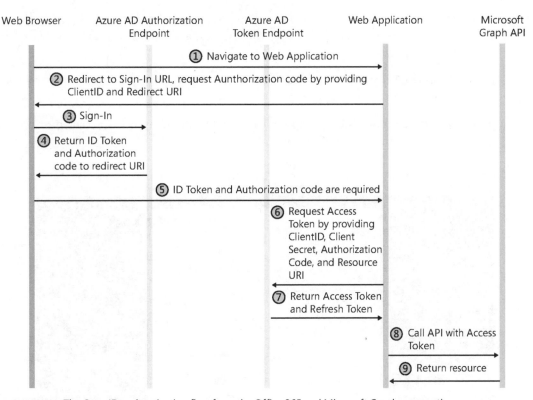

FIGURE 4-14 The OpenID authentication flow from the Office 365 and Microsoft Graph perspective

Under the cover of OpenID Connect and OAuth 2.0

The best way to understand the flow described in the previous section and to inspect what is happening under the cover is to use a tool like Fiddler[2] and look at what's happening on the wire.

Let's go into the Azure AD management portal, select a target app (like the one you have just registered), and click the View Endpoints command button that is available in the lower part of the screen. A dialog like the one shown in Figure 4-15 will appear, presenting the entire list of endpoint URLs for consuming the app. Here is the full list of available endpoints:

- **Federation Metadata Document**   Represents the URL for the federation metadata XML document the app uses for authentication through Azure AD

- **WS-Federation Sign-On Endpoint**   Declares the URL to use for sending sign-on and sign-out requests using the WS-Federation protocol

- **SAML-P Sign-On Endpoint**   Defines the URL to use for sending SAML-P sign-on requests

- **SAML-P Sign-Out Endpoint**   Defines the URL to use for sending SAML-P sign-out requests

---

[2] Fiddler is a free web debugging proxy that is available at the following URL: *http://www.fiddler2.com/*. It is a fundamental tool for creating real web-based and REST-based solutions.

- **Microsoft Azure AD Graph API Endpoint** Represents the endpoint at which an application can access directory data in your Windows Azure AD directory by using the Microsoft Graph API

- **OAuth 2.0 Token Endpoint** Declares the URL at which an app can obtain an access token according to the OAuth 2.0 protocol

- **OAuth 2.0 Authorization Endpoint** Defines the URL at which an app can obtain an authorization code according to the OAuth 2.0 protocol

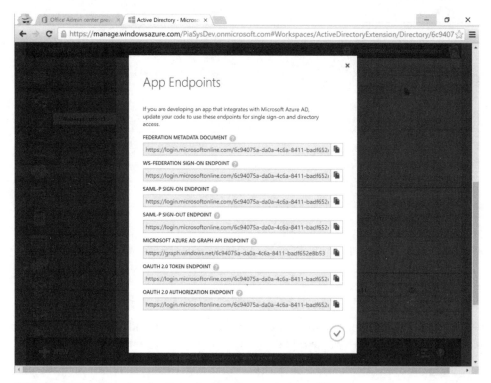

FIGURE 4-15 The dialog showing the endpoints of an app in Azure AD

As you can see by reading the declared URLs, all the addresses include a GUID that is the tenant ID, which varies for every Azure AD tenant. If your app is configured to support multitenancy, and if you want to use these URLs independently from any specific tenant, you can replace the GUID with the *common* keyword.

Getting an authorization code

Now let's say that you want to manually play with OAuth 2.0 and OpenID Connect to consume the Microsoft Graph API. Copy the URL of the OAuth 2.0 authorization endpoint and add some query string parameters, as shown here:

> *https://login.microsoftonline.com/common/oauth2/authorize?api-version=1.0&redirect_uri =[RedirectURL]&response_type=code&client_id=[ClientId]*

As you can see, in the above URL there is the *common* keyword instead of the tenant GUID because the sample app you are using should be configured as a multitenant app. Moreover, there are some variable arguments that the OAuth 2.0 protocol expects, like the *redirect_uri*, the *response_type*, and the *client_id*. The *redirect_uri* argument should assume as a value any of the Reply URL values defined in the Configure panel of the app. The *response_type* argument can assume a value of *code* whenever you want to get back an authorization code, which is the case in the current example. However, *code* is not the only accepted response type from an OpenID Connect specification perspective.[3] Last, the *client_id* argument can be copied from the Client ID available in the Configure panel of the app.

Replace the tokens with proper values according to the above explanation. Then, open a new browser session using the Private Browsing or the Incognito mode or at least without any logged-in user session from a Microsoft Azure or Office 365 perspective. Paste the customized OAuth 2.0 authorization URL into the browser's address bar. As you will see, your browsing session will be redirected to the Azure AD login page, which is the Azure AD authorization endpoint.

For a better understanding of what is happening under the cover, you can run the Fiddler tool to trace the HTTP(S) communication flow.

In this example, let's authenticate using an identity related to the tenant in which you registered the app. If you provide a valid set of credentials, the browser will be redirected (HTTP Status Code 302) to the URL provided in the *redirect_uri* query string argument with the addition of a query string argument with name *code*, which will hold the authorization code released by the OAuth 2.0 server. Putting the authorization code in the query string of the *redirect_uri* is the default behavior from an OpenID Connect Core specification perspective. Your browser will be redirected to a URL like the following:

[redirect_uri]?code=[Authorization Code]&session_state=[GUID]

For the sake of completing this sample journey, you should grab the value of the return authorization code and store it in a safe place.

In contrast, if you provide a valid set of credentials but configure the *redirect_uri* with a value that is not defined in the Configure panel of the app, you will get back an exception, even if you provide valid credentials during login. The exception will be something like the following:

AADSTS50011: The reply address '[your not properly configured redirect URL]' does not match the reply addresses configured for the application: [the ClientID of your app].

Now, let's play with multitenancy. First, if you try to use the app from a tenant that is not the one in which you have registered the app and have not configured the app to be multitenant, as soon as you authenticate providing third-party tenant's credentials, you will get back the following error:

AADSTS70001: Application with identifier [the ClientID of your app] was not found in the directory [third party tenant].

---

[3] For further details about the available response types, you can read the online documentation for the OpenID protocol available here: *http://openid.net/specs/oauth-v2-multiple-response-types-1_0.html*.

If you properly configured the app to support multitenancy and authenticate providing credentials of a third-party tenant, before redirecting the browser to the *redirect_uri* the Azure AD infrastructure will ask you to grant (consent) permissions to the app, according to the permissions configured in the Permissions To Other Applications section of the Configure panel of the app. In Figure 4-16, you can see the webpage that asks for a user's consent.

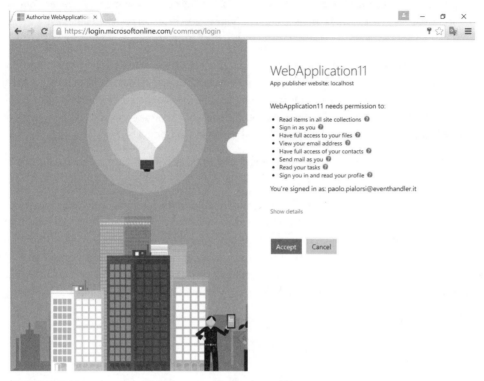

FIGURE 4-16 The consent user interface provided by Azure AD

By clicking the Accept button, the app will be registered in the third-party tenant automatically, and the web browser will be redirected to the app website (*redirect_uri*) providing the authorization code, as in the previous example.

Now, your user has been authenticated and you have the authorization code.

Getting an access token

The next step to access the Microsoft Graph API securely is to get an access token. To do this, get the OAuth 2.0 token endpoint from the list of app endpoints in Azure AD. It should be something like the following:

https://login.microsoftonline.com/common/oauth2/token

Notice that the URL is still targeting a multitenant environment because of the *common* keyword instead of the tenant GUID in the URL path. Start any HTTP(S) client tool like the Fiddler Composer, cURL, or whatever else you like. Fire an HTTP POST request targeting that URL and providing a body like the following:

```
grant_type=authorization_code&redirect_uri=[redirect_uri]&client_id=[ClientID]&client_secret=[Cl
ientSecret]&code=[Authorization_Code]&resource=[target_resource_identifier]
```

The *grant_type* argument instructs the target authorization server about the kind of authorization grant that the client is presenting. In the current example, you are providing an authorization code, hence the *authorization_code* value for the *grant_type* argument. Moreover, the POST request will include information about the *redirect_uri* for the app requesting the token and the *client_id* and *client_secret* of the app (registered in the Configure tab of Azure AD) to authenticate the app, not only the user. The authorization code will follow the app credentials included in the *code* argument. Last, there is a fundamental piece of information about the target resource/service that the app wants to consume: the *resource* argument, which generally is a unique URI representing the target resource/service. To consume the Microsoft Graph API, you should provide a value of *https://graph.microsoft.com/* to the token endpoint.

After sending the HTTP POST request, if the authorization code and the app credentials are valid and the request to consume the target resource is authorized, you will get back a JSON serialized response object,[4] which will include the following properties:

- **access_token**   The requested access token, formatted as a Base64 encoded JWT token, that you can use to consume the target service. Store it in a safe place.

- **expires_in**   The lifetime in seconds of the access token. Usually, the access token released by Azure AD lasts for one hour.[5]

- **expires_on**   The access token expire date formatted in Unix time format, which is the number of seconds elapsed since 00:00:00 UTC of Thursday, January 1, 1970 (1970-01-01T0:0:0Z), not including leap seconds.

- **id_token**   A Base64 encoded JWT token that defines the user's identity.

- **not_before**   The access token validity start date, represented in Unix time format.

- **refresh_token**   Optional; provides a token that can be used to refresh/renew access tokens when they expire.

- **resource**   The source for which the access token has been released.

- **scope**   The permissions that the access token contains/allows.

- **token_type**   The type of the access token. It is always Bearer.

---

[4] For further details about OAuth 2.0 token response, you can read the following document: *https://tools.ietf.org/html/rfc6749#section-4.1.4.*

[5] If you want to learn more about tokens validation, you can read the document "Azure AD Token Lifetime," which was written by Vittorio Bertocci and is available at the following URL: *http://www.cloudidentity.com/blog/2015/03/20/azure-ad-token-lifetime/.*

In the following code excerpt, you can see a sample response in JSON format, with an intentionally omitted *id_token*, *access_token*, and *refresh_token*.

```
{
    "expires_in":"3599",
    "token_type":"Bearer",
    "scope":"AllSites.Read Files.Read MyFiles.Read MyFiles.Write UserProfile.Read",
    "expires_on":"1435318185",
    "not_before":"1435314285",
    "resource":"https://graph.microsoft.com/",
    "access_token":"eyJ0eXAiOiJ…",
    "refresh_token":"AAABAAAAi…",
    "id_token":"eyJ0eXAiOiJKV1…"
}
```

If you get the value of the *id_token* argument and decode it using any JWT token decoder available on the Internet network, you will see that it includes a bunch of claims about the current user. Here, you can see a code excerpt presenting the decoded ID token in JSON format.

```
{
    "aud": "aa76451e-c09f-40a2-8714-9d7ea3f617ee",
    "iss": "https://sts.windows.net/f1aaea4d-8d94-4a74-9147-28d8691a325a/",
    "iat": 1435314285,
    "nbf": 1435314285,
    "exp": 1435318185,
    "ver": "1.0",
    "tid": "f1aaea4d-8d94-4a74-9147-28d8691a325a",
    "oid": "214aacc1-44f6-4a3f-8e6e-ed3a10c726c9",
    "upn": "paolo@pialorsi.onmicrosoft.com",
    "sub": "h_P28X9nnA4_ph-HdMhqTQZV3S5wRN10i1x4yZlRs5o",
    "given_name": "Paolo",
    "family_name": "Pialorsi",
    "name": "Paolo Pialorsi",
    "amr": [
        "pwd"
    ],
    "unique_name": "paolo@pialorsi.onmicrosoft.com"
}
```

In Table 4-2, you can see an explanation of the returned claims.

TABLE 4-2 Claims usually presented inside JWT-formatted OAuth 2.0 ID token

Claim	Description
aud	Stands for Audience and represents the target audience of the current token. In the current scenario, it is the ClientID of the app (your app) that requested the access token.
iss	Represents the principal that issued the ID token, also known as the Issuer of the token. In the current sample flow, it is the security token service (STS) of Azure AD and assumes a value like: *https://sts. windows.net/[Azure-AD-tenant-ID]/*.
iat	Defines the Issued At Time and represents the time when the JWT token was issued. The value is represented in Unix time.

Claim	Description
nbf	Defines the Not Before Time and represents the time when the JWT token becomes effective. The value is represented in Unix time.
exp	Defines the Expire Time and represents the time when the JWT token expires. The value is represented in Unix time.
ver	Declares the Version of the token. It usually assumes the value of 1.0.
tid	Represents the Azure AD Tenant Identifier and corresponds to the ID (GUID) declared in the Issuer URL.
oid	Defines the User Identifier of the current User Object in Azure AD. It is a GUID value.
upn	Represents the User Principal Name of the current user.
sub	Stands for Token Subject Identifier and is a persistent and immutable value for the user whom the token describes. Can be used for caching purposes.
given_name	The user's first name.
family_name	The user's last name.
amr	Stands for Authentication Methods References and defines the techniques used to authenticate the current user. It is a JSON array of case-sensitive strings and can contain values like *pwd* (user name and password authentication), *mfa* (multifactor authentication), *otp* (one-time password), and so on.
unique_name	Declares a unique descriptive name for the current user and usually corresponds to a UPN.

Now, let's do the same with the access token. The following is the JSON representation of the content of the access token.

```
{
    "aud": "https://graph.microsoft.com/",
    "iss": "https://sts.windows.net/f1aaea4d-8d94-4a74-9147-28d8691a325a/",
    "iat": 1435314285,
    "nbf": 1435314285,
    "exp": 1435318185,
    "ver": "1.0",
    "tid": "f1aaea4d-8d94-4a74-9147-28d8691a325a",
    "oid": "214aacc1-44f6-4a3f-8e6e-ed3a10c726c9",
    "upn": "paolo@pialorsi.onmicrosoft.com",
    "puid": "10030000828C6116",
    "sub": "dcxDje8sxZyw5KTJoZZxvKohnU9g_KjLutGU8eXXUS4",
    "given_name": "Paolo",
    "family_name": "Pialorsi",
    "name": "Paolo Pialorsi",
    "amr": [
        "pwd"
    ],
    "unique_name": "paolo@pialorsi.onmicrosoft.com",
    "appid": "aa76451e-c09f-40a2-8714-9d7ea3f617ee",
    "appidacr": "1",
    "scp": "AllSites.Read Files.Read MyFiles.Read MyFiles.Write UserProfile.Read",
    "acr": "1"
}
```

In Table 4-3, you can see the claims usually defined inside an OAuth 2.0 access token.

TABLE 4-3 Claims usually presented inside JWT-formatted OAuth 2.0 access token

Claim	Description
aud	Stands for Audience and represents the target audience of the current token. In the current scenario, it is the Resource ID of the resource/service that the access token targets. If you requested an access token to consume the Microsoft Graph API, the value will be something like: *https://graph.microsoft .com/*.
iss	Represents the principal that issued the ID token, also known as the Issuer of the token. In the current sample flow, it is the STS of Azure AD and assumes a value like: *https://sts.windows.net/[Azure-AD -tenant-ID]/*.
iat	Defines the Issued At Time and represents the time when the JWT token was issued. The value is represented in Unix time.
nbf	Defines the Not Before Time and represents the time when the JWT token becomes effective. The value is represented in Unix time.
exp	Defines the Expire Time and represents the time when the JWT token expires. The value is represented in Unix time.
ver	Declares the Version of the token. It usually assumes the value of 1.0.
tid	Represents the Azure AD Tenant Identifier and corresponds to the ID (GUID) declared in the Issuer URL.
oid	Defines the User Identifier of the current User Object in Azure AD. It is a GUID value.
upn	Represents the User Principal Name of the current user.
puid	Stands for Passport Unique Identifier and represents a unique identifier for the current user.
sub	Stands for Token Subject Identifier and is a persistent and immutable value for the user whom the token describes. Can be used for caching purposes.
given_name	The user's first name.
family_name	The user's last name.
name	The full name of the current user.
amr	Defines the techniques used to authenticate the current user. Can be an array of values in the case of multiple kinds of authentications and can assume values like *pwd* (user name and password authentication), *mfa* (multifactor authentication), and so on.
unique_name	Declares a unique descriptive name for the current user and usually corresponds to a UPN.
appid	The App Identifier. In the current scenario, it is the ClientID of the app (your app) that requested the access token.
appidacr	Stands for App Authentication Context Class Reference and defines how the client was authenticated. For a public client, the value is 0. For an authentication process with ClientID and ClientSecret, it assumes a value of 1, which is the case in the current example.
scp	Represents the Scope of the current access token and declares the permissions that the token grants.
acr	Stands for Authentication Context Class Reference and defines how the subject who is consuming the client/app was authenticated. A value of 0 means the end user authentication did not meet the ISO/IEC 29115 requirements[1] level 1. For security reasons, these kinds of authentications should not be allowed to access any resource of any monetary value. Parties using this claim will need to agree upon the meanings of the values used, which may be context-specific.

[1] For further details about the ISO/IEC 29115 requirements, you can read the following document: *http://www.iso.org/iso/iso_catalogue/catalogue _tc/catalogue_detail.htm?csnumber=45138*.

Accessing a resource or a service

You are now ready to leverage the access token to access the target resource or service. To do that, you just need to copy the access token value and provide it as an Authorization header of type Bearer while executing the HTTP request against the target service.

Let's say that you want to consume the Microsoft Graph API and you want to retrieve some generic information about the currently logged-in user's profile. You also want to access some files stored in the current user's OneDrive for Business.

Thanks to the new architecture of the Microsoft Graph API, the access token you retrieved in the previous section can be used to consume all the API published through the *https://graph.microsoft .com/* endpoint. Start invoking the *https://graph.microsoft.com/v1.0/me* endpoint to retrieve a user's profile information. You will have to make an HTTP request using the GET method and providing an authorization token like the following:

```
Authorization: Bearer [Access Token Value]
```

If you provided a valid access token (one that is not expired) that grants the right to retrieve the user's profile information, you will get back a JSON response with some useful information like:

- Business telephone, office location, mobile phone, and so on

- Main email address

- Preferred language for UI

- Registered devices

- Contacts and calendars

- User principal name

- Photo

Moreover, you can invoke the OneDrive for Business endpoints to retrieve, for example, the list of files in the user's personal storage. To do this, you just need to use the same request format as before (GET with HTTP Authorization Bearer Header), targeting the URL *https://graph.microsoft.com/v1.0/me /drive*. This time, the response will be a JSON object with pointers to the root folder of the OneDrive for Business drive and to the items within the drive.

These examples illustrate the power of the new Microsoft Graph API. In the past and without leveraging the Microsoft Graph API, you had to retrieve one dedicated access token for each service endpoint. Moreover, you had to find the target service URI through the Office 365 Discovery Service. Now, thanks to the new unified model, you just need to retrieve one unique access token for the unified endpoint, and you are ready to consume almost every service with a unique security handshake.

Refreshing an access token

In the previous sections, you saw that an access token has a validity time frame, and maybe you are wondering what happens when an access token expires. You cannot use an expired token. However, when you request an access token through the OAuth 2.0 token endpoint by providing an authorization code, you usually also get back a refresh token. That refresh token usually expires much later than the access token. The refresh token expiration depends on the authorization server configuration, and it can vary from hours (10 to 15 hours) to days or even months. At the time of this writing, Azure AD provides refresh tokens that last for 14 days and that will be renewed automatically for another 14 days whenever you use them within the 14 days of validity. You can repeat the process for up to 90 days. After 90 days, you will have to repeat the authentication process from scratch. Refresh tokens for Microsoft account guest accounts last only 12 hours. Furthermore, a refresh token can suddenly become invalid for many reasons; for instance, when an end user changes her password, any previously released refresh token expires immediately. In general, you cannot assume a specific and fixed lifetime for any refresh token, but you can assume that a refresh token will survive longer than the access token to which it is related. You can use a refresh token to request a new access token through the OAuth 2.0 token endpoint. You just need to submit an HTTP POST request with a body like the following:

```
grant_type=refresh_token&redirect_uri=[redirect_uri]&client_id=[ClientID]&client_
secret=[ClientSecret]&refresh_token=[Refresh_Token]&resource=[target_resource_identifier]
```

In the previous HTTP body excerpt, the *grant_type* argument has a value of *refresh_token*, which means that we are granting the consumer's identity through a refresh token, which is provided through the *refresh_token* argument, instead of by using an authorization code like in the previous examples. If the refresh token provided to the authorization server is expired or revoked, be ready to handle an Invalid Grant exception like the following:

> *AADSTS70002: Error validating credentials. AADSTS70008: The provided access grant is expired or revoked.*

In that case, you will have to discard the refresh token and restart the handshake process, requesting a new authorization code through the OAuth 2.0 authorization endpoint.

Security flow summary

If you have read this section until this point, you know the inner workings of OpenID Connect authentication and OAuth 2.0 authorization. It should be clear that the entire process has to be secured using SSL and HTTPS; otherwise, any "man in the middle" could steal any of the authorization code, access token, or refresh token and be able to act on behalf of someone else. That is the main reason for having all the modern web-based services provided over HTTPS instead of HTTP (think about Office 365, the Microsoft Graph API, the SharePoint Add-in model, Facebook, Twitter, and so on). Whenever OAuth 2.0 and OpenID Connect are involved, the communication channel has to be encrypted.

In the next section, you will learn how to leverage these security protocols through high-level libraries and tools that will make the entire authentication and authorization process easy. Nevertheless, knowing how the entire flow works makes you more independent from any helper or utility library and allows you to debug or inspect what is happening if necessary.

Active Directory Authentication Library

If you read the previous section, you learned the inner workings of OAuth 2.0 and OpenID Connect within an application registered in Azure AD. However, since late 2013, Microsoft provides a high-level library, which is called Active Directory Authentication Library (ADAL). At the time of this writing, ADAL is available in version 3.10 and allows you to consume OAuth 2.0 and OpenID Connect easily with multiple flavors[6] such as the following:

- Microsoft .NET Client: .NET Client, Windows Store, Windows Phone (8.1)

- Microsoft .NET Server: ASP.NET Open Web Interface, ASP.NET MVC

- Java

- JavaScript

- OS X, iOS

- Android

- Node.js

The most interesting information about ADAL is that the various flavors are all available as open source projects on GitHub. Thus, you can leverage them as is, but you can also see their source code, contribute, and provide fixes and new capabilities if you like.

In this last section, you will have a quick overview of ADAL and learn the basics about how to use ADAL in your own .NET projects.

Using ADAL in an ASP.NET MVC web application

Assume that you have the ASP.NET MVC application that you created in the previous topic "Using Microsoft Visual Studio" in the section "Configuring apps and services in Azure AD." In that case, you are using Microsoft Visual Studio 2015 and the Open Web Interface for .NET (OWIN) middleware to authenticate end users with Azure AD, thanks to OpenID Connect.

Supporting single tenancy with ADAL

It is now time to open the source code of the project and inspect the class file named *Startup.Auth. cs*, which is located under the App_Start folder of the web application. In Listing 4-1, you can see an excerpt of the *Startup.Auth.cs* file.

---

[6] For further information about the available flavors of ADAL, you can read the document "Azure Active Directory Authentication Libraries," which is available at the following URL: *https://msdn.microsoft.com/en-us/library/azure /dn151135.aspx*.

LISTING 4-1 An excerpt of the *Startup.Auth.cs* file of a web application with OWIN and Cloud – Single Organization authentication configuration

```
public partial class Startup {
    private static string clientId = ConfigurationManager.AppSettings["ida:ClientId"];
    private static string appKey = ConfigurationManager.AppSettings["ida:ClientSecret"];
    private static string aadInstance = ConfigurationManager.
AppSettings["ida:AADInstance"];
    private static string tenantId = ConfigurationManager.AppSettings["ida:TenantId"];
    private static string postLogoutRedirectUri =
        ConfigurationManager.AppSettings["ida:PostLogoutRedirectUri"];
    public static readonly string Authority = aadInstance + tenantId;

    // This is the resource ID of the AAD Graph API.  We'll need this to request
    // a token to call the Graph API.
    string graphResourceId = "https://graph.windows.net";

    public void ConfigureAuth(IAppBuilder app) {
        ApplicationDbContext db = new ApplicationDbContext();
        app.SetDefaultSignInAsAuthenticationType(
            CookieAuthenticationDefaults.AuthenticationType);
        app.UseCookieAuthentication(new CookieAuthenticationOptions());

        app.UseOpenIdConnectAuthentication(
            new OpenIdConnectAuthenticationOptions {
                ClientId = clientId,
                Authority = Authority,
                PostLogoutRedirectUri = postLogoutRedirectUri,
                Notifications = new OpenIdConnectAuthenticationNotifications() {
                    AuthorizationCodeReceived = (context) => {
                        var code = context.Code;
                        ClientCredential credential = new ClientCredential(
                            clientId, appKey);
                        string signedInUserID =
                            context.AuthenticationTicket.Identity.FindFirst(
                            ClaimTypes.NameIdentifier).Value;
                        AuthenticationContext authContext = new AuthenticationContext(
                            Authority, new ADALTokenCache(signedInUserID));
                        AuthenticationResult result =
                            authContext.AcquireTokenByAuthorizationCode(code,
                            new Uri(HttpContext.Current.Request.Url
                            .GetLeftPart(UriPartial.Path)), credential, graphResourceId);
                        return Task.FromResult(0);
                    }
                }
            });
    }
}
```

The excerpt defines a single-tenant scenario in which the startup code initializes some useful variables that will store information like the ClientID and Client Secret from an OAuth 2.0 perspective, the target Tenant ID, and so on. The first point of interest is the *UseOpenIdConnectAuthentication* method invocation, which is highlighted in bold text and which engages the OWIN OpenID Connect middleware. Inside the method invocation, the *AuthorizationCodeReceived* anonymous delegate implementation corresponds to the handling of the authorization code that we handled manually in the previous sections. The implementation uses the *AuthenticationContext* type, which is part of ADAL and is available in namespace *Microsoft.IdentityModel.Clients.ActiveDirectory*.

The *AuthenticationContext* type can be used to retrieve authentication tokens from Azure AD or ADFS 3.0. As you can see, the type constructor accepts a token cache object implementation, which is used to do token (access tokens and refresh tokens) caching based on the user ID. Through the invocation of the *AcquireTokenByAuthorizationCode* method of the *AuthenticationContext* instance, the class retrieves an object of type *AuthenticationResult*, which holds information like the access token and a refresh token. These tokens will be cached in the token cache and will be used to consume the Microsoft Graph API of Azure AD for reading the profile information of the currently logged-in user.

By using the *AuthenticationContext* type, you can also retrieve access tokens for consuming other services like the Microsoft Graph API and all the other API that are published and secured through a Microsoft Azure AD tenant, for instance. The *AuthenticationContext* type offers methods like *AquireToken*, *AcquireTokenByRefreshToken*, *AcquireTokenSilent*, and others that can be used to request access tokens for consuming specific resources.

For example, if you want to acquire an access token to consume the Microsoft Graph API, you can use the following syntax:

```
String graphAPIResourceId = "https://graph.microsoft.com/";

var graphAPIAuthenticationResult = authContext.AcquireTokenSilent(
    graphAPIResourceId
    credential,
    UserIdentifier.AnyUser);

var accessTokenValue = graphAPIAuthenticationResult.AccessToken;
```

In the previous code excerpt, you will find in the *accessTokenValue* variable the value of the access token that you can inject as an Authorization Bearer header within any further REST request against the Microsoft Graph API endpoints.

Supporting multitenancy with ADAL

If you want to manage a multitenant solution, first you have to configure the app as multitenant in the Azure AD application configuration.

You have to change the web.config file of the application slightly to support the *common* Tenant ID instead of a specific value. Thus, the *ida:TenantId* setting item will look like the following excerpt:

```
<add key="ida:TenantId" value="common" />
```

Just after that, you have to adapt the *Startup.Auth.cs* file to support a multitenancy scenario. In Listing 4-2, you can see a new version of that file.

LISTING 4-2 An excerpt of the *Startup.Auth.cs* file of a web application with OWIN and Cloud – Multiple Organization authentication configuration

```
public partial class Startup {
    private static string clientId = ConfigurationManager.AppSettings["ida:ClientId"];
    private static string appKey = ConfigurationManager.AppSettings["ida:ClientSecret"];
    private static string aadInstance = ConfigurationManager.
AppSettings["ida:AADInstance"];
    private static string tenantId = ConfigurationManager.AppSettings["ida:TenantId"];
    private static string postLogoutRedirectUri =
        ConfigurationManager.AppSettings["ida:PostLogoutRedirectUri"];
    public static readonly string Authority = aadInstance + tenantId;

    // This is the resource ID of the AAD Graph API.  We'll need this to request
    // a token to call the Graph API.
    string graphResourceId = "https://graph.windows.net";

    public void ConfigureAuth(IAppBuilder app) {
        ApplicationDbContext db = new ApplicationDbContext();
        app.SetDefaultSignInAsAuthenticationType(
            CookieAuthenticationDefaults.AuthenticationType);
        app.UseCookieAuthentication(new CookieAuthenticationOptions());

        app.UseOpenIdConnectAuthentication(
            new OpenIdConnectAuthenticationOptions {
                ClientId = clientId,
                Authority = Authority,
                PostLogoutRedirectUri = postLogoutRedirectUri,
                TokenValidationParameters = new System.IdentityModel.Tokens
                    .TokenValidationParameters {
                        // instead of using the default validation
                        // (validating against a single issuer value, as we do
                        // in line of business apps),
                        // we inject our own multitenant validation logic
                        ValidateIssuer = false,
                        // If the app needs access to the entire organization,
                        // then add the logic of validating the Issuer here.
                        // IssuerValidator
                },
                Notifications = new OpenIdConnectAuthenticationNotifications() {
                    AuthorizationCodeReceived = (context) => {
                        var code = context.Code;
                        ClientCredential credential = new ClientCredential(
                            clientId, appKey);
                        string signedInUserID =
                            context.AuthenticationTicket.Identity.FindFirst(
                            ClaimTypes.NameIdentifier).Value;

                        string tenantID =
                            context.AuthenticationTicket.Identity.FindFirst(
                            "http://schemas.microsoft.com/identity/claims/tenantid")
                            .Value;
                        AuthenticationContext authContext = new AuthenticationContext(
                            aadInstance + tenantID, new ADALTokenCache(signedInUser
```

```
                    ID));

                                AuthenticationResult result =
                                    authContext.AcquireTokenByAuthorizationCode(code,
                                    new Uri(HttpContext.Current.Request.Url
                                    .GetLeftPart(UriPartial.Path)), credential, graphResourceId);
                                return Task.FromResult(0);
                            }
                        }
                });
            }
        }
```

The code excerpt of Listing 4-2 is similar to the one of Listing 4-1. The only difference is that we need to retrieve the Tenant ID from the claims of the currently logged-in user, if any. Then, the Tenant ID is used to create the *AuthenticationContext* instance that will be used to retrieve tokens.

Moreover, in Listing 4-2 there is a custom configuration for the *TokenValidationParameters* property that allows you to inject a custom token issuer validation logic, if needed. In the code excerpt, there is a fake validation logic, but in your real business-level solutions you should validate token issuers carefully.

ADAL wrap-up

As you have just seen in practice, the ADAL library makes it easy to authenticate and to acquire access tokens and refresh tokens. Moreover, the ADAL library is able to renew access tokens automatically upon expiration by using the cached refresh token values.

Almost the same capabilities are available in all the other supported framework/technologies. Thus, feel free to leverage ADAL and all of its flavors in your real solutions to avoid doing a manual handshake with Azure AD and the OpenID Connect protocol.

Summary

In this chapter, you learned about the architecture of Azure AD and the key role Azure AD plays in the architecture of Office 365.

Moreover, you saw how you can leverage OAuth 2.0 and OpenID Connect to authenticate users and authorize access to the Microsoft Graph API on behalf of those users. You also inspected how the OAuth 2.0 and OpenID Connect protocols work under the cover during these authentication and authorization processes. Last, you saw how to leverage the ADAL to interact with Azure AD and to manage authentication identities and authorization tokens in Microsoft .NET.

If you would like to walk through all the configuration and development steps illustrated in this chapter, you can download the source code of the application that will be illustrated and built in Chapter 10. That sample application is available on GitHub at the following URL:

https://github.com/OfficeDev/PnP/tree/master/Samples/BusinessApps.O365ProjectsApp

In the next chapters, you will benefit from the information you learned in this chapter while consuming the Microsoft Graph API.

Consuming Office 365

Part III explains how to consume the Microsoft Graph API and services from a developer's perspective by using Microsoft .NET and C#. Through a set of practical examples, you will learn how to leverage Microsoft Office 365 in your custom software solutions.

The journey starts with the mail services, which are explained in Chapter 5, "Mail, calendar, and contact services." You will see how to read mailboxes and navigate through their folders. You will understand how to send, reply to, and forward mail messages and how to manage attachments. Chapter 5 also illustrates the most common tasks for managing contacts and calendars. You will see how to retrieve the list of contacts; how to create, update, or delete a contact; and how to manage contact folders. Moreover, the chapter illustrates how to manage users' calendar meetings; how to create, update, or delete events; and how to manage events and meeting requests.

Chapter 6, "Users and Groups services," covers Users and Groups services. You will learn how to browse groups, how to create or update groups, and how to manage groups' membership. Moreover, you will see how to manage conversations, files, and calendars for Office 365 Groups.

In Chapter 7, "File services," you will learn about the File services, which are a fundamental component to access files stored in Microsoft OneDrive for Business. The chapter explains how to create, update, read, and download files and how to manage folders.

The code samples of all the chapters included in this part are freely accessible through the OfficeDev Patterns & Practices (PnP) project, which is available at the following URL: *http://aka.ms/OfficeDevPnP*. The Microsoft Graph API samples of this part are available in the GitHub repository, which is available at the URL *https://github.com/OfficeDev/PnP* under the project named OfficeDevPnP.MSGraphAPIDemo, which is available at the following friendly URL: *http://aka.ms/ OfficeDev365ProgrammingSamples*.

## CHAPTER 5

Mail, calendar, and contact services

This chapter explains how to leverage the Microsoft Graph API services related to mail, calendar, and contacts. First, the chapter illustrates how to set up your development environment to consume the Microsoft Graph API. Then, the chapter covers the various flavors of available API in the fields of services related to Microsoft Exchange Online.

Setting up the environment

To develop a .NET solution that leverages the Microsoft Graph API, you need to create a new project, which can be almost any kind of project. It can be a console application, an ASP.NET MVC or Web Forms application, a WPF desktop application, and so on. Regardless of the kind of application you plan to develop, you will have to reference some .NET client libraries, and you will be able to play with REST and OData manually by using the *HttpClient* type of .NET.

The examples in this chapter will be based on an ASP.NET MVC application, which can be, for example, a Microsoft Office 365 application. The user interface (UI) of the sample application is out of scope of this part of the book. The UI elements will mainly leverage the Office UI Fabric components, which were introduced in Chapter 2, "Overview of Office 365 development," and which will be explained in detail in Chapter 10, "Creating Office 365 applications," to provide a consistent UI and user experience (UX) to the end users of the application. In the code samples related to this book, which are on GitHub (*http://aka.ms/OfficeDev365ProgrammingSamples*), you can see all the implementation details.

As you learned in Chapter 4, "Azure Active Directory and security," to consume the Microsoft Graph API you need to register your application within the Microsoft Azure Active Directory (Azure AD) tenant, and you need to configure the application permissions properly. For further details about how to register an application in Azure AD, please refer to the section "Configuring apps and services in Azure AD" in Chapter 4.

The easiest way to create a project like the demo that you will see in the following paragraphs is to create a new ASP.NET web application, choose the ASP.NET MVC 4.x template, and configure the web application authentication to use Work And School Accounts, as illustrated in the section "Using Visual Studio" in Chapter 4. This way, your application will already be registered in the Azure AD tenant of your choice. You will also need to install the Active Directory Authentication Library (ADAL) for .NET, which is available as a NuGet package with name "Microsoft.IdentityModel.Clients.ActiveDirectory." At the time of this writing, the latest released version of ADAL is 3.x.

Once you have set up the project references and the NuGet packages, to consume any of the services available through the Microsoft Graph API you need to acquire an OAuth access token via ADAL, as you learned in Chapter 4, and to set up an *HttpClient* object that will consume the API by providing that specific OAuth access token within the HTTP headers of the request. However, before you are able to acquire an access token through ADAL, you will need to customize the initialization code of the ASP. NET MVC project slightly. You will need to open the *Startup.Auth.cs* file, which is located under the App_Start folder of the ASP.NET MVC project, and add some logic to handle the OAuth 2.0 authorization flow. By default, configuring the application for Work And School Accounts authentication will set up an initial light version of that file, which looks like the code excerpt illustrated in Listing 5-1.

LISTING 5-1 The out-of-box *Startup.Auth.cs* file in an ASP.NET project configured for Work And School Accounts authentication

```
public partial class Startup {

    private static string clientId = ConfigurationManager.AppSettings["ida:ClientId"];
    private static string aadInstance = ConfigurationManager.AppSettings["ida:AADInstance"];
    private static string tenantId = ConfigurationManager.AppSettings["ida:TenantId"];
    private static string postLogoutRedirectUri =
      ConfigurationManager.AppSettings["ida:PostLogoutRedirectUri"];
    private static string authority = aadInstance + tenantId;

    public void ConfigureAuth(IAppBuilder app) {

        app.SetDefaultSignInAsAuthenticationType(
          CookieAuthenticationDefaults.AuthenticationType);

        app.UseCookieAuthentication(new CookieAuthenticationOptions());

        app.UseOpenIdConnectAuthentication(
          new OpenIdConnectAuthenticationOptions {
            ClientId = clientId,
            Authority = authority,
            PostLogoutRedirectUri = postLogoutRedirectUri
        });
    }
}
```

These lines of code define the Open Web Interface for .NET (OWIN) pipeline and declare that the ASP.NET MVC web application will use cookie-based authentication, followed by OpenID Connect authentication. The latter is also configured with a specific Client ID, Authority, and post logout redirect URL. By default, all these custom configuration parameters are loaded from the web.config of the web application. In the code samples related to the current book part, these values are retrieved through a static class that shares all the general settings across the entire application. In Listing 5-2, you can see the revised version of the *Startup.Auth.cs* file, which includes the OAuth access token handling logic.

```
public partial class Startup {
  public void ConfigureAuth(IAppBuilder app) {

    app.SetDefaultSignInAsAuthenticationType(
      CookieAuthenticationDefaults.AuthenticationType);

    app.UseCookieAuthentication(new CookieAuthenticationOptions());

    app.UseOpenIdConnectAuthentication(
      new OpenIdConnectAuthenticationOptions {
        ClientId = MSGraphAPIDemoSettings.ClientId,
        Authority = MSGraphAPIDemoSettings.Authority,
        PostLogoutRedirectUri = MSGraphAPIDemoSettings.PostLogoutRedirectUri,
        Notifications = new OpenIdConnectAuthenticationNotifications() {
          SecurityTokenValidated = (context) => {
            return Task.FromResult(0);
          },
          AuthorizationCodeReceived = (context) => {
            var code = context.Code;

            ClientCredential credential = new ClientCredential(
              MSGraphAPIDemoSettings.ClientId,
              MSGraphAPIDemoSettings.ClientSecret);

            string signedInUserID = context.AuthenticationTicket.Identity.FindFirst(
              ClaimTypes.NameIdentifier).Value;

            AuthenticationContext authContext = new AuthenticationContext(
              MSGraphAPIDemoSettings.Authority,
              new SessionADALCache(signedInUserID));

            AuthenticationResult result = authContext.AcquireTokenByAuthorizationCode(
              code,
              new Uri(HttpContext.Current.Request.Url.GetLeftPart(UriPartial.Path)),
              credential,
              MSGraphAPIDemoSettings.MicrosoftGraphResourceId);

            return Task.FromResult(0);
          },
          AuthenticationFailed = (context) => {
            context.OwinContext.Response.Redirect("/Home/Error");
            context.HandleResponse(); // Suppress the exception
            return Task.FromResult(0);
          }
        }
      });
  }
}
```

Within the *OpenIdConnectAuthenticationOptions* constructor, there is the configuration of the *Notifications* property, which is of type *OpenIdConnectAuthenticationNotifications* and allows you to intercept and handle some interesting events related to the OpenID authentication flow. In particular, the event called *AuthorizationCodeReceived* allows you to handle the OpenID Connect authorization code, which was discussed in Chapter 4, and to request an OAuth access token and a refresh token based on that. Inside the *AuthorizationCodeReceived* notification implementation, you can see the request for an access token through the invocation of method *AcquireTokenByAuthorizationCode* of an object of type *AuthenticationContext*. The result will be an object of type *AuthenticationResult*, which will include both an OAuth access token and a refresh token. Notice also that the *AuthenticationContext* instance is created by providing an object of type *SessionADALCache*. This is a custom cache object that ADAL will use to cache both the access token and the refresh token for a single user, based on the user ID passed to the constructor of the cache object. The session-based ADAL cache sample is simple, and in a real scenario you should use another kind of cache based, for example, on a SQL Server database and some Entity Framework code or even based on the Redis Cache of Microsoft Azure if your application will be hosted on Microsoft Azure.

> **Note** For further details about ADAL, the ADAL cache, and the OpenID Connect notifications, you can read the book *Modern Authentication with Azure Active Directory for Web Applications*, written by Vittorio Bertocci and published by Microsoft Press in 2015 (ISBN: 978-0-7356-9694-5).

Aside from the initialization code, which is executed whenever the user's authentication flow starts, to access the Microsoft Graph API you will have to provide a valid OAuth access token. In Listing 5-3, you can see a helper function, which is part of the sample project, to retrieve an access token either from the ADAL cache or by refreshing a new one through the refresh token stored in the ADAL cache. If neither the access token nor the refresh token is valid, the helper method will handle a full refresh of the authentication context by invoking the *Challenge* method of the current OWIN *Authentication* context.

LISTING 5-3 A helper method to get an OAuth access token for accessing the Microsoft Graph API

```
/// <summary>
/// This helper method returns an OAuth Access Token for the current user
/// </summary>
/// <param name="resourceId">The resourceId for which we are requesting the token</param>
/// <returns>The OAuth Access Token value</returns>
public static String GetAccessTokenForCurrentUser(String resourceId = null) {

  String accessToken = null;
  if (String.IsNullOrEmpty(resourceId)) {
    resourceId = MSGraphAPIDemoSettings.MicrosoftGraphResourceId;
  }

  try {
    ClientCredential credential = new ClientCredential(
      MSGraphAPIDemoSettings.ClientId,
      MSGraphAPIDemoSettings.ClientSecret);
```

```
        string signedInUserID = System.Security.Claims.ClaimsPrincipal.Current
          .FindFirst(ClaimTypes.NameIdentifier).Value;

        AuthenticationContext authContext = new AuthenticationContext(
          MSGraphAPIDemoSettings.Authority,
          new SessionADALCache(signedInUserID));

        AuthenticationResult result = authContext.AcquireTokenSilent(
          MSGraphAPIDemoSettings.MicrosoftGraphResourceId,
          credential,
          UserIdentifier.AnyUser);

        accessToken = result.AccessToken;
    }
    catch (AdalException ex) {
      if (ex.ErrorCode == "failed_to_acquire_token_silently") {
        // Refresh the access token from scratch
        HttpContext.Current.GetOwinContext().Authentication.Challenge(
          new AuthenticationProperties {
            RedirectUri = HttpContext.Current.Request.Url.ToString(),
          },
          OpenIdConnectAuthenticationDefaults.AuthenticationType);
      }
      else {
        // Rethrow the exception
        throw ex;
      }
    }
    return (accessToken);
}
```

Notice the *AcquireTokenSilent* method invocation, which will get the access token from the ADAL cache or refresh it based on the cached refresh token. The ADAL cache, as described previously, is built based on the current user ID. In case of an exception with an error code with a value of *failed_to_ac-quire_token_silently*, the helper will invoke the *Challenge* method to start a new authentication flow, as discussed previously.

In Listing 5-4, you can see a code excerpt that illustrates how to use the method *GetAccessTokenForCurrentUser* described in Listing 5-3.

LISTING 5-4 An excerpt of code that initializes an instance of the *HttpClient* leveraging the OAuth access token retrieved by invoking the *GetAccessTokenForCurrentUser* helper method

```
/// <summary>
/// This helper method makes an HTTP request and eventually returns a result
/// </summary>
/// <param name="httpMethod">The HTTP method for the request</param>
/// <param name="requestUrl">The URL of the request</param>
/// <param name="accept">The content type of the accepted response</param>
/// <param name="content">The content of the request</param>
/// <param name="contentType">The content  type of the request</param>
```

```
/// <param name="resultPredicate">The predicate to retrieve the result, if any</param>
/// <typeparam name="TResult">The type of the result, if any</typeparam>
/// <returns>The value of the result, if any</returns>
private static TResult MakeHttpRequest<TResult>(
    String httpMethod,
    String requestUrl,
    String accept = null,
    Object content = null,
    String contentType = null,
    Func<HttpResponseMessage, TResult> resultPredicate = null) {

    // Prepare the variable to hold the result, if any
    TResult result = default(TResult);

    // Get the OAuth Access Token
    Uri requestUri = new Uri(requestUrl);
    Uri graphUri = new Uri(MSGraphAPIDemoSettings.MicrosoftGraphResourceId);
    var accessToken =
        GetAccessTokenForCurrentUser(requestUri.DnsSafeHost != graphUri.DnsSafeHost ?
            ($"{requestUri.Scheme}://{requestUri.Host}") :
            MSGraphAPIDemoSettings.MicrosoftGraphResourceId);

    if (!String.IsNullOrEmpty(accessToken)) {
        // If we have the token, then handle the HTTP request
        HttpClient httpClient = new HttpClient();

        // Set the Authorization Bearer token
        httpClient.DefaultRequestHeaders.Authorization =
            new AuthenticationHeaderValue("Bearer", accessToken);

        // If there is an accept argument, set the corresponding HTTP header
        if (!String.IsNullOrEmpty(accept)) {
            httpClient.DefaultRequestHeaders.Accept.Clear();
            httpClient.DefaultRequestHeaders.Accept.Add(
                new MediaTypeWithQualityHeaderValue(accept));
        }

        // Prepare the content of the request, if any
        HttpContent requestContent =
            (content != null) ?
            new StringContent(JsonConvert.SerializeObject(content,
                Formatting.None,
                new JsonSerializerSettings {
                    NullValueHandling = NullValueHandling.Ignore,
                    ContractResolver = new CamelCasePropertyNamesContractResolver(),
                }),
            Encoding.UTF8, contentType) : null;

        // Prepare the HTTP request message with the proper HTTP method
        HttpRequestMessage request = new HttpRequestMessage(
            new HttpMethod(httpMethod), requestUrl);

        // Set the request content, if any
        if (requestContent != null) {
            request.Content = requestContent;
```

```
    }

    // Fire the HTTP request
    HttpResponseMessage response = httpClient.SendAsync(request).Result;

    if (response.IsSuccessStatusCode) {
        // If the response is Success and there is a
        // predicate to retrieve the result, invoke it
        if (resultPredicate != null) {
            result = resultPredicate(response);
        }
    }
    else {
        throw new ApplicationException(
            String.Format("Exception while invoking endpoint {0}.", graphRequestUri),
            new HttpException(
                (Int32)response.StatusCode,
                response.Content.ReadAsStringAsync().Result));
    }
    }
    return (result);
}
```

As you can see, the generic method called *MakeHttpRequest* internally handles any kind of HTTP request, based on the *httpMethod* and the *graphRequestUri* input arguments. Moreover, it sets up the HTTP Authorization header of type *Bearer* by using the value of the OAuth access token retrieved through the *GetAccessTokenForCurrentUser* method illustrated in Listing 5-3. The generic type *TResult* defines the type of the result, if any. In that case, the optional *resultPredicate* argument is used to retrieve a typed result for the HTTP request.

Notice the excerpt highlighted in bold, where the content of the HTTP request is defined. The syntax leverages the *JsonConvert* object, providing some custom serialization settings to suppress any *null* property that otherwise would be noisy for the target Microsoft Graph API.

The *MakeHttpRequest* method will be used internally by the *MicrosoftGraphHelper* class to fire any HTTP request in the following sections. In the *MicrosoftGraphHelper* class, there are a bunch of HTTP-related methods to make it easy to handle any kind of request. In Listing 5-5, you can see the definition of these methods.

LISTING 5-5 Code excerpt of the HTTP-related methods defined in the *MicrosoftGraphHelper* class

```
/// <summary>
/// This helper method makes an HTTP GET request and returns the result as a String
/// </summary>
/// <param name="graphRequestUri">The URL of the request</param>
/// <returns>The String value of the result</returns>
public static String MakeGetRequestForString(String graphRequestUri) {
    return (MakeHttpRequest<String>("GET",
        graphRequestUri,
```

```
            resultPredicate: r => r.Content.ReadAsStringAsync().Result));
}


/// <summary>
/// This helper method makes an HTTP GET request and returns the result as a Stream
/// </summary>
/// <param name="graphRequestUri">The URL of the request</param>
/// <param name="accept">The accept header for the response</param>
/// <returns>The Stream  of the result</returns>
public static System.IO.Stream MakeGetRequestForStream(String graphRequestUri,
        String accept) {
    return (MakeHttpRequest<System.IO.Stream>("GET",
        graphRequestUri,
        resultPredicate: r => r.Content.ReadAsStreamAsync().Result));
}


/// <summary>
/// This helper method makes an HTTP POST request without a response
/// </summary>
/// <param name="graphRequestUri">The URL of the request</param>
/// <param name="content">The content of the request</param>
/// <param name="contentType">The content/type of the request</param>
public static void MakePostRequest(String graphRequestUri,
        Object content = null,
        String contentType = null) {
    MakeHttpRequest<String>("POST",
        graphRequestUri,
        content: content,
        contentType: contentType);
}


/// <summary>
/// This helper method makes an HTTP POST request and returns the result as a String
/// </summary>
/// <param name="graphRequestUri">The URL of the request</param>
/// <param name="content">The content of the request</param>
/// <param name="contentType">The content/type of the request</param>
/// <returns>The String value of the result</returns>
public static String MakePostRequestForString(String graphRequestUri,
        Object content = null,
        String contentType = null) {
    return (MakeHttpRequest<String>("POST",
        graphRequestUri,
        content: content,
        contentType: contentType,
        resultPredicate: r => r.Content.ReadAsStringAsync().Result));
}


/// <summary>
/// This helper method makes an HTTP PATCH request and returns the result as a String
/// </summary>
/// <param name="graphRequestUri">The URL of the request</param>
/// <param name="content">The content of the request</param>
/// <param name="contentType">The content/type of the request</param>
/// <returns>The String value of the result</returns>
```

```
public static String MakePatchRequestForString(String graphRequestUri,
        Object content = null,
        String contentType = null) {
    return (MakeHttpRequest<String>("PATCH",
        graphRequestUri,
        content: content,
        contentType: contentType,
        resultPredicate: r => r.Content.ReadAsStringAsync().Result));
}


/// <summary>
/// This helper method makes an HTTP DELETE request
/// </summary>
/// <param name="graphRequestUri">The URL of the request</param>
/// <returns>The String value of the result</returns>
public static void MakeDeleteRequest(String graphRequestUri) {
    MakeHttpRequest<String>("DELETE", graphRequestUri);
}


/// <summary>
/// This helper method makes an HTTP PUT request without a response
/// </summary>
/// <param name="requestUrl">The URL of the request</param>
/// <param name="content">The content of the request</param>
/// <param name="contentType">The content/type of the request</param>
public static void MakePutRequest(String requestUrl,
    Object content = null, String contentType = null) {
    MakeHttpRequest<String>("PUT",
        requestUrl,
        content: content,
        contentType: contentType);
}


/// <summary>
/// This helper method makes an HTTP PUT request and returns the result as a String
/// </summary>
/// <param name="requestUrl">The URL of the request</param>
/// <param name="content">The content of the request</param>
/// <param name="contentType">The content/type of the request</param>
/// <returns>The String value of the result</returns>
public static String MakePutRequestForString(String requestUrl,
    Object content = null, String contentType = null) {
    return(MakeHttpRequest<String>("PUT",
        requestUrl,
        content: content,
        contentType: contentType,
        resultPredicate: r => r.Content.ReadAsStringAsync().Result));
}
```

You are now ready to consume the Microsoft Graph API within your code by leveraging these helper methods and the setup environment.

Mail services

As you saw in Chapter 3, "Microsoft Graph API reference," to consume the mail services you will need to access the proper REST endpoint and process the related JSON responses. However, from a .NET perspective, you will have to deserialize every JSON response into something that can be handled by your code. To achieve this, you can, for example, use the Newtonsoft.Json package, which is available through NuGet.

Reading folders, messages, and attachments

When playing with the mail services, the first and most common thing to do is to enumerate the email messages that you have in a mailbox. In Listing 5-6, you can see a code excerpt about how to retrieve the list of mail folders in the current user's mailbox.

LISTING 5-6 Code excerpt to enumerate the email folders in a mailbox

```
/// <summary>
/// This method retrieves the email folders of the current user
/// </summary>
/// <param name="startIndex">The startIndex (0 based) of the folders to retrieve</param>
/// <returns>A page of up to 10 email folders</returns>
public static List<MailFolder> ListFolders(Int32 startIndex = 0) {
    String jsonResponse = MicrosoftGraphHelper.MakeGetRequestForString(
        String.Format("{0}me/mailFolders?$skip={1}",
            MicrosoftGraphHelper.MicrosoftGraphV1BaseUri,
            startIndex));

    var folders = JsonConvert.DeserializeObject<MailFolderList>(jsonResponse);
    return (folders.Folders);
}
```

As you can see, the method leverages the helper method *MakeGetRequestForString*, which is illustrated in Listing 5-5. It uses the *JsonConvert* type of *Newtonsoft.Json* to convert the JSON response string into a custom type (*MailFolderList*) that holds a collection of objects of type *MailFolder*. These types are defined in Listing 5-7.

Moreover, as you can see in the code highlighted in bold, the URL of the request handles paging of responses by leveraging the OData *$skip* query string parameter. By default, the Microsoft Graph API will return results in chunks of no more than 10 elements, skipping a number of elements based on the *$skip* parameter value. Thanks to this out-of-box behavior of the Microsoft Graph API, you easily can do paging of every result set with pages of up to 10 elements each.

LISTING 5-7 Code excerpt that defines the *MailFolderList* and the *MailFolder* model types

```
/// <summary>
/// Defines a list of email message folders
/// </summary>
```

```
public class MailFolderList {

    /// <summary>
    /// The list of email message folders
    /// </summary>
    [JsonProperty("value")]
    public List<MailFolder> Folders { get; set; }
}

/// <summary>
/// Defines an email Folder
/// </summary>
public class MailFolder : BaseModel {

    /// <summary>
    /// The display name of the email folder
    /// </summary>
    [JsonProperty("displayName")]
    public String Name { get; set; }

    /// <summary>
    /// Total number of items
    /// </summary>
    public Int32 TotalItemCount { get; set; }

    /// <summary>
    /// Number of unread items
    /// </summary>
    public Int32 UnreadItemCount { get; set; }
}
```

Notice that the *MailFolder* type provides just a subset of the properties defined in a mail folder, but the *JsonConvert* engine will handle that, including any property remapping, by leveraging the *JsonProperty* attribute. Shaping the *MailFolder* type and any other domain model type is a task you must perform based on your real business requirements if you want to consume the Microsoft Graph API manually and at low level, with pure HTTP, REST, and JSON.

Once you have the list of folders for the current user, you can access the email messages of a specific folder by making a REST request for a URL like the following:

https://graph.microsoft.com/v1.0/me/mailFolders/<Folder ID>/messages

In Listing 5-8, you can see a code excerpt of a method that retrieves such a list of email messages.

LISTING 5-8 Code excerpt of a method that retrieves the email messages of a mail folder

```
/// <summary>
/// This method retrieves the email messages from a folder in the current user's mailbox
/// </summary>
/// <param name="folderId">The ID of the target folder, optional</param>
/// <param name="startIndex">The startIndex (0 based) of the messages to retrieve</param>
```

```
/// <param name="includeAttachments">Defines whether to include attachments</param>
/// <returns>A page of up to 10 email messages in the folder</returns>
public static List<MailMessage> ListMessages(String folderId = null, Int32 startIndex = 0,
Boolean includeAttachments = false) {

    String targetUrl = null;
    if (!String.IsNullOrEmpty(folderId)) {
        targetUrl = String.Format("{0}me/mailFolders/{1}/messages?$skip={2}",
            MicrosoftGraphHelper.MicrosoftGraphV1BaseUri,
            folderId, startIndex);
    }
    else {
        targetUrl = String.Format("{0}me/messages?$skip={1}",
            MicrosoftGraphHelper.MicrosoftGraphV1BaseUri,
            startIndex);
    }

    String jsonResponse = MicrosoftGraphHelper.MakeGetRequestForString(targetUrl);
    var messages = JsonConvert.DeserializeObject<MailMessageList>(jsonResponse);

    if (includeAttachments)
        foreach (var message in messages.Messages.Where(m => m.HasAttachments)) {
            message.LoadAttachments();
        }
    }

    return (messages.Messages);
}
```

The logic of the *ListMessages* method illustrated in Listing 5-8 is similar to that of the *ListFolders* method illustrated in Listing 5-6, including how the paging of results is handled. However, in the *ListMessages* method there is also some business logic to retrieve the attachments of the messages, if requested with the *includeAttachments* Boolean argument, by leveraging an extension method called *LoadAttachments* that extends the *MailMessage* custom type. In Listing 5-9, you can see how the *MailMessageList* and the *MailMessage* types are defined.

LISTING 5-9 Code excerpt that defines the *MailMessageList* and the *MailMessage* types

```
/// <summary>
/// Defines a list of email messages
/// </summary>
public class MailMessageList {

    /// <summary>
    /// The list of messages
    /// </summary>
    [JsonProperty("value")]
    public List<MailMessage> Messages { get; set; }
}

/// <summary>
```

```
/// Defines an email message
/// </summary>
public class MailMessage : BaseModel {

    public MailMessage() {
        this.Attachments = new List<MailAttachment>();
    }

    /// <summary>
    /// The importance of the email message
    /// </summary>
    [JsonConverter(typeof(StringEnumConverter))]
    public ItemImportance Importance { get; set; }

    /// <summary>
    /// The sender email address
    /// </summary>
    [JsonProperty("from")
    public MailMessageRecipient From { get; set; }

    /// <summary>
    /// The list of email address TO recipients
    /// </summary>
    [JsonProperty("toRecipients")]
    public List<MailMessageRecipient> To { get; set; }

    /// <summary>
    /// The list of email address CC recipients
    /// </summary>
    [JsonProperty("ccRecipients")]
    public List<MailMessageRecipient> CC { get; set; }

    /// <summary>
    /// The list of email address BCC recipients
    /// </summary>
    [JsonProperty("bccRecipients")]
    public List<MailMessageRecipient> BCC { get; set; }

    /// <summary>
    /// The subject of the email message
    /// </summary>
    public String Subject { get; set; }

    /// <summary>
    /// The body of the email message
    /// </summary>
    public ItemBody Body { get; set; }

    /// <summary>
    /// The UTC sent date and time of the email message
    /// </summary>
    public Nullable<DateTime> SentDateTime { get; set; }

    /// <summary>
    /// The UTC received date and time of the email message
```

```csharp
        /// </summary>
        public Nullable<DateTime> ReceivedDateTime { get; set; }


        /// <summary>
        /// Defines whether the email message is read on unread
        /// </summary>
        public Boolean IsRead { get; set; }


        /// <summary>
        /// Defines whether the email message is a draft
        /// </summary>
        public Boolean IsDraft { get; set; }


        /// <summary>
        /// Defines whether the email has attachments
        /// </summary>
        public Boolean HasAttachments { get; set; }


        /// <summary>
        /// The list of email message attachments, if any
        /// </summary>
        public List<MailAttachment> Attachments { get; private set; }
    }


    /// <summary>
    /// Defines the importance of an email message
    /// </summary>
    public enum ItemImportance {
        /// <summary>
        /// Low importance
        /// </summary>
        Low,
        /// <summary>
        /// Normal importance, default value
        /// </summary>
        Normal,
        /// <summary>
        /// High importance
        /// </summary>
        High,
    }


    /// <summary>
    /// Defines a recipient of an email message/meeting
    /// </summary>
    public class UserInfoContainer {
        /// <summary>
        /// The email address of the recipient
        /// </summary>
        [JsonProperty("emailAddress")]
        public EmailAddress Recipient { get; set; }
    }


    /// <summary>
    /// Defines a user info
```

```
/// </summary>
public class UserInfo {
    /// <summary>
    /// The email address
    /// </summary>
    public String Address { get; set; }

    /// <summary>
    /// The description of the email address
    /// </summary>
    public String Name { get; set; }
}
```

The layouts of the custom *MailMessage* and *MailMessageList* types are defined to make it easier to deserialize the JSON response retrieved from the Microsoft Graph API into .NET complex types. You can also think about using some custom *JsonConvert* types to customize the out-of-box behavior of the Newtonsoft.Json library, transforming the results into something different from the JSON response structure. For example, within the definition of the *MailMessage* type there is the custom converter of type *StringEnumConverter* applied to the *Importance* property of type *ItemImportance*, which is highlighted in bold in Listing 5-9, to serialize the value of the *enum* type as a JSON string instead of using a number. Moreover, the properties called *SentDateTime* and *ReceivedDateTime* are of type *Nullable<DateTime>* to customize the behavior of the Newtonsoft.Json library while serializing an email message instance. These settings will be helpful later in this chapter in the section "Sending an email message," when we will send email messages through the Microsoft Graph API.

In Listing 5-10, you can see how the *LoadAttachments* extension method is defined.

LISTING 5-10 Code excerpt of the *LoadAttachments* extension method to retrieve the attachments of an email message

```
/// <summary>
/// Extension method to load the attachments of an email message
/// </summary>
/// <param name="message">The target email message</param>
public static void LoadAttachments(this MailMessage message) {

    if (message.HasAttachments) {
        String jsonResponse = MicrosoftGraphHelper.MakeGetRequestForString(
            String.Format("{0}me/messages/{1}/attachments",
            MicrosoftGraphHelper.MicrosoftGraphV1BaseUri,
            message.Id));

        var attachments = JsonConvert.DeserializeObject<MailAttachmentList>(jsonResponse);
        message.Attachments.AddRange(attachments.Attachments);

        foreach (var attachment in message.Attachments) {
            attachment.ParentMessageId = message.Id;
        }
    }
}
```

The business logic makes an HTTP request for the URL of the Microsoft Graph API that retrieves the attachments of the current message. Then, it deserializes the JSON response into a list of .NET complex types and loads each instance of the *MailAttachment* type into the collection of attachments of the target *MailMessage* instance. The binary content of every attachment is handled automatically by the Newtonsoft.Json library, and you will find it in the *Byte* array property with name *Content* of the custom type *MailAttachment*.

Unfortunately, if the email message for which you are downloading the attachments has one or more big files attached, executing the request illustrated in Listing 5-10 could become expensive and slow, depending on the available bandwidth. It is better to leverage the OData querying capabilities and query for the list of attachments, including their size and excluding their binary content. Later, you can download just the necessary content of those attachments by accessing their URL endpoint directly. In Listing 5-11, you can see a revised sample according to these new requirements.

LISTING 5-11 Code excerpt of the *LoadAttachments* extension method to retrieve the attachments of an email message, with improved code quality

```
/// <summary>
/// Extension method to load the attachments of an email message in a smart way
/// </summary>
/// <param name="message">The target email message</param>
public static void LoadAttachments(this MailMessage message) {
    if (message.HasAttachments) {
        String jsonResponse = MicrosoftGraphHelper.MakeGetRequestForString(
        String.Format("{0}me/messages/{1}/attachments?$select=contentType,id,name,size",
            MicrosoftGraphHelper.MicrosoftGraphV1BaseUri,
            message.Id));

        var attachments = JsonConvert.DeserializeObject<MailAttachmentList>(jsonResponse);
        message.Attachments.AddRange(attachments.Attachments);

        foreach (var attachment in message.Attachments) {
            attachment.ParentMessageId = message.Id;
        }
    }
}

/// <summary>
/// Extension method to load the content of a specific attachment
/// </summary>
/// <param name="message">The target email message</param>
public static void EnsureContent(this MailAttachment attachment) {
    String jsonResponse = MicrosoftGraphHelper.MakeGetRequestForString(
        String.Format("{0}me/messages/{1}/attachments/{2}",
        MicrosoftGraphHelper.MicrosoftGraphV1BaseUri,
        attachment.ParentMessageId,
        attachment.Id));

    var result = JsonConvert.DeserializeObject<MailAttachment>(jsonResponse);
    attachment.Content = result.Content;
}
```

The *EnsureContent* method, which is illustrated in Listing 5-11, takes care of downloading the binary content of a single attachment if it is needed.

Sending an email message

Another common use case is sending an email message through the Microsoft Graph API. Achieving this result with ASP.NET MVC is straightforward. In Listing 5-12, there is a code excerpt to show how to leverage the *microsoft.graph.sendMail* action of the *me* entity.

LISTING 5-12 Code excerpt showing how to send an email message

```
MailHelper.SendMessage(new Models.MailMessageToSend {
    Message = new Models.MailMessage {
        Subject = "Test message",
        Body = new Models.ItemBody {
            Content = "<html><body><h1>Hello from ASP.NET MVC calling " +
                "the Microsoft Graph API!</h1></body></html>",
            Type = Models.BodyType.Html,
        },
        To = new List<Models.UserInfoContainer>(new Models.UserInfoContainer[] {
        new Models.UserInfoContainer {
            Recipient = new Models.UserInfo {
                Name = "Paolo Pialorsi",
                Address = "paolo@pialorsi.com",
            }
        }
    }),
    },
    SaveToSentItems = true,
});

/// <summary>
/// This method sends an email message
/// </summary>
/// <param name="message"></param>
public static void SendMessage(MailMessageToSend message) {
    MicrosoftGraphHelper.MakePostRequest(
        String.Format("{0}me/microsoft.graph.sendMail",
        MicrosoftGraphHelper.MicrosoftGraphV1BaseUri),
        message, "application/json");
}
```

In Listing 5-12, the content of the request is an object of type *MailMessageToSend*, which represents the structure of the JSON message expected by the *microsoft.graph.sendMail* method.

The *SendMessage* method internally uses the helper method called *MakePostRequest*, which is illustrated in Listing 5-5. It makes an HTTP POST request, providing the body content of the request as a JSON-serialized object.

As you can see from these examples, the processes for every kind of mail API call and every kind of complex type are similar. You have to make a REST request, with or without a request content, depending on the API you want to consume. You have to define a .NET complex type to hold the JSON serialization/deserialization of the request and the response. Last, you have to do some custom mapping or additional REST requests to enrich the resulting object model. From an ASP.NET MVC application perspective, you also have to implement the controllers to handle the requests and the views to present the output to the end users.

> **Note** Implementing an ASP.NET MVC application is out of the scope of this book. If you need to improve your knowledge about how to create an ASP.NET MVC application, you can read the web section "Learn About ASP.NET MVC," which is available at the following URL: *http://www.asp.net/mvc.*

Reply, reply all, and forward email messages

Sending an email message is just one option you have. You can also reply to a received message, reply all, or forward a received message. As you have seen in Chapter 3, to accomplish these tasks you can rely on the actions *reply*, *replyAll*, and *forward* that are available through the Microsoft Graph API and apply to any object that represents an email message. In Listing 5-13, you can see a code excerpt of three helper methods that reply, reply all, and forward an email message.

LISTING 5-13 Code excerpt to show the implementation of helper methods to reply, reply all, and forward an email message

```
/// <summary>
/// This method sends a reply to an email message
/// </summary>
/// <param name="messageId">The ID of the message to reply to</param>
/// <param name="comment">Any comment to include in the reply, optional</param>
public static void Reply(String messageId, String comment = null) {
    MicrosoftGraphHelper.MakePostRequest(
        String.Format("{0}me/messages/{1}/reply",
        MicrosoftGraphHelper.MicrosoftGraphV1BaseUri, messageId),
        content: !String.IsNullOrEmpty(comment) ? new { Comment = comment } : null,
        contentType: "application/json");
}

/// <summary>
/// This method sends a reply all to an email message
/// </summary>
/// <param name="messageId">The ID of the message to reply all to</param>
/// <param name="comment">Any comment to include in the reply all, optional</param>
public static void ReplyAll(String messageId, String comment = null) {
    MicrosoftGraphHelper.MakePostRequest(
        String.Format("{0}me/messages/{1}/replyAll",
        MicrosoftGraphHelper.MicrosoftGraphV1BaseUri, messageId),
        content: !String.IsNullOrEmpty(comment) ? new { Comment = comment } : null,
        contentType: "application/json");
}
```

```
/// <summary>
/// This method forwards an email message to someone else
/// </summary>
/// <param name="messageId">The ID of the message to forward</param>
/// <param name="recipients">The recipients of the forward</param>
/// <param name="comment">Any comment to include in the reply all, optional</param>
public static void Forward(String messageId,
    List<UserInfoContainer> recipients, String comment = null) {
    MicrosoftGraphHelper.MakePostRequest(
        String.Format("{0}me/messages/{1}/forward",
        MicrosoftGraphHelper.MicrosoftGraphV1BaseUri, messageId),
        content: new {
            Comment = !String.IsNullOrEmpty(comment) ? comment : null,
            ToRecipients = recipients,
        }, contentType: "application/json");
}
```

In the sample, the URL of the actions and the content of the reply/reply all messages that will be sent is highlighted in bold. Notice also the use of an anonymous type to hold the value of the response content. The same applies to the method for forwarding an email message, in which the HTTP request content is built as an anonymous type made of the *Comment*, which represents the body on top of the forward, and the *ToRecipients*, which are those to whom the message is forwarded. Using these methods to handle email responses is straightforward.

Calendar services

When developing custom Office 365 applications, it is often useful to interact with users' calendars and events to provide functionalities around the basic calendar features. As with users' mailboxes, here you will learn how to enumerate calendars and events and how to send, accept, and reject meeting requests by using C# within the ASP.NET MVC sample application.

Reading calendars and events

Browsing the list of a current user's calendars—or anybody else's calendars, as long as you have proper permissions—requires you to make an HTTP GET request for the *calendars* navigation property of the target user. In Listing 5-14, you can see the implementation of a helper method called *ListCalendars* that you can use to target the current user's calendars.

LISTING 5-14 Code excerpt to show the implementation of the *ListCalendars* method

```
/// <summary>
/// This method retrieves the calendars of the current user
/// </summary>
/// <param name="startIndex">The startIndex (0 based) of the folders to retrieve</param>
/// <returns>A page of up to 10 calendars</returns>
```

```
public static List<Calendar> ListCalendars(Int32 startIndex = 0) {
    String jsonResponse = MicrosoftGraphHelper.MakeGetRequestForString(
        String.Format("{0}me/calendars?$skip={1}",
            MicrosoftGraphHelper.MicrosoftGraphV1BaseUri,
            startIndex));

    var calendarList = JsonConvert.DeserializeObject<CalendarList>(jsonResponse);
    return (calendarList.Calendars);
}
```

The *calendars* navigation property supports OData querying and paging through the *$skip* query string argument. The result has to be deserialized into a typed object like the *CalendarList* type illustrated in Listing 5-15, which internally holds a collection of objects of type *Calendar*.

LISTING 5-15 Code excerpt to show the definition of the *CalendarList* type

```
/// <summary>
/// Defines a list of calendars
/// </summary>
public class CalendarList {
    /// <summary>
    /// The list of calendars
    /// </summary>
    [JsonProperty("value")]
    public List<Calendar> Calendars { get; set; }
}

/// <summary>
/// Defines a user's calendar
/// </summary>
public class Calendar : BaseModel {
    /// <summary>
    /// The color of the calendar
    /// </summary>
    public String Color { get; set; }

    /// <summary>
    /// The name of the calendar
    /// </summary>
    public String Name { get; set; }
}
```

Once you have the list of calendars, you can retrieve a single calendar object by ID by using a syntax like the one shown in Listing 5-16, where the *GetCalendar* helper method makes an HTTP GET request for a specific calendar item.

LISTING 5-16 Code excerpt to show the *GetCalendar* method

```
/// <summary>
/// This method retrieves a calendar of the current user
/// </summary>
/// <param name="id">The ID of the calendar</param>
/// <returns>The calendar</returns>
public static Calendar GetCalendar(String id) {
    String jsonResponse = MicrosoftGraphHelper.MakeGetRequestForString(
        String.Format("{0}me/calendars/{1}",
            MicrosoftGraphHelper.MicrosoftGraphV1BaseUri,
            id));

    var calendar = JsonConvert.DeserializeObject<Calendar>(jsonResponse);
    return (calendar);
}
```

The result of the HTTP request illustrated in Listing 5-16 is a JSON string that can be deserialized into an object of custom type *Calendar*. To browse the events in the calendar, you will need to have a collection of objects of type *Event*, which can be retrieved by invoking the *events* navigation property of a calendar. The JSON response will be deserialized into the collection. In Listing 5-17, you can see a helper method to retrieve a calendar's events with paging.

LISTING 5-17 Code excerpt to show the definition of the *ListEvents* helper method

```
/// <summary>
/// This method retrieves the events of the current user's calendar
/// </summary>
/// <param name="calendarId">The ID of the calendar</param>
/// <param name="startIndex">The startIndex (0 based) of the items to retrieve</param>
/// <returns>A page of up to 10 events</returns>
public static List<Event> ListEvents(String calendarId, Int32 startIndex = 0) {
    String jsonResponse = MicrosoftGraphHelper.MakeGetRequestForString(
        String.Format("{0}me/calendars/{1}/events?$skip={2}",
            MicrosoftGraphHelper.MicrosoftGraphV1BaseUri,
            calendarId,
            startIndex));

    var eventList = JsonConvert.DeserializeObject<EventList>(jsonResponse);
    return (eventList.Events);
}
```

Every event is made of a lot of properties. For the sake of simplicity, the current sample handles just the main properties, which are those defined in the custom type *Event* illustrated in Listing 5-18.

```
/// <summary>
/// Defines a list of calendar's events
/// </summary>
public class EventList {
    /// <summary>
    /// The list of calendar's events
    /// </summary>
    [JsonProperty("value")]
    public List<Event> Events { get; set; }
}

/// <summary>
/// Defines a user's calendar
/// </summary>
public class Event : BaseModel {
    /// <summary>
    /// The list of email address for the event's attendees
    /// </summary>
    public List<UserInfoContainer> Attendees { get; set; }

    /// <summary>
    /// The body of the email message for the event
    /// </summary>
    public ItemBody Body { get; set; }

    /// <summary
    /// The subject of the event
    /// </summary>
    public String Subject { get; set; }

    /// <summary>
    /// The Type of the event
    /// </summary>
    [JsonConverter(typeof(StringEnumConverter))]
    public EventType Type { get; set; }

    /// <summary>
    /// Date and time of creation
    /// </summary>
    public Nullable<DateTime> CreatedDateTime { get; set; }

    /// <summary>
    /// Defines whether the event is an all day event
    /// </summary>
    public Boolean IsAllDay { get; set; }

    /// <summary>
    /// Defines whether the current user is the organizer of the event
    /// </summary>
    public Boolean IsOrganizer { get; set; }

    /// <summary>
    /// The importance of the email message for the event
```

```
        /// </summary>
        [JsonConverter(typeof(StringEnumConverter))]
        public ItemImportance Importance { get; set; }

        /// <summary>
        /// The location of the event
        /// </summary>
        public EventLocation Location { get; set; }

        /// <summary>
        /// The event organizer
        /// </summary>
        public UserInfo Organizer { get; set; }

        /// <summary>
        /// The Original Zone of the end time
        /// </summary>
        public String OriginalStartTimeZone { get; set; }

        /// <summary>
        /// The Original Zone of the end time
        /// </summary>
        public String OriginalEndTimeZone { get; set; }

        /// <summary>
        /// The start date and time of the event
        /// </summary>
        public TimeInfo Start { get; set; }

        /// <summary>
        /// The end date and time of the event
        /// </summary>
        public TimeInfo End { get; set; }

        /// <summary>
        /// The status (show as) of the event
        /// </summary>
        [JsonConverter(typeof(StringEnumConverter))]
        public EventStatus ShowAs { get; set; }

        /// <summary>
        /// The ID of the Master Event of the Series of events
        /// </summary>
        public String SeriesMasterId { get; set; }

        /// <summary>
        /// The Recurrence pattern for the Series of events
        /// </summary>
        public EventRecurrence Recurrence { get; set; }
}

/// <summary>
/// Defines the type of event
/// </summary>
public enum EventType {
```

```
    /// <summary>
    /// Single instance event
    /// </summary>
    SingleInstance,
    /// <summary>
    /// Master of a Series of events
    /// </summary>
    SeriesMaster,
    /// <summary>
    /// Recurring event
    /// </summary>
    Occurrence,
    /// <summary>
    /// Exception of a Recurring event
    /// </summary>
    Exception,
}

/// <summary>
/// Defines the status (show as) of an event
/// </summary>
public enum EventStatus {
    /// <summary>
    /// Free
    /// </summary>
    Free,
    /// <summary>
    /// Tentative
    /// </summary>
    Tentative,
    /// <summary>
    /// Busy
    /// </summary>
    Busy,
    /// <summary>
    /// Out of Office
    /// </summary>
    Oof,
    /// <summary>
    /// Working elsewhere
    /// </summary>
    WorkingElsewhere,
    /// <summary>
    /// Unknown
    /// </summary>
    Unknown,
}
```

An event is similar to an email message; the custom *Event* type shares many properties, which are highlighted in bold, with the *MailMessage* type. If you like, you could do some refactoring and share an abstract base class between the *MailMessage* and *Event* types. Moreover, every *Event* type includes information specific to the event like the location, the start and end date, the event type and status, and so on. Most of these properties are defined through enumerations, and maybe you are wondering how to find the possible values for these enum types. The metadata document of the Microsoft Graph API provides you with all the needed information. If you browse to the metadata URL (*https://graph.microsoft.com/v1.0/$metadata*), at the beginning of the XML metadata document you will find the definition of all the enumerations and their possible values.

Browsing calendar views

As you probably noticed while playing with the code samples illustrated in the previous section, when you query the Microsoft Graph API for the events of a calendar, you get back up to 10 current and past events. You probably will also need to play with events in the future. As you saw in Chapter 3, it is possible to retrieve a calendar view targeting a specific calendar time frame. In Listing 5-19, you can see a code excerpt that shows how to retrieve the events within a specific and customizable date range.

LISTING 5-19 Code excerpt that shows how to retrieve the events within a specific date range

```
/// <summary>
/// Retrieves the events of the current user's calendar within a specific date range
/// </summary>
/// <param name="calendarId">The ID of the calendar</param>
/// <param name="startDate">The start date of the range</param>
/// <param name="endDate">The end date of the range</param>
/// <param name="startIndex">The startIndex (0 based) of the items to retrieve</param>
/// <returns>A page of up to 10 events</returns>
public static List<Event> ListEvents(String calendarId, DateTime startDate,
    DateTime endDate, Int32 startIndex = 0) {
    String jsonResponse = MicrosoftGraphHelper.MakeGetRequestForString(
        String.Format("{0}me/calendars/{1}/calendarView?" +
            "startDateTime={2:o}&endDateTime={3:o}&$skip={4}",
            MicrosoftGraphHelper.MicrosoftGraphV1BaseUri,
            calendarId,
            startDate.ToUniversalTime(),
            endDate.ToUniversalTime(),
            startIndex));

    var eventList = JsonConvert.DeserializeObject<EventList>(jsonResponse);
    return (eventList.Events);
}
```

The URL of the request targets the *calendarView* navigation property of the target *calendar* object and is built providing the arguments *startDateTime* and *endDateTime* within the query string. Notice that the values of the two date and time arguments are converted into UTC time zone and formatted according to the OData protocol format requirements. You will still get back objects of type *Event*, divided in pages of no more than 10 items. Thus, if you want to download all the events or multiple pages of events, you will still have to make multiple requests, leveraging the *$skip* query string argument. Keep in mind that you are not obliged to download the entire set of properties for every event. You can use the *$select* query string argument introduced earlier to project a subset of the properties to download only what you need.

Managing series of events

Another interesting scenario is recurring events and series of events. From a business requirements perspective, you may need to create a custom Office 365 application that enriches the capabilities around an event series. As you have seen in the previous section, every event has a *Type* property. When that property assumes a value of *SeriesMaster*, *Occurrence*, or *Exception*, it means that the event is part of a series. Aside from the event of type *SeriesMaster*, which is the main event of a series as the type implies, the two other kinds of events have a property called *SeriesMasterId*, which is a reference to the ID of the master event for the series of events. The events of type *Occurrence* are regular events based on a series, while the events of type *Exception* correspond to modified items of a series. Moreover, in every recurring event there is a complex property called *Recurrence* that defines the recurrence pattern and range for the series of events. In Listing 5-20, you can see the outline of the *EventRecurrence* type, which has been defined in the sample application to hold the JSON serialization of a recurrence.

LISTING 5-20 Code excerpt showing the definition of the *EventRecurrence* type

```
/// <summary>
/// Defines the Recurrence for a series of events
/// </summary>
public class EventRecurrence {
    /// <summary>
    /// The Recurrence Pattern
    /// </summary>
    public EventRecurrencePattern Pattern { get; set; }

    /// <summary>
    /// The Recurrence Range
    /// </summary>
    public EventRecurrenceRange Range { get; set; }
}

/// <summary>
/// Defines the Recurrence Pattern for a series of events
/// </summary>
public class EventRecurrencePattern {
    /// <summary>
    /// The day of the month for the recurrence
    /// </summary>
    public Int32 DayOfMonth { get; set; }

    /// <summary>
    /// The days of the week for the recurrence
    /// </summary>
    [JsonProperty(ItemConverterType = typeof(StringEnumConverter))]
    public DayOfWeek[] DaysOfWeek { get; set; }

    /// <summary>
    /// The first day of the week
    /// </summary>
    [JsonConverter(typeof(StringEnumConverter))]
```

```csharp
    public DayOfWeek FirstDayOfWeek { get; set; }

    /// <summary>
    /// The week of the month
    /// </summary>
    [JsonConverter(typeof(StringEnumConverter))]
    public WeekIndex Index { get; set; }

    /// <summary>
    /// The interval for repeating occurrences
    /// </summary>
    public Int32 Interval { get; set; }

    /// <summary>
    /// The month for the recurrence
    /// </summary>
    public Int32 Month { get; set; }

    /// <summary>
    /// The type of recurrence
    /// </summary>
    [JsonConverter(typeof(StringEnumConverter))]
    public RecurrenceType Type { get; set; }
}

/// <summary>
/// Defines the Recurrence Range for a series of events
/// </summary>
public class EventRecurrenceRange
{
    /// <summary>
    /// The Start Date of the recurrence
    /// </summary>
    [JsonConverter(typeof(Converters.DateOnlyConverter))]
    public Nullable<DateTime> StartDate { get; set; }

    /// <summary>
    /// The End Date of the recurrence
    /// </summary>
    [JsonConverter(typeof(Converters.DateOnlyConverter))]
    public Nullable<DateTime> EndDate { get; set; }

    /// <summary>
    /// The number of occurrences
    /// </summary>
    public Int32 NumberOfOccurrences { get; set; }

    /// <summary>
    /// The reference TimeZone for the recurrence
    /// </summary>
    public String RecurrenceTimeZone { get; set; }

    /// <summary>
    /// The type of recurrence
    /// </summary>
```

```
    [JsonConverter(typeof(StringEnumConverter))]
    public RecurrenceRangeType Type { get; set; }
}
```

There are some infrastructural enumerations under the cover of some properties. However, for the sake of simplicity, they are not illustrated in the code excerpt of Listing 5-20. You can also see that some of the properties are decorated with custom attributes to adapt the Newtonsoft.Json serialization engine to the context. For example, the *StartDate* and *EndDate* properties of the *EventRecurrenceRange* type have a custom JSON converter to serialize date-only values, skipping the time part. In addition, the *DaysOfWeek* property of the *EventRecurrencePattern* type has a *JsonProperty* attribute to instruct the serialization engine to handle every item of the array with the custom *StringEnumConverter* converter provided by the Newtonsoft.Json library.

If you want to retrieve all the occurrences of a specific series of events, you can leverage the *instances* navigation property of the event that is master of the series. To invoke the *instances* navigation property, you have to provide a *startDateTime* and an *endDateTime* query string parameter to declare the boundaries of the range of dates from which you want to retrieve the instances. You cannot retrieve all the instances at once; the events will be divided into chunks of up to 10 items, and you can leverage the *$skip* query string argument to move across pages of instances. In Listing 5-21, you can see a code excerpt to retrieve the event occurrences of an event series based on the ID of the master event.

LISTING 5-21 Code excerpt to retrieve the events of a series of events from a target calendar

```
/// <summary>
/// This method retrieves the events of a series within a specific date range
/// </summary>
/// <param name="calendarId">The ID of the calendar</param>
/// <param name="masterSeriesId">The ID of the master event of the series</param>
/// <param name="startDate">The start date of the range</param>
/// <param name="endDate">The end date of the range</param>
/// <param name="startIndex">The startIndex (0 based) of the items to retrieve</param>
/// <returns>A page of up to 10 events</returns>
public static List<Event> ListSeriesInstances(String calendarId,
    String masterSeriesId,
    DateTime startDate,
    DateTime endDate,
    Int32 startIndex = 0) {
    String jsonResponse = MicrosoftGraphHelper.MakeGetRequestForString(
        String.Format("{0}me/calendars/{1}/events/{2}/instances?" +
        "startDateTime={3:o}&endDateTime={4:o}&$skip={5}",
            MicrosoftGraphHelper.MicrosoftGraphV1BaseUri,
            calendarId,
            masterSeriesId,
            startDate.ToUniversalTime(),
            endDate.ToUniversalTime(),
            startIndex));

    var eventList = JsonConvert.DeserializeObject<EventList>(jsonResponse);
```

```
        return (eventList.Events);
}
```

The helper method builds the URL of the request, setting the ID of the calendar and of the master event of the series. Moreover, it configures the *startDateTime*, *endDateTime*, and *$skip* query string arguments.

Creating and updating events

Now let's say you want to create an event, which can be a single instance event or an event series. You will need to create a typed object that can be serialized into a JSON representation of the event type expected by the Microsoft Graph API. Then, you will have to send it through an HTTP POST request, targeting the URL endpoint of the collection of events where you want to create the new item. In Listing 5-22, you can see an example of how to create a single instance event.

LISTING 5-22 Code excerpt to create a new single instance event in a target calendar

```
var singleEvent = CalendarHelper.CreateEvent(calendars[0].Id,
    new Models.Event {
        Attendees = new List<Models.UserInfoContainer>(
            new Models.UserInfoContainer[] {
                new Models.UserInfoContainer {
                    Recipient = new Models.UserInfo {
                        Address = "paolo@pialorsi.com",
                        Name = "Paolo Pialorsi",
                    }
                },
                new Models.UserInfoContainer {
                    Recipient = new Models.UserInfo {
                        Address = "someone@company.com",
                        Name = "Someone Else",
                    }
                },
            }),
        Start = new Models.TimeInfo {
            DateTime = DateTime.Now.AddDays(2).ToUniversalTime(),
            TimeZone = "UTC"
        },
        OriginalStartTimeZone = "UTC",
        End = new Models.TimeInfo {
            DateTime = DateTime.Now.AddDays(2).AddHours(1).ToUniversalTime(),
            TimeZone = "UTC"
        },
        OriginalEndTimeZone = "UTC",
        Importance = Models.ItemImportance.High,
        Subject = "Introducing the Microsoft Graph API",
        Body = new Models.ItemBody {
            Content = "<html><body><h2>Let's talk about the " +
                "Microsoft Graph API!</h2></body></html>",
```

```
                Type = Models.BodyType.Html,
        },
        Location   = new Models.EventLocation {
            Name = "PiaSys.com Head Quarters",
        },
        IsAllDay = false,
        IsOrganizer = true,
        ShowAs = Models.EventStatus.WorkingElsewhere,
        Type = Models.EventType.SingleInstance,
    });
```

As you can see, the excerpt creates an instance of an object of type *Event* and submits it to the *CreateEvent* helper method of the *CalendarHelper* class. Notice that the event is a meeting request because the *Attendees* property is configured to contain a couple of people. The Microsoft Graph API will take care of sending all the invitations for you. The result of this HTTP method invocation will be the just-created instance of the event, so you don't need to make another query to retrieve it.

If you want to create an event series, you can submit an *Event* instance configured accordingly, providing a recurrence pattern and a range for the occurrences. In Listing 5-23, you can see an example to create an event series that recurs until the end of the current month, every Monday from 9.00 A.M. to 10.00 A.M.

LISTING 5-23 Code excerpt to create an event series in a target calendar

```
var eventSeries = CalendarHelper.CreateEvent(calendars[0].Id,
    new Models.Event {
        Start = new Models.TimeInfo {
            DateTime = nextMonday9AM.ToUniversalTime(),
            TimeZone = "UTC"
        },
        OriginalStartTimeZone = "UTC",
        End = new Models.TimeInfo {
            DateTime = nextMonday9AM.AddHours(1).ToUniversalTime(),
            TimeZone = "UTC"
        },
        OriginalEndTimeZone = "UTC",
        Importance = Models.ItemImportance.Normal,
        Subject = "Recurring Event about Microsoft Graph API",
        Body = new Models.ItemBody {
            Content = "<html><body><h2>Let's talk about the " +
                "Microsoft Graph API!</h2></body></html>",
            Type = Models.BodyType.Html,
        },
        Location = new Models.EventLocation {
            Name = "Paolo's Office",
        },
        IsAllDay = false,
        IsOrganizer = true,
        ShowAs = Models.EventStatus.Busy,
        Type = Models.EventType.SeriesMaster,
```

```
            Recurrence = new Models.EventRecurrence {
                Pattern = new Models.EventRecurrencePattern {
                    Type = Models.RecurrenceType.Weekly,
                    DaysOfWeek = new DayOfWeek[] { DayOfWeek.Monday },
                    Interval = 1,
                },
                Range = new Models.EventRecurrenceRange {
                    StartDate = nextMonday9AM.ToUniversalTime(),
                    Type = Models.RecurrenceRangeType.EndDate,
                    EndDate = lastDayOfMonth.ToUniversalTime(),
                }
            }
        });
```

It is clear that the only differences between a single instance event and a series of events are the configuration of the *Recurrence* property and the value of the *Type* property, which has a value of *SeriesMaster*. Aside from that, the just-created event is like any other object of type *Event*. Under the cover, the Microsoft Graph API will create for you all the series of events in the target calendar and will send the invitations if the recurring event is a meeting request.

Now, suppose you want to change one event in the series or another event that you have in a calendar. To accomplish this, you will need to get the event instance from the calendar, apply any changes, and resubmit the event to the calendar by using an HTTP PATCH method, as you learned in Chapter 3. In Listing 5-24, you can see a sample helper method to retrieve a single event instance from a calendar.

LISTING 5-24 Code excerpt of a helper method to retrieve a single event from a target calendar

```
/// <summary>
/// This method retrieves an event from a calendar
/// </summary>
/// <param name="calendarId">The ID of the calendar</param>
/// <param name="eventId">The ID of the event</param>
/// <returns>The retrieved event</returns>
public static Event GetEvent(String calendarId, String eventId) {
    String jsonResponse = MicrosoftGraphHelper.MakeGetRequestForString(
        String.Format("{0}me/calendars/{1}/events/{2}",
            MicrosoftGraphHelper.MicrosoftGraphV1BaseUri,
            calendarId, eventId));

    var calendarEvent = JsonConvert.DeserializeObject<Event>(jsonResponse);
    return (calendarEvent);
}
```

In Listing 5-25 you can see the definition of a helper method to update an event, leveraging the HTTP PATCH method.

LISTING 5-25 Code excerpt of a helper method to update a single event in a target calendar

```
/// <summary>
/// This method updates an event in a calendar
/// </summary>
/// <param name="calendarId">The ID of the calendar</param>
/// <param name="eventId">The event to update</param>
/// <returns>The updated event</returns>
public static Event UpdateEvent(String calendarId, Event eventToUpdate) {
    String jsonResponse = MicrosoftGraphHelper.MakePatchRequestForString(
        String.Format("{0}me/calendars/{1}/events/{2}",
            MicrosoftGraphHelper.MicrosoftGraphV1BaseUri,
            calendarId, eventToUpdate.Id),
        eventToUpdate, "application/json");

    var updatedEvent = JsonConvert.DeserializeObject<Event>(jsonResponse);
    return (updatedEvent);
}
```

Notice that the Microsoft Graph API returns the updated event as the result of the HTTP PATCH method. This behavior is useful if you want to refresh the event view in your business logic because you don't have to make another request to refresh your local copy of the updated event.

If you want to delete an event from a calendar, you can make an HTTP DELETE request against the URL of the event to remove. In Listing 5-26, you can see a code excerpt of the helper method to do that.

LISTING 5-26 Code excerpt of a helper method to delete a single event from a target calendar

```
/// <summary>
/// This method deletes an event from a calendar
/// </summary>
/// <param name="calendarId">The ID of the calendar</param>
/// <param name="eventId">The ID of the event to delete</param>
public static void DeleteEvent(String calendarId, String eventId) {
    MicrosoftGraphHelper.MakeDeleteRequest(
        String.Format("{0}me/calendars/{1}/events/{2}",
            MicrosoftGraphHelper.MicrosoftGraphV1BaseUri,
            calendarId, eventId));
}
```

Again, the powerful Microsoft Graph API will send for you a cancellation email if the event deleted is a meeting request that involves someone else.

Managing invitations for meeting requests

What if you get an invitation for a meeting request? Let's say you want to write a custom Office 365 application to automate the process of handling meeting request invitations. You can use the HTTP helper methods that we have to send feedbacks for meeting requests. In Chapter 3, you saw that every meeting request has the *ResponseStatus* property and that you can leverage the operations *Accept*, *Decline*, and *TentativelyAccept* to provide your feedback to the meeting organizer. In Listing 5-27, you can see a code excerpt to give a feedback for a received meeting request.

LISTING 5-27 Code excerpt of a helper method to provide a feedback for a received meeting request

```
/// <summary>
/// This method provides a feedback for a received meeting request
/// </summary>
/// <param name="calendarId">The ID of the calendar</param>
/// <param name="eventId">The ID of the meeting request</param>
/// <param name="feedback">The feedback for the meeting request</param
/// <param name="comment">Any comment to include in the feedback, optional</param>
public static void SendFeedbackForMeetingRequest(String calendarId,
    String eventId,
    MeetingRequestFeedback feedback,
    String comment = null) {
    MicrosoftGraphHelper.MakePostRequest(
        String.Format("{0}me/calendars/{1}/events/{2}/{3}",
            MicrosoftGraphHelper.MicrosoftGraphV1BaseUri,
            calendarId, eventId, feedback),
            content: !String.IsNullOrEmpty(comment) ? new { Comment = comment } : null,
            contentType: "application/json");
}
```

Note that the feedback is represented using a custom enumeration of possible feedbacks, which is called *MeetingRequestFeedback*. Moreover, every meeting request feedback can include a comment that will be sent to the meeting organizer with the feedback. Thus, the custom helper method accepts a *comment* argument of type *String*, which is provided within the HTTP request content using an anonymous type that will be serialized in JSON according to the content structure expected by the backing Microsoft Graph API.

Contact services

The last group of services provided by the Microsoft Graph API against Microsoft Exchange Online are those related to handling contacts. In this section, you will learn how to retrieve, add, update, or delete users' personal contacts.

Reading contacts

Like mailboxes and calendars, you can access a user's default folder of contacts by making a request for the *contacts* navigation property of a user, whether it is the current user (that is, *me*) or any other user for whom you have the permission to read contacts. For example, in Listing 5-28 there is a helper method to retrieve the contacts of the current user.

LISTING 5-28 Code excerpt of a helper method to get the contacts of the current user

```
/// <summary>
/// This method retrieves the contacts of the current user
/// </summary>
/// <param name="startIndex">The startIndex (0 based) of the contacts to retrieve</param>
/// <returns>A page of up to 10 contacts</returns>
public static List<Contact> ListContacts(Int32 startIndex = 0) {
    String jsonResponse = MicrosoftGraphHelper.MakeGetRequestForString(
        String.Format("{0}me/contacts?$skip={1}",
            MicrosoftGraphHelper.MicrosoftGraphV1BaseUri,
            startIndex));

    var contactList = JsonConvert.DeserializeObject<ContactList>(jsonResponse);
    return (contactList.Contacts);
}
```

As expected, the method retrieves contacts in pages of up to 10 items each. There is nothing special in the code sample of Listing 5-28 when compared to those related to email messages, calendars, or events. The only interesting difference is the outline of the *Contact* type, which presents some of the main properties returned by the Microsoft Graph API for every contact object. In Listing 5-29, you can see the definition of the custom *Contact* and *ContactList* types.

LISTING 5-29 Code excerpt to define the *Contact* and *ContactList* types

```
/// <summary>
/// Defines a list of contacts
/// </summary>
public class ContactList {
    /// <summary>
    /// The list of contacts
    /// </summary>
    [JsonProperty("value")]
    public List<Contact> Contacts { get; set; }
}

/// <summary>
/// Defines a user's contact
/// </summary>
public class Contact : BaseModel {
    /// <summary>
    /// The business address of the contact
    /// </summary>
```

```
public PhysicalAddress BusinessAddress { get; set; }

/// <summary>
/// The business phones of the contact
/// </summary>
public List<String> BusinessPhones { get; set; }

/// <summary>
/// The business home page of the contact
/// </summary>
public String BusinessHomePage { get; set; }

/// <summary>
/// The company name of the contact
/// </summary>
public String CompanyName { get; set; }

/// <summary>
/// The department name of the contact
/// </summary>
public String Department { get; set; }

/// <summary
/// The display name of the contact
/// </summary>
public String DisplayName { get; set; }

/// <summary>
/// The list of email addresses of the contact
/// </summary>
public List<UserInfo> EmailAddresses { get; set; }

/// <summary>
/// The "File As" of the contact
/// </summary>
public String FileAs { get; set; }

/// <summary>
/// The home address of the contact
/// </summary>
public PhysicalAddress HomeAddress { get; set; }

/// <summary>
/// The home phones of the contact
/// </summary>
public List<String> HomePhones { get; set; }

/// <summary>
/// The office location of the contact
/// </summary>
public String OfficeLocation { get; set; }

/// <summary>
/// The other address of the contact
/// </summary>
```

```csharp
    public PhysicalAddress OtherAddress { get; set; }

        /// <summary>
        /// Personal notes about the contact
        /// </summary>
        public String PersonalNotes { get; set; }

        /// <summary>
        /// The first name of the contac
        /// </summary>
        public String GivenName { get; set; }

        /// <summary>
        /// The family name of the contac
        /// </summary>
        public String Surname { get; set; }

        /// <summary>
        /// The title of the contact
        /// </summary>
        public String Title { get; set; }
    }

    /// <summary>
    /// Defines a physical address
    /// </summary>
    public class PhysicalAddress {
        /// <summary>
        /// The Street part of the address
        /// </summary>
        public String Street { get; set; }

        /// <summary>
        /// The City part of the address
        /// </summary>
        public String City { get; set; }

        /// <summary>
        /// The State part of the address
        /// </summary>
        public String State { get; set; }

        /// <summary>
        /// The Country or Region part of the address
        /// </summary>
        public String CountryOrRegion { get; set; }

        /// <summary>
        /// The Postal Code part of the address
        /// </summary>
        public String PostalCode { get; set; }
    }
```

You can define these types as you like, as long as they can be used to deserialize the JSON response returned by the service. When looking at how the code samples related to this book implement these types, it is interesting to notice how the properties *HomeAddress*, *BusinessAddress*, and *OtherAddress* are defined by leveraging the *PhysicalAddress* type. Moreover, note that the property *EmailAddresses* of every contact is a collection of instances of type *UserInfo*, which is also used to define the recipients of an email message. Thus, you can reuse this property to send an email message directly to a specific contact.

Furthermore, like with email messages and calendars, with contacts you can browse multiple contact folders. Every user object has a navigation property called *contactFolders* that represents a container folder for contacts. By default, every user's account has a default contact folder that is the root folder, which can contain a hierarchy of child folders. Using the navigation properties *contactFolders* and *childFolders*, you can browse all these folders. For example, in Listing 5-30 you can see a code excerpt of a helper method to retrieve the contacts of a specific contacts folder.

LISTING 5-30 Code excerpt to retrieve the contacts of a contacts folder

```
/// <summary>
/// This method retrieves the contacts of a contacts folder for the current user
/// </summary>
/// <param name="contactFolderId">The ID of the contacts folder</param>
/// <param name="startIndex">The startIndex (0 based) of the contacts to retrieve</param>
/// <returns>A page of up to 10 contacts</returns>
public static List<Contact> ListContacts(String contactFolderId, Int32 startIndex = 0) {
    String jsonResponse = MicrosoftGraphHelper.MakeGetRequestForString(
        String.Format("{0}me/contactFolders/{1}/contacts?$skip={2}",
            MicrosoftGraphHelper.MicrosoftGraphV1BaseUri,
            contactFolderId,
            startIndex));

    var contactList = JsonConvert.DeserializeObject<ContactList>(jsonResponse);
    return (contactList.Contacts);
}
```

Every contact can have a picture to better define the contact in the address list. To access the contact's picture, as you will do in Chapter 6, you can make an HTTP GET request for the navigation property *photo* and extract its *$value*. In Listing 5-31, you can see a helper method to get a contact's picture.

LISTING 5-31 Code excerpt of a helper method to get a contact's picture

```
/// <summary>
/// Retrieves the picture of a contact, if any
/// </summary>
/// <param name="contactId">The ID of the contact</param>
/// <returns>The picture as a binary Stream</returns>
public static Stream GetContactPhoto(String contactId) {
    Stream result = null;
    String contentType = "image/png";
```

```
        try {
            result = MicrosoftGraphHelper.MakeGetRequestForStream(
                String.Format("{0}me/contacts/{1}/photo/$value",
                    MicrosoftGraphHelper.MicrosoftGraphV1BaseUri, contactId),
                contentType);
        }
        catch (HttpException ex) {
            if (ex.ErrorCode == 404) {
                // If 404 -> The contact does not have a picture
                // Keep NULL value for result
                result = null;
            }
        }
        return (result);
    }
```

When you request the photo of a contact that does not have an associated image, the Microsoft Graph API will return an HTTP Status Code with a value of 404 (Not Found) and an error message with a value of "The specified object was not found in the store." That's why the code excerpt of Listing 5-31 handles this kind of HTTP response.

Managing contacts

Another set of common tasks when you work with contacts is updating existing contacts and adding new contacts. As you can imagine, updating an existing contact is just a matter of making an HTTP PATCH request, providing the JSON serialized representation of the contact to update. The *Contact* type defined in Listing 5-29 is also suitable for this task. In Listing 5-32, there is a code excerpt to accomplish the update task.

LISTING 5-32 Code excerpt of a helper method to update a contact

```
/// <summary>
/// This method updates a contact
/// </summary>
/// <param name="contact">The contact to update</param>
/// <returns>The updated contact</returns>
public static Contact UpdateContact(Contact contact) {
    String jsonResponse = MicrosoftGraphHelper.MakePatchRequestForString(
        String.Format("{0}me/contacts/{1}",
            MicrosoftGraphHelper.MicrosoftGraphV1BaseUri,
            contact.Id),
            contact,
            "application/json");

    var updatedContact = JsonConvert.DeserializeObject<Contact>(jsonResponse);
    return (updatedContact);
}
```

In Listing 5-33, you can see how to add a new contact.

LISTING 5-33 Code excerpt of a helper method to add a new contact

```
/// <summary>
/// This method adds a contact
/// </summary>
/// <param name="contact">The contact to add</param>
/// <returns>The added contact</returns>
public static Contact AddContact(Contact contact) {
    String jsonResponse = MicrosoftGraphHelper.MakePostRequestForString(
        String.Format("{0}me/contacts",
            MicrosoftGraphHelper.MicrosoftGraphV1BaseUri),
            contact,
            "application/json");

    var addedContact = JsonConvert.DeserializeObject<Contact>(jsonResponse);
    return (addedContact);
}
```

Both the methods return the updated or added contact object to make it easier for you to handle the refresh of the UI, if needed.

Deleting a contact is also straightforward. In Listing 5-34, you can see the corresponding helper method, which accepts the ID of the contact to delete.

LISTING 5-34 Code excerpt of a helper method to delete a contact

```
/// <summary>
/// This method deletes a contact
/// </summary>
/// <param name="contactId">The ID of the contact to delete</param>
public static void DeleteContact(String contactId) {
    MicrosoftGraphHelper.MakeDeleteRequest(
        String.Format("{0}me/contacts/{1}",
            MicrosoftGraphHelper.MicrosoftGraphV1BaseUri
            contactId));
}
```

Summary

In this chapter, you saw how to set up an ASP.NET MVC application to authenticate with Microsoft Azure Active Directory and how to register the application in the Azure AD tenant that sits under the cover of a Microsoft Office 365 tenant. Moreover, you saw how to leverage the Microsoft Active Directory Authentication Library (ADAL) to acquire an OAuth access token and how to store that token and a refresh token in a temporary cache.

Next, you saw how to leverage a helper class to manage the OAuth access token and make all the required HTTP requests to consume the Microsoft Graph API.

Last, you saw how to build a client application on top of these foundations that can consume the mail, calendar, and contact services provided by the Microsoft Graph API. You can use the code you saw in this chapter and the related code samples you can find on the Internet (*(http://aka.ms /OfficeDev365ProgrammingSamples))* as a starting point for writing you own software solutions that leverage the powerful capabilities of the Microsoft Graph.

CHAPTER 6

Users and Groups services

This chapter covers the services related to managing users and groups, which can be security or dynamic groups or the new Microsoft Office 365 Groups. The chapter covers the most useful API entities, entity sets, actions, and navigation properties to handle these resources and services.

You can continue to refer to the sample application that was introduced in Chapter 5, "Mail, calendar, and contact services" and is available at this URL: *http://aka.ms /OfficeDev365ProgrammingSamples*.

Users services

As you saw in Chapter 5, the main step for consuming some resources through the Microsoft Graph API in Microsoft .NET is to define the domain model types that can be used to serialize and deserialize the exchanged JSON messages. From a Users services perspective, the main type to define is the *User* class. In Listing 6-1, you can see an excerpt of the *User* type definition.

LISTING 6-1 Code excerpt to define the *User* type for consuming the Users services

```
/// <summary>
/// Defines a single tenant user
/// </summary>
public class User : BaseModel {
    /// <summary>
    /// Defines whether the user's account is enabled or not
    /// </summary>
    public Boolean AccountEnabled;

    /// <summary>
    /// List of licenses assigned to the user
    /// </summary>
    public List<AssignedLicense> AssignedLicenses;

    /// <summary>
    /// List of Office 365 plans assigned to the user
    /// </summary>
    public List<AssignedPlan> AssignedPlans;

    /// <summary>
    /// List of user's business phones
```

```
        /// </summary>
        public List<String> BusinessPhones;

        /// <summary>
        /// City of the user
        /// </summary>
        public String City;

        /// <summary>
        /// Company of the user
        /// </summary>
        public String CompanyName;

        /// <summary>
        /// Display Name of the user
        /// </summary>
        public String DisplayName;

        /// <summary>
        /// Mail of the user
        /// </summary>
        public String Mail;

        /// <summary>
        /// UPN for the user
        /// </summary>
        public String UserPrincipalName;

        // ... omissis ...
    }
```

The list of the user's attributes handled by the service is long, and for the sake of simplicity in Listing 6-1 you can see just a few of them. Some of the most important are *UserPrincipalName*, *Mail*, and *AccountEnabled*. In the following sections, you will see how to handle users instances like this.

Reading users

To browse the list of users registered in an Office 365 tenant, you can make an HTTP GET request for the *users* endpoint of the Microsoft Graph, as illustrated in Listing 6-2.

LISTING 6-2 Code excerpt to enumerate the users registered in the current tenant

```
/// <summary>
/// This method retrieves the list of users registered in Azure AD
/// </summary>
/// <param name="numberOfItems">Defines the TOP number of items to retrieve</param>
/// <returns>The list of users in Azure AD</returns>
public static List<User> ListUsers(Int32 numberOfItems = 100) {
    String jsonResponse = MicrosoftGraphHelper.MakeGetRequestForString(
        String.Format("{0}users?$top={1}",
```

```
        MicrosoftGraphHelper.MicrosoftGraphV1BaseUri,
        numberOfItems));

    var usersList = JsonConvert.DeserializeObject<UsersList>(jsonResponse);
    return (usersList.Users);
}
```

As you can see, the method internally leverages the helper method *MakeGetRequestForString* that we used in Chapter 5. Notice the *$top* query string parameter to retrieve just a subset of users. By default, if you don't specify any value for the *$top* parameter, the query returns the top 100 items. The values allowed for the *$top* parameter are between 1 and 999. Thus, you cannot retrieve more than 999 users per query, but you can apply some partitioning rules using the *$filter* query string parameter to reduce the result set according to the filtering rules supported by the *users* collection.

Thus, if you would like to filter the result—for example, extracting only the users working in a specified department—you can use a code excerpt like the one illustrated in Listing 6-3.

LISTING 6-3 Code excerpt to enumerate all the users working in a specified department

```
/// <summary>
/// This method retrieves the list of users working in a specific department
/// </summary>
/// <param name="department">The department to filter the users on</param>
/// <param name="numberOfItems">Defines the TOP number of items to retrieve</param>
/// <returns>The list of users in Azure AD</returns>
public static List<User> ListUsersByDepartment(String department,
    Int32 numberOfItems = 100) {

    String jsonResponse = MicrosoftGraphHelper.MakeGetRequestForString(
        String.Format("{0}users?$filter=department%20eq%20'{1}'&$top={2}",
            MicrosoftGraphHelper.MicrosoftGraphV1BaseUri,
            department,
            numberOfItems));

    var usersList = JsonConvert.DeserializeObject<UsersList>(jsonResponse);
    return (usersList.Users);
}
```

In Listing 6-3, you can see the OData *$filter* query string parameter, which selects those user items that have the *department* field equal to a specific filter value.

Another interesting filtering option is based on the *userType* property, which assumes a value of *Guest* for the external users. Thus, if you would like to select all the external users registered in the current tenant, you can use a query like the one defined in Listing 6-4.

LISTING 6-4 Code excerpt to enumerate all the external users for a target tenant

```
/// <summary>
/// This method retrieves the list of all the external users for a tenant
/// </summary>
/// <param name="numberOfItems">Defines the TOP number of items to retrieve</param>
/// <returns>The list of externa users in Azure AD</returns>
public static List<User> ListExternalUsers(Int32 numberOfItems = 100) {

    String jsonResponse = MicrosoftGraphHelper.MakeGetRequestForString(
        String.Format("{0}users?$filter=userType%20eq%20'Guest'&$top={1}",
            MicrosoftGraphHelper.MicrosoftGraphV1BaseUri,
            numberOfItems));

    var usersList = JsonConvert.DeserializeObject<UsersList>(jsonResponse);
    return (usersList.Users);
}
```

Moreover, because the full user's profile could be big and rich in attributes, querying the list of users you will get back the following attributes by default: *businessPhones*, *displayName*, *givenName*, *id*, *jobTitle*, *mail*, *mobilePhone*, *officeLocation*, *preferredLanguage*, *surname*, and *userPrincipalName*. You can leverage the OData *$select* query string parameter to change the default behavior of the service, selecting a custom set of attributes like the code excerpt in Listing 6-5 does.

LISTING 6-5 Code excerpt that retrieves a list of users with some custom fields

```
/// <summary>
/// This method retrieves the list of users registered in Azure AD with custom fields
/// </summary>
/// <param name="fields">The list of fields to retrieve</param>
/// <param name="numberOfItems">Defines the TOP number of items to retrieve</param>
/// <returns>The list of users in Azure AD</returns>
public static List<User> ListUsers(String[] fields = null, Int32 numberOfItems = 100) {

    String selectFilter = String.Empty;
    if (fields != null) {
        selectFilter = "&$select=";
        foreach (var field in fields) {
            selectFilter += HttpUtility.UrlEncode(field) + ",";
        }
    }

    String jsonResponse = MicrosoftGraphHelper.MakeGetRequestForString(
        String.Format("{0}users?$top={1}{2}",
            MicrosoftGraphHelper.MicrosoftGraphV1BaseUri,
            numberOfItems,
            selectFilter));

    var usersList = JsonConvert.DeserializeObject<UsersList>(jsonResponse);
    return (usersList.Users);
}
```

In Listing 6-6, you can see a code excerpt that invokes the helper method illustrated in Listing 6-5.

LISTING 6-6 Code excerpt that invokes the helper method illustrated in Listing 6-5

```
var usersWithCustomAttributes = UsersGroupsHelper.ListUsers(
    new String[] { "id", "userPrincipalName", "mail",
        "department", "country", "preferredLanguage",
        "onPremisesImmutableId", "onPremisesSecurityIdentifier",
        "onPremisesSyncEnabled", "userType" },
    600);
```

Another interesting option to consider is the capability to leverage some navigation properties of the user object. For example, every user has the *manager* navigation property that allows you to discover the manager of the current user, if any. Similarly, by using the *directReports* navigation property, you can see the list of the people managed by a specific user. From a SharePoint Online development perspective, it is important to underline that these properties and organizational relationships refer to those defined in Microsoft Azure Active Directory (Azure AD), and they are not necessarily the ones defined in the User Profile Service (UPS) of Microsoft SharePoint Online (SPO). Having the same values in Azure AD and in the UPS of SPO depends on the configuration of the UPS.

Note If you want to learn more about the fields that are synchronized by default by the UPS in Microsoft SharePoint, you can read the article "Default user profile property mappings in SharePoint Server 2013," which is available at the following URL: *https://technet .microsoft.com/library/hh147510.aspx*. If you want to import custom properties in the UPS of SPO, you can refer to the "User Profile Batch Update" sample that is available in the Office 365 Developer Patterns & Practices (PnP) project repository on GitHub. It can be found at the following friendly URL: *http://aka.ms/PnPUserProfileBatchUpdateAPI*.

In Listing 6-7, you can see the definition of a couple of helper methods to retrieve the manager and the direct reports of a user.

LISTING 6-7 Code excerpt to retrieve the manager and the direct reports of a user

```
/// <summary>
/// This method returns the manager of a user
/// </summary>
/// <param name="upn">The UPN of the user</param>
/// <returns>The user's manager</returns>
public static User GetUserManager(String upn) {
    String jsonResponse = MicrosoftGraphHelper.MakeGetRequestForString(
        String.Format("{0}users/{1}/manager",
            MicrosoftGraphHelper.MicrosoftGraphV1BaseUri,
            upn));

    var user = JsonConvert.DeserializeObject<User>(jsonResponse);
    return (user);
```

```
    }

    /// <summary>
    /// This method returns the direct reports of a user
    /// </summary>
    /// <param name="upn">The UPN of the user</param>
    /// <returns>The user's direct reports</returns>
    public static List<User> GetUserDirectReports(String upn) {
        String jsonResponse = MicrosoftGraphHelper.MakeGetRequestForString(
            String.Format("b",
                MicrosoftGraphHelper.MicrosoftGraphV1BaseUri,
                upn));

        var directReports = JsonConvert.DeserializeObject<UsersList>(jsonResponse);
        return (directReports.Users);
    }
```

There are many other navigation properties that you can use to go through the users' calendars, events, mailboxes and mail folders, drives on OneDrive for Business, and so on. To access these navigation properties, you must have the proper account delegations and proper permissions in Azure AD. Aside from the authorization rules, you can apply to these items the same development techniques that you saw in Chapter 5 and that you will learn about in Chapter 7, "File services."

Just as you can read a list of users, you can get a single user object. You just need to make an HTTP GET request providing, for example, the User Principal Name (UPN) just after the *users* endpoint. In Listing 6-8, you can see a sample helper method to accomplish this task.

LISTING 6-8 Code excerpt to retrieve a single user instance

```
    /// <summary>
    /// This method retrieves a single user from Azure AD
    /// </summary>
    /// <param name="upn">The UPN of the user to retrieve</param>
    /// <returns>The user retrieved from Azure AD</returns>
    public static User GetUser(String upn) {
        String jsonResponse = MicrosoftGraphHelper.MakeGetRequestForString(
            String.Format("{0}users/{1}",
                MicrosoftGraphHelper.MicrosoftGraphV1BaseUri,
                upn));

        var user = JsonConvert.DeserializeObject<User>(jsonResponse);
        return (user);
    }
```

From a user interface perspective, an interesting property of every user object is the photo. In fact, modern UI applications often show the lists of users not as text but by using their profile pictures. For example, think about what happens in Skype for Business or in the web UI of the Contacts list in Office 365: you have a list of profile pictures, each one wrapped in a circle. If you want to get the profile picture of a specific user, you have to leverage the *photo* property of that user. Specifically, to get the binary value of the photo, you have to query the *$value* property of the *photo* by using the common OData syntax. In Listing 6-9, you can see a helper method that retrieves a user's photo as a stream of bytes.

LISTING 6-9 Code excerpt of a helper method to retrieve a user's photo as a stream of bytes

```
/// <summary>
/// This method retrieves the photo of a single user from Azure AD
/// </summary>
/// <param name="upn">The UPN of the user</param>
/// <returns>The user's photo retrieved from Azure AD</returns>
public static Stream GetUserPhoto(String upn) {
    String contentType = "image/png";

    var result = MicrosoftGraphHelper.MakeGetRequestForStream(
        String.Format("{0}users/{1}/photo/$value",
            MicrosoftGraphHelper.MicrosoftGraphV1BaseUri, upn),
        contentType);

    return (result);
}
```

The resulting stream can be used wherever you like. For example, in the sample application related to this chapter, the user's photo is used to reproduce the current user's profile picture in the Office 365 suite bar. To achieve this result, the sample application uses a dedicated action in an ASP.NET MVC controller where the stream is returned as a binary file together with a specific image content type (image/png).

Groups services

Whenever you think about users in an enterprise scenario, you also have to think about groups to better manage permissions and authorizations and perform general management and governance. In Office 365, groups are managed in Azure AD, like users' accounts, and you can also manage them through the Microsoft Graph API. In this section, you will learn how to do that.

Browsing groups

First, you can query the list of groups by querying the *groups* endpoint of the Microsoft Graph API. The result will be a collection of objects that have a structure like the one illustrated in Listing 6-10.

LISTING 6-10 Code excerpt to define the *Group* type for consuming the Groups services

```
/// <summary>
/// Defines a Group
/// </summary>
```

```
public class Group : BaseModel {
    public String Description;
    public String DisplayName;
    public List<String> GroupTypes;
    public String Mail;
    public Boolean MailEnabled;
    public String MailNickname;
    public Nullable<DateTimeOffset> OnPremisesLastSyncDateTime;
    public String OnPremisesSecurityIdentifier;
    public Nullable<Boolean> OnPremisesSyncEnabled;
    public List<String> ProxyAddresses;
    public Boolean SecurityEnabled;
    public String Visibility;
    public Boolean AllowExternalSenders;
    public Boolean AutoSubscribeNewMembers;
    public Boolean IsSubscribedByMail;
    public Int32 UnseenCount;
}
```

As you can see, there are some descriptive properties, like the *DisplayName* and the *Description*, and more functional properties, like those related to the *Mail* address of the group, the *ProxyAddresses*, and so on. Moreover, there are the *GroupTypes* collection property and the Boolean *SecurityEnabled* property that are useful to disambiguate among the classic security groups (which are mainly used for members' authorization), the dynamic groups, and the new Office 365 Unified Groups. These enable you to provide a better collaboration experience for users, and they will be covered in the upcoming section. In general, at the time of this writing there are three flavors of groups:

- **Security Groups** Groups used for security authorization. They have the *GroupTypes* collection property empty and the *SecurityEnabled* property set to *true*.

- **Unified Groups** The Office 365 Groups. They have the *GroupTypes* collection property with a value of *Unified* and the *SecurityEnabled* property set to *false*.

- **Dynamic Groups** Groups with rule-based membership. This capability requires Azure AD Premium in the back end. They have the *GroupTypes* collection property with a value of *DynamicMembership* and the *SecurityEnabled* property set to *false*.

By playing with these properties and querying the *groups* endpoint via OData, you can start consuming the groups as you see in Listing 6-11.

LISTING 6-11 Code excerpt of a helper method to query for groups in Office 365 and Azure AD

```
/// <summary>
/// This method retrieves the list of groups registered in Azure AD
/// </summary>
/// <param name="numberOfItems">Defines the TOP number of items to retrieve</param>
/// <returns>The list of groups in Azure AD</returns>
public static List<Group> ListGroups(Int32 numberOfItems = 100) {
    String jsonResponse = MicrosoftGraphHelper.MakeGetRequestForString(
```

```
        String.Format("{0}groups?$top={1}",
            MicrosoftGraphHelper.MicrosoftGraphV1BaseUri,
            numberOfItems));

    var groupsList = JsonConvert.DeserializeObject<GroupsList>(jsonResponse);
    return (groupsList.Groups);
}
```

You can leverage the *$top* query string parameter to select a subset of group items. If you want to retrieve a specific set of groups, like the security enabled groups, you can apply a filtering condition by leveraging the *$filter* query string parameter, as illustrated in Listing 6-12.

LISTING 6-12 Code excerpt of a helper method to query for security groups in Office 365 and Azure AD

```
/// <summary>
/// This method retrieves the list of Security Groups
/// </summary>
/// <param name="numberOfItems">Defines the TOP number of items to retrieve</param>
/// <returns>The list of Security Groups</returns>
public static List<Group> ListSecurityGroups(Int32 numberOfItems = 100) {
    String jsonResponse = MicrosoftGraphHelper.MakeGetRequestForString(
        String.Format("{0}groups?$filter=SecurityEnabled%20eq%20true" +
            "&$top={1}", MicrosoftGraphHelper.MicrosoftGraphV1BaseUri,
            numberOfItems));

    var groupsList = JsonConvert.DeserializeObject<GroupsList>(jsonResponse);
    return (groupsList.Groups);
}
```

Moreover, if you want to retrieve a specific group, you can use the ID of the group object to make a direct HTTP GET request. In Listing 6-13, you can see how to do that.

LISTING 6-13 Code excerpt to retrieve a specific group by ID

```
/// <summary>
/// This method retrieves a specific group registered in Azure AD
/// </summary>
/// <param name="groupId">The ID of the group</param>
/// <returns>The group instance</returns>
public static Group GetGroup(String groupId) {
    String jsonResponse = MicrosoftGraphHelper.MakeGetRequestForString(
        String.Format("{0}groups/{1}",
            MicrosoftGraphHelper.MicrosoftGraphV1BaseUri,
            groupId));

    var group = JsonConvert.DeserializeObject<Group>(jsonResponse);
    return (group);
}
```

Managing groups

The basic purpose of having groups is to cluster users for authorization and targeting goals. Thus, it is often necessary to retrieve the members of a group or to manage groups' membership. Every group has some useful navigation properties to accomplish these tasks. For example, you can use the *members* navigation property to see the members of a group. In Listing 6-14, you can see a helper method to do that.

LISTING 6-14 Code excerpt to retrieve the members of a group

```
/// <summary>
/// This method retrieves the list of members of a group
/// </summary>
/// <param name="groupId">The ID of the group</param>
/// <returns>The members of the group</returns>
public static List<User> ListGroupMembers(String groupId) {
    String jsonResponse = MicrosoftGraphHelper.MakeGetRequestForString(
        String.Format("{0}groups/{1}/members",
            MicrosoftGraphHelper.MicrosoftGraphV1BaseUri,
            groupId));

    var usersList = JsonConvert.DeserializeObject<UsersList>(jsonResponse);
    return (usersList.Users);
}
```

It is interesting to note that the result of the *members* navigation property is an array of objects of type *User*. Thus, you can leverage the capabilities illustrated in the previous section against each *User* item. For example, you can retrieve the personal picture of every member, or you can retrieve the email addresses, the manager, the direct reports, and so on. If you have proper permissions, you can also access the user's mailbox, calendars, contacts, drives, and so on.

You can also get a reference to the owners of a group by using the *owners* navigation property, as illustrated in Listing 6-15.

LISTING 6-15 Code excerpt to retrieve the owners of a group

```
/// <summary>
/// This method retrieves the list of owners of a group
/// </summary>
/// <param name="groupId">The ID of the group</param>
/// <returns>The owners of the group</returns>
public static List<User> ListGroupOwners(String groupId) {
    String jsonResponse = MicrosoftGraphHelper.MakeGetRequestForString(
        String.Format("{0}groups/{1}/owners",
            MicrosoftGraphHelper.MicrosoftGraphV1BaseUri,
            groupId));

    var usersList = JsonConvert.DeserializeObject<UsersList>(jsonResponse);
    return (usersList.Users);
}
```

Because the *owners* navigation property returns an array of objects of type *User*, the same ideas that we applied to the members of a group can be applied to the owners of a group.

Managing group membership

You can also use the Microsoft Graph API to add members or owners to or remove them from a group. To achieve this result, you have to target the reference instance of the *members* and *owners* navigation properties of a group. This can be done by appending the *$ref* property to the URL of the target navigation property. Moreover, you will have to provide the ID of the user object you want to add. In Listing 6-16, you can see a helper method to add a new member to a group.

LISTING 6-16 Code excerpt of a helper method to add a member to a group

```
/// <summary>
/// This method adds a new member to a group
/// </summary>
/// <param name="user">The user to add as a new group's member</param>
/// <param name="groupId">The ID of the target group</param>
public static void AddMemberToGroup(User user, String groupId) {
    MicrosoftGraphHelper.MakePostRequest(
        String.Format("{0}groups/{1}/members/$ref",
            MicrosoftGraphHelper.MicrosoftGraphV1BaseUri,
            groupId),
        new GroupMemberToAdd
        {
            ObjectId = String.Format("{0}users/{1}/id",
            MicrosoftGraphHelper.MicrosoftGraphV1BaseUri, user.UserPrincipalName)
        },
        "application/json");
}
```

Notice the *GroupMemberToAdd* type used to describe the new member to add. It is a type that will serialize a JSON request body like the one illustrated in the following excerpt:

```
{"@odata.id":"https://graph.microsoft.com/v1.0/users/<UPN>/id"}
```

In Listing 6-17, you can see the definition of the *GroupMemberToAdd* type.

LISTING 6-17 The definition of the *GroupMemberToAdd* type

```
/// <summary>
/// This type defines a new member to add to a group
/// </summary>
public class GroupMemberToAdd {
    [JsonProperty("@odata.id")]
    public String ObjectId { get; set; }
}
```

Notice the *JsonProperty* attribute of the *Newtonsoft.Json* library applied to the *ObjectId* property to customize the JSON serialization of the request body, according to the functional requirements of the Microsoft Graph API.

If you try to add a member who already exists in the group's members list, you will get back an HTTP 400 response with an error message like the following:

> *One or more added object references already exist for the following modified properties: 'members'.*

If you want to remove a member or an owner from a group, you have to make an HTTP DELETE request targeting the specific user object reference inside the entity set from which you want to do the removal. In Listing 6-18, you can see the corresponding helper method.

LISTING 6-18 Code excerpt of a helper method to remove a member from a group

```
/// <summary>
/// This method removes a member from a group
/// </summary>
/// <param name="user">The user to remove from the group</param>
/// <param name="groupId">The ID of the target group</param>
public static void RemoveMemberFromGroup(User user, String groupId) {
    MicrosoftGraphHelper.MakeDeleteRequest(
        String.Format("{0}groups/{1}/members/{2}/$ref",
            MicrosoftGraphHelper.MicrosoftGraphV1BaseUri,
            groupId, user.Id));
}
```

Notice the $ref URL property at the end of the member user's URL. It is mandatory to reference the specific membership object to delete it.

Office 365 Groups services

The Office 365 Groups, also known as Unified Groups, deserve a dedicated section of this chapter. As you learned in Chapter 1, "Microsoft Office 365: A quick tour," and Chapter 2, "Overview of Office 365 development," the Office 365 Groups are an exciting new feature of the Office 365 ecosystem. Thus, it is a common business requirement to be able to query, add, update, or delete Office 365 Groups programmatically. In this section, you will learn how to master the most common needs in these fields.

Querying Office 365 Groups

First of all, querying the Office 365 Groups is similar to querying other groups, but you have to filter the results based on the *GroupType* collection property values. As you saw in the previous sections, a *GroupType* property that contains the *Unified* value describes an Office 365 Group. However, because the *GroupType* is a property of type collection of strings, you cannot compare its value with the Unified string. Instead, you have to search for the *Unified* value in the collection of values contained in the

GroupType property. In Listing 6-19, you can see how to achieve this result by leveraging the power of OData querying.

LISTING 6-19 Code excerpt of a helper method to query for the list of Office 365 Groups

```
/// <summary>
/// This method retrieves the list of Office 365 Groups
/// </summary>
/// <param name="numberOfItems">Defines the TOP number of items to retrieve</param>
/// <returns>The list of Office 365 Groups</returns>
public static List<Group> ListUnifiedGroups(Int32 numberOfItems = 100) {
    String jsonResponse = MicrosoftGraphHelper.MakeGetRequestForString(
        String.Format("{0}groups?$filter=groupTypes/any(gt:%20gt%20eq%20'Unified')" +
            "&$top={1}", MicrosoftGraphHelper.MicrosoftGraphV1BaseUri,
            numberOfItems));

    var groupsList = JsonConvert.DeserializeObject<GroupsList>(jsonResponse);
    return (groupsList.Groups);
}
```

Notice the use of the *any* function of OData applied to the *GroupTypes* collection property. Removing the URL encoding, the search query looks like the following:

```
$filter=groupTypes/any(gt: gt eq 'Unified')
```

In this example, the arguments of the *any* function are similar to a lambda expression (from a C# developer perspective), and the *gt* keyword represents every instance of the values contained in the *groupTypes* collection. When the instance value equals *Unified*, the *any* function will yield the containing group.

Typically, every Office 365 Group also has a picture to better describe the group and to make it easier for the users to recognize that group within hundreds or thousands of groups. Through the Microsoft Graph API, you can easily retrieve the picture of a group by consuming the *photo* property, like you can for a user. In Listing 6-20, you can see a helper method to retrieve a group's picture as a stream of bytes.

LISTING 6-20 Code excerpt of a helper method to retrieve the picture of a group

```
/// <summary>
/// This method retrieves the photo of a group from Azure AD
/// </summary>
/// <param name="groupId">The ID of the group</param>
/// <returns>The group's photo retrieved from Azure AD</returns>
public static Stream GetGroupPhoto(String groupId) {
    String contentType = "image/png";

    var result = MicrosoftGraphHelper.MakeGetRequestForStream(
        String.Format("{0}groups/{1}/photo/$value",
            MicrosoftGraphHelper.MicrosoftGraphV1BaseUri, groupId)
```

```
        contentType);

    return (result);
}
```

The stream can be used wherever you need it to save or show the corresponding image file.

Office 365 Groups capabilities

The main reason to access an Office 365 Group is to leverage the capabilities the new Unified Groups model provides. For example, imagine that you want to consume the conversation threads related to a specific Office 365 Group. To do that, you can make an HTTP GET request for the *conversations* or for the *threads* navigation properties. In Listing 6-21, you can find the corresponding sample helper method.

LISTING 6-21 Code excerpt of a helper method to retrieve the conversation threads of an Office 365 Group

```
/// <summary>
/// This method retrieves the list of threads of an Office 365 Group
/// </summary>
/// <param name="groupId">The ID of the group</param>
/// <returns>The threads of an Office 365 Group</returns>
public static List<ConversationThread> ListUnifiedGroupThreads(String groupId) {
    String jsonResponse = MicrosoftGraphHelper.MakeGetRequestForString(
        String.Format("{0}groups/{1}/threads",
            MicrosoftGraphHelper.MicrosoftGraphV1BaseUri,
            groupId));

    var conversationThreadsList =
        JsonConvert.DeserializeObject<ConversationThreadsList>(jsonResponse);
    return (conversationThreadsList.Threads)
}
```

The returned list of threads is represented by a collection of objects of custom type *ConversationThread*, which provides information about the topic, the recipients, any file attachment, and so on. However, a conversation thread is usually interesting because of its messages, which are accessible through the navigation property called *posts*. By querying that navigation property, you can access every post of the thread, and you can even programmatically reply to the thread by sending a new post message. In Listing 6-22, you can see how to consume a single post.

LISTING 6-22 Code excerpt of a helper method to retrieve a single post in a conversation thread of an Office 365 Group

```
/// <summary>
/// This method retrieves a single post of a conversation thread for an Office 365 Group
/// </summary>
```

```
/// <param name="groupId">The ID of the thread</param>
/// <param name="threadId">The ID of the thread</param>
/// <param name="postId">The ID of the post</param>
/// <returns>The post of the conversation thread for an Office 365 Group</returns>
public static ConversationThreadPost GetUnifiedGroupThreadPost(String groupId,
    String threadId, String postId) {

    String jsonResponse = MicrosoftGraphHelper.MakeGetRequestForString(
        String.Format("{0}groups/{1}/threads/{2}/posts/{3}",
            MicrosoftGraphHelper.MicrosoftGraphV1BaseUri,
            groupId,
            threadId,
            postId));

    var conversationThreadPost =
        JsonConvert.DeserializeObject<ConversationThreadPost>(jsonResponse);

    return (conversationThreadPost);
}
```

In Listing 6-23, you can see how to send a new post into an existing thread. Just invoke the *reply* action of the thread object, providing at least the body of the message and then providing the categories, any new message recipient, attachment, and whatever else pertains to the post.

LISTING 6-23 Code excerpt of a helper method to reply to a thread of an Office 365 Group

```
/// <summary>
/// This method replies to a thread of an Office 365 Group
/// </summary>
/// <param name="groupId">The ID of the thread</param>
/// <param name="threadId">The ID of the thread</param>
/// <param name="post">The post to send as the reply</param>
public static void ReplyToUnifiedGroupThread(String groupId,
    String threadId, ConversationThreadPost post) {

    MicrosoftGraphHelper.MakePostRequest(
        String.Format("{0}groups/{1}/threads/{2}/reply",
            MicrosoftGraphHelper.MicrosoftGraphV1BaseUri,
            groupId,
            threadId), new { post }, "application/json");
}
```

Notice the use of the anonymous type as the content argument for the *MakePostRequest* method invocation. The *reply* action signature of a conversation thread accepts a complex type, serialized in JSON, with a *post* property that represents the post with which to reply. In Listing 6-24, you can see a code excerpt that uses the previous helper method.

```
UnifiedGroupsHelper.ReplyToUnifiedGroupThread(group.Id, threads[0].Id,
    new Models.ConversationThreadPost {
        Body = new Models.ItemBody {
            Type = Models.BodyType.Html,
            Content = "<html><body><div>This is the body of a post created via" +
                "the Microsoft Graph API!</div></body></html>",
        },
        NewParticipants = new List<Models.UserInfoContainer>(
            new Models.UserInfoContainer[] {
                new Models.UserInfoContainer {
                    Recipient = new Models.UserInfo {
                        Name = "Paolo Pialorsi",
                        Address = "paolo@pialorsi.com",
                    }
                }
            }),
    });
```

As you can see, the sample code excerpt of Listing 6-24 replies to the thread and includes a new recipient through the *NewParticipants* collection property of the *ConversationThreadPost* type.

Another interesting capability of an Office 365 Group is the group-related calendar. Using the *calendar* navigation property of the group endpoint, you can access both the calendar of a Unified Group and the events stored in that calendar. In Listing 6-25, you can see the helper method to access a calendar of a Unified Group.

LISTING 6-25 Definition of the helper method to access the calendar of an Office 365 Group.

```
/// <summary>
/// This method retrieves the calendar of an Office 365 Group
/// </summary>
/// <param name="groupId">The ID of the group</param>
/// <returns>The calendar of an Office 365 Group</returns>
public static Calendar GetUnifiedGroupCalendar(String groupId) {
    String jsonResponse = MicrosoftGraphHelper.MakeGetRequestForString(
        String.Format("{0}groups/{1}/calendar",
            MicrosoftGraphHelper.MicrosoftGraphV1BaseUri,
            groupId));

    var calendar = JsonConvert.DeserializeObject<Calendar>(jsonResponse);
    return (calendar);
}
```

As you can see, the type of the result of the *calendar* navigation property is identical to that of the services illustrated in Chapter 5. Thus, with the calendars of Unified Groups, you can leverage all the functionalities and capabilities that you saw in Chapter 5. As an example, in Listing 6-26 you see how to consume the list of calendar events for a specific Office 365 Group.

```
/// <summary>
/// Retrieves the events of an Office 365 Group calendar within a specific date range
/// </summary>
/// <param name="groupId">The ID of the group</param>
/// <param name="startDate">The start date of the range</param>
/// <param name="endDate">The end date of the range</param>
/// <param name="startIndex">The startIndex (0 based) of the items to retrieve</param>
/// <returns>A page of up to 10 events</returns>
public static List<Event> ListUnifiedGroupEvents(String groupId, DateTime startDate,
    DateTime endDate, Int32 startIndex = 0) {

    String jsonResponse = MicrosoftGraphHelper.MakeGetRequestForString(
        String.Format("{0}groups/{1}/calendarView?startDateTime={2:o}&" +
            "endDateTime={3:o}&$skip={4}",
            MicrosoftGraphHelper.MicrosoftGraphV1BaseUri,
            groupId,
            startDate.ToUniversalTime(),
            endDate.ToUniversalTime(),
            startIndex));

    var eventList = JsonConvert.DeserializeObject<EventList>(jsonResponse);
    return (eventList.Events);
}
```

Again, the result is a collection of JSON objects that correspond to the custom *Event* type that we used in Chapter 5 when consuming the calendar services.

One last interesting capability of every Office 365 Group is the OneDrive for Business dedicated folder. From a Microsoft Graph API perspective, you can access the OneDrive for Business drive by using the *drive* navigation property, which will give you access to a JSON object that defines the *owner* and the *quota* of the drive. In Chapter 7, you will learn more about the *drive* object. For now, it will suffice to know that you can access the folders and files of an Office 365 Group. In Listing 6-27, you can see a code excerpt to access the drive's general information.

LISTING 6-27 The helper method to retrieve the drive of an Office 365 Group

```
/// <summary>
/// This method retrieves the OneDrive for Business of an Office 365 Group
/// </summary>
/// <param name="groupId">The ID of the group</param>
/// <returns>The OneDrive for Business of an Office 365 Group</returns>
public static Drive GetUnifiedGroupDrive(String groupId) {
    String jsonResponse = MicrosoftGraphHelper.MakeGetRequestForString(
        String.Format("{0}groups/{1}/drive",
            MicrosoftGraphHelper.MicrosoftGraphV1BaseUri,
            groupId));

    var drive = JsonConvert.DeserializeObject<Drive>(jsonResponse);
```

```
        return (drive);
    }
```

The type with name *Drive* will be defined and detailed in Chapter 7.

Creating or updating Office 365 Groups

Sometime it could be useful to create Unified Groups, not only to consume existing ones. For example, you could have an Office 365 application that creates a Unified Group for managing the approval process of a manual or another type of document, and you want to automate the group creation process and the group deletion once the document is completed and approved. By using the Microsoft Graph API, it is easy to create a new Office 365 Group.

To create an Office 365 Group, you just need to make an HTTP POST request against the *groups* entity set, providing the new group object as JSON serialized content within the body of the request. In Listing 6-28, you can see a helper method to achieve this result.

LISTING 6-28 The helper method to create a new Office 365 Group

```
/// <summary>
/// Creates/Adds a new Office 365 Group
/// </summary>
/// <param name="group">The group to add/create</param>
/// <returns>The just added group</returns>
public static Group AddUnifiedGroup(Group group) {
    String jsonResponse = MicrosoftGraphHelper.MakePostRequestForString(
        String.Format("{0}groups",
            MicrosoftGraphHelper.MicrosoftGraphV1BaseUri),
        group, "application/json");

    var addedGroup = JsonConvert.DeserializeObject<Group>(jsonResponse);
    return (addedGroup);
}
```

As you see, the helper method uses the *MakePostRequestForString* helper function because when you add a new group, the response will be the JSON serialization of the newly created group. Notice that there are some mandatory fields for creating a group. These are the *displayName*, *mailEnabled*, *mailNickname*, *GroupTypes*, and *securityEnabled* fields. Moreover, to create an Office 365 Group via the Microsoft Graph API, you have to provide a valid access token for delegation of an authorized user. You cannot create Office 365 Groups by providing an app-only access token. In Listing 6-29, you can see a code excerpt that invokes the *AddUnifiedGroup* helper method.

LISTING 6-29 A sample code excerpt that uses the i helper method

```
var newUnifiedGroup = UnifiedGroupsHelper.AddUnifiedGroup(
    new Models.Group {
        DisplayName = "Created via API",
        MailEnabled = true,
        SecurityEnabled = false,
        GroupTypes = new List<String>(new String[] { "Unified"}),
        MailNickname = "APICreated",
    });
```

Notice that the value for the *GroupTypes* collection property is *Unified*. If you like, you can configure many more properties while creating a new Office 365 Group. However, those highlighted in the demo will suffice. When you create a new group, the email address of the group—if any—will be generated automatically by the Exchange Online service, which sits under the cover of the mail capabilities of a group, and you cannot force any explicit value because the mail property of the group is read-only.

Because you could have many Office 365 Groups in your tenant, it is a good habit to set up every group with a specific and identifying group icon. Setting the group image/icon is straightforward: you just need to make an HTTP PATCH request against the *photo/$value* property of the target group. The approach to use is similar to the one for setting a single user's picture. In Listing 6-30, you can see the corresponding helper method.

LISTING 6-30 The definition of a helper method to set the picture of an Office 365 Group

```
/// <summary>
/// Updates the photo of an Office 365 Group
/// </summary>
/// <param name="groupId">The ID of the target group</param>
/// <param name="photo">The byte array of the photo</param>
public static void UpdateUnifiedGroupPhoto(String groupId, Stream photo) {
    MicrosoftGraphHelper.MakePatchRequestForString(
        String.Format("{0}groups/{1}/photo/$value",
            MicrosoftGraphHelper.MicrosoftGraphV1BaseUri,
            groupId),
        photo, "image/jpeg");
}
```

The request will contain the image content as a raw stream of bytes, provided with a specific content/type for the request body. The response—if successful—will be an HTTP Status Code with a value of 200 (OK), with no specific text or echo of the request.

If you want to delete an existing Office 365 Group, you can make an HTTP DELETE request targeting the URL of the group that you want to delete. In Listing 6-31, you can see a code excerpt to accomplish this task.

LISTING 6-31 The definition of a helper method to delete an Office 365 Group

```
/// <summary>
/// Deletes an Office 365 Group
/// </summary>
/// <param name="groupId">The ID of the group to delete</param>
public static void DeleteUnifiedGroup(String groupId) {
    MicrosoftGraphHelper.MakeDeleteRequest(
        String.Format("{0}groups/{1}",
            MicrosoftGraphHelper.MicrosoftGraphV1BaseUri, groupId));
}
```

Summary

In this chapter, you learned how to read and manage users and groups in an Office 365 tenant. In particular, you saw how to browse the groups according to group type (Security, Dynamic, and Unified). Furthermore, you saw how to query existing Office 365 Groups and how to browse conversations, threads, calendars, and drives of Unified Groups. Last, you learned how to create, update, and delete an Office 365 Group by using the Microsoft Graph API.

## CHAPTER 7

File services

OneDrive for Business is one of the most used services of Microsoft Office 365, together with Microsoft Exchange Online. In fact, almost every Office 365 user uses a personal drive on OneDrive for Business and has a mailbox.

In this chapter, we will see how to leverage the File services, which enable us to consume and manage drives and files in OneDrive for Business. As in the previous chapters of Part III, the code samples illustrated in this chapter are available at the URL: *http://aka.ms/OfficeDev365ProgrammingSamples*.

Working with drives, files, and folders

When consuming OneDrive for Business, the first thing to do is to get a reference to the current user's drive. As in the previous chapters, you can make an HTTP GET request targeting the drive navigation property of the current user (*me*). The *me/drive* property represents the main entry point for the current user's OneDrive for Business drive. In Listing 7-1, you can see the helper method to access the current user's personal drive.

LISTING 7-1 Code excerpt of the helper method to access the current user's personal drive

```
/// <summary>
/// This method returns the personal drive of the current user
/// </summary>
/// <returns>The current user's personal drive</returns>
public static Drive GetUserPersonalDrive() {
    String jsonResponse = MicrosoftGraphHelper.MakeGetRequestForString(
        String.Format("{0}me/drive",
            MicrosoftGraphHelper.MicrosoftGraphV1BaseUri));

    var drive = JsonConvert.DeserializeObject<Drive>(jsonResponse);
    return (drive);
}
```

The result will be an instance of a custom *Drive* type that defines the drive object and can be serialized into and deserialized from the JSON representation of a drive provided by the Microsoft Graph API. The custom *Drive* type is defined in Listing 7-2.

```
/// <summary>
/// Defines a drive of OneDrive for Business
/// </summary>
public class Drive : BaseModel {
    /// <summary>
    /// The type of the current Drive
    /// </summary>
    public String DriveType { get; set; }

    /// <summary>
    /// The drive's owner
    /// </summary>
    public IdentitySet Owner { get; set; }

    /// <summary>
    /// The storage quota of the drive
    /// </summary>
    public Quota Quota { get; set; }
}
```

As you can see, there is a *DriveType* property of type *String*, which assumes a value of *business* for a OneDrive for Business drive.

> **Note** You may be wondering why there is a property that declares the type of the drive. In the long term, it is reasonable to support multiple types of drives. For example, you could have a OneDrive for Business drive, or you could have a OneDrive Personal drive. Both the flavors of OneDrive can be accessed through a REST API, which is the OneDrive REST API v2.0, and it makes sense to think about a convergence of this API with the Microsoft Graph API.

Through the *Drive* instance, you can also access the *Owner* of the drive and the *Quota* numbers of the current drive. For example, by leveraging the *Owner* property of the drive object, you can access the user who owns that drive directly. This could be useful when you are browsing third parties' drives (as long as you have proper permissions to do that) and want to traverse the graph to gain a user from her drive object.

Browsing for files and folders

Once you have a reference to the drive object, you can access its root folder by making an HTTP GET request for the root navigation property, which represents the root folder of the drive. In Listing 7-3, you can see a helper method to get the root folder.

LISTING 7-3 Code excerpt of the helper method to access the root folder of the current user's personal drive

```
/// <summary>
/// This method returns the root folder of the personal drive of the current user
/// </summary>
/// <returns>The root folder of the current user's personal drive</returns>
public static DriveItem GetUserPersonalDriveRoot() {
    String jsonResponse = MicrosoftGraphHelper.MakeGetRequestForString(
        String.Format("{0}me/drive/root",
            MicrosoftGraphHelper.MicrosoftGraphV1BaseUri));

    var folder = JsonConvert.DeserializeObject<DriveItem>(jsonResponse);
    return (folder);
}
```

The result of querying the root folder is an object that can be serialized/deserialized into a custom type called *DriveItem* that corresponds to the general-purpose *driveItem* defined in the metadata documentation of the Microsoft Graph API and is described in Listing 7-4. If you browse to the Microsoft Graph API metadata endpoint (*https://graph.microsoft.com/v1.0/$metadata*) and search for the *EntityType* element with the attribute *Name* with a value of *driveItem*, you will see that the *driveItem* type can hold any kind of drive item: a folder, a generic file, an audio file, a video file, and so on. Based on the instance of *driveItem* you retrieve, you will get a value for some of the properties declared in the *DriveItem* type.

LISTING 7-4 The definition of the custom *DriveItem* type

```
/// <summary>
/// Defines any generic item of a drive
/// </summary>
public class DriveItem : BaseModel {
    public System.IO.Stream Content;
    public IdentitySet CreatedBy;
    public Nullable<DateTimeOffset> CreatedDateTime;
    public String CTag;
    public String Description;
    public String ETag;
    public IdentitySet LastModifiedBy;
    public Nullable<DateTimeOffset> LastModifiedDateTime;
    public String Name;
    public ItemReference ParentReference;
    public Nullable<Int64> Size;
    public String WebDavUrl;
    public String WebUrl;
    public Audio Audio;
    public Deleted Deleted;
    public File File;
    public FileSystemInfo FileSystemInfo;
    public Folder Folder;
    public Image Image;
    public GeoCoordinates Location;
```

```
    public Photo Photo;
    public SearchResult SearchResult;
    public Shared Shared;
    public SpecialFolder SpecialFolder;
    public Video Video;
}
```

For example, the root folder of a user's drive will hold just a few of the available properties. For the root folder and for folders in general, you will have at least the *Name*, the *WebUrl*, the *CreatedDateTime*, and the *LastModifiedDateTime*.

However, when you access a specific drive or folder, you usually are interested in consuming the files contained in that drive or folder. Let's say that you want to retrieve all the files stored in the root folder of the current user's drive. As you learned in Chapter 3, "Microsoft Graph API reference," you can make an HTTP GET request for the *children* navigation property of the folder you want to browse. For the root folder of the current user, the relative URL path could be like the following:

```
/me/drive/root/children
```

But to target any folder and any drive in general—not only the root folder of the current user's drive—you can use the ID of the drive and the ID of the folder to build a direct path to the collection of children items. So, you will have something like the following relative URL path:

```
/drives/<DriveID>/items/<FolderId>/children
```

In Listing 7-5, you can see a helper method that retrieves the children items of any folder for any target drive.

LISTING 7-5 The helper method to retrieve the children items of a target folder in a specific drive

```
/// <summary>
/// This method returns the children items of a specific folder
/// </summary>
/// <param name="driveId">The ID of the target drive</param>
/// <param name="folderId">The ID of the target folder</param>
/// <param name="numberOfItems">The number of items to retrieve</param>
/// <returns>The children items</returns>
public static List<DriveItem> ListFolderChildren(String driveId, String folderId,
    Int32 numberOfItems = 100) {

    String jsonResponse = MicrosoftGraphHelper.MakeGetRequestForString(
        String.Format("{0}drives/{1}/items/{2}/children?$top={3}",
            MicrosoftGraphHelper.MicrosoftGraphV1BaseUri,
            driveId,
            folderId,
            numberOfItems));

    var driveItems = JsonConvert.DeserializeObject<DriveItemList>(jsonResponse);
    return (driveItems.DriveItems);
}
```

By leveraging code recursion, you can then browse all the folders of a drive by using the ID of the folders and by accessing their children items. However, you should keep in mind that by default the Microsoft Graph API will return no more than 200 items for each request. Thus, you will have to leverage the @*odata.nextLink* property of the result with the $*top* OData query string parameter if you want to do paging of results and/or if you want to consume all the children items, page by page.

Consuming files

When you have identified a file that you want to consume, you can access it directly by ID, using the same syntax that you use for consuming a folder. Thus, the relative URL will look like the following:

```
/drives/<DriveID>/items/<FileId>
```

Of course, a file is made of much more information than a folder. For example, you have the size of the file, the user who created the file and when the file was created, the user who last updated the file and when, the MIME type of the file, and so on.

One of the most interesting properties of a file is its content, which can be accessed by using a helper method like the one shown in Listing 7-6.

LISTING 7-6 The helper method to consume the content of a file from OneDrive for Business

```
/// <summary>
/// This method returns the content of a specific file by ID
/// </summary>
/// <param name="driveId">The ID of the target drive</param>
/// <param name="fileId">The ID of the target file</param>
/// <returns>The content of the file as a Stream</returns>
public static Stream GetFileContent(String driveId, String fileId, String contentType) {
    Stream fileContent = MicrosoftGraphHelper.MakeGetRequestForStream(
        String.Format("{0}drives/{1}/items/{2}/content",
            MicrosoftGraphHelper.MicrosoftGraphV1BaseUri,
            driveId,
            fileId),
            contentType);

    return (fileContent);
}
```

As you saw in Chapter 3, the response will be an HTTP Redirect (Status Code 302) to the URL of the file. Thus, you will have to enable HTTP redirection in the *HttpClient* instance that you used to make the request.

However, often you don't know where a file is, and you want to search for it and then consume its content or properties. In that case, you can use the *microsoft.graph.search* (or *search*) action, which can be applied to any folder of OneDrive for Business. In Listing 7-7, you can see a function that leverages this search capability.

LISTING 7-7 The helper method to search for files in OneDrive for Business

```
/// <summary>
/// This method searches for a file in the target drive and optional target folder
/// </summary>
/// <param name="searchText">The text to search for</param>
/// <param name="driveId">The ID of the target drive</param>
/// <param name="folderId">The ID of the target folder, optional</param>
/// <returns>The list of resulting DriveItem objects, if any</returns>
public static List<DriveItem> Search(String searchText, String driveId,
    String folderId = null) {

    String requestUri = null;
    if (!String.IsNullOrEmpty(folderId)) {
        requestUri = String.Format("{0}drives/{1}/items/{2}/" +
            "search(q='{3}')",
            MicrosoftGraphHelper.MicrosoftGraphV1BaseUri,
            driveId, folderId, searchText);
    }
    else {
        requestUri = String.Format("{0}drives/{1}/root/search(q='{2}')",
            MicrosoftGraphHelper.MicrosoftGraphV1BaseUri,
            driveId, searchText);
    }

    String jsonResponse = MicrosoftGraphHelper.MakeGetRequestForString(requestUri);
    var driveItems = JsonConvert.DeserializeObject<DriveItemList>(jsonResponse);
    return (driveItems.DriveItems);
}
```

Notice that the function applies the action to a specific folder URL if the input argument *folderId* is provided. Otherwise, it applies the action to the root folder of the drive, which will search the content in the entire drive. Aside from that, it is just a common REST query that will return a set of objects of type *DriveItem* if there is any result corresponding to the provided query text. Nevertheless, you should consider that there could be some delay in finding newly added items due to the indexing engine that works in the background. Thus, don't be surprised if you do not instantly find any new file that you just uploaded.

When consuming files, sometimes it is also useful to present a list of files—for example, the list of search results—including a thumbnail of each file item. Luckily, OneDrive for Business and the Microsoft Graph API provide an out-of-box capability to generate and provide thumbnails for known file types. For every known file type—Office files, video, audio, images, and many others—you can have three different thumbnails: small, medium, and large. Depending on the user interface or the user experience that you want to provide, you can use any of these autogenerated thumbnails. You will need to make an HTTP GET request for the thumbnails navigation property of the *DriveItem* that you target, and the result will be the set of the three available thumbnails. You can also access a specific thumbnail size directly. In Listing 7-8, you can see a helper method to get these thumbnails for a specific file item.

LISTING 7-8 The helper method to retrieve thumbnail information for specific files in OneDrive for Business

```
/// <summary>
/// This method returns the thumbnails of a specific file by ID
/// </summary>
/// <param name="driveId">The ID of the target drive</param>
/// <param name="fileId">The ID of the target file</param>
/// <returns>The file thumbnails for the specific file</returns>
public static ThumbnailSet GetFileThumbnails(String driveId, String fileId) {
    String jsonResponse = MicrosoftGraphHelper.MakeGetRequestForString(
        String.Format("{0}drives/{1}/items/{2}/thumbnails",
            MicrosoftGraphHelper.MicrosoftGraphV1BaseUri,
            driveId,
            fileId));

    var thumbnails = JsonConvert.DeserializeObject<ThumbnailSetResponse>(jsonResponse);
    return (thumbnails.Value.Count > 0 ? thumbnails.Value[0] : null);
}

/// <summary>
/// This method returns a thumbnail by size of a specific file by ID
/// </summary>
/// <param name="driveId">The ID of the target drive</param>
/// <param name="fileId">The ID of the target file</param>
/// <param name="size">The size of the target thumbnail</param>
/// <returns>The file thumbnails for the specific file</returns>
public static Thumbnail GetFileThumbnail(String driveId, String fileId,
    ThumbnailSize size) {

    String jsonResponse = MicrosoftGraphHelper.MakeGetRequestForString(
        String.Format("{0}drives/{1}/items/{2}/thumbnails/0/{3}",
            MicrosoftGraphHelper.MicrosoftGraphV1BaseUri,
            driveId,
            fileId,
            size.ToString().ToLower()));

    var thumbnail = JsonConvert.DeserializeObject<Thumbnail>(jsonResponse);
    return (thumbnail);
}
```

Every thumbnail item will provide information about the height and width of the image file and the URL of the physical image file. If you want, you can even download the image file directly. For example, the URL of a thumbnail could be something like this:

https://<tenant>-my.sharepoint.com/personal/<user>/_api/v2.0/drive/items/<fileId>
/thumbnails/0/large/thumbnailContent

The URL of the thumbnail file content comes from the base URL of OneDrive for Business, which is related to the URL *https://<tenant>-my.sharepoint.com*. Thus, you cannot request this URL by providing the classic OAuth 2.0 access token that we used so far because that one targets the Microsoft Graph API resource identifier (*https://graph.microsoft.com*). As you learned in Chapter 4, "Azure Active Directory and security," you have to request an access token specific to every different resource by using the refresh token to request or refresh an access token. So to consume the image file of a thumbnail, you have to switch from the Microsoft Graph API to the OneDrive API, and you have to create a new access token. Aside from that, it will be a common HTTP request for a file stream, as you can see in Listing 7-9.

LISTING 7-9 The helper method to retrieve the image file of a thumbnail for specific files in OneDrive for Business

```
/// <summary>
/// This method returns the thumbnails of a specific file by ID
/// </summary>
/// <param name="driveId">The ID of the target drive</param>
/// <param name="fileId">The ID of the target file</param>
/// <returns>The file thumbnails for the specific file</returns>
public static Stream GetFileThumbnailImage(String driveId, String fileId,
    ThumbnailSize size) {

    String jsonResponse = MicrosoftGraphHelper.MakeGetRequestForString(
        String.Format("{0}drives/{1}/items/{2}/thumbnails/0/{3}",
            MicrosoftGraphHelper.MicrosoftGraphV1BaseUri,
            driveId,
            fileId,
            size.ToString().ToLower()));

    var thumbnail = JsonConvert.DeserializeObject<Thumbnail>(jsonResponse);
    var thumbnailImageStream = MicrosoftGraphHelper.MakeGetRequestForStream(
        thumbnail.Url,
        "image/jpeg");

    return (thumbnailImageStream);
}
```

Under the cover of the *MakeGetRequestForStream* method, the *MicrosoftGraphHelper* class will disambiguate among the various resource identifiers and request the proper access token to the Microsoft Azure AD OAuth 2.0 endpoint.

Uploading and updating files

So far, you have seen how to traverse the folders of a drive, how to browse and search for files, and how to browse and download the thumbnails of files, but you probably will also need to upload new files or update existing files. In this section, you will see how to write contents on OneDrive for Business through the Microsoft Graph API.

First, let's create a new folder that we will use for storing some sample files. Creating a folder is easy and requires almost the same procedure as creating a new file. The only difference is that a folder does not have any specific content, while a file is made mainly of content and content type. In Listing 7-10, you can see a function that creates a new folder in a parent folder of OneDrive for Business.

LISTING 7-10 Code excerpt of a helper method to create a new folder in OneDrive for Business

```
/// <summary>
/// This method creates a new folder in OneDrive for Business
/// </summary>
/// <param name="driveId">The ID of the target drive</param>
/// <param name="parentFolderId">The ID of the parent folder</param>
/// <param name="folder">The new folder object to create</param>
/// <returns>The just created folder</returns>
public static DriveItem CreateFolder(String driveId, String parentFolderId,
    DriveItem folder) {

    var jsonResponse = MicrosoftGraphHelper.MakePostRequestForString(
        String.Format("{0}drives/{1}/items/{2}/children",
            MicrosoftGraphHelper.MicrosoftGraphV1BaseUri,
            driveId,
            parentFolderId),
            folder,
            "application/json");

    var newFolder = JsonConvert.DeserializeObject<DriveItem>(jsonResponse);
    return (newFolder);
}
```

Invoking the helper method illustrated in Listing 7-10 is straightforward, and you can see a sample in Listing 7-11.

LISTING 7-11 Code excerpt to invoke the helper method illustrated in Listing 7-10

```
var newFolder = FilesHelper.CreateFolder(drive.Id, root.Id,
    new Models.DriveItem {
        Name = $"Folder Create via API - {DateTime.Now.GetHashCode()}",
        Folder = new Models.Folder { },
    });
```

Once you have a target folder, you can upload a new file into it. A file is a *DriveItem* like a folder, and you need to make an HTTP POST request against the children entity set of the parent folder where you want to create the file. However, a *DriveItem* that represents a file must have the *File* property assigned instead of the *Folder* property. Moreover, you will also have to upload the real file content, making an HTTP PUT request against the content property of the file item. In Listing 7-12, you can see a helper method that accepts the drive and parent folder in which you want to create a file and the file object of type *DriveItem* and a *System.IO.Stream* that will represent the real content for the file.

LISTING 7-12 Helper method to create and upload a file into a target parent folder

```
/// <summary>
/// This method creates and uploads a file into a parent folder
/// </summary>
/// <param name="driveId">The ID of the target drive</param>
/// <param name="parentFolderId">The ID of the parent folder</param>
/// <param name="file">The file object</param>
/// <param name="content">The binary stream of the file content</param>
/// <param name="contentType">The content type of the file</param>
/// <returns>The just created and uploaded file object</returns>
public static DriveItem UploadFile(String driveId, String parentFolderId,
    DriveItem file, Stream content, String contentType) {

    var jsonResponse = MicrosoftGraphHelper.MakePostRequestForString(
        String.Format("{0}drives/{1}/items/{2}/children",
            MicrosoftGraphHelper.MicrosoftGraphV1BaseUri,
            driveId,
            parentFolderId),
            file,
            "application/json");

    var uploadedFile = JsonConvert.DeserializeObject<DriveItem>(jsonResponse);

    try {
        MicrosoftGraphHelper.MakePutRequest(
            String.Format("{0}drives/{1}/items/{2}/content",
                MicrosoftGraphHelper.MicrosoftGraphV1BaseUri,
                driveId,
                uploadedFile.Id),
                content,
                contentType);
    }
    catch (ApplicationException ex) {
        // For whatever reason we come here ... the upload failed
        // and we need to delete the just created file
        FilesHelper.DeleteFile(driveId, uploadedFile.Id);

        // And then we re-throw the exception
        throw ex;
    }
    return (uploadedFile);
}
```

Notice that the helper method makes two requests against the Microsoft Graph API. In a real enterprise-level solution, you should provide some kind of logical transaction and a compensating transaction that will remove the file from the parent folder if the content upload fails for any reason. That's why there is a try catch statement wrapping the content upload stage. So, in case of any failure during content upload, the *DriveItem* will be deleted.

The previous helper method, in case of any failure, uses another helper method to delete a file, which makes an HTTP DELETE request against the target file item. In Listing 7-13, you can see the helper method to delete a file in OneDrive for Business.

LISTING 7-13 Helper method to delete a file in OneDrive for Business

```
/// <summary>
/// This method deletes a file in OneDrive for Business
/// </summary>
/// <param name="driveId">The ID of the target drive</param>
/// <param name="fileId">The ID of the target file</param>
public static void DeleteFile(String driveId, String fileId) {
    MicrosoftGraphHelper.MakeDeleteRequest(
        String.Format("{0}drives/{1}/items/{2}",
            MicrosoftGraphHelper.MicrosoftGraphV1BaseUri,
            driveId,
            fileId));
}
```

In Listing 7-14, you can see another option that you have to upload a new file, including its content, by making a unique HTTP request. If you make an HTTP PUT request—for example, providing the name of the target file instead of the ID in the target URL of the PUT request—the Graph API will create the file on the fly if it does not exist.

LISTING 7-14 Revised helper method to create and upload a file into a target parent folder

```
/// <summary>
/// This method creates and uploads a file into a parent folder with a unique request
/// </summary>
/// <param name="driveId">The ID of the target drive</param>
/// <param name="parentFolderId">The ID of the parent folder</param>
/// <param name="file">The file object</param>
/// <param name="content">The binary stream of the file content</param>
/// <param name="contentType">The content type of the file</param>
/// <returns>The just created and uploaded file object</returns>
public static DriveItem UploadFileDirect(String driveId, String parentFolderId,
    DriveItem file, Stream content, String contentType) {
    var jsonResponse = MicrosoftGraphHelper.MakePutRequestForString(
        String.Format("{0}drives/{1}/items/{2}/children/{3}/content",
            MicrosoftGraphHelper.MicrosoftGraphV1BaseUri,
            driveId,
            parentFolderId,
            file.Name),
            content,
            contentType);

    var uploadedFile = JsonConvert.DeserializeObject<DriveItem>(jsonResponse);
    return (uploadedFile);
}
```

In the previous sample, notice the target relative URL, which has a format like the following:

```
/drives/<DriveID>/items/<FolderId>/children/<TargetFileName>/content
```

Sometimes it is also useful to update an existing file. Maybe you need to update the file properties, like the file name, or maybe you want to update the file content. Depending on what you need, you could have to make an HTTP POST request against the *DriveItem* object, or maybe you have to make an HTTP PUT request to overwrite the target file content. In the former scenario, the coding is easy and intuitive. In the latter scenario, it is almost the same as the code sample illustrated in Listing 7-14. However, if you have the ID of the target file, it is safer to reference the file by ID than by using its file name because the ID already exists.

In Listing 7-15, you can see a code excerpt of a helper method that updates the content of an existing file and another helper method that renames an existing file.

LISTING 7-15 Helper methods to update name and/or content of an existing file

```csharp
/// <summary>
/// This method renames an already existing file in OneDrive for Business
/// </summary>
/// <param name="driveId">The ID of the target drive</param>
/// <param name="fileId">The ID of the target file</param>
/// <param name="newFileName">The new file name</param>
/// <returns>The updated DriveItem corresponding to the renamed file</returns>
public static DriveItem RenameFile(String driveId, String fileId, String newFileName) {
    var jsonResponse = MicrosoftGraphHelper.MakePatchRequestForString(
        String.Format("{0}drives/{1}/items/{2}",
            MicrosoftGraphHelper.MicrosoftGraphV1BaseUri,
            driveId,
            fileId),
            new DriveItem {
                Name = newFileName,
            },
            "application/json");

    var updatedFile = JsonConvert.DeserializeObject<DriveItem>(jsonResponse);
    return (updatedFile);
}


/// <summary>
/// Uploads a new file content on top of an already existing file
/// </summary>
/// <param name="driveId">The ID of the target drive</param>
/// <param name="fileId">The ID of the target file</param>
/// <param name="content">The binary stream of the file content</param>
/// <param name="contentType">The content type of the file</param>
public static void UpdateFileContent(String driveId, String fileId,
    Stream content, String contentType) {
    MicrosoftGraphHelper.MakePutRequest(
        String.Format("{0}drives/{1}/items/{2}/content",
            MicrosoftGraphHelper.MicrosoftGraphV1BaseUri,
            driveId,
```

```
            fileId),
            content,
            contentType);
    }
```

Updating the content of a file is straightforward. You need to make an HTTP PUT request against the content property of the target *DriveItem*, providing the new content as a *Stream* within the request body. You also have to provide a proper value for the request content type according to the content type of the new uploaded content. Last, notice that by using the PUT method, you can upload or update a file with a size up to 4 MB.

Renaming a file just requires you to provide a new *DriveItem* object within an HTTP PATCH request, configuring the *Name* property with the new name of the file. The same behavior can be used to rename a folder.

If you want to move a file or a folder instead of just renaming it, you can leverage the same approach. However, you will have to provide not only the name of the target *DriveItem*, but also the *parentReference* property, which represents the path of the parent for the current item. Changing the parent of an item implies moving that item under the new parent. In Listing 7-16, you can see a helper method to move a file (or a folder) from one parent to another.

LISTING 7-16 Helper method to move a *DriveItem* within a OneDrive for Business drive

```
/// <summary>
/// This method moves one item from one parent folder to another
/// </summary>
/// <param name="driveId">The ID of the target drive</param>
/// <param name="driveItemId">The ID of the target file</param>
/// <param name="newItemName">The new name for the item in the target folder</param>
/// <param name="newParent">The name of the new target folder</param>
/// <returns>The moved DriveItem instance</returns>
public static DriveItem MoveDriveItem(String driveId, String driveItemId,
    String newItemName, String newParent) {

    var jsonResponse = MicrosoftGraphHelper.MakePatchRequestForString(
        String.Format("{0}drives/{1}/items/{2}",
            MicrosoftGraphHelper.MicrosoftGraphV1BaseUri,
            driveId,
            driveItemId),
            new DriveItem {
                Name = newItemName,
                ParentReference = new ItemReference {
                    Path = $"/drive/root:/{newParent}"
                }
            },
            "application/json");

    var movedItem = JsonConvert.DeserializeObject<DriveItem>(jsonResponse);
    return (movedItem);
}
```

Permissions and sharing

One of the most powerful features of the cloud is the capability to share contents with colleagues or third parties easily. In this section, you will see topics related to managing permissions for files and folders, and you will learn how to share a file or a folder with someone.

Managing files permissions

A useful use case when handling contents of OneDrive for Business is browsing and managing permissions. Through the *permissions* navigation property, you can access and update item-level permissions where the target item is any *DriveItem*, like a file or a folder. In Listing 7-17, you can see a code excerpt to get the permissions for a *DriveItem*.

LISTING 7-17 Helper method to get the permissions for a *DriveItem* within a OneDrive for Business drive

```
/// <summary>
/// This method returns a list of permissions for a specific DriveItem in OneDrive for
Business
/// </summary>
/// <param name="driveItemId">The ID of the DriveItem</param>
/// <returns>The list of permission for the target object</returns>
public static List<Permission> GetDriveItemPermissions(String driveItemId, String
permissionId) {
    var jsonResponse = MicrosoftGraphHelper.MakeGetRequestForString(
        String.Format("{0}me/drive/items/{1}/permissions",
            MicrosoftGraphHelper.MicrosoftGraphV1BaseUri,
            driveItemId));

    var permission = JsonConvert.DeserializeObject<PermissionList>(jsonResponse);
    return (permission.Permissions);
}
```

Notice that the target in this scenario is the personal drive of the current user (*/me/drive*). At the time of this writing, you can only manage permissions of personal drives within the context of the current user.

The result will be a collection of objects of custom type *Permission*, which is defined in Listing 7-18 and which provides information about the target of the permission (*GrantedTo*), a *SharingLink* if any, and the permission *Roles* associated with the current permission.

LISTING 7-18 The definition of the custom type *Permission*

```
public class Permission: BaseModel {
    public IdentitySet GrantedTo;
    public SharingInvitation Invitation;
    public ItemReference InheritedFrom;
    public SharingLink Link;
```

```
    public List<String> Roles;
    public String ShareId;
}
```

If you want to retrieve a single object of type *Permission*, you can do that by directly querying the object by ID. In Listing 7-19, there is a helper method that retrieves by ID a single permission for a target *DriveItem*.

A helper method that retrieves a single permission of a target *DriveItem* in OneDrive for Business

```
/// <summary>
/// This method returns a permission of a specific DriveItem in OneDrive for Business
/// </summary>
/// <param name="driveItemId">The ID of the DriveItem</param>
/// <param name="permissionId">The ID of the permission</param>
/// <returns>The permission object</returns>
public static Permission GetDriveItemPermission(String driveItemId, String permissionId) {
    var jsonResponse = MicrosoftGraphHelper.MakeGetRequestForString(
        String.Format("{0}me/drive/items/{1}/permissions/{2}",
            MicrosoftGraphHelper.MicrosoftGraphV1BaseUri,
            driveItemId,
            permissionId));

    var permission = JsonConvert.DeserializeObject<Permission>(jsonResponse);
    return (permission);
}
```

Removing a permission is also a straightforward task. You need to make an HTTP DELETE request targeting the URL of the permission that you want to remove. In Listing 7-20, there is a helper method to achieve this result.

A helper method that deletes a permission from a target *DriveItem* in OneDrive for Business

```
/// <summary>
/// This method removes a permission from a target DriveItem
/// </summary>
/// <param name="driveItemId">The ID of the DriveItem</param>
/// <param name="permissionId">The ID of the permission</param>
public static void RemoveDriveItemPermission(String driveItemId, String permissionId) {
    MicrosoftGraphHelper.MakeDeleteRequest(
        String.Format("{0}me/drive/items/{1}/permissions/{2}",
            MicrosoftGraphHelper.MicrosoftGraphV1BaseUri
            driveItemId,
            permissionId));
}
```

Because this is the fourth chapter in which you see this kind of behavior while consuming entity sets through the Microsoft Graph API, you shouldn't be surprised by the syntax used in Listing 7-20.

Sharing a file

Sharing a file, which means creating a new permission for a target object of type *DriveItem*, is another interesting use case that can be helpful in real business and enterprise-level solutions. To share a file, you need to invoke with an HTTP POST request the *microsoft.graph.createLink* (or *createLink*) action, targeting the URL of the *DriveItem* that you want to share. Within the body of the HTTP request, you will have to provide a JSON object that defines the features of the sharing link that you want to create. As you saw in Chapter 3, every sharing link has a type, which can be *view*, *edit*, or *embed*, and a scope, which can be *organization* or *anonymous*.

In Listing 7-21, you can see another helper method that makes it easy to create a sharing link for a target *DriveItem*.

LISTING 7-21 A helper method that creates a sharing link for a target *DriveItem* in OneDrive for Business

```
/// <summary>
/// This method creates a sharing link for a target DriveItem
/// </summary>
/// <param name="driveItemId">The ID of the DriveItem</param>
/// <param name="type">The type of the sharing link</param>
/// <param name="scope">The scope of the sharing link</param>
/// <returns>The just added permission for the sharing link</returns>
public static Permission CreateSharingLink(String driveItemId,
    SharingLinkType type, SharingLinkScope scope) {

    var jsonResponse = MicrosoftGraphHelper.MakePostRequestForString(
        String.Format("{0}me/drive/items/{1}/createLink",
            MicrosoftGraphHelper.MicrosoftGraphV1BaseUri,
            driveItemId),
            new {
                @type = type.ToString().ToLower(),
                @scope = scope.ToString().ToLower(),
            },
            "application/json"
    );

    var addedPermission = JsonConvert.DeserializeObject<Permission>(jsonResponse);
    return (addedPermission);
}
```

Notice the use of the *anonymous* type for defining the type and scope of the sharing link. The result of the helper method will be a new object of custom type *Permission* that defines the newly added sharing permission for the target item.

Summary

In this chapter, you saw how to browse drives, folders, and files stored within OneDrive for Business. You learned how to consume files' content and files' thumbnails. You saw how to upload new files and update existing files. Moreover, you learned how to move a file or a folder around a drive and how to delete an item, whether it is a file or a folder. You also learned how to search for contents in OneDrive for Business. Last, you realized how to manage item-level permissions and how to share a file or a folder by creating a sharing link or by reading a list of permissions.

Now you have the knowledge and the power to manage the contents of OneDrive for Business programmatically through the Microsoft Graph API.

## CHAPTER 8

Microsoft Graph SDK for .NET

In the previous chapters, you played with the Microsoft Graph API by using low-level HTTP requests, which are a good option to keep control of what is travelling on the wire but can sometimes be painful to develop and maintain. Luckily, Microsoft released a NuGet package called Microsoft Graph SDK for .NET, which enables you to accomplish some of the most common and useful tasks by using a helper library, without having to dig into the details of the HTTP and REST protocols.

In this chapter, you will learn about the architecture, the functionalities, and the capabilities of the Microsoft Graph SDK for .NET and about the Microsoft Graph SDKs for all the other platforms. All the code samples and snippets illustrated in this chapter are available as a sample application on GitHub in the OfficeDev PnP repository at the following URL: *https://github.com/OfficeDev/PnP/tree/master /Samples/MicrosoftGraph.Office365.DotNetSDK*.

Introduction to the Microsoft Graph SDK

First of all, it is important to say that the Microsoft Graph SDK for .NET is just one flavor of many. At the time of this writing, the Microsoft Graph SDK is available for the following platforms:

- Microsoft .NET

- iOS

- Android

The SDKs for Node.js, PHP, Python, Ruby, and AngularJS are under development. The basic idea of this SDK is to leverage the Graph REST metadata to generate the domain model objects representing the entities provided by the Microsoft Graph, targeting all the main platforms. For example, the .NET SDK is made of a .NET Portable Library, which targets Microsoft .NET 4.5, .NET Windows Store apps, Universal Windows Platform (UWP) apps, and Windows Phone 8.1 or higher. All the types that define objects like *User*, *Contact*, *Group*, *Drive*, and so on are autogenerated. There are some more infrastructural and helper types that are written manually and made available as open source on GitHub (*https:// github.com/microsoftgraph/msgraph-sdk-dotnet/*), while the tool used to generate the domain model objects is based on VIPR (*https://github.com/microsoft/vipr*) and is available at the following URL: *https://github.com/microsoftgraph/MSGraph-SDK-Code-Generator*.

Registering the app and using the SDK

From a developer perspective, to use the Microsoft Graph SDK for .NET you just need to add the NuGet package with name Microsoft.Graph to your projects. Like many other packages, the package has a dependency on the Newtonsoft.Json package.

Once you have a reference to the Graph SDK, you will need to create a client session to consume the Microsoft Graph API. The first step to create a client session is to register your application to use the Graph API. At the time of this writing, it is possible to register an application through two different platforms:

- Microsoft Azure Active Directory (Azure AD): This is the registration you learned about in Chapter 4, "Azure Active Directory and security."

- Microsoft application registration portal: This is a new kind of registration that is still under preview at the time of this writing. It provides a unified authentication model that embraces both Azure AD organizational accounts (work and school accounts) and Microsoft accounts (personal accounts). Often, it is defined as the v2 authentication endpoint.

 More Information For further details about the v2 authentication endpoint, you can read the article "Authenticate Office 365 and Outlook.com APIs using the v2.0 authentication endpoint preview," which is available at the following URL: *https://msdn.microsoft.com /en-us/office/office365/howto/authenticate-Office-365-APIs-using-v2*. Moreover, if you want to learn about the current limitations of the v2 authentication endpoint, you can read the article "Should I use the v2.0 endpoint?" at the following URL: *https://azure.microsoft.com /en-us/documentation/articles/active-directory-v2-limitations/*.

In the following paragraphs, you will learn how to leverage each of these two registration models, which imply a corresponding authentication and authorization model. Regardless of the registration model, you will have to provide the authentication logic to the Microsoft Graph SDK to be able to consume the Graph API. Out of the box, the Microsoft Graph SDK does not have any authentication logic. Instead, there is an abstract interface called *IAuthenticationProvider* that has to be implemented by a class that implements the real authentication. In Listing 8-1, you can see the definition of the *IAuthenticationProvider* interface.

LISTING 8-1 The *IAuthenticationProvider* interface definition in the Microsoft Graph SDK

```
namespace Microsoft.Graph {
    using System.Net.Http;
    using System.Threading.Tasks;

    /// <summary>
    /// Interface for authenticating requests.
    /// </summary>
    public interface IAuthenticationProvider {
        /// <summary>
```

```
        /// Authenticates the specified request message.
        /// </summary>
        /// <param name="request">The <see cref="HttpRequestMessage"/>
        /// to authenticate.</param>
        /// <returns>The task to await.</returns>
        Task AuthenticateRequestAsync(HttpRequestMessage request);
    }
}
```

The interface defines only an asynchronous method called *AuthenticateRequestAsync*, which will be responsible for handling any authentication technique by managing the input object of type *HttpRequestMessage* before sending the request on the wire.

Out of the box, the SDK provides a class called *DelegateAuthenticationProvider*, which implements the *IAuthenticationProvider* interface and internally uses a delegate to process any authentication logic. If you registered your application in Azure AD, you will use Microsoft Active Directory Authentication Library (ADAL) to get an access token from the OAuth 2.0 endpoint and to put it into the headers of the *HttpRequestMessage*. If you registered the application in the Microsoft application registration portal, you will be able to use the new Microsoft Authentication Library (MSAL) to get the access token from the new v2 authentication endpoint, and you will put it into the headers of the *HttpRequestMessage* object.

> **More Information** The Microsoft Authentication Library (MSAL) is a new library, still under preview at the time of this writing, which has been announced at // Build 2016 and which targets the new v2 authentication endpoint. For further information about MSAL, you can read the document "Microsoft Identity at //build/ 2016," which is available at the following URL: *https://blogs.technet.microsoft.com/ad/2016/03/31/microsoft-identity-at-build-2016/*. You can also watch the video "Microsoft Identity: State of the Union and Future Direction" that is available at the following URL: *https://channel9.msdn.com/Events/Build/2016/B868*.

The Graph SDK is completely independent and agnostic from the authentication logic. Thus, if you like you can implement your own logic to retrieve an access token by using the OAuth 2.0 protocol at a low level.

Once you have defined the authentication technique, you are ready to create a Graph SDK client object, which is based on type *GraphServiceClient*. The constructor of the *GraphServiceClient* type accepts up to three arguments:

- **baseUrl** The base URL of the target service endpoint, which is the Microsoft Graph API endpoint. For example, it can be *https://graph.microsoft.com/v1.0*. By default, it assumes the value *https://graph.microsoft.com/currentServiceVersion*, and it is an optional argument.

- **authenticationProvider** Is of type *IAuthenticationProvider* and will handle the authentication logic. It is mandatory, and usually you can provide an anonymous delegate that implements the authentication logic.

- **httpProvider**   Is responsible for providing the HTTP protocol support together with the serialization of the messages. It is optional.

In Listing 8-2, you can see a code excerpt taken from an ASP.NET MVC web application, which is included in the code samples of this book, that initializes a *GraphServiceClient* instance by using ADAL. In such an example, you have to install the Microsoft.IdentityModel.Clients.ActiveDirectory (that is, ADAL) package from NuGet.

LISTING 8-2 Creation of the *GraphServiceClient* class using ADAL and Azure AD for authentication

```
var graphClient = new GraphServiceClient(
    new DelegateAuthenticationProvider(
        (requestMessage) => {
            // Get back the access token.
            var accessToken = ADALHelper.GetAccessTokenForCurrentUser();

            if (!String.IsNullOrEmpty(accessToken)) {
                // Configure the HTTP bearer Authorization Header
                requestMessage.Headers.Authorization = new
                    AuthenticationHeaderValue("bearer", accessToken);
            }
            else {
                throw new Exception("Invalid authorization context");
            }

            return (Task.FromResult(0));
        }));
```

In the code excerpt, there is a helper method called *GetAccessTokenForCurrentUser* that internally handles the retrieval of the OAuth 2.0 access token by using the *AuthenticationContext* of ADAL, as you saw in Chapter 4.

In Listing 8-3, you can see a code excerpt that uses the *DelegateAuthenticationProvider* class to authenticate against the v2 authentication endpoint by using MSAL. In this case, you have to install the Microsoft.Identity.Client (that is, MSAL) pre-release package from NuGet.

LISTING 8-3 Creation of the *GraphServiceClient* class by using MSAL and the v2 authentication endpoint

```
GraphServiceClient graphClient = new GraphServiceClient(
    new DelegateAuthenticationProvider(
        async (requestMessage) => {
            // Configure the permissions
            String[] scopes = {
                "User.Read",
                "Mail.Send",
            };

            // Create the application context.
            var clientApplication = new PublicClientApplication(MSAL_ClientID);
```

```
            // Acquire an access token for the given scope.
            clientApplication.RedirectUri = "urn:ietf:wg:oauth:2.0:oob";
            var authenticationResult = await clientApplication.AcquireTokenAsync(scopes);

            // Get back the access token.
            var accessToken = authenticationResult.Token;

            // Configure the HTTP bearer Authorization Header
            requestMessage.Headers.Authorization =
                new AuthenticationHeaderValue("bearer", accessToken);
    }));
```

The MSAL library requires you to create one object of type *PublicClientApplication* if you are in a native application, like we are in the console application from which the code excerpt of Listing 8-3 has been taken. Otherwise, if you are in a web application, you have to create an instance of the *ConfidentialClientApplication* type. The latter is defined "confidential" because it involves the use of a shared secret, which can be generated in the application registration portal, if needed.

As you can see, highlighted in bold is a set of scopes defined and provided to the *PublicClientApplication* instance to declare the permissions requested for the current authentication phase. Thus, instead of having to declare all the permissions while configuring the application, as with Azure AD and ADAL, with MSAL you can just ask for a set of permissions and try to get a consent for them. Depending on the requested permission scopes, you will need a user's consent or an administrator's consent.

The list of available permissions corresponds to the list of permissions defined in the Microsoft Graph and is available in the document "Microsoft Graph permission scopes" at the following URL: *http://graph.microsoft.io/en-us/docs/authorization/permission_scopes*. In case you provide an incorrect or nonexistent permission in the list of permissions scope, you will get back an exception like the following:

```
AADSTS70011: The provided value for the input parameter 'scope' is not valid. The scope <Wrong
list of permissions> openid email profile offline_access is not valid.
```

Notice that aside from the custom permissions that you provide to MSAL through the scope, internally it will always add permission requests for signing in the user (*openid*), reading the user's *email* and *profile*, and accessing the user's data any time (*offline_access*).

Moreover, the tenant scope is also implied by the provided user's credentials, and you don't need to register any specific tenant in the application registration portal or provide a target tenant to the *PublicClientApplication* instance. The v2 authentication endpoint and MSAL are multitenant by default.

For the sake of brevity, and because at the time of this writing MSAL is still under preview and in alpha release, we will not go deeper into this topic. However, we will use it in the code samples related to this chapter to keep the samples up to date.

Regardless of how you created the *GraphServiceClient* instance, once you have it you can just browse the properties of the object, which provide a fluent API of objects and a common and useful query model. The objects provided by the Graph SDK domain model map to the resources published by the Microsoft Graph REST API and are provided on the .NET side as property bag classes. For example, in Listing 8-4 you can see a code excerpt to query the *DisplayName* property of the current user (*me*).

LISTING 8-4 Code excerpt to query the current user's *DisplayName* property

```
var me = await graphClient.Me.Request().Select("DisplayName").GetAsync();
var displayName = me.DisplayName;
```

Notice that the Graph SDK object model is completely asynchronous and the syntax for querying objects looks similar to that of LINQ (Language Integrated Query), but it is not identical and you cannot use LINQ and *IQueryable<T>* to query the Graph SDK domain model.

Under the cover of every request, there will be an HTTP request handled by the Graph SDK engine through the implementation of the HTTP provider and a process of serialization/deserialization of JSON objects into domain model objects.

Request model

To better understand how the Microsoft Graph SDK works, it's worth digging a little deeper into the request model that sits under the cover of the library.

Whenever you want to access one or more resources, you have to ask the Graph SDK to make a REST request for you. Internally, the SDK has an engine made of request builders that are invoked whenever you call the *Request()* method of a target object. Because the Microsoft Graph API is continuously growing and evolving, the request builders are generated together with the domain model types that map the resources by using the *$metadata* endpoint of the target Graph API. The VIPR project, referenced earlier in this chapter, is responsible for the autogeneration of all these types. Moreover, to allow easy unit testing of custom developed solutions, all the request handlers implement a specific interface that is autogenerated by VIPR.

Listing 8-5 shows how the *GraphClientService* type is defined from an interface-level perspective at the time of this writing.

LISTING 8-5 The interface-level definition of the *GraphServiceClient* type

```
public class GraphServiceClient : BaseClient, IGraphServiceClient, IBaseClient {

    public GraphServiceClient(IAuthenticationProvider authenticationProvider,
        IHttpProvider httpProvider = null);

    public GraphServiceClient(string baseUrl,
        IAuthenticationProvider authenticationProvider,
        IHttpProvider httpProvider = null);
```

```
        public IGraphServiceDevicesCollectionRequestBuilder Devices { get; }

        public IGraphServiceDirectoryObjectsCollectionRequestBuilder DirectoryObjects { get; }

        public IGraphServiceDirectoryRolesCollectionRequestBuilder DirectoryRoles { get; }

        public IGraphServiceDirectoryRoleTemplatesCollectionRequestBuilder
            DirectoryRoleTemplates { get; }

        public IDriveRequestBuilder Drive { get; }

        public IGraphServiceDrivesCollectionRequestBuilder Drives { get; }

        public IGraphServiceGroupsCollectionRequestBuilder Groups { get; }

        public IUserRequestBuilder Me { get; }

        public IGraphServiceOrganizationCollectionRequestBuilder Organization { get; }

        public IGraphServiceSubscribedSkusCollectionRequestBuilder SubscribedSkus { get; }

        public IGraphServiceSubscriptionsCollectionRequestBuilder Subscriptions { get; }

        public IGraphServiceUsersCollectionRequestBuilder Users { get; }
}
```

As you can see, every complex property like the collection of *Users*, the collection of *Subscriptions*, the *Drive*, the current user (*Me*), and all the other properties are of type *I*RequestBuilder*, where the asterisk corresponds to the underling type name. For example, the *Me* property will return the current user resource object. Thus, it will be of type *IUserRequestBuilder*.

In the set of generated request builder types, there will be the *UserRequestBuilder* class, which implements the *IUserRequestBuilder* interface and internally prepares all the REST requests for a single user resource by leveraging the *UserRequest* type. For the sake of completeness, if you open the source code of the *UserRequest* type in the Microsoft Graph SDK, either by browsing it on GitHub (*https:// github.com/microsoftgraph/msgraph-sdk-dotnet/blob/master/src/Microsoft.Graph/Requests /Generated/UserRequest.cs*) or by forking the GitHub repository locally on your development environment, you will see that internally it handles the HTTP REST requests, including the proper HTTP methods, all the HTTP headers, and the query string parameters.

In the section "Reading users" in Chapter 6, "Users and Groups services," you saw how to select one or more properties of a user by querying the endpoint for the collection of users and providing the *$select* query string parameter. For example, a REST query to get the *DisplayName*, *UserPrincipalName*, and *Mail* address of all the users can be done by making a GET request for the following URL:

```
https://graph.microsoft.com/v1.0/users?$select=displayName,userPrincipalName,mail
```

Here, you can see the corresponding syntax if you want to make the same request by using the Microsoft Graph SDK:

```
var users = await
    graphClient.Users.Request().Select("DisplayName,UserPrincipalName,Mail").GetAsync();
```

As you can see, the request model is straightforward and clearly maps to the corresponding low-level REST approach.

For the request model, it is important to underline that to execute the HTTP request effectively against the target, you have to invoke the *GetAsync* method, which is an asynchronous method, as the name implies. In fact, the Graph SDK is completely asynchronous and ready for the asynchronous development model of .NET.

Querying resources

The situation becomes more challenging if you also want to filter, sort, or partition data. As you learned in the previous chapters, the Graph REST API is compliant with the OData v4 protocol specification. Thus, it supports query string parameters like *$filter*, *$orderBy*, *$skip*, *$top*, and *$expand*.

The Microsoft Graph SDK supports the same statements. In this section, you will see each of them in action.

Basic query operations

Let's start with the capability to filter resources. The SDK provides the *Filter* method for every *RequestBuilder* type. In Listing 8-6, you can see a sample code excerpt to query the list of users, filtered by work department.

LISTING 8-6 Code excerpt to query the users filtered by *Department* property value

```
var filteredUsers = await graphClient.Users.Request()
    .Select("DisplayName,UserPrincipalName,Mail")
    .Filter("department eq 'IT'")
    .GetAsync();
```

Notice that you can create a chain of methods so that, for example, in Listing 8-6 you apply the *Filter* method on top of the results of the *Select* method. The corresponding REST request will be something like the following:

```
https://graph.microsoft.com/v1.0/users?$select=displayName,userPrincipalName,mail,department&$fi
lter=department%20eq%20'IT'
```

As you can see, the string argument of the *Filter* method is what you can provide to the REST endpoint directly, without the URL encoding. Thus, using the new Microsoft Graph SDK you are free to make whatever query you like, but you will have to know the OData querying syntax because there are no high-level tools for building queries.

Another useful method you can use is *OrderBy*, which sorts the results of a query based on one or more property values. However, at the time of this writing you cannot combine the *OrderBy* method with the *Filter* method. This is highlighted in the REST API online documentation (see the "$orderby" section here: *http://graph.microsoft.io/en-us/docs/overview/query_parameters*). Moreover, depending on the target resource type, you could have to provide the properties' names with the same case that is used in the *$metada* document. For example, if you want to sort the users by *DisplayName*, you cannot use the *DisplayName* clause—you will have to use the *displayName* clause, with a lowercase trailing letter, according to its definition in the *$metadata* document. This is a requirement of the REST API, depending on the target type of resources, and not of the SDK because internally the SDK will build the REST request for the API, and the API refuses the query that has the wrong casing of properties, providing an exception message like the following:

```
Given expression for $orderby Microsoft.Data.OData.Query.SemanticAst.
SingleValueOpenPropertyAccessNode is not supported
```

In Listing 8-7, you can see a query with sorting based on *DisplayName* ascending.

LISTING 8-7 Code excerpt to query the users sorted by *DisplayName* ascending

```
var filteredUsers = await graphClient.Users.Request()
    .Select("DisplayName,UserPrincipalName,Mail")
    .OrderBy("displayName")
    .GetAsync();
```

If the target collection supports the capability, you can sort the resources in ascending (default) or descending order by providing the *desc* or *asc* keywords after the name of the sorting fields. You can even combine multiple fields to achieve multilevel hierarchical sorting.

Furthermore, you can partition results of queries by leveraging the *Top* and *Skip* methods. These are the counterparts of the *$top* and *$skip* query string parameters of the OData protocol. In Listing 8-8, you can see a query that retrieves the top 5 email messages in the inbox folder of the current user's mailbox, skipping the first 10 messages.

LISTING 8-8 Code excerpt to query the top 5 messages in inbox, skipping the first 10 messages

```
var partitionedMails = await graphClient.Me.MailFolders.Inbox.Messages.Request()
    .Select("subject,from,receivedDateTime")
    .OrderBy("receivedDateTime desc")
    .Skip(10)
    .Top(5)
    .GetAsync();
```

Again, depending on the target type of resource, some of these methods could be unsupported. For example, at the time of this writing, if you invoke the *Skip* method against the collection of users, you will get back an exception like the following:

```
'$skip' is not supported by the service.
```

The last method related to the querying capabilities of the Microsoft Graph SDK is the *Expand* method, which allows you to include in the results resources related to the main resource that is subject to query. For example, in Listing 8-9 you can see a code excerpt to retrieve a folder in a drive, together with (*Expand*) the children files and folders of that folder, within a unique request.

LISTING 8-9 Code excerpt to retrieve a folder and its children items

```
var expandedFiles = await graphClient.Me.Drive.Root.Request()
    .Expand("children($select=id,name,createdBy,lastModifiedBy)")
    .Select("id,name,webUrl")
    .GetAsync();
```

It is important to highlight that the *Select* method chained to the *Expand* method targets the root folder of the current user's OneDrive for Business drive and not the children items. To select a subset of properties for the children resources of the folder, you have to provide the list of properties through the input argument of the *Expand* method. Notice also that by design of the Graph REST API—independent from the Graph SDK—the *Expand* method can expand a maximum of 20 objects per request. If you are targeting a user resource, you can expand only one child resource or collection of resources for each request.

Handling paging of collections

In the previous paragraphs, you learned how to query collections of resources and how to filter, partition, and expand resulting data. However, in real business scenarios you could have large numbers of items. Thus, it is fundamental to also do paging of collections.

The Microsoft Graph API makes it possible to do paging by splitting the results in pages and providing the *@odata.nextLink* property in the result set. Thus, whenever you query the Graph API collections of resources, you can consume the query result and then make another query against the URL provided in the *@odata.nextLink* property of the result set. Considering a query for a set of users, the *@odata.nextLink* property value will be something like the following:

```
@odata.nextLink=https://graph.microsoft.com/v1.0/users?$skiptoken=X%2744537074020000203A666E3138
372E6C6E313837407368617265706F696E742D63616D702E636F6D29557365725F64393266313163652D326234322D34
3136662D386363302D61323639646265539663231360020203A666E3237372E6C6E323737407368617265706F696E742D63
616D702E636F6D29557365725F663861626433386662D653836332D3343639302D616637382D643939306434356366653534
34B900000000000000000000000%27
```

The *$skiptoken* query string argument instructs the REST service to provide the next page of the current page. Internally, the *$skiptoken* query string is an opaque token that identifies a starting point in the collection of resources identified by the current REST query. Basically, it defines the first record of the next page to query. If the query orders the resulting resources by using the *$orderby* query string argument, the results will be ordered according to the sorting rule. Otherwise—and by default—the results will be ordered by entity key (the ID).

When you query collections of resources by using the Microsoft Graph SDK, all the internals of paging and of the *$skiptoken* argument are hidden from you under the cover of the *ICollectionPage<T>* interface and a set of collection interfaces autogenerated by VIPR. For example, in Listing 8-10 you can see the definition of the *ICollectionPage<T>* interface.

LISTING 8-10 Definition of the *ICollectionPage<T>* interface of the Microsoft Graph SDK

```
/// <summary>
/// Interface for collection pages.
/// </summary>
/// <typeparam name="T">The type of the collection.</typeparam>
public interface ICollectionPage<T> : IList<T> {

    /// <summary>
    /// The current page of the collection.
    /// </summary>
    IList<T> CurrentPage { get; }

    IDictionary<string, object> AdditionalData { get; set; }
}
```

The interface definition is straightforward, and whenever you query a pageable collection you will get back a *CurrentPage* property and any additional data in the *AdditionalData* dictionary property, which will hold the values for the properties *@odata.context* and *@odata.nextLink*. For example, consider a collection of users. The result of the following query is an object of type *GraphServiceUsersCollectionPage* that implements the *IGraphServiceUsersCollectionPage* interface:

```
var pagedUsers = await graphClient.Users.Request().Select("id,DisplayName,Mail").GetAsync();
```

In Listing 8-11, you can see the definition of the *IGraphServiceUsersCollectionPage* interface, which implements the *ICollectionPage<T>* interface.

LISTING 8-11 Definition of the *IGraphServiceUsersCollectionPage* interface of the Microsoft Graph SDK

```
public interface IGraphServiceUsersCollectionPage : ICollectionPage<User> {

    /// <summary>
    /// Gets the next page <see cref="IGraphServiceUsersCollectionRequest"/> instance.
    /// </summary>
    IGraphServiceUsersCollectionRequest NextPageRequest { get; }

    /// <summary>
    /// Initializes the NextPageRequest property.
    /// </summary>
    void InitializeNextPageRequest(IBaseClient client, string nextPageLinkString);
}
```

Aside from the implemented interface, there is a property called *NextPageRequest* of type *IGraphServiceUsersCollectionRequest* that is an autogenerated interface, and that provides the shortcut to access the next page of the current page. When you invoke the *GetAsync* method to retrieve a result set of resources, internally that method will initialize the *NextPageRequest* property so that it will represent a request for the next page of resources. If you invoke the *GetAsync* method against the *NextPageRequest* property, you will get back the next page. By iterating through the collections of resources and invoking the *GetAsync* method of every *NextPageRequest*, as long as that property is not NULL you will get back all the resources page by page.

Thus, in Listing 8-12 you can see a full example of how you can browse all the pages of users by leveraging these interfaces and properties.

LISTING 8-12 Code sample of how to do paging of users by using the Microsoft Graph SDK

```
var pagedUsers = await graphClient.Users
    .Request()
    .Select("id,DisplayName,Mail")
    .GetAsync();

Int32 pageCount = 0;

while (true) {

    pageCount++;
    Console.WriteLine("Page: {0}", pageCount);



    foreach (var user in pagedUsers) {
        Console.WriteLine("{0} - {1} - {2}", user.Id, user.DisplayName, user.Mail);
    }

    if (pagedUsers.NextPageRequest != null) {
        pagedUsers = await pagedUsers.NextPageRequest.GetAsync();
    }
    else {
        break;
    }
}
```

You can implement the paging logic however you like; the key point is to request pages of resources as long as the *NextPageRequest* property is not NULL.

Managing resources

In the previous chapters, you saw that you can add, update, and delete the resources provided by the Microsoft Graph API. In this section, you will learn how to accomplish these tasks by using the Microsoft Graph SDK.

Adding a resource to a collection

You can add resources to collections by invoking the *AddAsync* method that is offered by any collection, thanks to the definition of the autogenerated *IGraphService*CollectionRequest* interfaces. Again, the asterisk has to be replaced with the name of every resource type.

Imagine that you want to create a new Office 365 Group, which is a useful business case for a real solution. First of all, you have to target the collection of groups, which is available through the *Groups* collection property of the *IGraphServiceClient* interface. Then, you have to invoke the *Request* method to get a reference to the REST request for the target resource collection. After that, you will be able to invoke the *AddAsync* method of the resulting object. In Listing 8-13, you can see a code excerpt that creates a new Office 365 Group.

LISTING 8-13 Code excerpt that creates a new Office 365 Group by using the Microsoft Graph SDK

```
String randomSuffix = Guid.NewGuid().ToString("N");

// Prepare the group resource object
Group newGroup = new Group {
    DisplayName = "SDK Group " + randomSuffix,
    Description = "This has been created via Graph SDK",
    MailNickname = "sdk-" + randomSuffix,
    MailEnabled = true,
    SecurityEnabled = false,
    GroupTypes = new List<string> { "Unified" },
};

// Add the group to the collection of groups
var addedGroup = await graphClient.Groups.Request().AddAsync(newGroup);
```

Notice that you have to configure the group completely in code. For example, to create an Office 365 Group, you have to specify the value for the *GroupTypes* property, selecting the *Unified* value.

Furthermore, when you create an Office 365 Group, usually you also would like to set up a photo for the group and to assign owners and members to the group. The group's photo can be configured by providing a *System.IO.Stream* object to the *PutAsync* method of the *Photo.Content.Request* of the target group. In Listing 8-14, you can see the corresponding code.

LISTING 8-14 Code excerpt that uploads a photo for an Office 365 Group by using the Microsoft Graph SDK

```
// Upload a new photo for the Office 365 Group
using (FileStream fs = new FileStream(@"..\..\AppIcon.png", FileMode.Open,
    FileAccess.Read, FileShare.Read)) {
    await graphClient.Groups[addedGroup.Id].Photo.Content.Request().PutAsync(fs);
}
```

If you are going to add a photo to a new group, you probably will need to provide a retry logic because usually it will take a few seconds after the creation for the group to be ready and available for uploading the photo.

The owners and members are more interesting. If you think about the Graph API from a REST perspective, the collections of members and owners of a group are accessible through the *$ref* keyword, which represents a reference to the underlying collection objects. Because the Graph SDK domain model is autogenerated from the *$metadata* definition of resources, the *$ref* endpoints are also made available through an autogenerated *References* property. That property gives us a reference to the underlying collection of items.

For example, if you reference a group item by using the *Groups* property of an *IGraphServiceClient* implementation, you will see that the *Owners* property will be of type *IGroupOwnersCollectionReferencesRequest*, where the interface name implies that there are also references included in the interface definition and that you can invoke the *Request* method against them. In general, in the autogenerated domain model there are a bunch of interfaces with name *I*CollectionReferencesRequest*, where the asterisk refers to the collection name.

If you get a reference to the collections of owners or members of a group, you can then invoke the *AddAsync* method of those collections and add new user objects of type *DirectoryObject* to them. In Listing 8-15, you can see a code excerpt that adds one owner and a couple of members to a just-created Office 365 Group.

LISTING 8-15 Code excerpt adding an owner and members to an Office 365 Group by using the Microsoft Graph SDK

```
// Add owners to the group
var ownerQuery = await graphClient.Users
    .Request()
    .Filter("userPrincipalName eq 'paolo.pialorsi@sharepoint-camp.com'")
    .GetAsync();

var owner = ownerQuery.FirstOrDefault();

if (owner != null) {
    try {
        await graphClient.Groups[addedGroup.Id].Owners
            .References.Request().AddAsync(owner);
    }
    catch (ServiceException ex) {
        Console.WriteLine(ex.Message);
    }
}

// Add members to the group
var memberOneQuery = await graphClient.Users
    .Request()
    .Filter("userPrincipalName eq 'paolo.pialorsi@sharepoint-camp.com'")
    .GetAsync();
var memberTwoQuery = await graphClient.Users
```

```
        .Request()
        .Filter("userPrincipalName eq 'john.white@sharepoint-camp.com'")
        .GetAsync();

var memberOne = memberOneQuery.FirstOrDefault();
var memberTwo = memberTwoQuery.FirstOrDefault();

if (memberOne != null) {
    try {
        await graphClient.Groups[addedGroup.Id].Members
            .References.Request().AddAsync(memberOne);
    }
    catch (ServiceException ex) {
        Console.WriteLine(ex.Message);
    }
}

if (memberTwo != null) {
    try {
        await graphClient.Groups[addedGroup.Id].Members
            .References.Request().AddAsync(memberTwo);
    }
    catch (ServiceException ex) {
        Console.WriteLine(ex.Message);
    }
}
```

Consider that if you try to add the same user object to the same target role (member or owner) more than once, you will get back an exception with an error message like the following, which is provided in the case of a duplicate owner:

```
One or more added object references already exist for the following modified properties:
'owners'.
```

Notice that if you access the *Owners* property of a *Group* instance retrieved using the *GetAsync* method, you will not have access to the *References* property. This is because the single instance of type *Group* does not expose the *Owners* as an implementation of *IGroupOwnersCollectionReferencesRequest*, but just as an implementation of the *IGroupOwnersCollectionWithReferencesPage* interface. This same is true for the *Members* property of a *Group* instance.

Last, consider that to add a new Office 365 Group, you will need to have the permission scope of type Group.ReadWrite.All, but if you also want to manage owners and members, you most likely will also need permissions to access the Azure AD tenant. For example, the permission scope Directory. AccessAsUser.All could be enough as long as you don't want to act with elevated privileges—for example, using an app-only access token. Nevertheless, keep in mind that at the time of this writing, you cannot create an Office 365 Group with an app-only access token.

Updating a resource

Now that you have seen how to add resources to collections, it is time to learn how to update an existing resource. The Microsoft Graph SDK provides the *UpdateAsync* method for this purpose.

The *UpdateAsync* method is available through the *I*Request* interface for objects that are updatable. For example, in Listing 8-16 you can see a code excerpt to update the *DisplayName* and *Description* properties of an Office 365 group.

LISTING 8-16 Code excerpt to update an Office 365 Group by using the Microsoft Graph SDK

```
var groupToUpdate = await graphClient.Groups[groupId]
    .Request()
    .GetAsync();

groupToUpdate.DisplayName = "SDK Group - Updated!";
groupToUpdate.Description += " - Updated!";

var updatedGroup = await graphClient.Groups[groupId]
    .Request()
    .UpdateAsync(groupToUpdate);
```

When you update a resource, particularly an Office 365 Group, you have to consider that there could be some delay due to data caching on the service side and because of asynchronous update operations that are working in the background. Thus, there is no guarantee that you will see your updates in real time.

Deleting a resource

Deleting a resource is another straightforward use case. You just need to get a reference to the resource object you want to delete and then invoke the *DeleteAsync* method on it.

In Listing 8-17, you can see a code excerpt to delete an existing Office 365 Group.

LISTING 8-17 Code excerpt to delete an Office 365 Group by using the Microsoft Graph SDK

```
await graphClient.Groups[groupId]
    .Request()
    .DeleteAsync();
```

As you can see, the *DeleteAsync* method is applied directly to the target resource. In case of success, it does not provide any kind of result. In case of failure, you will have to catch the proper exception type.

Handling exceptions and concurrency

Whenever you interact with a service layer, various kinds of exceptions can happen. The Microsoft Graph SDK will wrap all of the possible exceptions into the *ServiceException* type of the *Microsoft.Graph* namespace.

In Listing 8-18, you can see the definition of the *ServiceException* type.

LISTING 8-18 The definition of the *ServiceException* type of the Microsoft Graph SDK

```
public class ServiceException : Exception {

    public ServiceException(Error error, Exception innerException = null)
        : base(null, innerException) {
        this.Error = error;
    }

    public Error Error { get; private set; }

    public bool IsMatch(string errorCode) {
        if (string.IsNullOrEmpty(errorCode)) {
            throw new ArgumentException("errorCode cannot be null or empty", "errorCode");
        }

        var currentError = this.Error;
        while (currentError != null) {
            if (string.Equals(currentError.Code, errorCode,
                StringComparison.OrdinalIgnoreCase)) {
                    return true;
            }

            currentError = currentError.InnerError;
        }

        return false;
    }

    public override string ToString() {
        if (this.Error != null) {
            return this.Error.ToString();
        }

        return null;
    }
}
```

The main information provided by the *ServiceException* is the *Error* property, which provides detailed information about the service-side exception. The main information that you can find within the *Error* property, which is of type *Microsoft.Graph.Error*, is illustrated in Table 8.1:

TABLE 8-1 The properties of the *Microsoft.Graph.Error* type

Property	Description
Code	Represents an error code selected within a range of about 60 different error codes that are defined in type Microsoft.Graph.GraphErrorCode.
InnerError	Defines a nested error, if any.
Message	Defines the description message for the error.
ThrowSite	Declares the site that threw the error.
AdditionalData	Here, you can find information like the Request ID and the date and time of execution of the failed request.

Moreover, the *IsMatch* method of the *ServiceException* type enables you to double-check the type of the error, based on the error code. You can invoke the *IsMatch* method by providing a reference error code, and the method will give you back a *Boolean* value that enables you to verify if the exception corresponds to the provided error code. In Listing 8-19, you can see a sample of how to handle the *ServiceException* type.

LISTING 8-19 Sample of how to handle the *ServiceException* type with the Microsoft Graph SDK

```
try {

    // Do something with the Microsoft Graph SDK ...

}
catch (ServiceException ex) {
    Console.WriteLine(ex.Error);
    if (ex.IsMatch(GraphErrorCode.AccessDenied.ToString())) {
        Console.WriteLine("Access Denied! Fix permission scopes ...");
    }
    else if (ex.IsMatch(GraphErrorCode.ThrottledRequest.ToString())) {
        Console.WriteLine("Please retry ...");
    }
}
```

As you can see, the exception handling is clean and clear. It is also interesting to see that there is a specific error code for throttled requests, which is useful when you are consuming a cloud service like the Microsoft Graph API and you need to implement a retry logic.

Real-life examples

It is now time to play a little bit with the Microsoft Graph SDK, looking at how to accomplish some of the most common and useful tasks in real business scenarios.

Sending an email

Sending an email on behalf of the current user is one of the most common use cases. As you saw in Chapter 3, "Microsoft Graph API reference," and Chapter 5, "Mail, calendar, and contact services," there is an operation called *microsoft.graph.sendMail* available under the current user resource, which is called *Me*.

Using the Microsoft Graph SDK, you can invoke the *SendMail* method, which is available for the *Me* property of the *GraphServiceClient* object. In Listing 8-20, you can see a code excerpt that uses the *SendMail* method.

LISTING 8-20 Sample of how to send an email by using the Microsoft Graph SDK

```
try {
    await graphClient.Me.SendMail(new Message {
        Subject = "Sent from Graph SDK",
        Body = new ItemBody {
            Content = "<h1>Hello from Graph SDK!</h1>",
            ContentType = BodyType.Html,
        },
        ToRecipients = new Recipient[] {
            new Recipient {
                EmailAddress = new EmailAddress {
                    Address = recipientMail,
                    Name = recipientName,
                }
            }
        },
        Importance = Importance.High,
    },
    true).Request().PostAsync();
}
catch (ServiceException ex) {
    Console.WriteLine(ex.Error);
}
```

Notice that the *SendMail* method does not send the email message directly, but it returns a request builder of type *IUserSendMailRequestBuilder*. Thus, you have to invoke the *Request* method to retrieve the request object, and after that you have to POST over HTTP the request invoking the *PostAsync* method.

The main input of the *SendMail* method is an object of type *Microsoft.Graph.Message*, which is a domain model object autogenerated by VIPR and corresponding to the resource defined in the *$metadata* document.

Searching for Office 365 Groups

Another interesting and common use case is retrieving all the Office 365 Groups. We already saw that the *GraphServiceClient* object offers a *Groups* collection, but that collection returns all the available flavors of groups including security groups, Unified Groups (Office 365 Groups), and dynamic groups.

To select only the Office 365 Groups, you can use the *Filter* method applied to the *Request* for the *Groups* collection, searching for those groups that have the *GroupType* property containing a value of *Unified*. In Listing 8-21, you can see a code excerpt to accomplish this task.

LISTING 8-21 Code excerpt to retrieve all the Office 365 Groups page by page by using the Microsoft Graph SDK

```
var pagedGroups = await graphClient.Groups
    .Request()
    .Filter("groupTypes/any(grp: grp eq 'Unified')")
    .GetAsync();

Int32 pageCount = 0;

while (true) {
    pageCount++;
    Console.WriteLine("Page: {0}", pageCount);
    foreach (var group in pagedGroups) {
        Console.WriteLine("{0} - {1} - {2}", group.Id,
            group.DisplayName, group.Description);
    }

    if (pagedGroups.NextPageRequest != null) {
        pagedGroups = await pagedGroups.NextPageRequest.GetAsync();
    }
    else {
        break;
    }
}
```

The key point of the sample in Listing 8-21 is the argument provided to the *Filter* method. You can recognize the filtering criteria that we used in Chapter 3, in the section "Working with Office 365 Groups," within Listing 3-42.

Handling content of Office 365 Groups

Once you have a reference to an Office 365 Group resource, most likely you will have to retrieve information and content about the group.

For example, if you want to retrieve the files of a group, you can access the *Drive* property of the target group. From the group's drive, you will have access to the root folder and to its children items. Listing 8-22 illustrates how to retrieve the files and folders from the root folder of a group's drive.

LISTING 8-22 Code excerpt to retrieve all the files in the root folder of an Office 365 Group

```
var groupDriveItems = await graphClient
    .Groups[unifiedGroupId].Drive.Root.Children
    .Request()
    .GetAsync();
```

As usual, you have to build the request and then execute it asynchronously. If you are looking for a specific file by name or content, you can use the search capabilities of OneDrive for Business and SharePoint. In Listing 8-23, you can see how to search for a file.

LISTING 8-23 Code excerpt to search for files in the root folder of an Office 365 Group

```
var groupDriveItems = await graphClient
    .Groups[unifiedGroupId].Drive.Root.Search("query text")
    .Request()
    .GetAsync();
```

Another common need is the retrieval of conversations from the current group. To do this, you need to make a request for the *Conversations* collection resource. Listing 8-24 illustrates the corresponding sample.

LISTING 8-24 Code excerpt to retrieve all the conversations of an Office 365 Group

```
var groupDriveItems = await graphClient
    .Groups[unifiedGroupId].Conversations
    .Request()
    .GetAsync();
```

One last common use case is the retrieval of one or more events from the group's calendar. There is an *Events* collection property for the group, and you can make a request for it, like Listing 8-25 does.

LISTING 8-25 Code excerpt to retrieve all the events of an Office 365 Group

```
var groupEvents = await graphClient
    .Groups[unifiedGroupId].Events
    .Request()
    .GetAsync();
```

All of these collections are also available for management of their resources. For example, if you want to add a new topic to a group conversation, you can use a syntax like the one illustrated in Listing 8-26.

```
var posts = new ConversationThreadPostsCollectionPage();
posts.Add(new Post { Body = new ItemBody {
    Content = "Welcome to this group!",
    ContentType = BodyType.Text,
} });

var ct = new ConversationThread {
    Topic = "The Microsoft Graph SDK!",
    Posts = posts
};

var unifiedGroups = await graphClient.Groups
    .Request()
    .Filter("groupTypes/any(grp: grp eq 'Unified')")
    .GetAsync();

var groupEvents = await graphClient
    .Groups[unifiedGroups.FirstOrDefault().Id].Threads
    .Request()
    .AddAsync(ct);
```

As you can see from reading the code samples, you need to create an instance of type *ConversationThread*, providing the mandatory *Topic* property and one or more instances of *Post* resources.

In Listing 8-27, you can see how to add a new event in the group's calendar.

LISTING 8-27 Code excerpt to add a new event in the calendar of an Office 365 Group

```
Event evt = new Event {
    Subject = "Created with Graph SDK",
    Body = new ItemBody {
        Content = "<h1>Office 365 Party!</h1>",
        ContentType = BodyType.Html,
    },
    Start = new DateTimeTimeZone {
        DateTime = DateTime.Now.AddDays(1).ToUniversalTime()
            .ToString("yyyy-MM-ddThh:mm:ss"),
        TimeZone = "UTC",
    },
    End = new DateTimeTimeZone {
        DateTime = DateTime.Now.AddDays(2).ToUniversalTime()
            .ToString("yyyy-MM-ddThh:mm:ss"),
        TimeZone = "UTC",
    },
    Location = new Location {
        Address = new PhysicalAddress {
            City = "Redmond",
            CountryOrRegion = "USA",
            State = "WA",
```

```
            Street = "Microsft Way",
            PostalCode = "98052",
        },
        DisplayName = "Microsoft Corp. HQ",
    },
    Type = EventType.SingleInstance,
    ShowAs = FreeBusyStatus.Busy,
};

var groupEvents = await graphClient
    .Groups[unifiedGroups.FirstOrDefault().Id].Events
    .Request()
    .AddAsync(evt);
```

The syntax is pretty self-explanatory. First, you have to create an instance of the *Microsoft.Graph.Event* type. Then, you have to pass it to the *AddAsync* method of the collection of *Events* for the current group. Note that the *Start* and *End* properties of the *Event* type have to be provided in a specific date and time format. Thus, the code sample makes a custom *ToString* call to reproduce the required behavior.

Managing current user's photo

Managing the current user's photo is another frequently used capability, and it is similar to handling the photo of an Office 365 Group.

In Listing 8-28, you can see an excerpt of a code sample that retrieves the current user's photo.

LISTING 8-28 Code excerpt to retrieve the current user's photo by using the Microsoft Graph SDK

```
// Get the photo of the current user
var userPhotoStream = await graphClient.Me.Photo.Content.Request().GetAsync();

using (FileStream fs = new FileStream(@"..\..\user-photo-original.png",
    FileMode.OpenOrCreate, FileAccess.Write, FileShare.None)) {
        userPhotoStream.CopyTo(fs);
}
```

As you can see, any user resource—including the current user (*Me*)—has a *Photo* property that provides a *Content* property. You just need to invoke the *GetAsync* method against the *Request* method of the *Content*. The result of the *GetAsync* method is an object of type *System.IO.Stream* that you can consume freely. The code sample in Listing 8-28 saves the image on the local file system.

Updating the current user's photo is even more interesting, as illustrated in Listing 8-29.

```
// Upload a new photo for the current user
using (FileStream fs = new FileStream(@"..\..\user-photo-two.png", FileMode.Open,
    FileAccess.Read, FileShare.Read)) {
    try {
        await graphClient.Me.Photo.Content.Request().PutAsync(fs);
    }
    catch (ServiceException ex) {
        Console.WriteLine(ex.Error);
        if (ex.IsMatch(GraphErrorCode.AccessDenied.ToString()))
            Console.WriteLine("Access Denied! Fix permission scopes ...")
        }
        else if (ex.IsMatch(GraphErrorCode.ThrottledRequest.ToString())) {
            Console.WriteLine("Please retry ...");
        }
    }
}
```

The sample is straightforward. You have to get a reference to the *Content* property of the user's *Photo*, and after that you have to invoke the *PutAsync* method, providing an argument of type *System. IO.Stream* that represents the content of the image to upload. Of course, you will need to have proper permissions for the client application to be able to update the user's picture.

Managing current user's manager and direct reports

In real business solutions, you often have to provide organization charts or escalate tasks from direct reports to managers. Thus, being able to read who are the direct reports of a user or who is the manager of a user is really useful—as is managing users' hierarchical relationships in general.

The Microsoft Graph, as you saw in Chapter 6, provides a couple of operations for getting the manager or the direct reports of a user. In Listing 8-30, you can see how to retrieve the current user's manager, which is a use case that can be applied to any user resource, not only to the current user.

LISTING 8-30 Code excerpt to retrieve the current user's manager by using the Microsoft Graph SDK

```
var managerPointer = await graphClient.Me.Manager.Request().GetAsync();

var manager = await graphClient.Users[managerPointer.Id].Request()
    .Select("DisplayName").GetAsync();

if (manager != null) {
    Console.WriteLine("Your manager is: {0}", manager.DisplayName);
}
```

Notice that the *Manager* property of the user resource gives you back only the ID of the target manager, not the whole directory object. Thus, if you want to retrieve any property of the manager, you will have to make one more request, targeting the collection of *Users* of the *GraphServiceClient* object and providing the ID as the key to access the proper user resource. Moreover, the *Manager* property of the user object provides a *Reference* property, which can be retrieved through the *Request* method. The *Manager.Reference* resource provides a *DeleteAsync* method that can be used to unlink the current user from his manager.

Furthermore, the direct reports can be retrieved by querying the *DirectReports* collection property of the target user resource. Because there can be many direct reports, the collection supports paging. In Listing 8-31, you can see a sample of how to retrieve a list of direct reports for the current user, without paging.

LISTING 8-31 Code excerpt to retrieve the current user's direct reports by using the Microsoft Graph SDK

```
var reports = await graphClient.Me.DirectReports.Request().GetAsync();

if (reports.Count > 0) {
    Console.WriteLine("Here are your direct reports:");
    foreach (var r in reports) {
        var report = await graphClient.Users[r.Id].Request()
            .Select("DisplayName").GetAsync();

        Console.WriteLine(report.DisplayName);
    }
}
else {
    Console.WriteLine("You don't have direct reports!");
}
```

The sample is straightforward and just browses the direct report resources. Like the manager resource, the direct reports provide only the ID of the target directory object. Thus, you will have to query explicitly for every direct report resource that you want to use, if any.

To add a direct report to a user, you can invoke the *AddAsync* method against the *Request* provided by the *References* property of the *DirectReports* user's property.

Based on what you just saw, there are methods to add direct reports to a user and to delete the manager reference from a user. However, there are no direct methods to add or change the manager of a user or to delete the direct reports from a user. Nevertheless, you can achieve all of the possible results by leveraging the available methods in the right sequence.

If you want to add or change a manager of a user, you can just add that user as a direct report for her manager. If you want to remove a direct report of a user, you can delete his manager's reference. Last, if you want to change the direct reports of a user, you can assign them as direct reports of a new manager or delete their manager's reference.

Uploading a file to OneDrive for Business

A common use case in business solutions is to upload files onto OneDrive for Business.

As you saw in Chapter 7, "File services," in the section "Uploading and updating files," to upload a new file by using the Microsoft Graph you first need to create it as a new child of type *DriveItem* in the collection of children items of the target folder. In Listing 8-32, you can see how to create a new file in the root folder of the current user's OneDrive for Business.

LISTING 8-32 Code excerpt to create a new file in current user's OneDrive for Business root folder by using the Microsoft Graph SDK

```
var newFile = new Microsoft.Graph.DriveItem {
    File = new Microsoft.Graph.File(),
    Name = "filename.ext",
};

newFile = await graphClient.Me.Drive.Root.Children.Request().AddAsync(newFile);
```

Notice that the file has to be provided as a *DriveItem* instance and that at a minimum you have to configure the *File* property and the *Name* property. As you saw in Chapter 7, creating a folder or a specific file type like a picture or a video will use the same approach, setting the proper properties on the *DriveItem* instance.

Once you have created the *DriveItem* instance, you can add the item to the collection of children of the target folder, which is the root folder in Listing 8-32.

So far, you have only created a new item in the target folder. Now you need to upload the real content of the file, which is also useful if you need to update the content of an existing file. Every drive item resource provides the *Content* property, which can be used to update the file content by requesting the content resource and invoking the *PutAsync* method. The *PutAsync* method accepts an argument of type *System.IO.Stream*, which represents the binary content of the file. In Listing 8-33, you can see how to upload or update the content of a target file.

LISTING 8-33 Code excerpt to upload or update the content of a file in OneDrive for Business by using the Microsoft Graph SDK

```
using (FileStream fs = new FileStream(@"..\..\user-photo-two.png", FileMode.Open,
    FileAccess.Read, FileShare.Read)) {
    var newFileContent = await graphClient.Me.Drive.Items[newFile.Id].Content
        .Request().PutAsync<DriveItem>(fs);
}
```

Notice that the result of the *PutAsync* method will be the just-uploaded or updated *DriveItem*.

Searching for files in OneDrive for Business

Today, every user has a huge number of files and folders in her OneDrive for Business. Thus, being able to search for something is fundamental.

The Microsoft Graph SDK enables you to leverage the search capabilities of OneDrive for Business by invoking a *Search* method, which is available for every *DriveItem* resource, where the resource should be a folder. You saw this method when searching for files in an Office 365 Group.

In Listing 8-34, you can evaluate a code sample to make a free text search against the root folder of the current user's OneDrive for Business.

LISTING 8-34 Sample to search files in OneDrive for Business by using the Microsoft Graph SDK

```
var searchResults = await graphClient.Me.Drive.Root
    .Search(queryText).Request().GetAsync();

Int32 pageCount = 0;

while (true) {
    pageCount++;
    Console.WriteLine("Page: {0}", pageCount);
    foreach (var result in searchResults) {
        Console.WriteLine("{0} - {1}\n{2}\n", result.Id, result.Name, result.WebUrl);
    }
    if (searchResults.NextPageRequest != null) {
        searchResults = await searchResults.NextPageRequest.GetAsync()
    }
    else {
        break;
    }
}
```

Because the number of results is unpredictable and could be very large, the code sample leverages the paging capabilities of the Microsoft Graph SDK to browse all the results.

Moreover, consider that the search query results are provided through an instance type that implements the *IDriveItemSearchCollectionPage* interface. Thus, every result will be an object of type *Microsoft.Graph.DriveItem*, and you can apply querying methods like *Select*, *Filter*, *OrderBy*, and so on to the result so that you can partition, order, and project the results based on your needs.

Downloading a file from OneDrive for Business

The last use case that we will consider in this chapter is the download of a file. If you search for one or more files, you most likely will want to access the content of those files.

The Microsoft Graph SDK enables you to consume (that is, download) the content of a file with an easy technique. You just need to make a request for the *Content* property of an object of type *DriveItem*. In Listing 8-35, you can see how to achieve the result.

LISTING 8-35 Sample to download the content of a file stored in OneDrive for Business by using the Microsoft Graph SDK

```
var file = await graphClient.Me.Drive.Items[driveItemId]
    .Request().Select("id,Name").GetAsync();
var fileContent = await graphClient.Me.Drive.Items[driveItemId]
    .Content.Request().GetAsync();

using (FileStream fs = new FileStream(@"..\..\" + file.Name, FileMode.CreateNew,
    FileAccess.Write, FileShare.None)) {
        fileContent.CopyTo(fs);
}
```

Because by requesting the *Content* property you will get back an object of type *System.IO.Stream*, if you also want to retrieve metadata information like the file name or its content type you will have to make a separate request selecting what you need against the target resource.

In Listing 8-35, we just download the file and save it onto the file system, retrieving the name of the file from the Graph API.

Summary

In this chapter, you learned about the new Microsoft Graph SDK for .NET, which is an object model Microsoft provides to make it easy to consume the Microsoft Graph API without having to dig into the HTTP and REST protocol details.

Throughout the chapter, you examined the architecture of the SDK and saw how to authenticate by using either ADAL for Azure AD or MSAL for the new v2 authentication endpoint. Moreover, you learned about the request model and the querying model of the Graph SDK.

You saw how to do paging of collections, how to manage items of collections, and how to do exceptions handling properly.

Last, you had a preview of some of the most common use cases, which can be useful whenever you need to create real business-level solutions using the Microsoft Graph API and the Microsoft Graph SDK for .NET.

## CHAPTER 9

SharePoint REST API

Since Microsoft SharePoint 2013, SharePoint has included a rich set of REST (Representational State Transfer) API, which is useful for creating SharePoint Add-ins, SharePoint workflows, and other software solutions. The SharePoint REST API gives any platform access to many key objects, properties, and methods that are also available via the client-side object model (CSOM). The new API provides a rich set of REST URIs that you can access via HTTP and XML/JSON (JavaScript Object Notation) for consuming nearly every capability of the CSOM. All you need is a third-party technology capable of consuming REST services. In this chapter, you will learn about the architecture of this REST API and how to manage the most common tasks for everyday programming needs.

Introducing the REST API

The overall architecture of the REST API is based on the *client.svc* Windows Communication Foundation (WCF) service, which serves the classic CSOM and also implements an OData-compliant endpoint.

 More Information stands for Open Data Protocol, and you can read more about it at *http://www.odata.org/*.

You can access the REST API at the relative URL *_api/* of any SharePoint site. For example, to access the API targeting the root site collection of a target web application, you can open your browser and navigate to a URL such as the following:

> *https://<your-tenant>.sharepoint.com/_api/site*

where *<your-tenant>.sharepoint.com* is the host name of a sample web application hosted in Microsoft Office 365. However, the SharePoint REST API is also available on-premises. The previous URL is just an alias of the real URL of the WCF service under the cover of the REST API, which is:

> *https://<your-tenant>.sharepoint.com/_vti_bin/client.svc/site*

This is just an additional RESTful endpoint that publishes the capabilities of the classic CSOM through the OData protocol. By browsing to such a URL, you will see that the result is an XML representation—based on the ATOM protocol—of information about the current site collection. (When using Internet Explorer, be sure to disable the feed-reading view in the browser's content properties.) At the beginning of the ATOM response, there is a list of links targeting many additional URLs for accessing information and API related to the current site collection. At the end of the response, there are some properties specific to the current site collection.

Here are some other commonly used URLs of API, which are useful while developing on SharePoint:

- **https://<your-tenant>.sharepoint.com/_api/web** Use to access the information about the target website.

- **https://<your-tenant>.sharepoint.com/_api/web/lists** Use to access the collection of lists in the target website.

- **https://<your-tenant>.sharepoint.com/_api/web/lists/GetByTitle('Title of the List')** Use to access the information of a specific list instance, selected by title.

- **https://<your-tenant>.sharepoint.com/_api/search** Use to access the search query engine.

As you can see, the root of any relative endpoint is the _api/ trailer, which can be followed by many API targets (as the following section will illustrate) and corresponds to the most common artifacts of SharePoint. As with many REST services, you can communicate with this REST API not only by using the browser, invoking URLs with the HTTP GET method, but also by using a client capable of communicating over HTTP and parsing ATOM or JSON responses. Depending on the HTTP *Accept* header provided within the request, the REST service will provide ATOM (*Accept: application/atom+xml*) or JSON (*Accept: application/json;odata=verbose*) answers. By default, REST service responses are presented by using the ATOM protocol according to the OData specification.

Depending on the HTTP method and headers (*X-Http-Method*) you use, you can take advantage of various capabilities of the API, such as a complete CRUDQ (create, read, update, delete, and query) set of methods. The available HTTP methods and headers are as follows:

- **GET** These requests typically represent read operations that apply to objects, properties, or methods and return information.

- **POST** Without any additional *X-Http-Method* header, this method is used for creation operations. For example, you can use POST to post a file to a library, post an item to a list, or post a new list definition for creation in a target website. While invoking POST operations against a target object, any property that is not required and is not specified in the HTTP invocation will be set to its default value. If you provide a value for a read-only property, you will get an exception.

- **PUT, PATCH, and MERGE** These requests are used for update operations. You can use PUT to update an object. While invoking PUT operations, you should specify all writable properties. If any property is missing, the operation could fail or could set the missing properties back to their default values. The PATCH and MERGE operations are based on the POST method, with the addition of an *X-Http-Method* header with a value of *PATCH* or *MERGE*. They are equivalent, and you should always use the former because the latter is provided for backward compatibility only. Like PUT, PATCH and MERGE handle update operations. The big difference is that with PATCH and MERGE, any writeable property that is not specified will retain its current value.

- **DELETE** These requests are for deleting an item and can be implemented with POST plus the additional *X-Http-Method* header with a value of *DELETE*. If you invoke this operation against recyclable objects, SharePoint will move them to the Recycle Bin.

Listing 9-1 demonstrates how to use the new REST API from within PowerShell. The sample is intentionally written using a PowerShell script to demonstrate that the REST API is available to any platform and any technology landscape. The code reads the title of a list instance in a target website. Moreover, this sample leverages a useful and powerful set of PowerShell extensions for Microsoft SharePoint Online and Office 365, which are available through the Office 365 Developer Patterns & Practices (PnP) community project.[1]

LISTING 9-1 A sample PowerShell script for reading the title of a list instance in a target website using the REST API

```
# Connect to SharePoint Online
$targetSite = "https://<your-tenant>.sharepoint.com/sites/<Site-Name>/"
$targetSiteUri = [System.Uri]$targetSite
Connect-SPOnline $targetSite

# Retrieve the client credentials and the related Authentication Cookies
$context = (Get-SPOWeb).Context
$credentials = $context.Credentials
$authenticationCookies = $credentials.GetAuthenticationCookie($targetSiteUri, $true)

# Set the Authentication Cookies and the Accept HTTP Header
$webSession = New-Object Microsoft.PowerShell.Commands.WebRequestSession
$webSession.Cookies.SetCookies($targetSiteUri, $authenticationCookies)
$webSession.Headers.Add("Accept", "application/json;odata=verbose")

# Set request variables
$targetLibrary = "Documents"
$apiUrl = "$targetSite" + "_api/web/lists/getByTitle('$targetLibrary')"

# Make the REST request
$webRequest = Invoke-WebRequest -Uri $apiUrl -Method Get -WebSession $webSession

# Consume the JSON result
$jsonLibrary = $webRequest.Content | ConvertFrom-Json
Write-Host $jsonLibrary.d.Title
```

The sample code invokes a *GET* method through the *Invoke-WebRequest* cmdlet. However, before invoking the HTTP request, it logs into SharePoint Online using the custom *Connect-SPOnline* cmdlet and invokes the *GetAuthenticationCookie* method provided by the *SharePointOnlineCredentials* type, retrieving the authentication cookies required by SharePoint Online and Microsoft Azure Active Directory (Azure AD).

---

[1] For further details about the Office 365 Developer Patterns & Practices community project, you can browse to the following URL: *http://aka.ms/OfficeDevPnP*. The PowerShell extensions, which have been created by Erwin van Hunen (*https://twitter.com/erwinvanhunen*), can be installed from the following URL: *https://github.com/OfficeDev/PnP-PowerShell/tree/master/Binaries*. They are available in three flavors: SharePointPnPPowerShell2013.msi targets SharePoint 2013 on-premises, SharePointPnPPowerShell2016.msi targets SharePoint 2016 on-premises, and SharePointPnPPowerShellOnline.msi targets SharePoint Online.

You can achieve the same goal with any other programming or scripting language capable of communicating over HTTP and managing ATOM or JSON contents. For testing purposes, you can also play with tools like Fiddler Composer (*http://www.fiddler2.com*) to test the behavior and the responses provided by the REST API.

API reference

Every method offered by the REST API can be invoked by using a reference URL, which is made according to the schema illustrated in Figure 9-1.

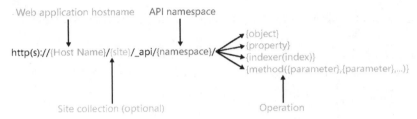

FIGURE 9-1 The schema of the URL of any REST API published by SharePoint

The protocol moniker can be *http* or *https*, depending on the web application configuration. If you target Microsoft SharePoint Online, it will be https. The *{hostname}* argument is the host name—which will include the fully qualified domain name—of the target web application. For Microsoft SharePoint Online, it will be *<your-tenant>.sharepoint.com*. The subsequent *{site}* is the target site collection and is optional because you could target the root site collection. Following the *_api* trailer is a *{namespace}* argument that corresponds to one of the target families of API. Table 9-1 lists some of the main available namespaces. The URL ends with a reference to an *{object}*, a specific *{property}*, an *{indexer}*, or a *{method}* call. Indexers will be followed by a numeric *{index}* argument, while method calls could be followed by *{parameter}* arguments. For some operations, the arguments can be provided as a JSON object in the HTTP POST request body.

TABLE 9-1 The main namespaces available in URLs of the REST API

Namespace	Target
site	The current site collection. Can be used to browse site collection properties and configuration and corresponds to the Microsoft.SharePoint.Client.Site class of the CSOM.
web	The current website. Can be used to browse website properties, configuration, and contents and corresponds to the Microsoft.SharePoint.Client.Web class of the CSOM.
SP.UserProfiles.PeopleManager	The APIs for working with the User Profile Service (UPS) within the context of the current user. Corresponds to the Microsoft.SharePoint.Client.UserProfiles.PeopleManager class of the CSOM.
ContextInfo	Retrieves the context of the current session, which corresponds to the serialization of an object of type Microsoft.SharePoint.SPContextWebInformation.
search	The search engine of SharePoint. Can be used to search content and suggestions.
social.feed	The social capabilities. Includes operations for accessing social feeds, followers, followed content, and so on. These capabilities are related to the early social features of SharePoint and are available for backward compatibility only.

The REST API offers about 2,000 classes and more than 6,000 members, which are available throughout the hierarchy of objects of the CSOM using the preceding namespaces as root objects. The first three namespaces are easy to manage and understand because you just need to reference the corresponding CSOM types and compose the request URLs. For example, the *Site* class of the *Microsoft. SharePoint.Client* namespace offers a property with name *Owner* and type *User*. By using the REST API, you can invoke the GET verb to retrieve the following URL:

```
https://<your-tenant>.sharepoint.com/_api/site/owner
```

To invoke the *GetWebTemplates* method, which accepts the *culture* parameter, you can invoke the following URL:

```
https://<your-tenant>.sharepoint.com/_api/site/GetWebTemplates(1033)
```

The value 1033 provided is the en-US culture. Consult the CSOM online reference (*http://msdn .microsoft.com/en-us/library/ee544361.aspx*) to see all the available properties, methods, and members.

Notice that for security reasons, all the operations that modify data will require a security form digest with a name of *X-RequestDigest* in the HTTP request headers. To retrieve the value needed for this header, you have a couple of options:

- Working in JavaScript, inside a webpage directly hosted in SharePoint or a SharePoint-hosted add-in, you can retrieve the value of the digest from a hidden *INPUT* field with an ID value of *__REQUESTDIGEST*. For example, using jQuery, you can reference the field with the following syntax: *$("#__REQUESTDIGEST").val()*.

- Working in any other context, you can invoke (using the *POST* method) the *ContextInfo* namespace and retrieve the form digest value from the ATOM or JSON response. By default, the form digest retrieved through this method will expire in 1,800 seconds.

Listing 9-2 shows the JSON output of the *ContextInfo* method invocation. The form digest value is highlighted in bold.

LISTING 9-2 The JSON output of the *ContextInfo* method invocation

```
{
  "d": {
    "GetContextWebInformation": {
      "__metadata": {
        "type":"SP.ContextWebInformation"
      },
      "FormDigestTimeoutSeconds":1800,
      "FormDigestValue":"0x3C8E83432D855AC62850B198CDE3D4A3CF
A2D081864200B78ED5A8A053014DB4DC5AA5733F34DE47419A87604
D86A186870353B830D9185F85A3770BA0888773,06 Jul 2015 21:19:58 -0000",
      "LibraryVersion":"16.0.4208.1220",
      "SiteFullUrl":"https://piasysdev.sharepoint.com/sites/ProgrammingOffice365",
      "SupportedSchemaVersions": {
        "__metadata": {
          "type":"Collection(Edm.String)"
```

```
      },
      "results": [
        "14.0.0.0",
        "15.0.0.0"
      ]
    },
    "WebFullUrl":"https://piasysdev.sharepoint.com/sites/ProgrammingOffice365"
    }
  }
}
```

Listing 9-3 provides a code excerpt of a PowerShell script that invokes the *EnsureUser* method of a target website, providing a value for the form digest HTTP header, which is called *X-RequestDigest*, after extracting that value from the *ContextInfo* method.

LISTING 9-3 A PowerShell code excerpt for invoking the *EnsureUser* method of a target website via the REST API

```
$global:webSession = New-Object Microsoft.PowerShell.Commands.WebRequestSession

function Initialize-SPOSecuritySession {
    param ($targetSite)

    # Connect to SharePoint Online
    $targetSiteUri = [System.Uri]$targetSite
    Connect-SPOnline $targetSite

    # Retrieve the client credentials and the related Authentication Cookies
    $context = (Get-SPOWeb).Context
    $credentials = $context.Credentials
    $authenticationCookies = $credentials.GetAuthenticationCookie($targetSiteUri, $true)

    # Set the Authentication Cookies and the Accept HTTP Header
    $global:webSession.Cookies.SetCookies($targetSiteUri, $authenticationCookies)
    $global:webSession.Headers.Add("Accept", "application/json;odata=verbose")
}

function Initialize-SPODigestValue {
    param ($targetSite)

    $contextInfoUrl = $targetSite + "_api/ContextInfo"

    $webRequest = Invoke-WebRequest -Uri $contextInfoUrl -Method Post
        -WebSession $global:webSession

    $jsonContextInfo = $webRequest.Content | ConvertFrom-Json

    $digestValue = $jsonContextInfo.d.GetContextWebInformation.FormDigestValue
    $global:webSession.Headers.Add("X-RequestDigest", $digestValue)
}

$targetSite = "https://<your-tenant>.sharepoint.com/sites/<Site-Name>/"
Initialize-SPOSecuritySession -targetSite $targetSite
```

```
Initialize-SPODigestValue -targetSite $targetSite

# Define the EnsureUser REST API call
$ensureUserUrl = $targetSite + "_api/web/EnsureUser('username@domain.tld')"

# Make the REST request
$webRequest = Invoke-WebRequest -Uri $ensureUserUrl -Method Post
    -WebSession $global:webSession

# Check the result
if ($webRequest.StatusCode -ne 200) {
    Write-Host "Error:" $webRequest.StatusDescription
}
else {
    Write-Host $webRequest.StatusDescription
}
```

So far, you have seen that all the REST requests were decorated with the *Accept* HTTP header and configured with a value of *application/json;odata=verbose*. This header instructs the OData engine to give back a JSON (application/json) response with a rich set of information (metadata) about the type of the result. This capability could be useful if you query unknown data structures and want to retrieve not only the data but also the data type because you want to update the data back to SharePoint. However, often you consume data sets by themselves, in read-only mode and with a fixed set of fields. Having all the metadata information of what is coming back from the server in every response could be noisy and expensive. That is why the international community defined the so-called JSON Light protocol and why Office 365 supports the JSON Light format since August 2014. JSON Light is an open standard that allows developers to provide in the HTTP headers of the REST requests how much metadata has to be returned. The supported values for the *Accept* HTTP header are:

- *application/json;odata=verbose*

- *application/json;odata=minimalmetadata*

- *application/json;odata=nometadata*

The first option is the most common and well known, and it retrieves all the metadata available from the HTTP server. In the following excerpt, you can see a JSON object retrieved with the *verbose* option by using a customized OData query that retrieves the ID and the Title of a single document from a library with the *EMail* field of the document's Author. The metadata information is highlighted in bold.

```
{"d":
  {"__metadata":
    {"id":"00af8a37-6fbd-454b-bd02-8fe1b74f8c41",
     "uri":"https://<your-tenant>.sharepoint.com/sites/<Site-Name>/_api/Web/...",
     "etag":"\"2\"",
     "type":"SP.Data.Sample_x0020_LibraryItem"},
   "Author":
    {"__metadata":
      {"id":"8d8bbb4d-aa28-4a9b-be38-30cb8667fb2e",
       "type":"SP.Data.UserInfoItem"},
```

```
     "EMail":"<author>@<your-tenant>.onmicrosoft.com"},
  "Id":1,
  "Title":"Sample-File-03",
  "ID":1}
}
```

The second option—which is now the default in Office 365 if you don't specify the *odata* attribute in the *Accept* request header—instructs the engine to release minimal metadata information. In the following excerpt, you can see the JSON result of the same query as before, but with the *minimalmetadata* option.

```
{"odata.metadata":"https://<your-tenant>.sharepoint.com/sites/<Site-Name>/_api/$metadata#...",
 "odata.type":"SP.Data.Sample_x0020_LibraryItem",
 "odata.id":"50be68eb-be36-46b0-a3ef-6a8452a134cd",
 "odata.etag":"\"2\"",
 "odata.editLink":"Web/Lists(guid'70473747-fda3-4a81-a16a-3231f2876aa7')/Items(1)",
 "Author@odata.navigationLinkUrl":"Web/Lists(guid'70473747-fda3-4a81-a16a-3231f2876aa7')/
Items(1)/Author",
 "Author":
   {"odata.type":"SP.Data.UserInfoItem",
    "odata.id":"4cdc633c-8f3a-41e5-87ec-8117256b409b",
    "EMail":"<author>@<your-tenant>.onmicrosoft.com"},
 "Id":1,
 "Title":"Sample-File-03",
 "ID":1
}
```

The last option, *nometadata*, declares to skip any metadata information. It is the lightest solution if you just need the data and don't want to focus on metadata. Here, you can see an excerpt of a JSON object, the same as before, retrieved with the *nometadata* option.

```
{"Author":
   {"EMail":"<author>@<your-tenant>.onmicrosoft.com"},
  "Id":1,
  "Title":"Sample-File-03",
  "ID":1}
```

In SharePoint on-premises, the JSON Light support is provided since SharePoint 2013 Service Pack 1.

Querying data

Another useful capability of the REST API is support for OData querying. Every time you invoke an operation that returns a collection of entities, you can also provide an OData-compliant set of query string parameters for sorting, filtering, paging, and projecting that collection. For example, imagine querying the list of items available in a document library. The URL would be:

https://<your-tenant>.sharepoint.com/_api/web/lists/GetByTitle('Documents')/Items

If you are interested in the list of files in the root folder of the library, the corresponding URL is:

https://<your-tenant>.sharepoint.com/_api/web/lists/GetByTitle('Documents')/RootFolder/Files

According to the OData specification, you can append the following querying parameters to the URL:

- **$filter** Defines partitioning criteria on the current entity set. For example, you can provide the query string argument *$filter=substringof('Budget',Name)%20eq%20true* to retrieve documents with *Budget* in their file name.

- **$select** Projects only a subset of properties (fields) of the entities in the current entity set. For example, you can provide a value of *$select=Name,Author* to retrieve only the file name and the author of every file in the entity set.

- **$orderby** Sorts data returned by the query. You can provide query string arguments with a syntax like *$sort=TimeLastModified%20desc,Name%20asc* to sort files descending by *TimeLastModified* and ascending by *Name*.

- **$top** Selects the first N items of the current entity set. Use the syntax *$top=5* to retrieve only the first five entities from the entity set.

- **$skip** Skips the first N items of the current entity set. Use the syntax *$skip=10* to skip the first 10 entities of the entity set.

- **$expand** Automatically and implicitly resolves and expands a relationship between an entity in the current entity set and another related entity. For example, you can use the syntax *$expand=Author* to retrieve the author of a file.

The arguments provided to an OData query must be URL encoded because they are passed to the query engine via REST, through the URL of the service. Space characters must be converted into *%20*, for example, and any other non-alphanumeric characters must be converted into their corresponding encoded values.

In the previous examples, you saw a quick preview of the available functions and operators for filtering entities with OData. Table 9-2 provides the full list of the available logical operations defined in the OData core specification. You can read the official core documentation of OData at *http://docs. oasis-open.org/odata/odata/v4.0/odata-v4.0-part1-protocol.html*. The operators in bold are supported by the SharePoint REST API.

TABLE 9-2 The logical operations available in the OData core specification

Operator	Description	Example
eq	Equal	/Suppliers?$filter=Address/City eq 'Redmond'
ne	Not equal	/Suppliers?$filter=Address/City ne 'London'
gt	Greater than	/Products?$filter=Price gt 20
ge	Greater than or equal to	/Products?$filter=Price ge 10
lt	Less than	/Products?$filter=Price lt 20
le	Less than or equal to	/Products?$filter=Price le 100
has	Has flags	/Products?$filter=Style has Sales.Color'Yellow'

Operator	Description	Example
and	Logical and	/Products?$filter=Price le 200 and Price gt 3.5
or	Logical or	/Products?$filter=Price le 3.5 or Price gt 200
not	Logical negation	/Products?$filter=not endswith(Description,'milk')

There are also some arithmetic operators, which are listed in Table 9-3.

TABLE 9-3 The arithmetic operators available in the OData core specification

Operator	Description	Example
add	Addition	/Products?$filter=Price add 5 gt 10
sub	Subtraction	/Products?$filter=Price sub 5 gt 10
mul	Multiplication	/Products?$filter=Price mul 2 gt 2000
div	Division	/Products?$filter=Price div 2 gt 4
mod	Modulo	/Products?$filter=Price mod 2 eq 0

None of the arithmetic operators defined in the OData core specification are supported by the SharePoint REST API. While defining a query, you can compose operators using parentheses ( ) to group elements and define precedence. For example, you can write the following:

```
/Products?$filter=(Price sub 5) gt 10
```

Last, in queries for partitioning data, you can also use functions for strings, dates, math, and types. Table 9-4 provides the full list of functions available in the OData specification. Again, the operators highlighted in bold are those supported by the SharePoint REST API.

TABLE 9-4 The functions available in the OData core specification for querying entities

Function	Description	Example
bool contains(string searchInString, string searchString)	Returns a Boolean value stating whether the field provided in the first argument contains the string value of the second argument.	contains(CompanyName, 'Alfreds')
bool substringof(string searchString, string searchInString)	Returns a Boolean value stating whether the value provided in the first argument is a substring of the second argument. Can be used as a replacement for the contains method.	substringof('Alfreds',CompanyName)
bool endswith(string string, string suffixString)	Returns a Boolean value declaring whether the string provided in the first argument ends with the string provided in the second argument.	endswith(CompanyName,'Futterkiste')
bool startswith(string string, string prefixString)	Returns a Boolean value declaring whether the string provided in the first argument starts with the string provided in the second argument.	startswith(CompanyName,'Alfr')

Function	Description	Example
int length(string string)	Returns an integer value representing the length of the string provided as the argument.	length(CompanyName) eq 19
int indexof(string searchInString, string searchString)	Returns an integer value representing the index of the string provided in the second argument, which is searched within the string provided in the first argument.	indexof(CompanyName,'lfreds') eq 1
string replace(string searchInString, string searchString, string replaceString)	Replaces the string provided in the second argument with the string provided in the third argument, searching within the first string argument.	replace(CompanyName,' ', '') eq 'AlfredsFutterkiste'
string substring(string string, int pos)	Returns a substring of the string provided in the first argument, starting from the integer position provided in the second argument.	substring(CompanyName,1) eq 'lfreds Futterkiste'
string substring(string string, int pos, int length)	Returns a substring of the string provided in the first argument, starting from the integer position provided in the second argument and stopping after a number of characters provided in the third integer argument.	substring(CompanyName,1, 2) eq 'lf'
string tolower(string string)	Returns a string that is the lowercase conversion of the string provided as the string argument.	tolower(CompanyName) eq 'alfreds futterkiste'
string toupper(string string)	Returns a string that is the uppercase conversion of the string provided as the string argument.	toupper(CompanyName) eq 'ALFREDS FUTTERKISTE'
string trim(string string)	Returns a string trimmed of spaces based on the string provided as the argument.	trim(CompanyName) eq 'Alfreds Futterkiste'
string concat(string string1, string string2)	Returns a string that is the concatenation of the two string arguments provided.	concat(concat(City,', '), Country) eq 'Berlin, Germany'
int year(DateTime datetimeValue)	Returns an integer that corresponds to the year of the datetime value provided as the argument.	year(BirthDate) eq 1948
int month(DateTime datetimeValue)	Returns an integer that corresponds to the month of the datetime value provided as the argument.	month(BirthDate) eq 12
int day(DateTime datetimeValue)	Returns an integer that corresponds to the day of the datetime value provided as the argument.	day(BirthDate) eq 8
int hour(DateTime datetimeValue)	Returns an integer that corresponds to the hour of the datetime value provided as the argument.	hour(StartTime) eq 1
int minute(DateTime datetimeValue)	Returns an integer that corresponds to the minute of the datetime value provided as the argument.	minute(StartTime) eq 0

Function	Description	Example
int second(DateTime datetimeValue)	Returns an integer that corresponds to the seconds of the datetime value provided as the argument.	second(StartTime) eq 0
int fractionalseconds(DateTime datetimeValue)	Returns an integer that corresponds to the fractional seconds of the date-time value provided as the argument.	fractionalsecond(StartTime) eq 0
date date(DateTime value)	Returns a value of type date.	date(BirthDate) eq now()
time time(DateTime value)	Returns a value of type time.	time(StartTime) eq now()
totaloffsetminutes	Returns a minutes total offset of the current time.	totaloffsetminutes(StartTime) eq 60
now	Returns the current date and time.	BirthDate ge now()
mindatetime	Returns the minimum datetime value.	StartTime eq mindatetime()
maxdatetime	Returns the maximum datetime value.	EndTime eq maxdatetime()
double round(double doubleValue)	Returns a double number that is the rounded value of the double value provided as the argument.	round(Freight) eq 32
decimal round(decimal decimalValue)	Returns a decimal number that is the rounded value of the decimal value provided as the argument.	round(Freight) eq 32
double floor(double doubleValue)	Returns a double number that is the floor value of the double value provided as the argument.	floor(Freight) eq 32
decimal floor(decimal datetimeValue)	Returns a decimal number that is the floor value of the decimal value provided as the argument.	floor(Freight) eq 32
double ceiling(double doubleValue)	Returns a double number that is the ceiling value of the double value provided as the argument.	ceiling(Freight) eq 33
decimal ceiling(decimal datetime-Value)	Returns a decimal number that is the ceiling value of the decimal value provided as the argument.	ceiling(Freight) eq 33
bool IsOf(type value)	Returns a Boolean value stating if the target entity is of the type provided as the argument.	isof('NorthwindModel.Order')
bool IsOf(expression value, type targetType)	Returns a Boolean value stating if the expression provided as the first argument is of the type provided as the second argument.	isof(ShipCountry,'Edm.String')
geo.distance	Measures the distance between two geolocation places.	geo.distance(CurrentPosition, TargetPosition)
geo.length	Returns the total path length of a linestring.	geo.length(DirectRoute)
geo.intersects	Identifies whether a point is contained within the enclosed space of a polygon.	geo.intersects(Position,TargetArea)

Based on all the information provided in previous paragraphs, you should now be able to understand the following query:

```
https://<your-tenant>.sharepoint.com/_api/web/lists/GetByTitle('Documents')/
RootFolder/Files?$expand=Author&$select=Name,Author/EMail,TimeLastModified&$sort=TimeLastModifi
ed%20desc,Name&$skip=20&$top=10&$filter=substringof('Chapter',Name)%20eq%20true
```

You can disassemble and decode the query string parameters with the information provided in Table 9-5.

TABLE 9-5 The sample query string parameters explained

Query part	Explanation
$expand=Author	Expand the related object author while retrieving the documents.
$select=Name,Author/EMail,TimeLastModified	Retrieve the fields Name, Author/EMail, and TimeLastModified.
$sort=TimeLastModified desc,Name	Sort the output descending by TimeLastModified and ascending by Name.
$skip=20	Skip the first 20 items of the result set (the first two pages of 10 items).
$top=10	Retrieve only the first 10 items of the result set (the third page of 10 items).
$filter= substringof('Chapter',Name) eq true	Retrieve only files with a file name that contains Chapter.

More Information For quick testing and definition of OData queries, you can use LINQPad, which is a smart tool available at the following URL: *http://www.linqpad.net*.

If you are working with the .NET Framework, the OData client library creates such queries for you, allowing you to write LINQ queries on the consumer side. If you are working with any other development technology, you need to understand and write this kind of query.

Managing data

Creating, updating, deleting, and otherwise managing entities by using OData and the REST API is simple if you remember a few rules. First, as you have seen, you must provide the *X-RequestDigest* HTTP header whenever you want to change some data. Second, when managing lists and list items, you need to avoid concurrency conflicts by specifying an additional HTTP header with the name *IF-MATCH*, which assumes a value of *ETag*. To avoid concurrency conflicts, read the *ETag* value by retrieving the target entity (list or list item) with a *GET* method. The *ETag* value will be included in the response HTTP headers and in the response content, regardless of whether it is formatted in ATOM or JSON. Listing 9-4 includes a sample set of HTTP response headers returned by SharePoint Online while selecting a list item via the REST API. The *ETag* header is highlighted in bold, together with the OData version supported (3.0) and the SharePoint build version (16.0.0.4208).

Note The *IF-MATCH* header applies only to lists and list items and can assume a value of *
for situations in which you do not care about concurrency and want to force your action.

LISTING 9-4 A sample set of HTTP response headers returned while querying a list item via the REST API

```
HTTP/1.1 200 OK
Cache-Control: private, max-age=0
Content-Type: application/json;odata=verbose;charset=utf-8
Expires: Sun, 21 Jun 2015 22:48:18 GMT
Last-Modified: Mon, 06 Jul 2015 22:48:18 GMT
ETag: "2"
Server: Microsoft-IIS/8.5
X-SharePointHealthScore: 0
X-SP-SERVERSTATE: ReadOnly=0
DATASERVICEVERSION: 3.0
SPClientServiceRequestDuration: 109
X-AspNet-Version: 4.0.30319
SPRequestGuid: b17b179d-f0b2-2000-3929-0362939a61f8
request-id: b17b179d-f0b2-2000-3929-0362939a61f8
X-FRAME-OPTIONS: SAMEORIGIN
X-Powered-By: ASP.NET
MicrosoftSharePointTeamServices: 16.0.0.4208
X-Content-Type-Options: nosniff
X-MS-InvokeApp: 1; RequireReadOnly
P3P: CP="ALL IND DSP COR ADM CONo CUR CUSo IVAo IVDo PSA PSD TAI TELo OUR SAMo CNT COM INT
NAV ONL PHY PRE PUR UNI"
Date: Mon, 06 Jul 2015 22:48:19 GMT
Content-Length: 2713
```

To better understand how to manage data via the REST API, switch to some JavaScript code
samples, which likely are similar to what you will need while writing SharePoint Add-ins and SharePoint
Framework solutions. For example, the code excerpt of the JavaScript function in Listing 9-5 updates
the title of an item by using the REST API and provides a value for the *ETag* parameter.

LISTING 9-5 A sample code excerpt to update the title of a list item by using JavaScript and the REST API

```
var hostweburl;
var appweburl;
var eTag;

// This code runs when the DOM is ready and creates a context object
// which is needed to use the SharePoint object model
$(document).ready(function () {
    //Get the URI decoded URLs.
    hostweburl = decodeURIComponent(getQueryStringParameter("SPHostUrl"));
    appweburl = decodeURIComponent(getQueryStringParameter("SPAppWebUrl"));

    var scriptbase = hostweburl + "/_layouts/15/";
```

```
        $.getScript(scriptbase + "SP.RequestExecutor.js", execCrossDomainRequest);
});

function execCrossDomainRequest() {
    var contextInfoUri = appweburl + "/_api/contextinfo";
    var itemUri = appweburl +
"/_api/SP.AppContextSite(@target)/web/lists/GetByTitle('Documents')/Items(1)?@target='" +
        hostweburl + "'";

    var executor = new SP.RequestExecutor(appweburl);

    // First request, to retrieve the form digest
    executor.executeAsync({
        url: contextInfoUri,
        method: "POST",
        headers: { "Accept": "application/json; odata=verbose" },
        success: function (data) {
            var jsonObject = JSON.parse(data.body);
            formDigestValue = jsonObject.d.GetContextWebInformation.FormDigestValue;
            updateListItem(formDigestValue, itemUri);
        },
        error: function (data, errorCode, errorMessage) {
            var errMsg = "Error retrieving the form digest value: "
                + errorMessage;
            $("#error").text(errMsg);
        }
    });
}

function updateListItem(formDigestValue, itemUri) {
    var executor = new SP.RequestExecutor(appweburl);
    var newContent = JSON.stringify({ '__metadata': { 'type': 'SP.Data.Shared_x0020_
DocumentsItem' }, 'Title': 'Changed by REST API' });

    // Second request, to retrieve the ETag of the target item
    executor.executeAsync({
        url: itemUri,
        method: "GET",
        headers: { "Accept": "application/json; odata=verbose" },
        success: function (data) {
            $("#message").text('ETag: ' + data.headers["ETAG"]);
            eTag = data.headers["ETAG"];
            internalUpdateListItem(formDigestValue, itemUri, eTag, newContent);
        },
        error: function (data, errorCode, errorMessage) {
            var errMsg = "Error retrieving the eTag value: "
                + errorMessage;
            $("#error").text(errMsg);
        }
    });
}

function internalUpdateListItem(formDigestValue, itemUri, eTag, newContent) {
    var executor = new SP.RequestExecutor(appweburl);
```

```
    // Third request, to change the title of the target item
    executor.executeAsync({
        url:
            appweburl +
"/_api/SP.AppContextSite(@target)/web/lists/GetByTitle('Documents')/Items(1)?@target='" +
            hostweburl + "'",
        method: "POST",
        body: newContent,
        headers: {
            "Accept": "application/json;odata=verbose",
            "content-type": "application/json;odata=verbose",
            "content-length": newContent.length,
            "X-RequestDigest": formDigestValue,
            "X-HTTP-Method": "MERGE",
            "IF-MATCH": eTag
        },
        success: function (data) {
            $("#message").text('Item successfully updated!');
        },
        error: function (data, errorCode, errorMessage) {
            var errMsg = "Error updating list item: "
                + errorMessage;
            $("#error").text(errMsg);
        }
    });
}

// Function to retrieve a query string value.
// For production purposes you may want to use
// a library to handle the query string.
function getQueryStringParameter(paramToRetrieve) {
    var params =
        document.URL.split("?")[1].split("&");
    var strParams = "";
    for (var i = 0; i < params.length; i = i + 1) {
        var singleParam = params[i].split("=");
        if (singleParam[0] == paramToRetrieve)
            return singleParam[1];
    }
}
```

Executing as soon as the DOM document is ready, Listing 9-5 first configures both the app web URL and the host web URL. Then, it configures a scripting file (SP.RequestExecutor.js), which will be discussed in the section "Cross-domain calls" that follows. After startup, the sample code requests the *ContextInfo* via a POST request to extract a valid value for the form digest. If your code runs inside a SharePoint-hosted app, you can read the form digest value from the current page (a hidden field with name __*REQUESTDIGEST*). After retrieving the form digest, the sample gets the item to update to access its *ETag* value. Last, the code runs a POST request against the target item URI, providing the JSON serialization of the changes to apply, the form digest, and the *ETag*.

In the "Common REST API usage" section later in this chapter, you will see many samples based on the concepts demonstrated here. For now, notice that the JavaScript code for invoking the REST API uses an object of type *SP.RequestExecutor* to invoke the service endpoints instead of a classic *jQuery. Ajax* method. In the next section, "Cross-domain calls," you will learn how it works.

One last thing to understand about data management is how the REST API behaves in case of a concurrency conflict. Remember, providing the *ETag* value enables you to identify and manage conflicts; it does not prevent you from experiencing them unless you provide a value of * for the *IF-MATCH* header. For example, imagine that while you're executing the code of Listing 9-5, someone else changes the same target item, confirming the updates before the execution of your code. In a real-world scenario, you should retrieve the *ETag* value as soon as the user starts editing the target item, and you should provide it back to the server while saving your changes. Thus, you could have a short-term concurrency conflict. Every time someone changes an item and saves it, the *ETag* value will change. It is a numeric value, and it will increment by 1 unit whenever a change happens. If a conflict does occur, the update or delete action will fail, and your HTTP request will get back a 412 HTTP status code, which is the Precondition Failed status. Moreover, in the response body, you will find an XML or JSON representation of the error. For example, the JSON response error message will look like the following excerpt:

```
{"error":{"code":"-1, Microsoft.SharePoint.Client.ClientServiceException","message":{"lang":"en-
US","value":"The request ETag value '\"4\"' does not match the object's ETag value '\"5\"'."}}}
```

You can find this object serialized inside the *data* argument of the function invoked if the HTTP request fails due to a concurrency conflict, and the *errorCode* variable will assume a value of –1002. In your custom code, you should catch this kind of exception, prompt the user with a concurrency conflict error, and download the updated item from SharePoint to let the user compare data and make a choice.

Cross-domain calls

When developing SharePoint Add-ins, you typically need to make cross-domain JavaScript calls between the app web, which is the website in which your add-in executes, and the host web, which is the website that is extended through your SharePoint Add-in. Because the domain of the app web is always different from the domain of the host web, this can cause complications. Specifically, browsers prohibit this kind of behavior by default in an effort to avoid cross-domain attacks and related security issues. Luckily, SharePoint provides a JavaScript library to help you satisfy the browsers and keep the calls flowing: the SP.RequestExecutor.js library.

Found in the _layouts/15 folder of every SharePoint site, the SP.RequestExecutor.js library provides out-of-box capabilities to make cross-domain calls against trusted and registered domains. When you instantiate the library's *SP.RequestExecutor* type in your client-side code, it uses a hidden *IFRAME* element and some POST messages and a proxy page (*AppWebProxy.aspx*) to enable you to make highly secure calls—even cross-domain calls.

In Listing 9-5, the startup code adds a reference to the library for making cross-domain calls. Then, it creates an instance of the *SP.RequestExecutor* type, providing the URL of the app web in the object constructor. Behind the scenes, the object injects an IFrame rendering the *AppWebProxy.aspx* page, which calls the host web. When the call to the host web completes, the client instance of the

SP.RequestExecutor retrieves the result from the IFrame and provides it to the calling add-in. Figure 9-2 diagrams this process.

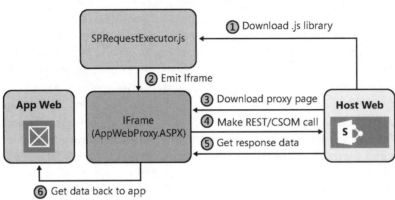

FIGURE 9-2 The steps of a cross-domain call using the SP.RequestExecutor.js library

To use the SP.RequestExecutor.js library while invoking the REST API, you need to create an instance of the *SP.RequestExecutor* type. In addition, you must invoke the *executeAsync* method and provide the necessary arguments, including the following:

- **url**   Represents the target URL of the REST API. While using the code from an app web, you can provide a reference to the host web by using the *SP.AppContextSite()* function, as illustrated in Listing 9-5.

- **method**   Defines the HTTP method to use while invoking the target URL.

- **body**   Declares the content of the message body that will be posted to the target URL in case you have message content to send.

- **headers**   Allows defining a list of HTTP headers to provide while invoking the target URL. As you can see from Listing 9-5, you can provide headers such as *Accept, X-RequestDigest, X-HTTP-Method, IF-MATCH*, and so on.

- **success**   Is the pointer to a function that will be invoked in case of a successful call.

- **error**   Is the pointer to a function that will be invoked in case of a failed call.

Security

By default, the REST API requires that the consumers act in an authenticated session for security purposes. From a SharePoint on-premises perspective, the authenticated session can be gained through Windows integrated security, browser-based direct authentication (in the case of a SharePoint-hosted app), or by using OAuth (in any other situation). From a SharePoint Online perspective, the session can be authenticated only by using the Azure AD user's credentials or by using the OAuth protocol.

In the case of integrated security, you need to enable the automatic flow of integrated security credentials in the HTTP client library you will use. For example, if you're working in JavaScript within a web browser and using SharePoint-hosted add-in or application pages, the flow of integrated security credentials will be automatic. In contrast, when working in a Universal Windows Platform app for Windows 10, for example, you must request permission for the enterprise authentication capability in the *AppManifest.xml* file of the app.

If you want to use OAuth—for example, if you're executing JavaScript code within a provider-hosted SharePoint Add-in on a third-party site—you first need to retrieve and store the access token provided during the OAuth handshake. For example, you can use the ADAL.JS library that was introduced in Chapter 4, "Azure Active Directory and security." Then, you must provide that access token to every request to the REST API, embedded in a dedicated *Authorization* HTTP header, as you did in the PowerShell sample in Listing 9-1. The JavaScript code excerpt in Listing 9-6 configures that HTTP header using an access token stored in a hypothetical *accessToken* variable.

LISTING 9-6 A code excerpt for invoking the REST API with OAuth authentication

```
jQuery.ajax({
  url: "http://hostname/_api/contextinfo",
  type: "POST",
  headers: {
    "Authorization": "Bearer " + accessToken,
    "accept": "application/json;odata=verbose",
    "contentType": "text/xml"
  },
})
```

Within Office 365, you can also leverage Azure AD to get an access token to access SharePoint Online as long as you register your application in the directory and assign proper permissions to it, as you saw in Chapter 4.

If you target an on-premises farm, you can enable anonymous access to read-only operations of the REST API if you want to publish your contents to the public Internet. To configure this capability, you will need to edit the Anonymous permission of the target website. Figure 9-3 shows the configuration panel for setting this option. You can find the panel by choosing Site Settings | Site Permissions | Anonymous Access. However, you should be really careful and disable this flag only in specific scenarios and after having considered all pros and cons.

If you turn off Require Use Remote Interfaces Permission, all anonymous users will be able to invoke the read-only operations of the REST API. Only authorized users can change this option, but they may do so from the web interface, by working within PowerShell, or by using the CSOM. For security reasons, this option is not available in Microsoft SharePoint Online.

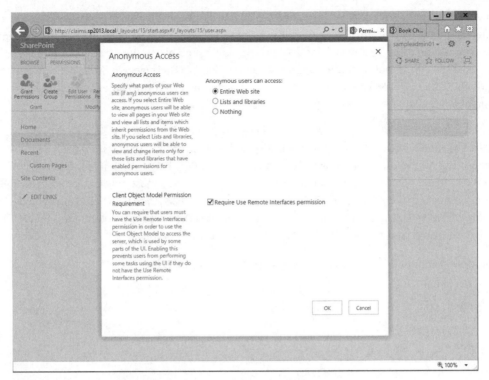

FIGURE 9-3 The UI for configuring anonymous access to the REST API

Common REST API usage

For the remainder of the chapter, you will learn how to use the REST API while executing common and useful tasks. All the code samples are provided in JavaScript and run in a SharePoint Add-in that uses cross-domain calls. Thus, you will be able to reuse all the code excerpts illustrated by copying and pasting the code and adapting the values of the arguments and HTTP headers provided to the methods.

> **Important** The code samples are available through the PnP repository on GitHub. To access them, follow the instructions provided in the introduction of this book. The code samples illustrated here come from a SharePoint-hosted add-in, so they do not need to provide an OAuth access token. Please refer to the "Security" section earlier in this chapter if you need to use the code sample from a provider-hosted app.

For the sake of simplicity, all the code samples assume that you have the set of global and predefined variables illustrated in Listing 9-7 and some common startup code.

LISTING 9-7 A code excerpt for the startup phase of the code samples illustrated in the current section

```
var hostweburl;
var appweburl;
var eTag;
var formDigestValue;

$(document).ready(function () {
    // Get the URI-decoded URLs.
    hostweburl = decodeURIComponent(getQueryStringParameter("SPHostUrl"));
    appweburl = decodeURIComponent(getQueryStringParameter("SPAppWebUrl"));

    var scriptbase = hostweburl + "/_layouts/15/";
    $.getScript(scriptbase + "SP.RequestExecutor.js", retrieveFormDigest);
});

// Function to retrieve a query string value.
// For production purposes you may want to use
// a library to handle the query string.
function getQueryStringParameter(paramToRetrieve) {
    var params =
        document.URL.split("?")[1].split("&");
    var strParams = "";
    for (var i = 0; i < params.length; i = i + 1) {
        var singleParam = params[i].split("=");
        if (singleParam[0] == paramToRetrieve)
            return singleParam[1];
    }
}

function retrieveFormDigest() {
    var contextInfoUri = appweburl + "/_api/contextinfo";
    var executor = new SP.RequestExecutor(appweburl)

    executor.executeAsync({
        url: contextInfoUri,
        method: "POST",
        headers: { "Accept": "application/json; odata=verbose" },
        success: function (data) {
            var jsonObject = JSON.parse(data.body);
            formDigestValue = jsonObject.d.GetContextWebInformation.FormDigestValue;
        },
        error: function (data, errorCode, errorMessage) {
            var errMsg = "Error retrieving the form digest value: "
                + errorMessage;
            $("#error").text(errMsg);
        }
    });
}
```

All the code samples illustrated in the following sections will behave as event handlers for HTML *Button* input elements.

Creating a new list

To create a new list instance via the REST API and JSON, you first need to prepare a JSON representation of the list to create. Then, you must send it through AJAX, including the *X-RequestDigest* HTTP header. Listing 9-8 provides a function for this.

LISTING 9-8 A JavaScript function for creating a list instance by using the REST API

```
function createNewList() {
    var executor = new SP.RequestExecutor(appweburl);
    var operationUri = appweburl +
        "/_api/SP.AppContextSite(@target)/web/lists?@target='" +
        hostweburl + "'";

    var bodyContent = JSON.stringify({
            '__metadata': { 'type': 'SP.List' },
            'AllowContentTypes': true,
            'BaseTemplate': 100,
            'ContentTypesEnabled': true,
            'Description': 'Custom List created via REST API',
            'Title': 'RESTCreatedList'
    });

    executor.executeAsync({
        url: operationUri,
        method: "POST",
        headers: {
            "Accept": "application/json;odata=verbose",
            "content-type": "application/json;odata=verbose",
            "content-length": bodyContent.length,
            "X-RequestDigest": formDigestValue,
        },
        body: bodyContent,
        success: function (data) {
            var jsonObject = JSON.parse(data.body);
        },
        error: function (data, errorCode, errorMessage) {
            var jsonObject = JSON.parse(data.body);
            var errMsg = "Error: " + jsonObject.error.message.value;
            $("#error").text(errMsg);
        }
    });
}
```

Notice that Listing 9-8 creates the list in the host web; your app will need specific permissions to accomplish this task.

Creating and updating a list item

Now, imagine that you want to add one or more items to the list you just created. The code will be similar to Listing 9-8, but you will need to define the JSON structure of a list item. Moreover, you will need to change the URI of the operation to map to the collection of items of the target list. Listing 9-9 shows the necessary code.

LISTING 9-9 A JavaScript function for creating a list item in a list instance by using the REST API

```
function createNewListItem() {
    var executor = new SP.RequestExecutor(appweburl);
    var operationUri = appweburl +
"/_api/SP.AppContextSite(@target)/web/lists/GetByTitle('RESTCreatedList')/Items?@target='"
+ hostweburl + "'";

    var bodyContent = JSON.stringify({
            '__metadata': { 'type': 'SP.Data.RESTCreatedListListItem' },
            'Title': 'Item created via REST API'
    });

    executor.executeAsync({
        url: operationUri,
        method: "POST",
        headers: {
            "Accept": "application/json;odata=verbose",
            "content-type": "application/json;odata=verbose",
            "content-length": bodyContent.length,
            "X-RequestDigest": formDigestValue,
        },
        body: bodyContent,
        success: function (data) {
            var jsonObject = JSON.parse(data.body);
        },
        error: function (data, errorCode, errorMessage) {
            var jsonObject = JSON.parse(data.body);
            var errMsg = "Error: " + jsonObject.error.message.value;
            $("#error").text(errMsg);
        }
    });
}
```

Notice the value assigned to the *type* property of the *__metadata* of the target item. It defines the data type name corresponding to a list item of the current list. Listing 9-9 assumes a value of *SP.Data. RESTCreatedListListItem*.

Updating an existing item is almost the same as creating a new one, except that you need to provide the *ETag* value in the request headers and synchronize the execution of parallel operations. Listing 9-10 shows an example that changes the *title* property of an existing list item.

LISTING 9-10 A JavaScript function for updating a list item in a list instance by using the REST API

```
function updateListItem() {
    var executor = new SP.RequestExecutor(appweburl);
    var operationUri = appweburl +
"/_api/SP.AppContextSite(@target)/web/lists/GetByTitle('RESTCreatedList')/Items(1)?@
target='" + hostweburl + "'";
    var bodyContent = JSON.stringify({
            '__metadata': { 'type': 'SP.Data.RESTCreatedListListItem' },
            'Title': 'Item changed via REST API'
    });

    // Retrieve the ETag value
    executor.executeAsync({
        url: operationUri,
        method: "GET",
        headers: { "Accept": "application/json; odata=verbose" },
        success: function (data) {
            $("#message").text('ETag: ' + data.headers["ETAG"]);
            eTag = data.headers["ETAG"];

            // Invoke the real update operation
            executor.executeAsync({
                url: operationUri,
                method: "POST",
                headers: {
                    "Accept": "application/json;odata=verbose",
                    "content-type": "application/json;odata=verbose",
                    "content-length": bodyContent.length,
                    "X-RequestDigest": formDigestValue,
                    "X-HTTP-Method": "MERGE",
                    "IF-MATCH": eTag
                },
                body: bodyContent,
                success: function (data) {
                    $("#message").text("Operation completed!");
                },
                error: function (data, errorCode, errorMessage) {
                    var jsonObject = JSON.parse(data.body);
                    var errMsg = "Error: " + jsonObject.error.message.value;
                    $("#error").text(errMsg);
                }
            });
        },
        error: function (data, errorCode, errorMessage) {
            var jsonObject = JSON.parse(data.body);
            var errMsg = "Error retrieving the eTag value: " +
                jsonObject.error.message.value;
            $("#error").text(errMsg);
        }
    });
}
```

Note that Listing 9-10 uses a nested *SP.RequestExecutor* instance, which will run just after successful completion of the external operation invocation.

Deleting an existing list item

If you want to recycle one or more of the items you created in the previous examples, you need to provide the *ETag* value of the current item, as shown in Listing 9-11.

LISTING 9-11 A JavaScript function for deleting a list item in a list instance by using the REST API

```
function deleteListItem() {
    var executor = new SP.RequestExecutor(appweburl);
    var operationUri = appweburl +
"/_api/SP.AppContextSite(@target)/web/lists/GetByTitle('RESTCreatedList')/Items(1)?@
target='" + hostweburl + "'";

    // Retrieve the eTag value
    executor.executeAsync({
        url: operationUri,
        method: "GET",
        headers: { "Accept": "application/json; odata=verbose" },
        success: function (data) {
            $("#message").text('ETag: ' + data.headers["ETAG"]);
            eTag = data.headers["ETAG"];

            // Invoke the real delete operation
            executor.executeAsync({
                url: operationUri,
                method: "POST",
                headers: {
                    "Accept": "application/json;odata=verbose",
                    "content-type": "application/json;odata=verbose",
                    "X-RequestDigest": formDigestValue,
                    "X-HTTP-Method": "DELETE",
                    "IF-MATCH": eTag
                },
                success: function (data) {
                    $("#message").text("Operation completed!");
                },
                error: function (data, errorCode, errorMessage) {
                    var jsonObject = JSON.parse(data.body);
                    var errMsg = "Error: " + jsonObject.error.message.value;
                    $("#error").text(errMsg);
                }
            });
        },
        error: function (data, errorCode, errorMessage) {
            var jsonObject = JSON.parse(data.body);
            var errMsg = "Error retrieving the eTag value: " +
                jsonObject.error.message.value;
            $("#error").text(errMsg);
```

```
        }
    });
}
```

Listing 9-11 uses an HTTP POST method and an *X-HTTP-Method* header with a value of *DELETE*. If you want to force the deletion, you can provide a value of * for the *ETag* header.

Querying a list of items

A common and useful operation is querying a list of items. As shown in the "Querying data" section earlier in this chapter, you just need to invoke an endpoint providing an OData query as a set of query string parameters. If you're working in JavaScript on the client side, the result will be a collection of items presented in JSON format. Listing 9-12 demonstrates how to query the items in a hypothetical list of contacts.

LISTING 9-12 A JavaScript function for querying a list of contacts by using the REST API

```
function queryListItems() {
    var executor = new SP.RequestExecutor(appweburl);
    var operationUri = appweburl +
    "/_api/SP.AppContextSite(@target)/web/lists/GetByTitle('Sample%20Contacts')/" +
    "Items?@target='" + hostweburl + "'&$filter=Company%20eq%20'DevLeap'";

    executor.executeAsync({
        url: operationUri,
        method: "GET",
        headers: { "Accept": "application/json;odata=verbose" },
        success: function (data) {
            var jsonObject = JSON.parse(data.body);
            $("#result").empty();

            for (var i = 0; i < jsonObject.d.results.length; i++) {
                var item = jsonObject.d.results[i];
                $("#result").append("<div>" + item.Title + "</div>");
            }
        },
        error: function (data, errorCode, errorMessage) {
            var jsonObject = JSON.parse(data.body);
            var errMsg = "Error: " + jsonObject.error.message.value;
            $("#error").text(errMsg);
        }
    });
}
```

The HTTP request for querying items is a GET; it does not require a form digest, and it will suffice that the app and the current user both have permissions to read the target list. The response is a JSON serialized array of items that is browsed by code.

Creating a new document library

Most SharePoint solutions use documents and document libraries. Listing 9-13 shows you how to create a document library via the REST API.

LISTING 9-13 A JavaScript function for creating a document library via the REST API

```
function createNewLibrary() {
    var executor = new SP.RequestExecutor(appweburl);
    var operationUri = appweburl +
        "/_api/SP.AppContextSite(@target)/web/lists?@target='" +
        hostweburl + "'";

    var bodyContent = JSON.stringify( {
            '__metadata': { 'type': 'SP.List' },
            'AllowContentTypes': true,
            'BaseTemplate': 101,
            'ContentTypesEnabled': true,
            'Description': 'Custom Library created via REST API',
            'Title': 'RESTCreatedLibrary'
        });

    executor.executeAsync({
        url: operationUri,
        method: "POST",
        headers: {
            "Accept": "application/json;odata=verbose",
            "content-type": "application/json;odata=verbose",
            "content-length": bodyContent.length,
            "X-RequestDigest": formDigestValue,
        },
        body: bodyContent,
        success: function (data) {
            var jsonObject = JSON.parse(data.body);
        },
        error: function (data, errorCode, errorMessage) {
            var jsonObject = JSON.parse(data.body);
            var errMsg = "Error: " + jsonObject.error.message.value;
            $("#error").text(errMsg);
        }
    });
}
```

The procedure is almost identical to that for creating a custom list. The only difference is that here you provide a *BaseTemplate* value compliant with a document library. The example provides a value of *101*, which corresponds to a generic document library. When you successfully create the library, you will get back a JSON serialization of its definition in the success event.

Uploading or updating a document

Once you have one or more document libraries, you can use the REST API to upload documents into them. Listing 9-14 uploads an example XML file into a document library. The URL of the operation for adding the new file is highlighted in bold, as are the HTTP headers that are required for the correct and secure execution of the operation.

LISTING 9-14 A JavaScript function for uploading a document into a document library via the REST API

```
function uploadFile() {
    var executor = new SP.RequestExecutor(appweburl);
    var operationUri = appweburl + "/_api/SP.AppContextSite(@target)/web/lists/" +
        "GetByTitle('Documents')/RootFolder/Files/Add" +
        "(url='SampleFile.xml',overwrite=true)?@target='" + hostweburl + "'";

    var xmlDocument = "<?xml version='1.0'?><document>" +
        "<title>Uploaded via REST API</title></document>";

    executor.executeAsync({
        url: operationUri,
        method: "POST",
        headers: {
            "Accept": "application/json;odata=verbose",
            "content-type": "text/xml",
            "content-length": xmlDocument.length,
            "X-RequestDigest": formDigestValue,
        },
        body: xmlDocument,
        success: function (data) {
            var jsonObject = JSON.parse(data.body);
            $("#message").text("Operation completed!");
        },
        error: function (data, errorCode, errorMessage) {
            var jsonObject = JSON.parse(data.body);
            var errMsg = "Error: " + jsonObject.error.message.value;
            $("#error").text(errMsg);
        }
    });
}
```

If you want to update a published file, you can use a procedure like the one illustrated in Listing 9-15.

LISTING 9-15 A JavaScript function for updating a document in a document library via the REST API

```
function updateFile() {
    var executor = new SP.RequestExecutor(appweburl);
    var operationUri = appweburl +
        "/_api/SP.AppContextSite(@target)/web/" +
        "GetFileByServerRelativeUrl('/sites/AppsDevelopmentSite/" +
        "Shared%20Documents/SampleFile.xml')/$value?@target='" +
        hostweburl + "'";
```

```
        var xmlDocument = "<?xml version='1.0'?><document>" +
            "<title>File updated via REST API</title></document>";

    executor.executeAsync({
        url: operationUri,
        method: "POST",
        headers: {
            "Accept": "application/json;odata=verbose",
            "content-type": "text/xml",
            "content-length": xmlDocument.length,
            "X-HTTP-Method": "PUT",
            "X-RequestDigest": formDigestValue,
        },
        body: xmlDocument,
        success: function (data) {
            $("#message").text("Operation completed!");
        },
        error: function (data, errorCode, errorMessage) {
            var jsonObject = JSON.parse(data.body);
            var errMsg = "Error: " + jsonObject.error.message.value;
            $("#error").text(errMsg);
        }
    });
s}
```

As you can see, the REST endpoint for the operation is the *$value* of the file, and the file will be over-written by the *body* content submitted through the HTTP request.

Checking in and checking out documents

Another vital component of many business-level solutions is the ability to control document versioning through the check-in and check-out capabilities of SharePoint. Listing 9-16 shows you how to check out a document.

LISTING 9-16 A JavaScript function for checking out a document from a document library via the REST API

```
function checkOutFile() {
    var executor = new SP.RequestExecutor(appweburl);
    var operationUri = appweburl +
        "/_api/SP.AppContextSite(@target)/web/" +
        "GetFileByServerRelativeUrl('/sites/AppsDevelopmentSite/" +
        "Shared%20Documents/SampleFile.xml')/CheckOut()?@target='" +
        hostweburl + "'";

    executor.executeAsync({
        url: operationUri,
        method: "POST",
        headers: {
            "Accept": "application/json;odata=verbose",
            "X-RequestDigest": formDigestValue,
```

```
        },
        success: function (data) {
            var jsonObject = JSON.parse(data.body);
            $("#message").text("Operation completed!");
        },
        error: function (data, errorCode, errorMessage) {
            var jsonObject = JSON.parse(data.body);
            var errMsg = "Error: " + jsonObject.error.message.value;
            $("#error").text(errMsg);
        }
    });
}
```

Listing 9-17 shows how to check in a checked-out document.

LISTING 9-17 A JavaScript function for checking a document into a document library via the REST API

```
function checkInFile() {
    var executor = new SP.RequestExecutor(appweburl);
    var operationUri = appweburl +
        "/_api/SP.AppContextSite(@target)/web/" +
        "GetFileByServerRelativeUrl('/sites/AppsDevelopmentSite/" +
        "Shared%20Documents/SampleFile.xml')/CheckIn?@target='" +
        hostweburl + "'";

    var bodyContent = JSON.stringify({
            'comment': 'Checked in via REST',
            'checkInType': 1
        });

    executor.executeAsync({
        url: operationUri,
        method: "POST",
        headers: {
            "Accept": "application/json;odata=verbose",
            "Content-type": "application/json;odata=verbose",
            "Content-length": bodyContent.length,
            "X-RequestDigest": formDigestValue,
        },
        body: bodyContent,
        success: function (data) {
            var jsonObject = JSON.parse(data.body);
            $("#message").text("Operation completed!");
        },
        error: function (data, errorCode, errorMessage) {
            var jsonObject = JSON.parse(data.body);
            var errMsg = "Error: " + jsonObject.error.message.value;
            $("#error").text(errMsg);
        }
    });
}
```

The check-out phase just requires an operation URI to be invoked via HTTP POST. In contrast, the check-in phase requires posting some arguments, which in the current example are presented as a JSON object. This posted JSON object represents the arguments for the standard *CheckIn* method of the CSOM.

Deleting a document

The last action related to managing single files is deleting a document. As shown at the beginning of this chapter, to delete a document you need to make an HTTP POST request to the service, providing an *ETag* for security validation rules and an HTTP header of type *X-HTTP-Method* with a value of *DELETE*. Listing 9-18 demonstrates the process.

LISTING 9-18 A JavaScript function for deleting a document from a document library via the REST API

```
function deleteFile() {
    var executor = new SP.RequestExecutor(appweburl);
    var operationUri = appweburl + "/_api/SP.AppContextSite(@target)/web/" +
        "GetFileByServerRelativeUrl('/sites/AppsDevelopmentSite/" +
        "Shared%20Documents/SampleFile.xml')?@target='" +
        hostweburl + "'";

    executor.executeAsync({
        url: operationUri,
        method: "POST",
        headers: {
            "Accept": "application/json;odata=verbose",
            "X-HTTP-Method": "DELETE",
            "X-RequestDigest": formDigestValue,
            "IF-MATCH": "*", // Discard concurrency checks
        },
        success: function (data) {
            $("#message").text("Operation completed!");
        },
        error: function (data, errorCode, errorMessage) {
            var jsonObject = JSON.parse(data.body);
            var errMsg = "Error: " + jsonObject.error.message.value;
            $("#error").text(errMsg);
        }
    });
}
```

Notice that Listing 9-18 retrieves the file itself as an *SP.File* object instead of the bare content (*$value*) of the file. The code then deletes that file without performing a concurrency check, thanks to the *IF-MATCH* header with a value of *.

Querying a list of documents

Querying a list of documents from a document library is almost the same as querying a list of items. The main difference is the URL of the endpoint, which targets the *Files* collection instead of the *Items* collection. Furthermore, every file of a document library is an object of type *SP.File*, not *SP.ListItem*.

LISTING 9-19 A JavaScript function for querying files from a document library via the REST API

```
function queryDocuments() {
    var executor = new SP.RequestExecutor(appweburl);
    var operationUri = appweburl +
        "/_api/SP.AppContextSite(@target)/web/lists/" +
        "GetByTitle('Documents')/RootFolder/Files?@target='" +
        hostweburl + "'";

    executor.executeAsync({
        url: operationUri,
        method: "GET",
        headers: { "Accept": "application/json;odata=verbose" },
        success: function (data) {
            var jsonObject = JSON.parse(data.body);
            $("#message").empty();

            for (var i = 0; i < jsonObject.d.results.length; i++) {
                var item = jsonObject.d.results[i];
                $("#message").append("<div>" + item.Name + "</div>");
            }
        },
        error: function (data, errorCode, errorMessage) {
            var jsonObject = JSON.parse(data.body);
            var errMsg = "Error: " + jsonObject.error.message.value;
            $("#error").text(errMsg);
        }
    });
}
```

Notice that the HTTP query uses an HTTP GET method and provides only the *Accept* HTTP header. It does not require any other extended header or information.

Summary

In this chapter, you learned about the REST API introduced in SharePoint 2013 and available in Microsoft SharePoint Online. You examined the architecture and the capabilities of this tool, which can be consumed by any platform capable of making HTTP requests. In addition, you learned how to implement the REST API in real projects with JavaScript, addressing a set of common scenarios.

#### PART IV

SharePoint and Office apps

## CHAPTER 10

Creating Office 365 applications

So far, you have seen how to consume Microsoft Office 365 from a general viewpoint. However, as a developer you need to create real business solutions that leverage the Office 365 ecosystem. In this chapter, you will walk through a set of real-life examples that can give you inspiration about how to empower your solutions with what you learned in the previous chapters.

Solution overview

Throughout this chapter, you will see how to create a solution that leverages some of the most interesting capabilities of Office 365 and the Microsoft Graph. The goal is to create a custom ASP.NET MVC solution that extends Office 365 to create custom digital workplaces to manage business projects.

The resulting application will be accessible through a tile in the app launcher and by extending the out-of-box UI of SharePoint Online with some custom actions. The sample solution provides some collaboration-oriented capabilities, enabling you to start a new business project with a focus group of people working on it. Under the cover of every project, there will be an Office 365 Group that will hold the documents, a shared calendar, and the communications related to the project. The custom application will provide some customized UI elements to interact with each project and to monitor the overall process by sending automated email messages and feeding the Office 365 Group custom notifications and events by leveraging the Office 365 Connectors.

Overall, the solution will give you some guidance about how to accomplish the following tasks:

- Creating an Office 365 application by using Microsoft Visual Studio 2015

- Configuring the application to act on behalf of the current user via OAuth 2.0 or with an app-only access token

- Leveraging the Office UI Fabric to provide a common and well-known user experience to the application users

- Using the Microsoft Graph to interact with Office 365 Groups and Microsoft Exchange Online

- Using the Microsoft SharePoint REST API to consume SharePoint Online

- Leveraging controls and libraries provided by the Office 365 Developer Patterns & Practices (PnP) community project

- Leveraging an asynchronous development pattern and a Microsoft Azure WebJob to create more scalable and reliable solutions

- Creating an Office 365 Connector to asynchronously interact with an Office 365 Group

In Figure 10-1, you can see the overall architecture of the solution, and in the following sections you will dig into each of its key points.

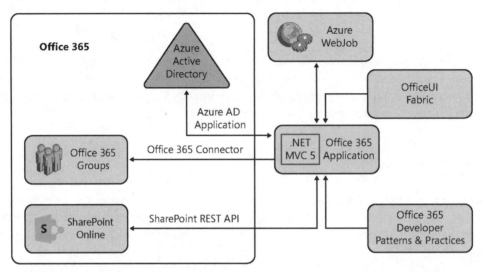

FIGURE 10-1 The overall architecture of the sample project's management solution illustrated in this chapter

Most of the topics covered in this chapter will be useful for your everyday work when you are developing custom solutions for Office 365.

Creating and registering the Office 365 application

The development platform for the sample application will be Microsoft Visual Studio 2015 (Update 2). First, you have to create a new empty solution, which in the samples related to this chapter is called *BusinessApps.O365ProjectsApp*, together with a new project of type ASP.NET web application, which in the current sample is called *BusinessApps.O365ProjectsApp.WebApp*.

> **Note** You can download the full sample solution from GitHub at the following URL: *https:// github.com/OfficeDev/PnP/tree/master/Samples/BusinessApps.O365ProjectsApp*. Within the same GitHub repository, you will find other useful samples and solutions, ready to be used for creating your own solutions.

You can select to create a new ASP.NET 4.5.x MVC web application, which will provide both MVC and Web API capabilities. Moreover, as you learned in Chapter 4, "Azure Active Directory and security," you will have to select an authentication model. To target Office 365, you have to select the Work

And School Accounts authentication model, providing the target tenant name. You should also select to have read access to directory data so that Visual Studio will register a new Client Secret for your application, from an Open Authorization perspective. This will also enrich the *Startup.Auth.cs* file with statements to handle not only the OpenID Connect authentication, but also the OAuth 2.0 authorization. For further details about these dynamics, see Chapter 4.

Try to start your application by pressing F5 in Visual Studio, and you will be prompted for authentication against the Microsoft Azure Active Directory (Azure AD) tenant that is under the cover of your target Office 365 tenant. Just after the authentication phase, you will see the home page of the ASP. NET MVC site. So far, starting the application will give you quite a bitter feeling because the UI will be the one available out of the box for any ASP.NET MVC application, which is unlike the user interface and experience of Office 365. In the section "Basic UI elements with Office UI Fabric" later in this chapter, you will learn how to customize the UI to adhere to the common and well-known user experience of Office 365. Nevertheless, even with the out-of-box ASP.NET MVC UI, you will see the currently logged-in user name in the upper-right corner of the screen.

Azure AD application general registration

So far, you have created and registered the application in Azure AD. However, to set up the application properly, you probably will also need to configure a custom logo for it. The custom logo will be used in the Office 365 app launcher to show your application. To configure a custom logo, go to the Azure AD tenant under the cover of your Office 365 tenant, open the Applications tab, search for your custom application (by using either the Client ID or the application name), and open the application Configuration tab. At the beginning of the page, you will find the default application logo, and in the lower part of the screen you will have an Upload Logo button. Click that button and choose a custom logo image, which has to adhere to the following requirements:

- Image dimensions of 215 × 215 pixels

- Central image dimensions of 94 × 94 pixels, with the remainder of the image as a solid field

- Supported file types: BMP, JPEG, and PNG

- File size less than 100 KB

In the current sample, we will use the OfficeDev PnP logo because this sample application will be hosted under the PnP family of samples.

After registering the application logo, you can open the browser and go to your Office 365 tenant account. Click the app launcher and select the View All My Apps link in the lower-left corner of the app launcher. There, you will find the full list of native and custom Office 365 applications available to your user, including the just-configured application. If you want to pin the new application to the app launcher, you can click the ellipses in the upper-right corner of the app logo and select the Pin To App Launcher menu item. See Figure 10-2 to have a look at the overall result.

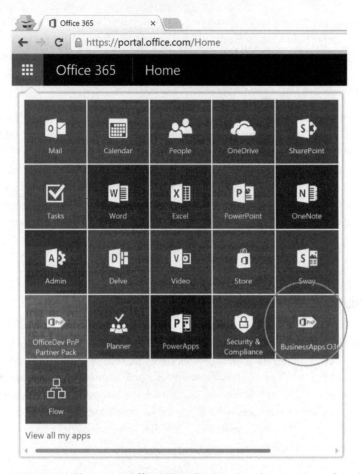

FIGURE 10-2 The custom Office 365 application pinned to a user's app launcher

If later you would like to remove the application from the app launcher, just come back to the View All My Apps page, select the app, click the ellipses, and select the Unpin From App Launcher menu item.

> **Note** At the time of this writing, is not possible to automate the process of pinning an application to the app launcher. In the future, Microsoft may make an API to automate the process, but this is not guaranteed.

App-only authorization registration

The sample application that is built throughout this chapter requires you to accomplish some tasks acting as "app-only" from an authorization perspective. Thus, in this section you will learn how to configure the application in Azure AD to be able to interact with SharePoint Online and the Microsoft Graph with an app-only token.

First of all, you will need to create a self-signed X.509 certificate that will be used to authenticate your application against Azure AD while providing the app-only access token. The certificate can be created using the makecert.exe command-line tool, which is included in the Windows SDK. In the following excerpt, you can see the syntax to invoke the *makecert* command:

```
makecert -r -pe -n "CN=ApplicationName" -b 05/01/2016 -e 05/01/2018 -ss my -len 2048
```

The statement instructs the tool to create a self-signed certificate (option -*r*), with an exportable private key (option -*pe*), with a common name value of "CN=ApplicationName" (option -*n*), valid from May 1 2016 (-*b*) to May 1 2018 (-*e*). Moreover, the certificate will be stored in the personal certificates secure store of the current user (-*ss my*), and the generated key length will be 2,048 bits (-*len 2048*).

Another option that you have is to leverage the PowerShell cmdlet called *New-SelfSignedCertificate*, which is newer and more powerful. This option is my favorite because you can easily create a PowerShell script that automates the configuration process. However, if you don't like PowerShell, or if you are not familiar with it, you can fall back to the makecert option.

> **Note** You can find further details about the makecert tool at the following URL: *htps:// msdn.microsoft.com/en-us/library/bfsktky3(v=vs.100).aspx*. You can find more information about the *New-SelfSignedCertificate* cmdlet at the following URL: *https://technet.microsoft .com/en-us/library/hh848633*.

There is a sample solution called PnP Partner Pack that is available in the OfficeDev PnP offering at the following URL: *http://aka.ms/OfficeDevPnPPartnerPack*. That sample solution uses the app-only authorization, like the sample application about which you are learning in this chapter. One key benefit of having a look at the PnP Partner Pack is that the setup guide of the project provides you with a PowerShell script (*https://github.com/OfficeDev/PnP-Partner-Pack/blob/master/scripts/Create -SelfSignedCertificate.ps1*) that gives you a ready-to-go solution for creating a self-signed certificate, which will be automatically installed in the certificate store and also saved in the local file system.

> **More info** The PnP Partner Pack is a sample solution provided to the community as an open source project in GitHub. The goal of the PnP Partner Pack is to show how to leverage the patterns, guidance, and tools that PnP provides through a real solution that can be considered a startup project for real business use cases. The main capabilities of the PnP Partner Pack are: it is an Office 365 application; it provides the capability to do self-service site and site collection creation based on PnP provisioning templates; it allows you to save a site as a template (PnP provisioning template) directly from the web UI of SharePoint; and it provides sample jobs for governance purposes. The PnP Partner Pack is available at the following URL: *http://aka.ms/OfficeDevPnPPartnerPack*.

Once you have created the certificate, you can browse to the Configuration page of the Office 365 application in the Azure AD management portal and click the Manage Manifest button, which is available in the lower part of the screen. Select the Download Manifest option, and the browser will start to download a .JSON file that represents the manifest of the app. In Figure 10-3, you can see a screenshot of the Manage Manifest menu item.

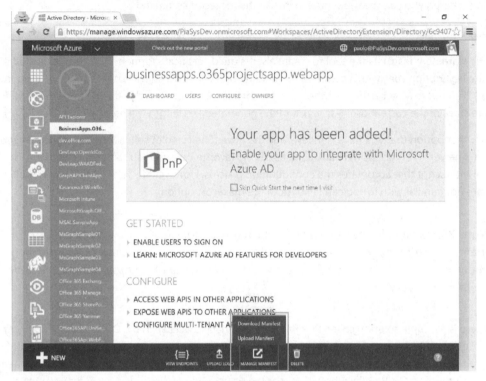

FIGURE 10-3 The Manage Manifest command in Azure AD

When you open the file, it will look like the excerpt illustrated in Listing 10-1.

LISTING 10-1 The .JSON manifest file of an Office 365 application registered in Azure AD

```
{
  "appId": "74c393a9-b865-48b7-b2b6-0efa7a2305a1",
  "appRoles": [],
  "availableToOtherTenants": false,
  "displayName": "BusinessApps.O365ProjectsApp.WebApp",
  "errorUrl": null,
  "groupMembershipClaims": null,
  "homepage": "https://localhost:44304/",
  "identifierUris": [
    "https://tenant.onmicrosoft.com/BusinessApps.O365ProjectsApp.WebApp"
  ],
  "keyCredentials": [],
  "knownClientApplications": [],
  "logoutUrl": null,
  "oauth2AllowImplicitFlow": false,
  "oauth2AllowUrlPathMatching": false,
```

```
  "oauth2Permissions": [
    {
      "adminConsentDescription": "Allow the application to access BusinessApps.
O365ProjectsApp.WebApp on behalf of the signed-in user.",
      "adminConsentDisplayName": "Access BusinessApps.O365ProjectsApp.WebApp",
      "id": "11851dd6-95ef-4336-afca-8e8d9212d5ec",
      "isEnabled": true,
      "type": "User",
      "userConsentDescription": "Allow the application to access BusinessApps.
O365ProjectsApp.WebApp on your behalf.",
      "userConsentDisplayName": "Access BusinessApps.O365ProjectsApp.WebApp",
      "value": "user_impersonation"
    }
  ],
  "oauth2RequirePostResponse": false,
  "passwordCredentials": [
    {
      "customKeyIdentifier": null,
      "endDate": "2017-04-25T16:18:21.3676329Z",
      "keyId": "1892ef1f-f2c3-448c-89df-d3b77cf0628c",
      "startDate": "2016-04-25T16:18:21.3676329Z",
      "value": null
    },
    {
      "customKeyIdentifier": null,
      "endDate": "2017-04-25T15:56:46.1588957Z",
      "keyId": "8ff689f8-724a-417f-b754-a11ef88eff88",
      "startDate": "2016-04-25T15:56:46.1588957Z",
      "value": null
    }
  ],
  "publicClient": false,
  "replyUrls": [
    "https://localhost:44304/"
  ],
  "requiredResourceAccess": [
    {
      "resourceAppId": "00000002-0000-0000-c000-000000000000",
      "resourceAccess": [
        {
          "id": "311a71cc-e848-46a1-bdf8-97ff7156d8e6",
          "type": "Scope"
        },
        {
          "id": "5778995a-e1bf-45b8-affa-663a9f3f4d04",
          "type": "Scope"
        }
      ]
    }
  ],
  "samlMetadataUrl": null,
  "extensionProperties": [],
  "objectType": "Application",
  "objectId": "695258ca-fe41-44f8-8a56-2e3560164e7c",
  "deletionTimestamp": null,
```

```
        "createdOnBehalfOf": null,
        "createdObjects": [],
        "manager": null,
        "directReports": [],
        "members": [],
        "memberOf": [],
        "owners": [],
        "ownedObjects": []
}
```

So far, the interesting part for you is the property named *keyCredentials*, of type *array*, which is highlighted in bold. There are many other useful settings stored within the manifest file, but they are out of the scope of this book. To configure an X.509 certificate as a credential set for the application, you will have to provide a value for the *keyCredentials* array.

Luckily, by using another PowerShell cmdlet that is available within the set of PowerShell cmdlets of PnP, you will be able to use the following syntax to create the *KeyCredentials* array from the X.509 certificate that you have just created.

```
Get-SPOAzureADManifestKeyCredentials -CertPath <path to your .cer file> | clip
```

This statement will copy onto the clipboard of your machine a JSON excerpt like the following:

```
"keyCredentials": [
  {
    "customKeyIdentifier": "<Base64CertHash>",
    "keyId": "<KeyId>",
    "type": "AsymmetricX509Cert",
    "usage": "Verify",
    "value":   "<Base64Cert>"
  }
],
```

The values *<Base64CertHash>*, *<KeyId>*, and *<Base64Cert>* are just sample placeholders. In reality, they will hold the corresponding values generated from the X.509 certificate that you generated.

You just need to paste that JSON excerpt, replacing the empty *keyCredentials* array. Then, save the updated manifest file and upload it back to Azure by using the Upload Manifest option, which is available under the Manage Manifest menu item.

Later in this chapter, you will learn how to use the certificate to access resources with an app-only access token.

Setting Azure AD permissions

Setting up credentials of Office 365 applications enables you to leverage the authorization rules through Azure AD. Thus, it is now time to configure proper permissions for the application both when acting on behalf of the current user and when acting as app-only.

To support the capabilities the current sample application requires, you will need to configure the permissions illustrated in Table 10-1.

TABLE 10-1 Permissions configured for the sample Office 365 application

Application	Permission Type	Permission	Description
Windows Azure Active Directory	Application Permissions	-	-
	Delegated Permissions	Sign in and read user profile	Allows the application to sign in a user and read his profile data
		Read directory data	Allows the application to read the Azure AD directory on behalf of a user
Microsoft Graph	Application Permissions	Read and write all groups	Allows the application to read and write all the Azure AD Groups, including the Office 365 Groups
		Send mail as any user	Allows the application to send email messages using the mailbox of any tenant user
		Read and write directory data	Allows the application to read and write directory data
	Delegated Permissions	Read user contacts	Allows the application to read the contacts of authenticated users on their behalf
		Read and write all groups	Allows the application to read and write all groups on behalf of the current user, as long as the current user also has proper permissions
		Read and write directory data	Allows the application to read and write directory data on behalf of the current user, as long as the current user also has proper permissions
Office 365 SharePoint Online	Application Permissions	Have full control of all site collections	Allows the application to have full control of all site collections of SharePoint Online
		Read managed metadata	Allows the application to read the managed metadata store of SharePoint Online
	Delegated Permissions	Run search queries as a user	Allows the application to run search queries acting on behalf of the currently logged-in user
		Read and write items and lists in all site collections	Allows the application to read and write all items and lists in all site collections on behalf of the current user, as long as the current user has permissions on the target items or lists

You are now ready to implement the solutions, leveraging the services and capabilities provided by Azure AD and the Microsoft Graph.

Basic UI elements with Office UI Fabric

A professional and real business-level Office 365 application has to provide the users a UI/UX that makes them feel like they are using Office 365 and not an external solution. Most users already know how to interact with Office 365 and its core services by leveraging a set of well-known controls and icons.

Since late 2015, Microsoft has provided an open source project called Office UI Fabric, which you encountered in Chapter 2, "Overview of Office 365 development," and which provides a rich set of tools, markup, and styles to mimic the UI/UX of Office 365 in any custom software solution. You can find the Office UI Fabric entry point at the following URL: *http://dev.office.com/fabric*.

From a developer perspective, you can reference Office UI Fabric in many different ways, which are documented at the following URL: *http://dev.office.com/fabric/get-started*. In the current sample project, the easiest way to use Office UI Fabric is to reference its corresponding NuGet package, which is named OfficeUIFabric. Here, you can see the short command to install the package using the NuGet Package Manager Console:

```
PM> Install-Package OfficeUIFabric
```

The NuGet package will install all the needed .CSS and .JS files into your project so that you will be ready to benefit from using Office UI Fabric, as you will see in the following paragraphs. Another option you have is to reference those files directly from a content delivery network (CDN). Regardless of how you access the Office UI Fabric files, what matters is what you can do with them.

When getting the Office UI Fabric through NuGet, you will have to reference its .CSS and .JS files in the *BundleConfig.cs* file of the MVC project. Thus, open the *BundleConfig.cs* file under the App_Start folder and update it according to what is highlighted in bold in Listing 10-2.

LISTING 10-2 The updated version of *BundleConfig.cs*, with added or updated parts highlighted in bold

```
using System.Web;
using System.Web.Optimization;

namespace BusinessApps.O365ProjectsApp.WebApp {
    public class BundleConfig {
        public static void RegisterBundles(BundleCollection bundles) {

            bundles.Add(new ScriptBundle("~/bundles/jquery").Include(
                        "~/Scripts/jquery-{version}.js"));

            bundles.Add(new ScriptBundle("~/bundles/jqueryval").Include(
                        "~/Scripts/jquery.validate*"));

            bundles.Add(new ScriptBundle("~/bundles/modernizr").Include(
                        "~/Scripts/modernizr-*"));

            bundles.Add(new ScriptBundle("~/bundles/bootstrap").Include(
                        "~/Scripts/bootstrap.js",
                        "~/Scripts/respond.js"));

            bundles.Add(new ScriptBundle("~/bundles/fabric").Include(
                        "~/Scripts/jquery.fabric.*"));

            bundles.Add(new StyleBundle("~/Content/css").Include(
                        "~/Content/bootstrap.css",
                        "~/Content/Office365SuiteBar.css",
                        "~/Content/fabric.css",
```

```
                    "~/Content/fabric.components.css",
                    "~/Content/site.css"));
        }
    }
}
```

You need to add the script bundle named *~/bundles/fabric*, and you have to add the *fabric.css* and *fabric.components.css* files to the default style bundle named *~/Content/css*. In Listing 10-2, you can also see the *Office365SuiteBar.css* file, which will be explained in the following section and is not related directly to the Office UI Fabric project.

Moreover, you will need to update the shared layout CSHTML file to reference the new Office UI Fabric JavaScript bundle, as you will see in Listing 10-3 in the next section.

Office 365 suite bar and top navigation

The first UI element that you should provide within your application is the Office 365 suite bar, which is the one placed in the upper edge of the screen, with the app launcher, the title of the current application, the current user's picture and profile, and some other context-related links and menu items.

Unfortunately, at the time of this writing there isn't a ready-to-go component in the Office UI Fabric to provide the Office 365 suite bar to your custom applications. Maybe it will come in the future, but for now you have to build it yourself. Of course, you can try to copy and reuse as much as you can from the real suite bar. Nevertheless, it can be a painful task. In Listing 10-3, you can see a sample custom layout template for ASP.NET MVC, which reproduces a minimalist version of the UI and the behavior of the Office 365 suite bar, excluding the app launcher and some other functionalities.

LISTING 10-3 The CSHTML code of a *_Layout.cshtml* file that partially mimics the behavior of the Office 365 suite bar

```
<!DOCTYPE html>
<html>
<head>
    <meta charset="utf-8" />
    <meta name="viewport" content="width=device-width, initial-scale=1.0">
    <title>@ViewBag.Title</title>

    <script type="text/javascript" src="https://ajax.aspnetcdn.com/ajax/4.0/1/
MicrosoftAjax.js"></script>

    @Scripts.Render("~/bundles/jquery")
    @Styles.Render("~/Content/css")
    @Scripts.Render("~/bundles/modernizr")
</head>
<body>

    @Html.Partial("~/Views/Shared/_Office365SuiteBar.cshtml")
    @Html.Partial("~/Views/Shared/_Office365NavBar.cshtml")
```

```
    <div class="scrollableContent">
        <div id="mainContent">
            <div class="ms-Grid">
                <div class="ms-Grid-row">
                    <div class="ms-Grid-col ms-u-sm1 ms-u-md1 ms-u-lg2">
                        <img src="/AppIcon.png" class="siteIcon" />
                    </div>
                    <div class="ms-Grid-col ms-u-sm11 ms-u-md11 ms-u-lg10">
                        <h1>@ViewBag.Title</h1>
                    </div>
                </div>
                <div class="ms-Grid-row">
                    <div class="ms-Grid-col ms-u-sm1 ms-u-md1 ms-u-lg2">
                    </div>
                    <div class="ms-Grid-col ms-u-sm11 ms-u-md11 ms-u-lg10">
                        @RenderBody()
                    </div>
                </div>
                <div class="ms-Grid-row">
                    <div class="ms-Grid-col ms-u-sm12 ms-u-md12 ms-u-lg12">
                        <hr />
                        <footer>
                            (C) Office 365 Developers Patterns &amp; Practices, 2016
                        </footer>
                    </div>
                </div>
            </div>
        </div>
    </div>

    @Scripts.Render("~/bundles/jquery")
    @Scripts.Render("~/bundles/bootstrap")
    @Scripts.Render("~/bundles/fabric")
    @RenderSection("scripts", required: false)

    <script type="text/javascript">

        // Initialize the NavBar object
        if ($.fn.NavBar) {
            $(".ms-NavBar").NavBar();
        }

    </script>

</body>
</html>
```

As you can see, the *SuiteBar* is included through a couple of custom MVC partial views. The first one ("~/Views/Shared/_Office365SuiteBar.cshtml") mimics the top suite bar, while the second one ("~/Views/Shared/_Office365NavBar.cshtml") is a custom top navigation bar that looks like the top navigation bar of OneDrive for Business by leveraging the Office UI Fabric icons and menu styles.

Moreover, there are some statements to include the bundled scripts and styles that we discussed in the previous section. In Figure 10-4, you can see the overall result, rendered in a browser.

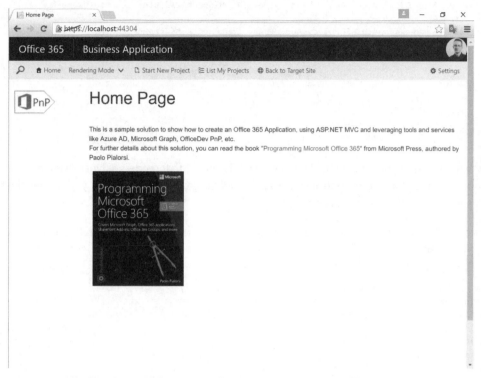

FIGURE 10-4 The home page of the custom Office 365 application with the Office 365 suite bar and top navigation bar

For the sake of brevity, this section will not show the entire content of the _Office365SuiteBar.cshtml_ partial view, which is available in the sample code related to this book. However, in Listing 10-4 you can see an interesting excerpt, in which the rendering of the current user's photo is managed by leveraging the Microsoft Graph API and a custom MVC controller. Moreover, in Listing 10-4 you can see the use of the _Persona_ control of Office UI Fabric, which renders a user's picture and online status by using a well-known layout.

LISTING 10-4 An excerpt of the CSHTML code of a _Office365SuiteBar.cshtml_ file that partially mimics the behavior of the Office 365 suite bar

```
@if (System.Security.Claims.ClaimsPrincipal.Current != null && System.Security.Claims.
ClaimsPrincipal.Current.Identity != null && System.Security.Claims.ClaimsPrincipal.
Current.Identity.IsAuthenticated) {
    <div role="banner" aria-label="User settings">
        <div class="o365cs-nav-topItem o365cs-rsp-tn-hideIfAffordanceOn">
            <div class="ms-Persona ms-Persona--s">
                <div class="ms-Persona-imageArea">
                    <div class="ms-Persona-initials ms-Persona-initials--
blue">@(BusinessApps.O365ProjectsApp.WebApp.Components.MSGraphAPIContext.
```

```
CurrentUserInitials)</div>
                    <img class="ms-Persona-image" src="/Persona/GetPhoto?upn=@
(BusinessApps.O365ProjectsApp.WebApp.Components.MSGraphAPIContext.CurrentUserUPN)&height=6
4&width=64"
title="@(BusinessApps.O365ProjectsApp.WebApp.Components.MSGraphAPIContext.
CurrentUserDisplayName)">
                </div>
                <div class="ms-Persona--offline"></div>
            </div>
        </div>
    </div>
}
```

As you can see, highlighted in bold there is an IMG element that renders a dynamic image, which is rendered through a custom controller named *PersonaController*. In Listing 10-5, you can see the full implementation of that *PersonaController*.

LISTING 10-5 The source code of the *PersonaController*, which renders the current user's profile picture by using the Microsoft Graph

```
using BusinessApps.O365ProjectsApp.WebApp.Components;
using System;
using System.Collections.Generic;
using System.Drawing;
using System.Drawing.Imaging;
using System.IO;
using System.Linq;
using System.Web;
using System.Web.Mvc;

namespace BusinessApps.O365ProjectsApp.WebApp.Controllers {

    [Authorize]
    public class PersonaController : Controller {
        public ActionResult GetPhoto(String upn, Int32 width = 0, Int32 height = 0) {
            Stream result = null;
            String contentType = "image/png";

            var sourceStream = GetUserPhoto(upn);

            if (sourceStream != null && width != 0 && height != 0) {
                Image sourceImage = Image.FromStream(sourceStream);
                Image resultImage = ScaleImage(sourceImage, width, height);
                result = new MemoryStream();
                resultImage.Save(result, ImageFormat.Png);
                result.Position = 0;
            }
            else {
                result = sourceStream;
            }

            if (result != null) {
```

```
                return base.File(result, contentType);
            }
            else {
                return new HttpStatusCodeResult(System.Net.HttpStatusCode.NoContent);
            }
        }


        /// <summary>
        /// This method retrieves the photo of a single user from Azure AD
        /// </summary>
        /// <param name="upn">The UPN of the user</param>
        /// <returns>The user's photo retrieved from Azure AD</returns>
        private static Stream GetUserPhoto(String upn) {
            String contentType = "image/png";

            var result = MicrosoftGraphHelper.MakeGetRequestForStream(
                String.Format("{0}users/{1}/photo/$value",
                    MicrosoftGraphHelper.MicrosoftGraphV1BaseUri, upn),
                contentType);

            return (result);
        }

        private Image ScaleImage(Image image, int maxWidth, int maxHeight) {
            var ratioX = (double)maxWidth / image.Width;
            var ratioY = (double)maxHeight / image.Height;
            var ratio = Math.Min(ratioX, ratioY);

            var newWidth = (int)(image.Width * ratio);
            var newHeight = (int)(image.Height * ratio);

            var newImage = new Bitmap(newWidth, newHeight);

            using (var graphics = Graphics.FromImage(newImage))
                graphics.DrawImage(image, 0, 0, newWidth, newHeight);

            return newImage;
        }
    }
}
```

The key implementation is in the *GetUserPhoto* method, which uses the Microsoft Graph API according to what you learned in Chapter 6, "Users and Groups services," to retrieve the binary content of the user's profile picture. There are also some plumbing functions to resize and convert the image into the proper output format for the target browser.

In Listing 10-6, you can see the content of the *_Office365NavBar.cshtml* partial view, which provides the UI for the top navigation bar. For the sake of completeness, the sample navigation bar leverages some of the most useful primitives of Office UI Fabric for creating menus, just to show you how to use them.

LISTING 10-6 The CSHTML code of the _Office365NavBar.cshtml_ file that provides the top navigation bar

```
<div class="ms-NavBar">
    <div class="ms-NavBar-openMenu js-openMenu">
        <i class="ms-Icon ms-Icon--menu"></i>
    </div>
    <div class="ms-Overlay"></div>
    <ul class="ms-NavBar-items">

        <!-- Search Text Box and Icon -->
        <li class="ms-NavBar-item ms-NavBar-item--search ms-u-hiddenSm">
            <div class="ms-TextField">
                <input class="ms-TextField-field">
            </div>
        </li>

        <!-- Home menu item -->
        <li class="ms-NavBar-item"><a class="ms-NavBar-link" href="/Home/Index">
            <i class="ms-Icon ms-Icon--home" aria-hidden="true"></i> Home</a></li>

        <!-- Rendering Mode dropdown menu item -->
        <li class="ms-NavBar-item ms-NavBar-item--hasMenu">
            <a class="ms-NavBar-link">Rendering Mode</a>
                <i class="ms-NavBar-chevronDown ms-Icon ms-Icon--chevronDown"
                    aria-hidden="true"></i>
            <ul class="ms-ContextualMenu">
                <li class="ms-ContextualMenu-item">
                    <a class="ms-ContextualMenu-link">Simple</a></li>
                <li class="ms-ContextualMenu-item">
                    <a class="ms-ContextualMenu-link">Normal</a></li>
                <li class="ms-ContextualMenu-item">
                    <a class="ms-ContextualMenu-link">Full</a></li>
            </ul>
        </li>

        <!-- Start New Process menu item -->
        <li class="ms-NavBar-item"><a class="ms-NavBar-link" href="/Home/StartNewProcess">
            <i class="ms-Icon ms-Icon--documentAdd"
                aria-hidden="true"></i> Start New Process</a></li>

        <!-- List My Processes menu item -->
        <li class="ms-NavBar-item"><a class="ms-NavBar-link" href="/Home/MyProcesses">
            <i class="ms-Icon ms-Icon--listCheckbox"
                aria-hidden="true"></i> List My Processes</a></li>

        <!-- Go back to default Site Collection -->
        <li class="ms-NavBar-item"><i class="ms-Icon ms-Icon--globe"
            aria-hidden="true"></i> <a class="ms-NavBar-link" href="@BusinessApps.
O365ProjectsApp.WebApp.Components.O365ProjectsAppContext.CurrentSiteUrl">Back to Target
Site</a></li>

        <!-- Settings menu item -->
        @if (BusinessApps.O365ProjectsApp.WebApp.Components.MSGraphAPIContext.
CurrentUserIsAdmin) {
            <li class="ms-NavBar-item ms-NavBar-item--right">
```

```
            <a class="ms-NavBar-link" href="/Home/Settings">
            <i class="ms-Icon ms-Icon--gear"
                aria-hidden="true"></i> Settings</a></li>
        }
    </ul>
</div>
```

Notice the search text box, which leverages a hidden text box that will be shown if necessary. Also notice the fake Rendering Mode menu, which is made of three sub-menu items and is also highlighted with the *--hasMenu* style. Last, look at the conditional code, highlighted in bold, that checks if the current user is an Admin before showing the Settings menu item. The Settings menu is rendered on the right side of the screen by using the *--right* version of the menu item CSS class.

To work properly, the top navigation bar will also need to have a bunch of JavaScript code, which has already been added to the project by the Office UI Fabric NuGet package and has been included in that page through the script bundle named *~/bundles/fabric*. Because you could have multiple navigation bars within a unique page, you also have to invoke the prototype JavaScript function called *NavBar* targeting the proper navigation bar. You can see the syntax to invoke the *NavBar* function at the end of Listing 10-3.

Furthermore, the menu items of the top navigation bar are branded with some fancy icons, which are available thanks to the Office UI Fabric project. At the time of this writing, there are about 338 custom icons that you can use in your projects to provide branding for menu items, buttons, and graphical elements in the UI of your software solutions. You can see the full list of available icons at the following URL: *http://dev.office.com/fabric/styles#icons*.

All the icons are based on a custom font that contains glyphs you can customize by changing their color, scale, and style. Every icon can be rendered by using an HTML syntax like the following:

```
<i class="ms-Icon ms-Icon--home" aria-hidden="true"></i>
```

The CSS class *ms-Icon* defines that the element represents an icon, and the *ms-Icon--[Icon Name]* class defines the specific kind of icon. The attribute *aria-hidden* with a value of *true* instructs any screen reader to skip the current icon, which is not text but just a glyphicon.

Responsive grid

So far, the UI of the custom Office 365 application has an Office 365 suite bar and a usable top navigation bar, but it would have awful page content and body—especially from a responsiveness perspective—unless you use the grid styles provided by Office UI Fabric.

The Office UI Fabric project provides a responsive grid made of up to 12 columns that behaves almost like the bootstrap grid. You just need to have a DIV element with the CSS class *.ms-Grid* and fill it with children DIV elements with the CSS class *.ms-Grid-row*. Each row can be made of one or more DIV elements styled with the CSS class *.ms-Grid-col*, followed by some other CSS classes that define how large the column will be on small, medium, and large devices. For the sake of completeness, in Listing 10-7 you can see a sample grid divided into the following three rows:

- **Row #1** Partitioned into three columns, each with a width of 4 blocks of 12

- **Row #2** Partitioned into four columns, each with a width of 3 blocks of 12

- **Row #3** Partitioned into two columns, the one on the left with a width of 4 blocks of 12 and the one on the right with a width of 8 blocks of 12

The styles applied to each column instruct the browser how to render the columns. The following is an explanation of the three kinds of styles:

- **ms-u-sm[size]** Defines the size, with values between 1 and 12, for small-screen devices

- **ms-u-md[size]** Defines the size, with values between 1 and 12, for medium-screen devices

- **ms-u-lg[size]** Defines the size, with values between 1 and 12, for large-screen devices

Of course, you can have different column sizes based on the size of the device. For the sake of simplicity, in Listing 10-7 the columns have the same width regardless of the device size.

LISTING 10-7 Sample HTML excerpt that renders a responsive grid of Office UI Fabric

```
<div class="ms-Grid">
    <div class="ms-Grid-row">
        <div class="ms-Grid-col ms-u-sm4 ms-u-md4 ms-u-lg4">First</div>
        <div class="ms-Grid-col ms-u-sm4 ms-u-md4 ms-u-lg4">Second</div>
        <div class="ms-Grid-col ms-u-sm4 ms-u-md4 ms-u-lg4">Third</div>
    </div>
    <div class="ms-Grid-row">
        <div class="ms-Grid-col ms-u-sm3 ms-u-md3 ms-u-lg3">First</div>
        <div class="ms-Grid-col ms-u-sm3 ms-u-md3 ms-u-lg3">Second</div>
        <div class="ms-Grid-col ms-u-sm3 ms-u-md3 ms-u-lg3">Third</div>
        <div class="ms-Grid-col ms-u-sm3 ms-u-md3 ms-u-lg3">Fourth</div>
    </div>
    <div class="ms-Grid-row">
        <div class="ms-Grid-col ms-u-sm4 ms-u-md4 ms-u-lg4">First</div>
        <div class="ms-Grid-col ms-u-sm8 ms-u-md8 ms-u-lg8">Second</div>
    </div>
</div>
```

Based on what you learned in this section, you can now understand the shared CSHTML page layout.

Custom components and styles

The Office UI Fabric provides not only the responsive grid styles, the glyphicons, the *Persona* control, and the *NavBar* control, but also about 30 different controls that we can use to improve the user experience of our projects. Moreover, because it is an open source project with tens of committed people contributing within the worldwide community of Office 365 developers, the Office UI Fabric is a continuously evolving project.

In Table 10-2, you can see the list of all the controls, together with a brief explanation of their purpose, to give you a "map" to navigate the Office UI Fabric project.

TABLE 10-2 The custom components available in Office UI Fabric

Component	Description
Breadcrumb	Common and well-known breadcrumb control to provide sitemap path capabilities.
Button	Classic button control, including the capability to define a button primary control. Also allows you to define compound buttons and the so-called Hero Buttons, which look like the New button in SharePoint Online document libraries, for example.
Callout	To provide callout messages within the UI of the application. It is useful to provide additional help or messages to the end users. You can bind actions or buttons to the callout element.
ChoiceField	Common choice fields like radio, checkbox, and radio groups.
CommandBar	Provides the capability to create a command bar like the one available in OneDrive for Business for uploading new files or handling existing files.
ContextualMenu	Gives the basic artifacts to implement a contextual menu with rich capabilities like grouping of menu items, sub-menus, and multiselect menu items.
DatePicker	A classic date picker control, with all the common capabilities to select day, month, year, and so on.
Dialog	Enables you to create nonmodal or modal dialogs with different styles for rendering the content and the title.
Dropdown	A classic drop-down list control.
Facepile	Useful to render a group (pile) of users' profile pictures with the classic circle typical of Office 365 and the online presence status.
Label	Renders a label with the required field marker.
Link	Renders a common hyperlink.
List	Enables you to implement a list of elements with a rich set of fields; for example, the list of email messages in the inbox. It can be used to render items in a vertical list or in a grid.
ListItem	Defines the layout of a single item of a list.
MessageBanner	Useful to provide messages to the user through a dynamic banner, which can be expanded to show the full message, if needed, and can be dismissed by clicking a button.
NavBar	The top navigation bar that we saw earlier in this chapter.
OrgChart	Represents an organizational chart with users' faces, either in circles or squares, and also can provide online presence information.
Overlay	Creates an overlay panel, either white or gray, on top of the current page/content.
Panel	Renders an information panel, which can be docked on the right side or the left side of the screen. The panel size can be normal, medium, large, or extra large.
PeoplePicker	Provides the UI for a rich people picker control, which provides users' metadata, profile pictures, online presence, and much more. Supported by various formats: normal, compact, disconnected, facepile.
Persona	Renders a single user's profile picture, either in a circle or square and with or without online presence information.

Component	Description
PersonaCard	Provides the well-known person card with picture, information about role, address, department, and so on. It is available in two flavors: circle or squared picture.
Pivot	Implements the pivot control to move across views or tabs within a page. Provides both text-based and button-based section titles.
ProgressIndicator	Renders the classic Office 365 progress indicator, useful for monitoring file uploads or other long-running processes.
SearchBox	The classic search box, typical of SharePoint, Delve, and Office 365 in general.
Spinner	A spinner control that spins during the execution of a long-running task.
Table	Renders a table with the capability to select one or more items and to present multiple fields through table columns.
TextField	A classic text field with a placeholder text. It can be single-line or multiline.
Toggle	The classic toggle to switch on or off one capability or option.

It is fundamental to stress that all the Office UI Fabric controls are responsive and support three different sizes/formats: SmartPhone (small: max width of 320 pixels), Tablet (medium: max width of 640 pixels), and Desktop (large: max width up to 840 pixels).

Last but not least, in the Office UI Fabric you also find typography styles, which provide about 10 base font classes that allow you to adhere to the Office Design Language. Moreover, there are some CSS styles to use predefined color palette sets and animations for showing or hiding elements (enter/exit animations), for moving or sliding elements (move up, down, left, right), and to control the duration of the animations in the UI.

> **Note** You can find further details about the Office Design Language and the general UI guidelines for creating Office 365 applications and Office Add-ins at the following URL: *https://dev.office.com/docs/add-ins/design/add-in-design*.

Extending and consuming SharePoint Online

Now that the UI and UX of the application are consistent with the Office Design Language, we can concentrate on the real implementation and business logic.

First of all, we need to choose how the application can be activated. In the previous section, "Azure AD application general registration," we saw that you can pin the application to the Office 365 app launcher. However, often the customers and end users want to be able to activate the application within the context of use and not only from a generic app launcher icon.

Let's say for example that the end users want to be able to activate the application through the ECB (Edit Control Block) menu of any document in a specific document library of SharePoint Online so that the document will be the main and startup element for every team project.

Extending the UI of SharePoint Online

To satisfy the business requirement described in the previous paragraph, you can create a SharePoint Online list custom action that extends a target document library, defining a custom ECB menu item. Under the cover, that item will use JavaScript code to activate the custom Office 365 application and to start or access the team project.

In the old server-side code development and feature framework development for SharePoint, to create a list custom action you need to create an XML feature that defines all the attributes of the custom action. Now, the server side in SharePoint Online is not available, and the feature framework can be used only with a sandboxed solution. This is a deprecated habit if it contains code, and it is not suggested even if it is just a container for feature framework elements.

Within a SharePoint Add-in, you can use the client-side object model (CSOM) to interact with SharePoint and create artifacts and customization. However, the project we created is an Office 365 application, not a SharePoint Add-in. Thus, you may be wondering how you can create a custom action in SharePoint Online using an Office 365 application.

> **Note** If you want to read more about developing SharePoint Add-ins, you can read the book *Microsoft SharePoint 2013 Developer Reference* from Microsoft Press (ISBN: 0735670714), most of which is still valid for SharePoint 2016 in the field of SharePoint Add-ins development.

When we registered the application in Azure AD, we requested to have the application (app-only) permission to "Have full control of all site collections." Thus, even if we are in an Office 365 application, we can use the SharePoint CSOM to create a list custom action onto a target site collection.

Moreover, if you are using the OfficeDev PnP Core library and the PnP Provisioning Engine, you can easily provision the custom action and the list to which the custom action applies. Thus, install the SharePointPnPCoreOnline NuGet package in the project, as you learned in Chapter 2.

First of all, let's see how to access the SharePoint Online infrastructure with an app-only access token to provision the artifacts. In Listing 10-8, you can see a code excerpt that is executed when the custom application starts and authenticates against SharePoint Online with an app-only token. Then, it provisions a custom library with a custom action for the ECB menu of the documents in that library, in case the library does not exist yet.

LISTING 10-8 Sample code excerpt that connects to SharePoint Online with an app-only token and provision some artifacts via CSOM

```
public static void Provision() {

    // Create a PnP AuthenticationManager object
    AuthenticationManager am = new AuthenticationManager();

    // Authenticate against SPO with an App-Only access token
```

```
using (ClientContext context = am.GetAzureADAppOnlyAuthenticatedContext(
    O365ProjectsAppContext.CurrentSiteUrl, O365ProjectsAppSettings.ClientId,
    O365ProjectsAppSettings.TenantId, O365ProjectsAppSettings.AppOnlyCertificate)) {

    Web web = context.Web;
    List targetLibrary = null;

    // If the target library does not exist (PnP extension method)
    if (!web.ListExists(O365ProjectsAppSettings.LibraryTitle)) {

        // Create it using another PnP extension method
        targetLibrary = web.CreateList(ListTemplateType.DocumentLibrary,
            O365ProjectsAppSettings.LibraryTitle, true, true);
    }
    else {
        targetLibrary = web.GetListByTitle(O365ProjectsAppSettings.LibraryTitle);
    }

    // If the target library exists
    if (targetLibrary != null) {
        // Try to get the user's custom action

        UserCustomAction customAction =
            targetLibrary.GetCustomAction(O365ProjectsAppConstants.ECB_Menu_Name);

        // If it doesn't exist
        if (customAction == null) {

            // Add the user custom action to the list
            customAction = targetLibrary.UserCustomActions.Add();
            customAction.Name = O365ProjectsAppConstants.ECB_Menu_Name;
            customAction.Location = "EditControlBlock";
            customAction.Sequence = 100;
            customAction.Title = "Manage Business Project";
            customAction.Url = $"{O365ProjectsAppContext.CurrentAppSiteUrl}Project/?Si
teUrl={{SiteUrl}}&ListId={{ListId}}&ItemId={{ItemId}}&ItemUrl={{ItemUrl}}";
        }
        else {
            // Update the already existing Custom Action
            customAction.Name = O365ProjectsAppConstants.ECB_Menu_Name;
            customAction.Location = "EditControlBlock";
            customAction.Sequence = 100;
            customAction.Title = "Manage Business Project";
            customAction.Url = $"{O365ProjectsAppContext.CurrentAppSiteUrl}Project/?Si
teUrl={{SiteUrl}}&ListId={{ListId}}&ItemId={{ItemId}}&ItemUrl={{ItemUrl}}";
        }
        customAction.Update();
        context.ExecuteQueryRetry();
    }
}
}
```

Notice the use of the *AuthenticationManager* class, which is part of the PnP Core library and provides some helper methods to create a CSOM *ClientContext* object using any of the available authentication techniques. In Listing 10-8, the *GetAzureADAppOnlyAuthenticatedContext* method uses the target URL of the site collection, the *ClientId* and *TenantId* defined in Azure AD, and the X.509 certificate that we registered in the section "App-only authorization registration" earlier in this chapter to create an authenticated context using an app-only access token.

The code sample hides the complexity of retrieving the X.509 certificate to authenticate against Azure AD through a global setting called *O365ProjectsAppSettings.AppOnlyCertificate*. In the full source code of the sample application, you will find the details about how to retrieve the certificate from a certificate store.

After creating an authenticated context, the code excerpt checks if the target library exists by using the *ListExists* extension method, which is available in the PnP Core library. If the list exists, the code gets a reference to it using another extension method called *GetListByTitle*. Otherwise, it creates the library using the *CreateList* extension method.

Regardless of whether the list already exists, after getting a reference to the library the code checks if the target library already has a user's custom action for the ECB menu. If the custom action does not exist, the code creates a new one. Otherwise, it updates the existing one.

The ECB menu item will drive the user's browser to the Office 365 application, providing in the query string the URL of the current document together with its *ListId*, *ItemId*, and the source site URL, leveraging the classic SharePoint URL tokens.

As you can see, the user's custom action creation requires you to invoke the *ExecuteQuery* method of the CSOM *ClientContext* object. However, Listing 10-8 uses another PnP Core library extension method called *ExecuteQueryRetry*, which is a powerfull method that internally handles any retry of the *ExecuteQuery* standard method of the *ClientContext* object. When you target SharePoint Online, some requests could fail or be rejected because of connectivity issues or throttling rules on the services side. The *ExecuteQueryRetry* method provided by PnP automatically handles retries and hides from your code the need to take care of any connectivity or throttling issues. You can even customize the *ExecuteQueryRetry* method, providing arguments for *retryCount* and *delay* between retries. By default, the *ExecuteQueryRetry* method will retry 10 times, with a 500 milliseconds delay between each retry.

Provisioning SharePoint artifacts

In the previous section, you saw how to create a library and a user's custom action in the target site by using CSOM and the PnP Core library. However, as you saw in Chapter 2, within the PnP Core library you can also find the PnP Remote Provisioning Engine. Through that engine, you can do remote provisioning by code or by applying a template file, which can be applied by using PowerShell or by writing .NET code.

For the sake of completeness, in this section you will see how to leverage an XML-based template file to provision artifacts by writing just a few lines of code. In Listing 10-9, you can see a PnP XML provisioning template that provisions the library that we discussed earlier in this chapter and its user's custom action.

LISTING 10-9 Sample PnP XML provisioning template that provisions a library with a user's custom action

```xml
<?xml version="1.0"?>
<pnp:Provisioning xmlns:pnp="http://schemas.dev.office.com/PnP/2016/05/
ProvisioningSchema">
  <pnp:Preferences Generator="OfficeDevPnP.Core, Version=2.5.1606.2, Culture=neutral, Publ
icKeyToken=3751622786b357c2">
    <pnp:Parameters>
      <pnp:Parameter Key="AppSiteUrl" Required="true" />
    </pnp:Parameters>
  </pnp:Preferences>
  <pnp:Templates ID="CONTAINER-TEMPLATE-O365ProjectsApp">
    <pnp:ProvisioningTemplate ID="TEMPLATE- O365ProjectsApp" Version="1">
      <pnp:Lists>
        <pnp:ListInstance Title="BusinessProjects" Description=""
DocumentTemplate="{site}/BusinessProjects/Forms/template.dotx" TemplateType="101"
Url="BusinessProjects" EnableVersioning="true" EnableMinorVersions="true"
MinorVersionLimit="0" MaxVersionLimit="0" DraftVersionVisibility="0"
TemplateFeatureID="00bfea71-e717-4e80-aa17-d0c71b360101" EnableAttachments="false">
          <pnp:ContentTypeBindings>
            <pnp:ContentTypeBinding ContentTypeID="0x0101" Default="true" />
            <pnp:ContentTypeBinding ContentTypeID="0x0120" />
          </pnp:ContentTypeBindings>
          <pnp:Views>
            <View Name="{632CEDCA-76C7-4C0E-AEED-4D343DB02B5B}" DefaultView="TRUE"
MobileView="TRUE" MobileDefaultView="TRUE" Type="HTML" DisplayName="All Documents" Url="/
sites/O365ProjectsAppSite/BusinessProjects/Forms/AllItems.aspx" Level="1" BaseViewID="1"
ContentTypeID="0x" ImageUrl="/_layouts/15/images/dlicon.png?rev=43">
              <Query>
                <OrderBy>
                  <FieldRef Name="FileLeafRef" />
                </OrderBy>
              </Query>
              <ViewFields>
                <FieldRef Name="DocIcon" />
                <FieldRef Name="LinkFilename" />
                <FieldRef Name="Modified" />
                <FieldRef Name="Editor" />
              </ViewFields>
              <RowLimit Paged="TRUE">30</RowLimit>
              <JSLink>clienttemplates.js</JSLink>
            </View>
          </pnp:Views>
          <pnp:FieldRefs>
            <pnp:FieldRef ID="ef991a83-108d-4407-8ee5-ccc0c3d836b9" Name="SharedWithUsers"
DisplayName="Shared With" />
            <pnp:FieldRef ID="d3c9caf7-044c-4c71-ae64-092981e54b33"
Name="SharedWithDetails" DisplayName="Shared With Details" />
            <pnp:FieldRef ID="3881510a-4e4a-4ee8-b102-8ee8e2d0dd4b" Name="CheckoutUser"
DisplayName="Checked Out To" />
          </pnp:FieldRefs>
          <pnp:UserCustomActions>
            <pnp:CustomAction
                Name="O365ProjectsApp.ManageBusinessProject"
                Location="EditControlBlock"
```

```
              Sequence="100"
              Rights="EditListItems,AddListItems,DeleteListItems"
              Title="Manage Business Project"              Url="{AppSiteUrl}/Project/?
SiteUrl={SiteUrl}&amp;ListId={ListId}&amp;ItemId={ItemId}&amp;ItemUrl={ItemUrl}"
              Enabled="true" />
        </pnp:UserCustomActions>
      </pnp:ListInstance>
    </pnp:Lists>
  </pnp:ProvisioningTemplate>
 </pnp:Templates>
</pnp:Provisioning>
```

The template file declares to provision a new library by using the *ListInstance* element highlighted in bold with a user's custom action, which is also highlighted in bold. Moreover, the template accepts a mandatory parameter named *AppSiteUrl*, which you can see at the beginning of the template, and which allows you to keep the URL of the site publishing the Office 365 application dynamic.

In Listing 10-10, you can see how to apply that provisioning template to a site, creating the artifacts or updating them if they already exist.

LISTING 10-10 Sample code excerpt that applies a provisioning template to a site

```
public static void Provision() {

    // Create a PnP AuthenticationManager object
    AuthenticationManager am = new AuthenticationManager();

    // Authenticate against SPO with an App-Only access token
    using (ClientContext context = am.GetAzureADAppOnlyAuthenticatedContext(
        O365ProjectsAppContext.CurrentSiteUrl, O365ProjectsAppSettings.ClientId,
        O365ProjectsAppSettings.TenantId, O365ProjectsAppSettings.AppOnlyCertificate)) {

        Web web = context.Web;

        // Load the template from the file system
        XMLTemplateProvider provider =
        new XMLFileSystemTemplateProvider(
            String.Format(HttpContext.Current.Server.MapPath(".")),
            "ProvisioningTemplates");

        ProvisioningTemplate template = provider.GetTemplate("O365ProjectsAppSite.xml");

        // Configure the AppSiteUrl parameter
        template.Parameters["AppSiteUrl"] = O365ProjectsAppContext.CurrentAppSiteUrl;

        // Apply the template to the target site
        template.Connector = provider.Connector;
        web.ApplyProvisioningTemplate(template);
    }
}
```

Notice the statement that loads the PnP provisioning template from the file system and then configures the current site URL, providing a value for the required template parameter. Last, by using the *ApplyProvisioningTemplate* extension method, the code applies the template to the target site.

Because internally the PnP Remote Provisioning Engine does delta handling and compares the target site with the source template, this technique will always keep the target site in sync and aligned with the requirements and capabilities defined in the application within the provisioning XML file.

> **Note** For further details about the XML schema available for defining PnP provisioning templates, you can browse the GitHub repository where the schema is defined and available as a community open source project: *https://github.com/OfficeDev/PnP-Provisioning -Schema/.* If you are interested in understanding details about the PnP Provisioning Engine, you can watch the following training video on Channel 9: *https://channel9.msdn.com/blogs /OfficeDevPnP/PnP-Core-Component-Site-Provisioning-Framework.*

Consuming SharePoint Online with delegated permissions

The initial provisioning of artifacts most likely will have to be done using app-only credentials because it requires high permission on the target SharePoint Online. Because the OAuth 2.0 authorization protocol intersects the app permissions with the current user's permissions, you cannot provision artifacts with every kind of user, and you can't assign full control permissions to all users, either. Thus, having the capability to act as app-only, only when needed, is powerful. We could say that the app-only technique, in the context of the Office 365 application model and in the SharePoint Add-in model, is like the *SPSecurity.RunWithElevatedPrivileges* of the old server-side development in SharePoint 201x, but with much more control on the permissions assigned to the app that will act as app-only.

However, in common tasks you probably will need to act with delegated permissions based on the currently logged-in user. In Listing 10-11, you can see a code excerpt that shows how to consume SharePoint Online via CSOM using the current user's identity and an OAuth 2.0 access token with both the user's token and the app token.

LISTING 10-11 Sample code excerpt that consumes SharePoint Online via CSOM using an OAuth 2.0 access token with user's token and app token

```
public static void BrowseLibraryFiles() {

    // Create a PnP AuthenticationManager object
    AuthenticationManager am = new AuthenticationManager();

    // Authenticate against SPO with an App-Only access token
    using (ClientContext context = am.GetAzureADWebApplicationAuthenticatedContext(
        O365ProjectsAppContext.CurrentSiteUrl, (url) => {
            return (MicrosoftGraphHelper.GetAccessTokenForCurrentUser(url));
        })) {
```

```
        Web web = context.Web;
        var targetLibrary = web.GetListByTitle(O365ProjectsAppSettings.LibraryTitle);

        context.Load(targetLibrary.RootFolder,
            fld => fld.ServerRelativeUrl,
            fld => fld.Files.Include(f => f.Title, f => f.ServerRelativeUrl));
        context.ExecuteQueryRetry();

        foreach (var file in targetLibrary.RootFolder.Files) {
            // Handle each file object
        }
    }
}
```

The sample code excerpt creates a *ClientContext* instance object authenticated against Azure AD and based on the current user's authorization context by using the *AuthenticationManager* class of PnP and leveraging its *GetAzureADWebApplicationAuthenticatedContext* method.

Notice that the above code will access the contents with a delegated permission. Thus, it will have access only to those contents that are accessible to both the application, based on its Azure AD delegated permissions, and the currently logged-in user. Because in Azure AD the application has the delegated permission "Read and write items and lists in all site collections" (see Table 10-1), the current user's permissions will determine the effective and resulting permissions.

Whether you want to use delegated permissions or app-only access tokens, by using the techniques illustrated in this and the previous section and having proper permissions in Azure AD and in SharePoint Online, you can do almost everything you need against SharePoint Online by using CSOM and the PnP extension methods and helper classes.

Using the Microsoft Graph

In the first section of this chapter, you saw that creating an Office 365 application enables you to consume not only SharePoint Online, but also the entire Office 365 ecosystem. Moreover, in Section III, "Consuming Office 365," you learned how to leverage the Microsoft Graph API and the Microsoft Graph SDK to interact with and consume the main services of Office 365. In this section, you will learn how to apply what you have learned in theory to a real use case.

In this section, the key point is how to leverage the OAuth access token to consume the Microsoft Graph API, not the specific actions executed. Nevertheless, discussing the potential and the capabilities through real examples makes it easier to understand the topic and to follow the flow.

Creating and consuming the project's Office 365 Group

One requirement of the business use case to which the sample Office 365 application refers is to create a new Office 365 Group for each project that has to be managed. In the code samples, you will find the full implementation of the solution. Here, we will discuss just what really matters from a learning perspective.

In Listing 10-12, you can see a code excerpt of a helper method that creates a new Office 365 Group, assigns some users as members of the just-created group, and optionally updates the image of the group.

LISTING 10-12 Helper method that uses the Microsoft Graph API to create and configure an Office 365 Group

```
/// <summary>
/// Creates a new Office 365 Group for a target Project
/// </summary>
/// <param name="group">The group to create</param>
/// <param name="membersUPN">An array of members' UPNs</param>
/// <param name="photo">The photo of the group</param>
/// <returns>The Office 365 Group created</returns>
public static Group CreateOffice365Group(Group group, String[] membersUPN,
    Stream photo = null) {

    // Create the Office 365 Group
    String jsonResponse = MicrosoftGraphHelper.MakePostRequestForString(
        String.Format("{0}groups",
            MicrosoftGraphHelper.MicrosoftGraphV1BaseUri),
        group, "application/json");

    var addedGroup = JsonConvert.DeserializeObject<Group>(jsonResponse);

    // Set users' membership
    foreach (var upn in membersUPN) {
        MicrosoftGraphHelper.MakePostRequest(
            String.Format("{0}groups/{1}/members/$ref",
                MicrosoftGraphHelper.MicrosoftGraphV1BaseUri,
                addedGroup.Id),
            new GroupMemberToAdd {
                ObjectId = String.Format("{0}users/{1}/id",
                MicrosoftGraphHelper.MicrosoftGraphV1BaseUri, upn)
            },
            "application/json");
    }

    // Update the group's picture, if any
    if (photo != null) {
        // Retry up to 10 times within 5 seconds, because the
        // Office 365 Group sometime takes long to be ready
        Int32 retryCount = 0;
        while (true) {
            retryCount++;
            try {
                if (retryCount > 10) break;
```

```
                System.Threading.Thread.Sleep(TimeSpan.FromMilliseconds(500));

                photo.Position = 0;
                MemoryStream photoCopy = new MemoryStream();
                photo.CopyTo(photoCopy);
                photoCopy.Position = 0;

                MicrosoftGraphHelper.MakePatchRequestForString(
                    String.Format("{0}groups/{1}/photo/$value",
                        MicrosoftGraphHelper.MicrosoftGraphV1BaseUri,
                        addedGroup.Id),
                    photoCopy, "image/jpeg");

                break;
            }
            catch {
                // Ignore any exception, just wait for a while and retry
            }
        }
    }

    return (addedGroup);
}
```

As you can see, all the tasks are handled by making some HTTPS direct requests against the Microsoft Graph API endpoints. From an authorization perspective, the code leverages the delegated permissions of type "Read and write directory data," and "Read and write all groups," which means that the user invoking the function must have at least the same permissions. Notice also that the upload of the custom image for the group implements a retry logic because often the image is available as a target endpoint a few milliseconds after the creation of the group. The group creation method returns the just-created group, which can be useful for further use.

In the sample project, whenever a user clicks the ECB menu item Manage Business Project, which has been created in the section "Extending and consuming SharePoint Online" earlier in this chapter, the MVC controller that will handle the request will check if the Office 365 Group backing the project exists. If the group exists, the controller will consume it, providing to the end user some high-level information about the group. If the group does not exist, the controller will use the method illustrated in Listing 10-12 to create the group.

In Listing 10-13, you can see a code excerpt used to test whether the Office 365 Group exists.

LISTING 10-13 Helper method that uses the Microsoft Graph API to check if an Office 365 Group exists

```
/// <summary>
/// Checks whether an Office 365 Group exists or not
/// </summary>
/// <param name="groupName">The name of the group</param>
/// <returns>Whether the group exists or not</returns>
public static Boolean Office365GroupExists(String groupName) {
```

```
String jsonResponse = MicrosoftGraphHelper.MakeGetRequestForString(
    String.Format("{0}groups?$select=id,displayName" +
        "&$filter=groupTypes/any(gt:%20gt%20eq%20'Unified')%20" +
        "and%20displayName%20eq%20'{1}'",
        MicrosoftGraphHelper.MicrosoftGraphV1BaseUri,
        HttpUtility.UrlEncode(groupName).Replace("%27", "''")));

var foundGroups = JsonConvert.DeserializeObject<GroupsList>(jsonResponse);
return (foundGroups != null && foundGroups.Groups.Count > 0);
}
```

The sample method makes a REST request against the collection of groups in the current tenant, filtering the items based on the values in the *groupTypes* collection and searching the target group by display name. If the response is a collection of at least one item, the group does exist; otherwise, it doesn't.

Sending notifications on behalf of users

After creating the Office 365 Group for the project, you may want to send an email message to the group members by leveraging the conversation panel of the just-created group.

Using the current user's context of authentication, you can automate the sending of the message on behalf of the current user. The group will get a message from the current user, but in reality the application will send the message automatically. To achieve the described result, the application must have proper permissions in Azure AD, as discussed at the beginning of this chapter.

In Listing 10-14, you can see a code excerpt that sends a new thread message to the conversation stream of the group.

LISTING 10-14 Helper method that uses the Microsoft Graph API to send a message to an Office 365 Group

```
/// <summary>
/// Creates a new thread in the conversation flow of a target Office 365 Group
/// </summary>
/// <param name="groupId">The ID of the target Office 365 Group</param>
public static void SendMessageToGroupConversation(String groupId) {
    var conversation = new Conversation {
        Topic = "Let's manage this Business Project!",
        Threads = new List<ConversationThread>(
            new ConversationThread[] {
                    new ConversationThread {
                    Topic = "I've just created this Business Project",
                    Posts = new List<ConversationThreadPost>(
                        new ConversationThreadPost[] {
                            new ConversationThreadPost {
                                Body = new ItemBody {
                                    Content = "<h1>Welcome to Project</h1>",
                                    Type = BodyType.Html,
                                },
```

```
                    }
                })
            }
        })
    };

    MicrosoftGraphHelper.MakePostRequest(
        String.Format("{0}groups/{1}/conversations",
            MicrosoftGraphHelper.MicrosoftGraphV1BaseUri, groupId),
            conversation, "application/json");
}
```

The key part of the code sample is the creation of the new *Conversation* object that is made of a new *ConversationThread*. As you can see in Figure 10-5, the result will be the creation of a new welcome thread in the new Office 365 Group.

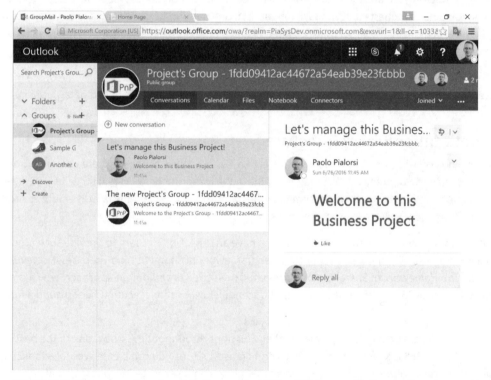

FIGURE 10-5 The conversation view of the just-created Office 365 Group, with the new thread created by code

Creating asynchronous jobs

As you probably experienced while playing with the examples of the previous section, the creation of an Office 365 Group can take a few seconds because under the cover it will create a SharePoint Online site collection and some other objects in Azure AD and Exchange Online. In general, many tasks can take quite a long time to complete or just an unpredictable amount of time to run whenever you interact with external services that are provided by a third party or by a cloud-based platform. Moreover, in Office 365 there are throttling rules that may cause some of your requests to fail, as you saw with SharePoint Online when talking about the benefits of using the *ExecuteQueryRetry* method of PnP compared with the standard *ExecuteQuery*.

Furthermore, while consuming such API and services within a web-based application, the HTTP requests from the web browser (that is, the client) to the web server that is providing the functionality can time out while waiting for back-end services. For example, if you host your ASP.NET MVC web application in Microsoft Azure, by default you will have one minute of request timeout. What if you want or need to manage requests that can take longer than one minute? In general, what can you do to have a stronger and more available software architecture, avoiding tight dependancies on unpredictable completion times of third-party services?

There are some good patterns that make your software architectures more solid. One of the most powerful patterns is the asynchronous job, which will be discussed in the following paragraphs.

Remote timer job architecture

The basic idea of the asynchronous job pattern is to avoid executing actions that are complex, long-running, or have an unpredictable completion time in the foreground and in real time, instead leveraging a queue of actions that will be performed in the background by an engine (a worker job) as soon as there are resources available for processing them.

Many enterprise-level platforms and solutions have an out-of-box system to provide such functionalities. For example, think about the TimerJob framework of SharePoint on-premises. However, the TimerJob framework of SharePoint requires a full trust code development approach, which is not suitable for Office 365. In Office 365, there isn't a scheduler service for executing background actions or tasks.

Nevertheless, as you have seen in many other situations throughout this book, one of the best friends of Office 365 is Microsoft Azure. By using Microsoft Azure, you can create WebJobs that can be scheduled to run at a specific time based on a schedule or can be executed on demand manually by users or triggered by some external event. One of the possible events that can be used to trigger an Azure WebJob is the presence of a message in an Azure Storage Queue.

Thus, whenever you are in an Office 365 application and need to perform an action that is business critical and can take an unpredictable amount of time to run, you can enqueue into an Azure Storage Queue a request to perform that action. Later, an Azure WebJob will be triggered and will perform the real action in the background. In Figure 10-6, you can see an architectural schema of the overall solution.

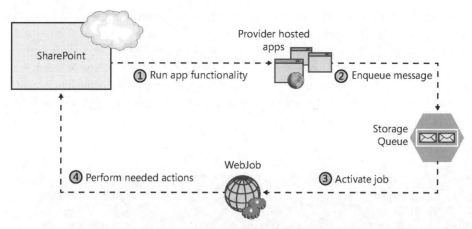

FIGURE 10-6 The architecture of an asynchronous WebJob for Office 365

The job is often referred to as a "remote timer job" because it mimics a classic SharePoint timer job, but it acts remotely by using the Microsoft Graph and the SharePoint REST API instead of any server-side code. Moreover, it can be a job that interacts with the entire Office 365 ecosystem using the Office 365 application model. From an authentication perspective, the job can access the Office 365 services either by using a set of application credentials (username and password) or—even better—by using a *ClientID* and *SharedSecret* by leveraging the OAuth 2.0 protocol and Azure AD, typically running in an app-only authorization context.

If you are targeting SharePoint Online only, you can even consider using the PnP remote timer job framework, which is part of the PnP Core library and provides some useful types (base abstract classes and helper types) to make it easier for you to create a remote timer job for SharePoint with this new model. For example, you could have a SharePoint Online remote timer job to check the security settings of sites. In fact, it is a good habit and a best practice to have at least two site collection administrators for each site collection, but SharePoint Online requires only one site collection administrator. Thus, you can create a SharePoint remote timer job that can go through all the existing site collections of a tenant and double-check the number of site collection administrators, adding a predefined second one where there is only one or sending an alert to the single site collection administrator. This is a perfect candidate for using the PnP remote timer job framework and for targeting SharePoint Online only. In the PnP Partner Pack sample solution, there is this kind of sample remote timer job for SharePoint Online.

However, there are many scenarios in which you will need to target the entire Office 365 ecosystem. For example, what we did in the previous section—creating an Office 365 Group, setting its image, and enabling members of the group—is a good candidate for such an asynchronous task.

Creating a remote timer job in Azure

Let's see how you can create a real remote timer job hosted in Azure that will create and configure Office 365 Groups with the asynchronous pattern described in the previous section.

First of all, you have to create a Microsoft Azure Blob Storage account that will host the Blob Queue. To do this, open the Microsoft Azure management portal (*https://portal.azure.com/*) and select a target subscription, which will be used for the required services. From the left menu of the portal (see Figure 10-7), you can select Storage Accounts and then select to Add A New Storage Account. Provide all the required information—the storage account name, the performance level, the deployment model, and so on. Aside from the name, from the current task perspective you can keep every option with its default value.

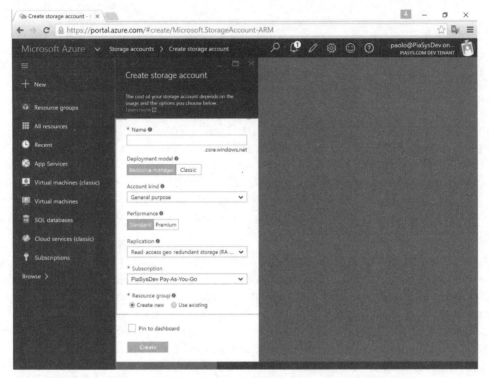

FIGURE 10-7 The UI of the Azure management portal while creating a new storage account

Once you have created the Azure Blob storage account, click the *Keys* button, which is in the upper-right corner of the panel of the just-created storage account. Copy the storage account name and the primary and secondary storage keys in a safe place because we will use them soon.

Now, create a new project of type Console Application, which can be added to the current solution. Reference the PnP Core library for SharePoint Online (SharePointPnPCoreOnline) via NuGet. Then, add the *Microsoft.Azure.WebJobs* package. For the sake of having better management of the overall solution, in the current sample solution it has been added as a class library project, which is used to share some types between the ASP.NET MVC web application and the console remote timer job. Thus, in the reference sample solution you will find a slightly refactored architecture, compared with what you have seen previously.

Add a new class to the console project, give it whatever name you like, and add a function like the one illustrated in Listing 10-15.

LISTING 10-15 Class and function triggered by a message in a Blob Storage Queue

```
public class JobActivator {
    // This function will get triggered/executed when a new message is written
    // on an Azure Queue called queue.
    public static void ProcessQueueMessage(
        [QueueTrigger(O365ProjectsAppConstants.Blob_Storage_Queue_Name)]
            GroupCreationInformation groupCreation,
            TextWriter log) {
        log.WriteLine(String.Format("Found Job: {0}", content));

        // Here will go you real code ...

        log.WriteLine("Completed Job");
    }
}
```

The method signature is simple, but notice the *QueueTrigger* attribute applied to the first argument. The purpose of the attribute is to instruct the job engine to trigger this method whenever there is a new message in a queue, whose name is provided as an argument to the attribute. To make the sample solution easier to maintain, we provide the name of the queue to poll via a string constant stored in a helper type, which is defined in the infrastructural class library. Moreover, the first argument of the method is a POCO (Plain Old CLR Object) instance of type *GroupCreationInformation*, which you can define freely and which will be used to hold the deserialized content of every enqueued message. The *QueueTrigger* attribute supports the following types as input arguments for the queue message:

- *String*

- *Byte[]*

- Any POCO type

- *CloudQueueMessage*

The second argument of the method allows you to keep track of the job activities by logging them through a *TextWriter* object.

In Listing 10-16, you can see how the *GroupCreationInformation* type is defined. It is a lightweight object with just a few properties that define the general information useful to create the Office 365 Group under the cover of the business project. It is fundamental to notice that any custom type used as a message for a Blob Storage Queue will have to be serializable through the NewtonSoft.Json library because internally the Azure WebJobs SDK will use that serialization engine to serialize and deserialize queued messages.

LISTING 10-16 The *GroupCreationInformation* type definition

```
public class GroupCreationInformation {
    public String AccessToken { get; set; }
    public Guid JobId { get; set; }
    public String Name { get; set; }
    public String[] Members { get; set; }
    public Byte[] Photo { get; set; }
}
```

In a real business job, you can handle the typed input argument and implement your own business logic, processing every queued message. In Listing 10-17, you can see the real implementation of the job related to the sample solution for this project.

LISTING 10-17 The real implementation of the queue triggered method of the job

```
// This function will get triggered/executed when a new message is written
// on an Azure Queue called queue.
public static void ProcessQueueMessage(
    [QueueTrigger(O365ProjectsAppConstants.Blob_Storage_Queue_Name)]
GroupCreationInformation groupCreation, TextWriter log) {

    log.WriteLine(String.Format("Starting Job: {0} - Creating Group: {1}",
        groupCreation.JobId, groupCreation.Name));

    // Convert photo into a MemoryStream
    MemoryStream photoStream = new MemoryStream();
    photoStream.Write(groupCreation.Photo, 0, groupCreation.Photo.Length);
    photoStream.Position = 0;

    // Create the Office 365 Group
    var group = GraphRemoteActions.CreateOffice365Group(
        new Group {
            DisplayName = groupCreation.Name,
            MailEnabled = true,
            SecurityEnabled = true,
            GroupTypes = new List<String>(new String[] { "Unified" }),
            MailNickname = groupCreation.Name,
        },
        groupCreation.Members,
        photoStream,
        accessToken: accessToken);

    // Send the welcome message into the group's conversation
    GraphRemoteActions.SendMessageToGroupConversation(group.Id,
        new Conversation {
            Topic = $"Let's manage the Project {groupCreation.Name}!",
            Threads = new List<ConversationThread>(
                new ConversationThread[] {
                    new ConversationThread {
                        Topic = "We've just created this Business Project",
```

```
                    Posts = new List<ConversationThreadPost>(
                        new ConversationThreadPost[] {
                        new ConversationThreadPost {
                            Body = new ItemBody {
                            Content = "<h1>Welcome to this Business Project</h1>",
                            Type = BodyType.Html,
                            },
                        }
                        })
                    }
            })
        },
        accessToken: accessToken);


    log.WriteLine("Completed Job");
}
```

As you can see, the method creates a new Office 365 Group, like in Listing 10-12. After that, it sends the welcome message, using the same syntax that we used in Listing 10-14. Overall, the method implementation is straightforward, and the only difference is that the method will be activated by a queued message.

Moreover, because the job will be executed in the background and without an interactive user's session, from an authentication and authorization perspective you have three options: passing the interactive user's OAuth access token to the background job; using an app-only access token with an X.509 certificate authentication; or using an explicit set of credentials (username and password) of an application account. Because in the current sample the Office 365 Group needs to be created by an explicit user's account that will automatically become the owner of the group, in Listing 10-17 you see the *accessToken* argument passed to both the methods that create the group and start the first conversation in the group. That access token is the one of the interactive user who enqueued the async job item in the Blob Storage Queue, and it is passed through the *AccessToken* property of the *GroupCreationInformation* instance. For security reasons, you should encipher the access token value to avoid having sensitive data represented in cleartext in the Blob Storage Queue.

To make the job effective, you will also need to add a couple of statements in the *Main* static method entry point of the console application. In Listing 10-18, you can see the *Main* method implementation.

LISTING 10-18 The *Main* method of the console application under the cover of the remote timer job

```
class Program {
    static void Main() {
        var host = new JobHost();
        // The following code ensures that the WebJob will be running continuously
        host.RunAndBlock();
    }
}
```

The *RunAndBlock* method of the *JobHost* type allows the WebJob to run continuously, waiting for external triggers (like a new message in the Blob Storage Queue), keeping the foreground thread on hold, and leveraging background threads for the asynchronous events.

Moreover, to run the job properly, you will have to configure a couple of connection strings in the *App.Config* of the console application. These settings reference the Azure Storage Queue and will be used by the Azure WebJobs infrastructure to run the job. In Listing 10-19, you can see an excerpt of the *App.Config* file showing those connection strings. You will also have to configure the *App.Config* file of the console application to have the settings related to the Office 365 application and the custom configuration settings for the app.

LISTING 10-19 An excerpt of the *App.Config* file of the remote timer job

```xml
<?xml version="1.0" encoding="utf-8"?>
<configuration>

    <!-Omissis, for the sake of simplicity ... -->

    <connectionStrings>
        <add name="AzureWebJobsDashboard"
            connectionString="[Azure Blob Storage Connection String]" />
        <add name="AzureWebJobsStorage"
            connectionString="[Azure Blob Storage Connection String]" />
    </connectionStrings>

    <!-Omissis, for the sake of simplicity ... -->

</configuration>
```

The *connectionString* attribute's values, which will be based on the storage account name and the primary or secondary storage keys that you saved previously, will look like the following excerpt:

```
"DefaultEndpointsProtocol=https;AccountName=[StorageAccountName];AccountKey=[Key]"
```

However, the key element of an asynchronous job like the one we are discussing is in the code that enqueues a new message in the Azure Blob Queue. Returning to the ASP.NET MVC application, we need to replace the code that creates the Office 365 Group in the controller with some new statements that will send the typed message to the queue. In Listing 10-20, you can see a sample implementation for the new MVC controller.

LISTING 10-20 An excerpt of the MVC controller implementation that creates a message and enqueues it into the Azure Blob Queue

```
try {
    // Get the storage account for Azure Storage Queue
    CloudStorageAccount storageAccount =
        CloudStorageAccount.Parse(ConfigurationManager
            .ConnectionStrings["AzureWebJobsStorage"].ConnectionString);
```

```
    // Get queue ... and create if it does not exist
    CloudQueueClient queueClient = storageAccount.CreateCloudQueueClient();
    CloudQueue queue = queueClient.GetQueueReference(
        O365ProjectsAppConstants.Blob_Storage_Queue_Name);
    queue.CreateIfNotExists();

    // Add entry to queue
    queue.AddMessage(new CloudQueueMessage(JsonConvert.SerializeObject(job)));
}
catch (Exception) {
    // TODO: Handle any exception thrown by the object of type CloudQueue
}
```

The first part of the excerpt creates an instance of the *CloudStorageAccount* type and of type *CloudQueueClient*, then it checks if the target queue already exists. If it doesn't, it creates it by using the method *CreateIfNotExists*, which is highlighted in bold. Next, the method enqueues an object of type *GroupCreationInformation*. On average, this is a very fast operation that will take no more than a few seconds or even milliseconds. In the background, the job will do the real work, taking all the time needed. To make the above code work, you will also have to configure the connection with name *AzureWebJobsStorage* in the web.config file of the ASP.NET MVC web application, providing the same connection string value that you used in Listing 10-19.

Be careful that the job activation is not in real time. For example, up to a minute could elapse between enqueueing a message and starting its processing. By default, the polling engine retrieves messages every two seconds, and if there are no messages in the queue it will wait for four seconds. If there are no messages in the queue after four seconds, the engine will wait much longer. As long as there are no new messages in the queue, the WebJobs SDK will increase the wait time between polls up to one minute, which is a configurable time span. Thus, a high-traffic queue will trigger events quickly, basically every two seconds, while a low-traffic queue will trigger events every minute.

Moreover, from a scalability perspective, you can run the WebJob on multiple App Service instances, and the WebJobs SDK will guarantee out of the box the synchronization and the concurrency lock to avoid processing a message multiple times on multiple instances. By default, the WebJobs SDK allows a single instance to process up to 16 messages concurrently, but you can customize the batch size setting.

Furthermore, in case of any issue while processing the message on the job side, you can even leverage an out-of-box retry logic. In fact, whenever an exception occurs in the job, if you throw it back, doing some logging or tracing, and you don't hide it from the calling process, the currently processed message will be put back into the queue, allowing for further processing with an out-of-box retry logic. If the issue that caused the exception can be fixed, this will give you the capability to improve the availability of the job. In contrast, if you hide the exception from the calling infrastructure, the queued message will be completely removed from the queue and you will lose it, even if an exception occurred. The out-of-box retry logic will retry processing a message up to five times, and the retry number is configurable. If the job cannot be processed within the boundaries of the retry logic, it will be moved into a poison queue with the name *[QueueName]-poison*. The content of the poison queue can be inspected by code, so you can do further investigation or reprocess any failing message after providing a proper solution to the blocking issue.

Maybe you are wondering how you can access the poison queue and, more generally, if there are any tools or techniques to inspect the content of the Azure Blob Queue. Aside from using the API, which is a suitable path even if challenging to implement, you can download and install tools like the Microsoft Azure Storage Explorer (*http://storageexplorer.com/*). Such tools allow you to browse the queues defined in an Azure Storage account. In Figure 10-8, you can see a screenshot of the tool while inspecting a real queue.

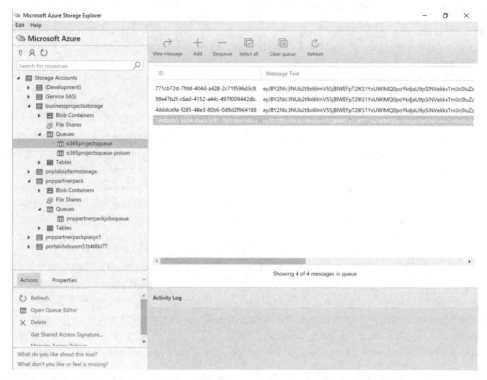

FIGURE 10-8 The UI of the Azure Storage Explorer tool while inspecting the content of a queue

Publishing the application on Azure

One fundamental step in the process of creating an Office 365 application is publishing the custom web application together with any additional services or jobs. The choice of the hosting infrastructure is up to you, and from an Office 365 perspective it doesn't really matter what you choose. However, publishing on Microsft Azure is often a good choice because it will allow you to easily leverage all the out-of-box capabilities of Microsoft's Platform as a Service (PaaS) offering.

Thus, in this section you will learn how to publish the full sample solution onto Microsoft Azure, using an Azure App Service and an Azure WebJob. As a reminder, the full source code of the sample solution illustrated in this chapter is available at the following URL: *https://github.com/OfficeDev/PnP /tree/master/Samples/BusinessApps.O365ProjectsApp*.

Publishing the Azure App Service

To publish the ASP.NET MVC web application, first you have to create a new Azure App Service. While creating the web application project, you can ask Microsoft Visual Studio 2015 to create it for you. However, I usually prefer to keep the publishing phase separate from the project creation phase.

So, access the Azure management portal and select to add a new Azure App Service, give it a name, choose a size (from a vertical scaling perspective) at least of type Basic to have support for custom certificates, and wait a few seconds for its creation. After creating the Azure App Service, you can download the publishing profile file from the portal UI. The publishing profile file will be useful for publishing the application to the just-created App Service from within Visual Studio. Another option that you have when working in Visual Studio 2015 is to right-click the web application project and select the Publish On Azure option. You will be prompted with information requests—for example, the name of the target Azure subscription and the target App Service, whether you want to build the project in release or in debug mode while publishing, and so on.

The publishing wizard is easy to follow, and the only key point is the request about the authentication model that you want to use for the published application, which is prompted in the Publish Web Wizard. Because you are targeting Microsoft Office 365 and have already configured the OpenID Connect authenticaton, which you did in the section "Creating and registering the Office 365 application" earlier in this chapter, you need to clear the Enable Organizational Account check box to ensure that the published application will not have the security settings scrambled.

Once you have published the application on the Azure App Service, you have to go back to the Azure management portal, select the just-created App Service, and open the Settings pane. There, you will have to configure a couple of settings to support the X.509 certificate authentication against Azure AD.

First of all, you need to upload the .PFX file of the X.509 certificate that you created. If you created the certificate using the PowerShell suggested in the section "App-only authorization registration" earlier in this chapter, you will find the .PFX file beside the .CER file in the same folder. Go back to the management UI of the Azure App Service object in the Azure management portal, select Settings, and then select Certificates. From there, you can upload a .PFX certificate as long as you have the password for accessing the private key. The certificate, together with its private key, will be stored in the current user's personal certificates store (CurrentUser/My). For an Azure App Service, the current user is the identity used for running the web application pools—that is, the identity running the service.

Moreover, you will need to authorize the Azure App Service to access that certificate. Luckily, in the Settings page of the Azure App Service, you can load custom configuration settings that will be similar to the AppSettings section of any .config XML file. There are some infrastructural settings that can be configured with the same approach, and they usually have a name starting with the trailer *WEBSITE_*. In particular, there is the *WEBSITE_LOAD_CERTIFICATES* setting, which instructs the Azure hosting environment about how to handle any custom certificates stored in the current user's personal certificates store. If you provide a value of * for that setting—without quotes—you instruct Azure to allow the App Service to load any of the certificates from the current user's personal certificates store. Otherwise, if you want to load just some specific certificates, you can provide the thumbprints of those certificates, comma separated.

In the infrastructural project, within the *O365ProjectSettings* class, you can find a bunch of code that loads the X.509 certificate from the current user's personal certificates store.

Let's publish the web application and play with it. However, to authenticate against Azure AD with the just-published Azure website, you will also have to update the Login URL and the Return URLs settings of the Office 365 application in Azure AD. So far, you have been using the localhost URLs, but now you need to replace them with the new Azure App Service URLs.

Publishing the WebJob

Another fundamental component of the current sample solution is the remote timer job, which will have to be published on Azure as an Azure WebJob. From a hosting perspective, an Azure WebJob is hosted within an Azure App Service. There are three main methods for activating an Azure WebJob:

- **Manual Activation**   The job is activated manually; for example, by using the Azure management portal UI.

- **Scheduled Activation**   The job is activated based on a predefined and customizable schedule. It requires you to use the Azure Scheduler service, and you will incur further billing for using this service.

- **Continuous**   The job is running continuously, like an always-on engine.

From our perspective, the Continuous model is the best one because the job will always be on, and upon receival of a message in the queue it will be activated promptly.

To publish the job on Microsoft Azure, you can right-click the console application project that implements the job and select the option Publish As Azure WebJob. A wizard will ask you to choose the activation model (select Continous) and the target Azure App Service that will host the job. You can select the same Azure App Service that you are using to host the web application.

It will take a while to publish the job, but after completion you will see the job in the Azure management portal and will be able to monitor it. If you go to the App Service management UI and select WebJobs, you will see the just-published job. By clicking/selecting the job, you will be able to open the web-based UI provided for managing jobs in Azure. In Figure 10-9, you can see the monitoring UI that is provided out of the box.

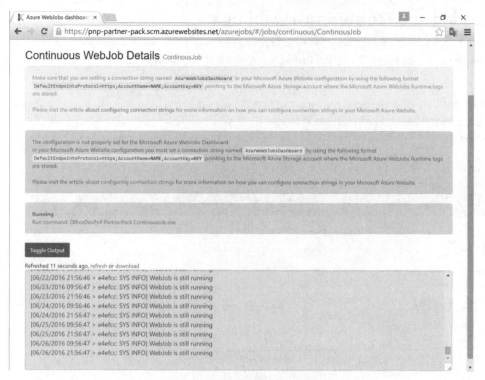

FIGURE 10-9 The web-based UI to manage an Azure WebJob

If you click the Logs command of a specific job instance, select a running instance, and click the Toggle Output button, you can see the WebJob monitoring UI, and you will be able to see all the logging messages written by the WebJobs SDK and from your job through the *TextWriter* object.

You can even inspect the logs of executed and completed jobs. However, in the case of a continuous job, you will have an always running process, and usually all the logs will be available in the unique logging session of the currently running instance. Nevertheless, you will still be able to inspect logs of previously completed batch processes.

Office 365 Connectors

One last interesting option for extending Office 365 and especially the Office 365 Groups are the Office 365 Connectors. In this section, you will learn how to leverage the out-of-box webhooks connectors and how to create completely custom connectors.

As you learned in Chapter 2, in the section "Office 365 Connectors," there are two flavors of connectors. The first are registered in Office 365 and available to multiple Office 365 Groups and are published on the public marketplace and available to any Office 365 tenant. The second are related to a single Office 365 Group and behave like a webhook communicating over HTTPS through JSON messages.

Creating and registering a webhook

The webhooks are the easiest way to implement connectors. However, as already stated, you have to register them for every Office 365 Group. Here, you will learn how to create and register a custom webhook.

First of all, you have to open the target Office 365 Group. In the UI of the group, you will see a Connectors tab panel, as you can see in Figure 10-10, which will give you the full list of available connectors.

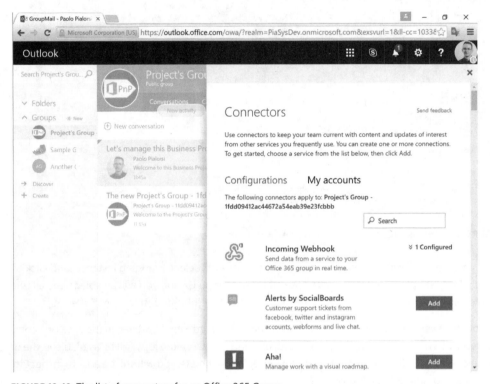

FIGURE 10-10 The list of connectors for an Office 365 Group

Select the connector with name Incoming Webhook and click the Add button to add a new instance. You will be prompted with a screen like the one shown in Figure 10-11.

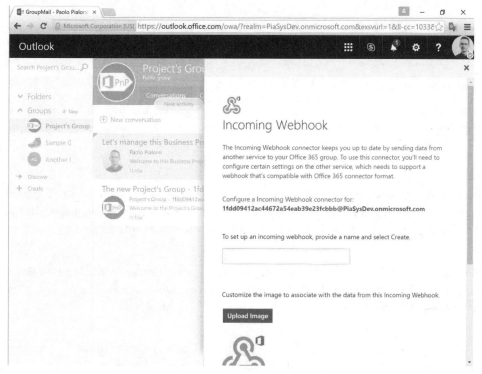

FIGURE 10-11 The UI to add an incoming webhook to an Office 365 Group

There, you have to provide a name for the incoming webhook, and you optionally can provide an image. Click the Create button, and the webhook will be registered. The resulting page will give you the URL to use as the target HTTPS endpoint for your messages. Copy that URL and store it in a safe place. The URL will look like the following sample:

> *https://outlook.office365.com/webhook/00395c37-b87b-4371-bf2a-9f94b66275fa@6c94075a*
> *-da0a-4c6a-8411-badf652e8b53/IncomingWebhook/2511ea6499824decb668b6c40b849f37*
> */bea7a848-0459-4bee-9034-5513ee7f66e0*

All the GUIDs within the URL define the references to the context of the current webhook.

To communicate with the target Office 365 Group by using that webhook, you need to send an anonymous HTTPS POST message, in JSON format, to the URL that you got. For the sake of simplicity, you can use tools like Fiddler or CURL to test the webhook and send a card to the target Office 365 Group. For example, you can send a message content like the following excerpt:

```
{"text":"This is your first message from the webhook!"}
```

The above card provides text content that will be the message body in the conversation. The content of the JSON message has to adhere to the card formats defined in the online documentation for Office 365 Connectors.

> **More info** You can find further details about the supported card formats at the following URL: *https://dev.outlook.com/Connectors/GetStarted*.

A more complex card could be the following:

```
{
 "title":"New card from a webhook!",
 "text":"Please visit the [OfficeDev PnP site](http://aka.ms/OfficeDevPnP)!",
 "themeColor":"C0C0C0"
}
```

This second sample sends a card with a title, a body that includes a hyperlink, and a custom color. As you can see, the syntax of the hyperlink in the body is based on the Markdown language, which is also used for editing .MD files on GitHub. You can do much more with the cards' content.

> **More info** For a full reference about the syntax for creating cards, you can read the document "Office 365 Connectors API Reference," which is available at the following URL: *https://dev.outlook.com/connectors/reference*.

If you want to send a message to the webhook using .NET code, you need to use the *HttpClient* type like we did in Section III, "Consuming Office 365," while consuming the Microsoft Graph.

Writing the project's connector

Even if the webhooks are easy to register and implement, adding them manually to every target Office 365 Group is not always the best option. Luckily, you can create much more structured connectors that can be registered at the corporate level and reused across multiple target groups. In this section, you will learn how to create this kind of connector.

The first step to create such a connector is to register it in the Connectors Developer Dashboard, which is available at the following URL: *http://go.microsoft.com/fwlink/?LinkID=780623*. To register a new connector, you will have to log in with your tenant-level credentials and click the New Connector button in the upper-left side of the webpage. The form illustrated in Figure 10-12 will prompt you for some information and configuration settings about the connector that you are creating.

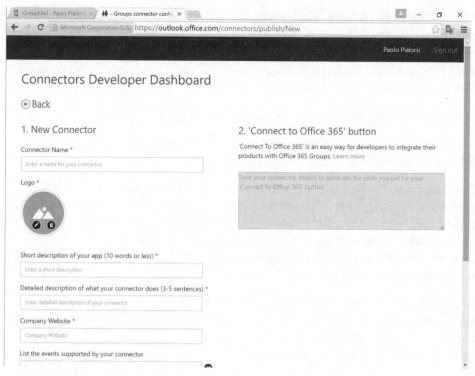

FIGURE 10-12 The UI of the Connectors Developer Dashboard for registering a new connector for an Office 365 Group

The fields of the form are:

- **Connector Name**   The name of the connector; a mandatory field.

- **Logo**   The logo of the connector; a mandatory field.

- **Short Description**   A short description of the connector; a mandatory field.

- **Detailed Description**   A detailed description of the connector; a mandatory field.

- **Company Website**   The URL of the company website, for marketing or reference purposes; a mandatory field.

- **List The Events Supported By Your Connector**   Optional list of events supported by the connector; an optional field.

- **Landing Page For Your Users**   The page to which the users will be brought while adding the connector to a target Office 365 Group; a mandatory field.

- **Redirect URL**   The URL to which the web browser of the end users will be redirected after configuring the group connector. The URL should be under HTTPS, and this is a mandatory field.

Provide at least the values of the mandatory fields and click the Save button. In the right side of the screen, you will see an autogenerated HTML code snippet of a Connect To Office 365 button, which you can embed in your application. If you want to publish the connector on the public market, you can click the Publish To Store button to make the connector publicly available, as long as it adheres to the validation rules of the Office Store.

See Also *For further details about publishing applications in the Office Store, please refer to Chapter 12, "Publishing your applications and add-ins."*

The Connect To Office 365 button will open a URL like the following:

https://outlook.office.com/connectors/Connect?state=myAppsState&app_id=440ae2b5-aa7e-4bbc-9145-ce57ec0fcdb9&callback_url=<Callback_URL>

The *state* argument in the query string defines a custom state that you can pass back to your application within the query string of the *callback_url*. The *app_id* argument in the query string is a GUID to uniquely identify your app. Last, the *callback_url* query string argument defines the URL of the page to which your users will be redirected after having configured the new connector, and it is the URL that you provided in the previous step. In Figure 10-13, you can see the UI of the Connect To Office 365 page, which is provided by clicking the Connect To Office 365 button.

The page will provide a list of Office 365 Groups, and by selecting a group and clicking the Allow button, the user's browser will be redirected to the *callback_url* defined in the query string, getting in the query string of the target page some useful arguments to properly register the webhook for the connector. The following is an example of the *callback_url* with the query string parameters:

*<Callback_URL>?state=myAppsState&webhook_url=https%3A%2F%2Foutlook.office365
.com%2Fwebhook%2Fc748625f-ece2-4951-bab7-6e89ad8b6f10%406c94075a-da0a-4c6a
-8411-badf652e8b53%2F440ae2b5-aa7e-4bbc-9145
-ce57ec0fcdb9%2Fbb274c954fbc4ce7b2996b1f90a5f0b4%2Fbea7a848
-0459-4bee-9034-5513ee7f66e0&group_name=Sample%20Group*

Notice the *webhook_url* argument, which defines the URL of the webhook to use for communicating with the target Office 365 Group. The URL will also provide the *group_name* argument, which defines the name of the target Office 365 Group. If you defined a custom *state* in the Connect To Office 365 button definition, you will get it back in the callback URL.

There is one more query string argument called *error*, which will be provided to the *callback_url* if the end user clicks the Deny button instead of clicking the Allow button to connect the connector with the target Office 365 Group. In this last scenario, the value of the *error* argument will be *AccessDenied*. There are some other possibile values for the *error* argument, but for the sake of brevity we will not cover them here.

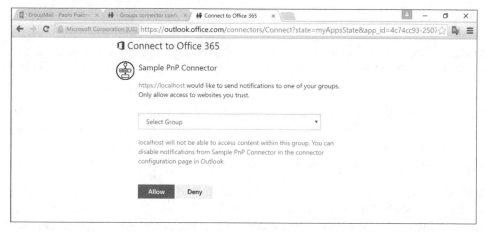

FIGURE 10-13 The UI of the Connect To Office 365 page for adding a custom connector to an Office 365 Group

Furthermore, if you want to play with the connectors without having to create and register a real application, you can leverage the Connectors Sandbox tool, which is available at the following URL: *http://connectplayground.azurewebsites.net/*. In Figure 10-14, you can see the UI of the Connectors Sandbox, which is basically a tool that allows you to send cards to an Office 365 Group using a web-based helper UI and inspect the JSON sent to the target group.

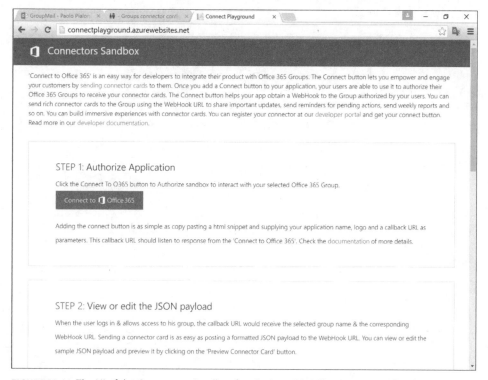

FIGURE 10-14 The UI of the Connectors Sandbox for playing with Office 365 Connectors

Summary

In this chapter, you learned a lot of information about how to create real enterprise-level solutions by leveraging Office 365, the services provided by this Platform as a Service (PaaS) offering, and Microsoft Azure.

In particular, you saw how to create and register an Office 365 application in Azure AD. You learned how to configure the application to leverage app-only authentication/authorization and how to set up app permissions properly. You discovered the purpose and the business value of Office UI Fabric to create professional UI and UX for your custom solutions.

Moreover, you saw how to extend SharePoint with custom UI elements and by provisioning custom artifacts like site columns, content types, lists and libraries, and so on. You also experienced how to consume the Microsoft Graph API in real enterprise-level scenarios, like automatically creating Office 365 Groups either in real time or by leveraging a background job. You learned how to create remote timer jobs for SharePoint Online and for Office 365 in general.

Then, you saw how to publish an Office 365 application and any remote timer job to an Azure App Service.

Last, you learned how to create connectors for Office 365 Groups, both simple webhooks registered for a single Office 365 Group and complex connectors available at the tenant level or even globally available in the Office Store.

CHAPTER 11

Overview of Office Add-ins

The Office Add-ins are another kind of custom developed solution that you can create to extend the Microsoft Office 365 ecosystem.

In this chapter, you will have an overview of the various flavors of Office Add-ins that you can create, and you will understand the potential of the Office Add-ins development model.

Introducing Office Add-ins

An Office Add-in is a custom developed extension that can add capabilities or functionalities to the Office client. One key feature of the Office Add-ins is that they can extend not only Office client for desktop, but also the Office Web Apps and the mobile apps for Office. In Figure 11-1, you can see a schema that explains the architecture of an Office Add-in.

XML manifest   Web application   Office add-in

FIGURE 11-1 Architectural schema of an Office Add-in

The Office Add-ins are built using HTML, CSS, and JavaScript and are published through any web hosting environment, such as Microsoft Azure. Moreover, every add-in is defined by a XML manifest file, which provides to Office all of the needed information to load and execute the add-in.

As a result, the Office Add-ins can be hosted and executed wherever you need, regardless of whether you are using Office for desktop or Office Web Apps. They are supported on Office 2013 or later, and they can be sold by using the Office Store or published by using a Corporate Catalog or a network shared folder. Further details about how to publish and sell your Office Add-ins are available in Chapter 12, "Publishing your applications and add-ins."

The Office Add-ins target only some of the applications that are included in the Microsoft Office family. For example, you can create add-ins for Word, Excel, PowerPoint, Project, and Outlook, but not all of the Office applications are extensible through add-ins, at least at the time of this writing. For example, you cannot create an add-in for Microsoft Visio or Office Publisher. Moreover, depending on the type of Office client application, you could have different capabilities and layouts available.

First of all, to understand what Office Add-ins are and how to build them, you need to figure out the various kinds of add-ins that you can build. There are two main groups of add-ins:

- Add-ins that add new functionalities to the target Office client

- Add-ins that provide interactive content that can be embedded into Office documents

For example, in Word, Excel, and PowerPoint, you can leverage add-ins that extend functionalities. In Excel and PowerPoint, you can also embed new contents in the documents. In Outlook, you can add functionalities. In Chapter 2, "Overview of Office 365 development," in Table 2-1 you saw the various flavors of add-ins and how they fit in the Office applications.

In this chapter, you will mainly see how to create Outlook Add-ins, but what you will learn is also valid for building add-ins for all the other Office clients. On GitHub (*https://github.com/OfficeDev/PnP -OfficeAddins/tree/master/Samples/Outlook.ConsumeGraphAPI*), you can find the source code of the sample Outlook Add-in solution that will be discussed in the following sections. You can also find a re- pository with some useful samples of Office Add-ins: *https://github.com/OfficeDev/PnP-OfficeAddins/.*

Tools for creating Office Add-ins

Based on the architecture of Office Add-ins, you can create a new add-in by using any tool that can manage editing of HTML, CSS, and JavaScript files, together with the XML manifest file.

For example, you can use Microsoft Visual Studio 2015 (or 2013) after the Office Developer Tools for Visual Studio are installed.

But you can also use any text/code editor, like Visual Studio Code and the webstack by leveraging tools like Node.js, npm, and Yeoman, which you encountered in Chapter 2 in the section "Preparing for the SharePoint Framework." Being able to use any editor, including Visual Studio Code, and the webstack means that you can also create and develop Office Add-ins using almost any development platform, like Mac OS—you're not forced to use a Microsoft Windows development machine.

Moreover, you can leverage a web-based tool called Napa, which is a SharePoint Add-in that you can use from wherever you like by using a web browser.

In this chapter, you will learn how to use Visual Studio 2015 and Visual Studio Code with the web- stack. The Napa SharePoint Add-in will not be covered.

Regardless of the tools you use to create an Office Add-in, the main steps to build your own solu- tions are:

- Create the add-in XML manifest file

- Create at least one HTML page that will be the entry point of your add-in

- Define the JavaScript logic under the cover of your add-in

Of course, you can create multiple pages to provide your add-in capabilities. However, it is useful to consider using JavaScript frameworks like AngularJS and KnockoutJS and adhering to the single-page application development model, which generally is more interesting from an add-in development perspective. By using the single-page application approach, you can think about the add-in as a whole application with multiple views and controls, all rendered and managed through a unique entry point, and with some data binding rules to render any supporting data source. It will be almost like a real desktop application with a form-based UI.

While writing the business logic under the cover of your add-in, you will leverage JavaScript and some supporting APIs like the Microsoft Graph, the SharePoint REST API, or any custom developed REST API. Moreover, you will be able to use the JavaScript API for Office targeting the specific Office client application that you are extending. For example, if you are creating a Task Pane Office Add-in for Microsoft Excel, you can use the Excel JavaScript API to interact with the current sheet and its content.

One last tool that you likely will use is the Office UI Fabric package, which you saw in practice in Chapter 10, "Creating Office 365 applications," and which provides you with a bunch of ready-to-go UI elements to enrich the user experience of your add-ins and to make them adhere to the UI guidelines and rules provided by Microsoft. By using the Office UI Fabric components in an Office Add-in, you will be able to make it behave exactly like the container Office client application, giving your end users an integrated and comprehensive user experience.

One last piece of fundamental information to keep in mind is that for security reasons, any Office Add-in has to be published over HTTPS. This includes any external JavaScript library consumed, for example, from an external CDN (content delivery network) and any UI element like images or CSS files. Thus, if you are hosting the Office Add-in on Microsoft Azure, you will be fine out of the box with this requirement because every Azure App Service can publish your Azure websites over HTTPS with an SSL certificate provided by Microsoft Azure and valid for any site with a common name like *.azureweb-sites.net. If you want to use a custom domain, you will have to buy a valid SSL certificate even if you will publish the add-in on Microsoft Azure. Furthermore, if you are hosting your add-in outside Microsoft Azure, you will have to ensure that the third-party hosting provider allows you to publish the add-in over HTTPS, and most likely you will have to acquire an SSL certificate.

Add-in manifest

As you just saw, one key component of every Office Add-in is the manifest file, which is an XML file that defines settings, capabilities, and information about an add-in. The XML manifest file contains information like the following:

- The display name of the add-in, its description, its version, the default locale, and a unique ID for the add-in

- How the add-in can integrate with the various Office client applications (Word, Excel, PowerPoint, Project, Outlook), including any custom UI element

- The permission levels and data access requirements for the add-in

The file by itself is simple and has to be validated against the XML Schema definition for Office Add-in manifests, for which you can find some useful samples at the following URL: *https://dev.office.com /docs/Add-ins/overview/Add-in-manifests*. Moreover, you can find the XSD (XML Schema Definition) files for the XML manifests at the following URL: *https://github.com/OfficeDev/office-js-docs/tree/master/docs/overview/schemas*.

If you are using Microsoft Visual Studio to create your add-ins, you don't need to dig into the details of the XML Schema. You will need to design the add-in settings by using the manifest designer provided by the Office Developer Tools for Visual Studio. In Figure 11-2, you can see the user interface of the manifest designer in Visual Studio 2015 for an Outlook Add-in.

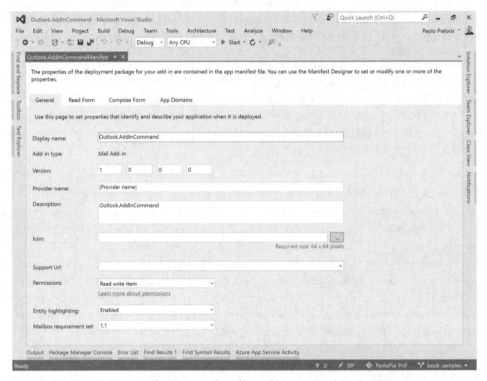

FIGURE 11-2 The UI of the manifest designer for Office Add-ins in Visual Studio 2015

In addition to the general information about the add-in, in the manifest file you can declare a lot of information about the UI elements (like buttons, tabs, menu items, and so on) if the add-in defines custom commands for the UI. In addition, depending on the type of add-in, the XML manifest file can have different shapes and different XML elements.

In the following sections, you will see some kinds of add-ins and have an overview of the most important settings in the corresponding XML manifest files.

Creating Outlook Add-ins

The first family of add-ins about which you will learn are those for extending Outlook client, Outlook Web Access (OWA), and the mailbox consumption in general.

Outlook Add-ins can extend the UI of the client by adding new commands to the ribbon, or they can add new functionalities by providing contextual objects while the users are viewing or composing new items like email messages, meetings, or appointments. Regardless of the target item of the add-in, the code under the cover of the add-in will be able to access the main properties of the current context item through a set of JavaScript API.

As a minimum requirement, Outlook Add-ins need to have the target mailbox hosted in Exchange Server 2013 on-premises or Exchange Online. Moreover, on the client side it is required to have Outlook 2013 or later, Outlook 2016 for Mac, Outlook Web App for Exchange 2013 on-premises, Outlook Web Access in Office 365, or Outlook.com. Last, Outlook Add-ins aren't supported in accounts consumed through IMAP or POP.

Add-in manifest for Outlook

As already stated, the XML manifest file is a fundamental component of an Office Add-in. When you develop an add-in for Outlook, the manifest designer of Visual Studio allows you to define multiple sections divided into tabs.

The first section is called General, and here you find settings about name, version, description, icon (a 64 × 64 pixel image of type PNG, BMP, GIF, JPEG, EXIF, or TIFF), and all the general information that will describe the add-in to the end users. Moreover, through this section you can define the permissions requirements for the add-in by choosing one of the following options: Restricted, Read Item, Read Write Item, or Read Write Mailbox. The permissions names are straightforward, but you can find further details at the following URL: *http://dev.office.com/docs/Add-ins/outlook/understanding -outlook-Add-in-permissions*.

There is also an option to set the mailbox requirement set, which declares the minimum version of APIs supported and requested by the Outlook Add-in to work properly. At the time of this writing, there are three versions: 1.1, 1.2, and 1.3. If you create an add-in with a mailbox requirement of 1.3, the add-in will not be available in any Outlook client that does not support that minimum requirement. In contrast, if your add-in has a minimum mailbox requirement of 1.1, it can be loaded in any Outlook client that supports APIs with a version equal to or higher than 1.1, and the add-in will also be able to use more recent versions of the APIs if needed. In Table 11-1, you can see the mapping between Outlook client versions and the API versions.

TABLE 11-1 Mapping between Outlook client versions and the API versions

Outlook Client	Supported API requirement sets
Outlook 2016	1.1, 1.2, 1.3
Mac Outlook 2016	1.1
Outlook 2013	1.1, 1.2, 1.3
Outlook on the web (Office 365 and Outlook.com)	1.1, 1.2, 1.3
Outlook Web App (Exchange 2013 on-premises)	1.1
Outlook Web App (Exchange 2016 on-premises)	1.1, 1.2, 1.3

Under the cover, the manifest designer defines in the XML file a *Requirements* element with the requirements sets using a syntax like the following:

```
<Requirements>
  <Sets>
    <Set Name="Mailbox" MinVersion="1.1" />
  </Sets>
</Requirements>
```

A second section of settings available in the manifest designer is called Read Form, and it defines if and when the Outlook Add-in will be activated while reading any target item. From this section, which you can see in Figure 11-3, you can define the activation rules for your Mail Add-in and the UI settings of the add-in.

The activation rules supported at the time of this writing are:

- Item is a message

- Item is an appointment

- Item matches a regular expression

- Items has an attachment

- Item contains an address

- Item contains a contact

- Item contains an email address

- Item contains a meeting suggestion

- Item contains a phone number

- Item contains a task suggestion

- Item contains a URL

It is interesting to notice that you can group rules in rule collections and combine rules with AND or OR logic operators to create tailored activation rules based on your real requirements.

Moreover, from the Read Form section you can define if the add-in will be available on tablets and/or on smartphones, and you can provide the relative URL of a custom HTML page for those devices. You can also share a unique HTML page for all of the devices, making the design of the page responsive.

The third section is called Compose Form, and it allows you to declare if you want to activate the add-in while composing an email message and/or while creating a new appointment. If you enable the add-in activation in any of the above scenarios, you will have to provide the relative URL of the HTML pages that provide the compose capability. Again, you can specify a different page for every target device (desktop, tablet, and smartphone), or you can share a unique responsive page.

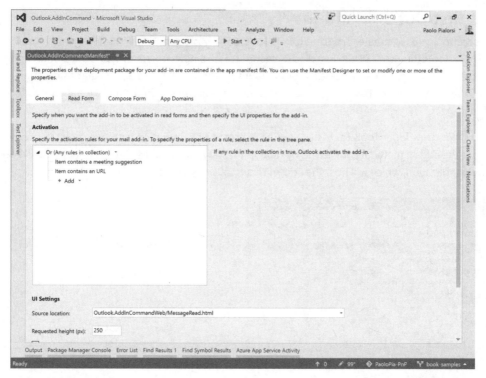

FIGURE 11-3 The Read Form tab of the manifest designer for Outlook Add-ins in Visual Studio 2015

The last section is called App Domains, and it can be used to declare the domains from which your add-in will consume pages, if any. By default, if an Office Add-in opens a URL outside the add-in base URL, the Office client will open a new web browser window to avoid any unexpected injection of HTML for the end user. However, if you really need to rely on a third-party site or content, you can declare its URL in this form, and the Office client will keep rendering that content within the add-in area without using an external web browser.

All the settings you can configure through the manifest designer will be converted into XML elements and attributes in the underlying XML manifest file. At the time of this writing, there are a bunch of new settings related to the new Add-in Commands functionality that are not yet supported in the designer. If you need to edit or configure any of these settings, you will have to open the XML manifest file using an XML text editor and apply changes manually to the file.

Note Be careful while changing the XML manifest manually. Any issue in the XML or any additional namespace that is not supported by Visual Studio could make the manifest designer unable to process the manifest, creating a situation in which you will have to manage the whole manifest manually with a text editor.

Your first Outlook Add-in

In this section, you will create an add-in for Outlook. Start Microsoft Visual Studio 2015 with the Office Developer Tools for Visual Studio installed. Select to create a new project of type Office/SharePoint > Outlook Add-in, give it a name (for example, Outlook.AddInSample) and a path, and start defining the Outlook Add-in. In Figure 11-4, you can see the Solution Explorer of Visual Studio for a new Outlook Add-in project.

The Office Developer Tools for Visual Studio will create a new solution with two projects: one that provides the add-in metadata, including by default the XML manifest file, and another that represents the web application, which will host the add-in UI and business logic.

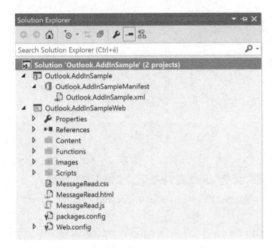

FIGURE 11-4 The outline of the Solution Explorer in Visual Studio 2015 for an Outlook Add-in

Double-click the manifest file (the one with the Office icon) to manage the XML manifest definition by using the manifest designer, as you saw in the previous section. Configure the add-in with proper display name, version, icon, and description. Give it the Read Write Item permission level, and configure the mailbox requirements to version 1.3 (for this example).

By default, the Visual Studio project template creates a sample custom pane add-in that will be activated whenever the end users read any email message. The web application project contains a MessageRead.html page on the root folder, which provides the UI of the add-in. Moreover, there is a *MessageRead.js* file and a *MessageRead.css* file that provide the JavaScript logic for the add-in and its UI style.

If you open the MessageRead.html page, you can see that there are just HTML elements and every logic is loaded from the supporting *MessageRead.js* file. The HTML page by default uses the Office UI Fabric components, downloaded from the public Microsoft CDN (*https://appsforoffice.microsoft.com/*), to give a standard UI to the sample add-in. Moreover, the page downloads the Office JavaScript APIs from the Microsoft CDN to leverage the Office object model for add-ins.

The add-in template will create an add-in that reads some properties from the current context item and shows them in the custom pane. You can start playing with the add-in by starting the project in Visual Studio by pressing F5. Visual Studio will start the deployment of the add-in and will prompt you for credentials of the target mailbox to which you want to install the add-in for testing and debugging purposes. In Figure 11-5, you can see the UI of Visual Studio 2015 prompting for target mailbox credentials.

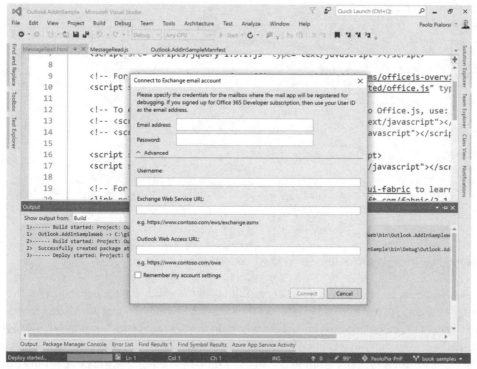

FIGURE 11-5 The dialog of Visual Studio 2015 to collect target mailbox credentials for testing and debugging an Outlook Add-in

If deployment succeeds, the default web browser will be started, and you will be brought to the Outlook Web Access site for the target mailbox. Select any email message, and you will see the add-in in action. In Figure 11-6, you can see the output in the web browser.

Under the cover, Visual Studio 2015 will attach the browser process for debugging of JavaScript code so that you easily can inspect what happens under the cover of the sample add-in. For the sake of simplicity, open the *MessageRead.js* file and browse the source code. At the beginning of the file, you will find the *Office.initialize* function implementation. The following section, "Office JavaScript APIs," will introduce the *Office* namespace in JavaScript. For now, it will suffice to know that the *Office.initialize* function is fundamental and must be defined for each page in your app for every kind of add-in.

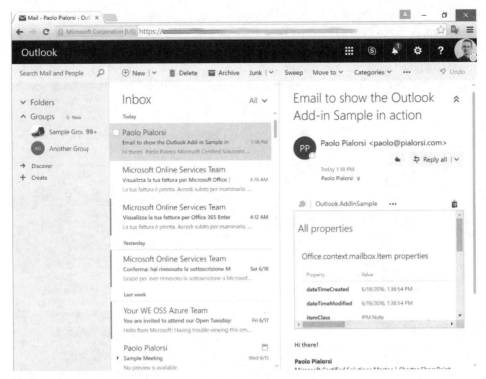

FIGURE 11-6 The sample Outlook Add-in rendered in Outlook Web Access

In the sample implementation of the current Outlook Add-in, inside the *Office.initialize* function there is the handling of a message banner and the invocation of a method that will load all of the properties from the current context item. Generally, from the *Office.initialize* function you will have to invoke all the JavaScript business logic of your add-in to shape the HTML output. The JavaScript business logic will use the Office JavaScript APIs to interact with the hosting Office application and with the current context item, if any.

A more realistic example

Let's say that you want to create an Outlook Add-in to interact by email with a new request for a quote coming from a customer. For example, you could have an activation rule for the add-in that makes it show up whenever the email subject contains a trailer like the following:

```
[Offer Request]
```

Here is the corresponding regular expression:

```
\[Offer Request\]
```

To make the add-in show up when the email subject satisfies the rule, you can edit the manifest file and add an activation rule of type Item Matches A Regular Expression, which will be in logical AND with the rule Item Is A Message. In Figure 11-7, you can see how the activation rules are configured.

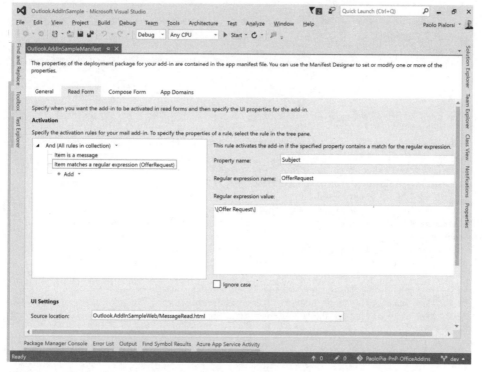

FIGURE 11-7 The Read Form rules to activate the add-in in Outlook

Once the add-in is activated, instead of rendering the properties of the current context item like the out-of-box add-in template does, the custom add-in will render some information about the current sender of the request for quote. First, the add-in will search for any existing contact in the current user's organization by using the Microsoft Graph API. Furthermore, the add-in gets the list of the top documents in the current user's OneDrive for Business with a reference to the customer's display name by using the search capabilities of OneDrive for Business in the Microsoft Graph API.

In Listing 11-1, you can see the updated HTML for the MessageRead.html page, including some HTML placeholder elements that will be used to render the output of the queries executed against the Microsoft Graph API.

LISTING 11-1 The modified source code of the MessageRead.html page for the Outlook Add-in

```
<!DOCTYPE html>
<html>
<head>
    <meta charset="UTF-8" />
    <meta http-equiv="X-UA-Compatible" content="IE=Edge" />
    <title></title>
    <script src="Scripts/jquery-1.9.1.js" type="text/javascript"></script>

    <!-- For the JavaScript APIs for Office, go to http://aka.ms/officejs-overview to
learn more. -->
```

```html
    <script src="https://appsforoffice.microsoft.com/lib/1/hosted/office.js" type="text/
javascript"></script>
    <script
src="https://secure.aadcdn.microsoftonline-p.com/lib/1.0.10/js/adal.min.js"></script>

    <!-- To enable offline debugging using a local reference to Office.js, use: -->
<!--
<script src="Scripts/Office/MicrosoftAjax.js" type="text/javascript"></script>
-->
    <!-- <script src="Scripts/Office/1/office.js" type="text/javascript"></script>  -->

    <script src="MessageRead.js" type="text/javascript"></script>
    <script src="Scripts/FabricUI/MessageBanner.js" type="text/javascript"></script>

    <!-- For the Office UI Fabric, go to http://aka.ms/office-ui-fabric to learn more. -->
    <link rel="stylesheet" href="https://appsforoffice.microsoft.com/fabric/2.1.0/fabric.
min.css" />
    <link rel="stylesheet" href="https://appsforoffice.microsoft.com/fabric/2.1.0/fabric.
components.min.css" />

    <!-- To enable the offline use of Office UI Fabric, use: -->
    <!-- link rel="stylesheet" href="Content/fabric.min.css" -->
    <!-- link rel="stylesheet" href="Content/fabric.components.min.css" -->
</head>
<body>
    <div id="content-header">
        <div class="padding">
            <p class="ms-font-xl ms-fontColor-themeDarkAlt ms-fontWeight-semilight">Sender
Details</p>
        </div>
    </div>
    <div id="content-main" class="ms-Grid">
        <div class="ms-Grid-row">
            <div class="ms-Grid-col ms-u-sm12">
                <h2 class="ms-font-l">Contact details</h2>
                <div class="ms-Table">
                    <div class="ms-Table-row">
                        <span class="ms-Table-cell">Property</span>
                        <span class="ms-Table-cell">Value</span>
                    </div>
                    <div class="ms-Table-row">
                        <span class="ms-Table-cell ms-fontWeight-semibold">Display Name</
span>
                        <span id="senderDisplayName" class="ms-Table-cell"></span>
                    </div>
                    <div class="ms-Table-row">
                        <span class="ms-Table-cell ms-fontWeight-semibold">Company</span>
                        <span id="senderCompanyName" class="ms-Table-cell"></span>
                    </div>
                    <div class="ms-Table-row">
                        <span class="ms-Table-cell ms-fontWeight-semibold">Mobile Phone</
span>
                        <span id="senderMobilePhone" class="ms-Table-cell"></span>
                    </div>
                </div>
```

```
                </div>
            </div>

            <div id="message-props" class="ms-Grid-row hidden">
                <div class="ms-Grid-col ms-u-sm12">
                    <h2 class="ms-font-l">Files related on OneDrive for Business</h2>
                    <div class="ms-Table" id="filesTable">
                        <div class="ms-Table-row">
                            <span class="ms-Table-cell">Filename</span>
                        </div>
                    </div>
                </div>
            </div>
        </div>

        <!-- FabricUI component used for displaying notifications -->
        <div class="ms-MessageBanner" style="position:absolute;bottom: 0;">
            <div class="ms-MessageBanner-content">
                <div class="ms-MessageBanner-text">
                    <div class="ms-MessageBanner-clipper">
                        <div class="ms-font-m-plus ms-fontWeight-semibold"
id="notificationHeader"></div>
                        <div class="ms-font-m ms-fontWeight-semilight"
id="notificationBody"></div>
                    </div>
                </div>
                <button class="ms-MessageBanner-expand" style="display:none"><i class="ms-Icon
ms-Icon--chevronsDown"></i> </button>
                <div class="ms-MessageBanner-action"></div>
            </div>
            <button class="ms-MessageBanner-close"> <i class="ms-Icon ms-Icon--x"></i> </
button>
        </div>
    </body>
</html>
```

Notice that we are using the Office UI Fabric styles to render the output of the add-in.

Before implementing the business logic of the add-in, go to the Azure management portal and—as you learned in Chapter 4, "Azure Active Directory and security"—configure the web application hosting the add-in to have access to Microsoft Azure Active Directory (Azure AD) and to the Microsoft Graph. You will have to provide the Name, the Sign-On URL, and the App ID URI for your application. For the Sign-On URL, provide the full URL of the MessageRead.html page and select proper values for all the other fields. After creating the new Azure AD application, configure it to consume the Microsoft Graph, granting the following delegated permissions:

- Read User Files

- Read User Contacts

Within the add-in, you will use the ADAL.JS (Active Directory Authentication Library for JavaScript) library to get an OAuth 2.0 access token from Azure AD, which will allow you to consume the Microsoft Graph. Because the add-in will consume the Azure AD and the Microsoft Graph from JavaScript, on the client side you will need to enable the OAuth 2.0 implicit flow capability, which is disabled by default in any Azure AD application.

See Also *For further details about the OAuth 2.0 implicit flow capability, you can read the official OAuth 2.0 specification—in particular, the section that explains the implicit flow—which is available at the following URL: https://tools.ietf.org/html/rfc6749#section-1.3.2.*

To configure the OAuth 2.0 implicit flow, while in the configuration page of the just-created Azure AD application, click the Manage Manifest command in the lower part of the screen and select the Download Manifest option. Save the manifest file and open it with a text editor of your choice. Search for the *oauth2AllowImplicitFlow* configuration option, which by default has a value of *false*, and change it to *true*. Save the manifest file and upload it back to Azure AD, overwriting the existing one (Manage Manifest > Upload Manifest).

Now, you have to configure the add-in manifest to allow access to the URL domains related to Azure AD from within the add-in frame. To do that, as you saw previously, you need to edit the App Domains section of the manifest. In Figure 11-8, you can see how the sample add-in is configured.

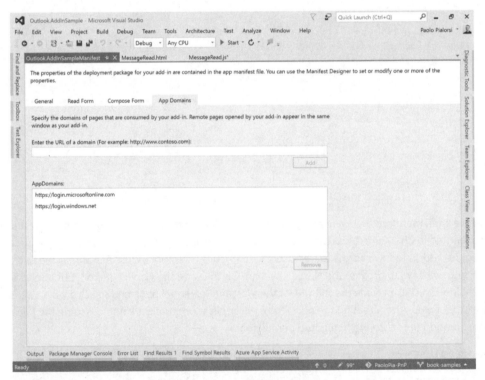

FIGURE 11-8 The App Domains settings for the sample Outlook Add-in

The domains to configure are:

- *https://login.microsoftonline.com*

- *https://login.windows.net*

Configuring these URLs in the manifest will enable your add-in to authenticate the current user and to retrieve an OAuth 2.0 access token without opening any pop-up browser window.

> **Note** If your customers use an external identity provider system, like Active Directory Federation Services (ADFS), you will also have to configure such domains in the App Domains settings of the add-in.

You are now ready to plug the ADAL.JS library and its related logic into the add-in business logic. First, you will have to reference the ADAL.JS library, which can be done by downloading the source code from GitHub (*https://github.com/AzureAD/azure-activedirectory-library-for-js*) or by referencing the official CDN provided by Microsoft through the following *script* tag:

```
<script src="https://secure.aadcdn.microsoftonline-p.com/lib/1.0.10/js/adal.min.js"></script>
```

You can add the previous *script* element to the headers of the MessageRead.html page in the add-in web application, just after the JavaScript APIs for Office *script* element and before the reference to the *MessageRead.js* file, as you can see highlighted in bold in Listing 11-1. If you are using the webstack, you can also reference ADAL.JS via some of the web package managers like npm (*https://www.npmjs.com/*) or Bower (*https://bower.io/*), and there are ADAL libraries for Angular.JS, Cordova, and so on.

Once you have referenced ADAL.JS, you are ready to use it. Open the *MessageRead.js* file and paste the code illustrated in Listing 11-2 at the beginning of the file.

LISTING 11-2 Code excerpt for using ADAL.JS in the Outlook Add-in *MessageRead.js* file

```
// Create ADAL.JS config and
// get the AuthenticationContext
var azureADTenant = "<your tenant>"; // Target Azure AD tenant
var azureADClientID = "<your client ID>"; // App ClientID

// General settings for ADAL.JS
window.config = {
    tenant: azureADTenant + ".onmicrosoft.com",
    clientId: azureADClientID,
    postLogoutRedirectUri: window.location.origin,
    endpoints: {
        graphApiUri: "https://graph.microsoft.com",
        sharePointUri: "https://" + azureADTenant + ".sharepoint.com",
    },
    cacheLocation: "localStorage"
};

// Create the AuthenticationContext object to play with ADAL.JS
```

```
var authContext = new AuthenticationContext(config);

// Check For & Handle Redirect From AAD After Login
var isCallback = authContext.isCallback(window.location.hash);
authContext.handleWindowCallback();

// Check Login Status, Update UI
if (isCallback && !authContext.getLoginError()) {
    window.location = authContext._getItem(authContext.CONSTANTS.STORAGE.LOGIN_REQUEST);
}
else {
    var user = authContext.getCachedUser();
    if (!user) {
        authContext.login();
    }
}
```

As you can see, the code excerpt registers some configuration variables, including the target Azure AD tenant name, the client ID for the current application, and the resources that you want to consume using ADAL for authorization. In Listing 11-2, the target resources are the Microsoft Graph API and SharePoint Online.

After you have prepared the configuration settings, you need to create an instance of the *AuthenticationContext* object of ADAL.JS. Then, the code excerpt checks if the current user is authenticated against Azure AD, and if she isn't, it fires a login request. In a common scenario, because the add-in usually is running within an authenticated context (Office client), the authentication flow will be just one round trip to Azure AD and back to the add-in implementation. You are now ready to consume the Microsoft Graph API with ADAL.JS, which will get an OAuth 2.0 access token for you. In Listing 11-3, you can see the remainder of the *MessageRead.js* file.

LISTING 11-3 Code excerpt of the remainder of *MessageRead.js* file, where the business logic consumes Microsoft Graph API

```
(function () {
  "use strict";

  var messageBanner;

  // The Office initialize function must be run each time a new page is loaded.
  Office.initialize = function (reason) {
    $(document).ready(function () {
      var element = document.querySelector('.ms-MessageBanner');
      messageBanner = new fabric.MessageBanner(element);
      messageBanner.hideBanner();
      loadContextData();
    });
  };

  function loadContextData() {
      var item = Office.context.mailbox.item;
```

```
        var senderDisplayName = item.sender.displayName;

    authContext.acquireToken(config.endpoints.graphApiUri, function (error, token) {
        if (error || !token) {
            console.log("ADAL error occurred: " + error);
            return;
        }
        else {
            var senderContactUri = config.endpoints.graphApiUri + "/v1.0/me/
contacts?$filter=displayName%20eq%20'" + senderDisplayName + "'&$top=1";
            $.ajax({
                type: "GET",
                url: senderContactUri,
                headers: {
                    "Authorization": "Bearer " + token
                }
            }).done(function (response) {
                console.log("Query for sender contact executed.");
                var items = response.value;
                for (var i = 0; i < items.length; i++) {
                    console.log(items[i].displayName);
                    $("#senderDisplayName").text(items[i].displayName);
                    $("#senderCompanyName").text(items[i].companyName);
                    $("#senderMobilePhone").text(items[i].mobilePhone);
                }
            }).fail(function () {
                console.log("Error while searching for sender contact.");
            });

            var filesUri = config.endpoints.graphApiUri + "/v1.0/me/drive/root/
search(q='" + senderDisplayName + "')";

            $.ajax({
                type: "GET",
                url: filesUri,
                headers: {
                    "Authorization": "Bearer " + token
                }
            }).done(function (response) {
                console.log("Successfully fetched files from OneDrive.");
                var items = response.value;
                for (var i = 0; i < items.length; i++) {
                    console.log(items[i].name);
                    $("#filesTable").append("<div class='ms-Table-row'><span class='ms-
Table-cell'><a href='" + items[i].webUrl + "'>" + items[i].name + "</a></span></div>");
                }
            }).fail(function () {
                console.log("Fetching files from OneDrive failed.");
            });
        }
    });
}

// Helper function for displaying notifications
function showNotification(header, content) {
```

```
      $("#notificationHeader").text(header);
      $("#notificationBody").text(content);
      messageBanner.showBanner();
      messageBanner.toggleExpansion();
   }
})();
```

The JavaScript code in Listing 11-3 invokes the *loadContextData* function within the *Office.initialize* method that we have already seen. The *loadContextData* function retrieves a reference to the current item (*Office.context.mailbox.item*) and determines the *displayName* property for the sender of the current email. After that, the code fires a couple of AJAX requests over HTTPS targeting the Microsoft Graph API. The first request retrieves the first contact, if any, who has a *displayName* that matches the name of the sender. The second request searches in the current user's OneDrive for Business root folder for the top files that have the sender's *displayName* in them. The results are bounded to the HTML placeholders illustrated in Listing 11-1.

In Figure 11-9, you can see a screenshot of the resulting add-in consuming a matching email message in Outlook Web Access.

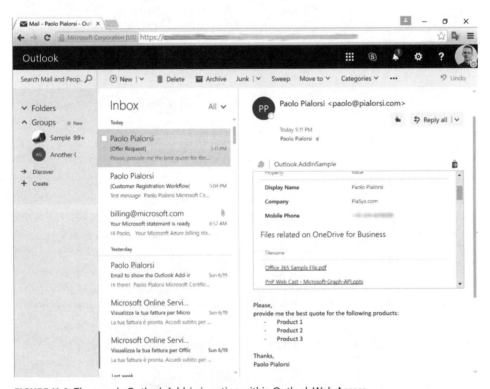

FIGURE 11-9 The sample Outlook Add-in in action within Outlook Web Access

This is a simple example of how to consume the Microsoft Graph API from within an Outlook Add-in. You can do much more, and you can always enrich the client-side development model of the Office

Add-in by implementing a set of custom REST API services (could be ASP.NET MVC *ApiController* types) that can provide custom and additional capabilities to the Office Add-in business logic.

> **Note** The sample Outlook Add-in illustrated in this section is available as an open source project on GitHub at the following URL: *https://github.com/OfficeDev/PnP-OfficeAddins /tree/master/Samples/Outlook.ConsumeGraphAPI.*

Using Yeoman generator

In the previous examples, we created the Outlook Add-ins by using Visual Studio 2015, which is a good option if you are a professional developer, you have proper licenses to run Visual Studio 2015, and you are working on a Windows development machine.

However, if you are working on a Mac OS machine or don't have Visual Studio 2015, you can develop an Office Add-in by using Visual Studio Code and leveraging the Yeoman generator, which we introduced in Chapter 2.

To play with this alternative scenario, start the Cmder console emulator that you installed by following the instructions provided in Chapter 2, in the section "Preparing for the SharePoint Framework." On your local file system, create a new folder that will host all the files related to the add-in that you will build. At the Cmder command prompt, run the following command:

```
yo office
```

The Yeoman generator will start a generation template for creating an Office Add-in.

> **Note** You can find further details about the Yeoman generator for Office and about all the available commands for Office Add-ins at the following URL: *https://github.com/OfficeDev/ generator-office.*

First, you have to provide a name for the add-in project that will be generated. Then, you have to select the target folder where all the autogenerated files will be stored. After that, you have to choose the kind of add-in you want to develop. At the time of this writing, the available options are:

- Mail Add-in (read & compose forms)
- Task Pane Add-in
- Content Add-in

Then, you can choose the technology you want to use for creating the Office Add-in. The available options are:

- HTML, CSS & JavaScript: The option we used earlier.
- Angular: Will use AngularJS only.

- Angular ADAL: Will use AngularJS together with ADAL.JS for Angular.

- Manifest.xml only (no application source files): Will just create the manifest file. Everything else will be in your charge.

Select the first option for the sake of comparing the Yeoman result with what you can get by using the project templates of Visual Studio 2015.

Because we chose to create a Mail Add-in, you have to select what kind of extension points you want to support with the target add-in. The available options are:

- Message read

- Message compose

- Appointment attendee

- Appointment organizer

- Custom pane (for message read and appointment attendee forms)

You can make multiple selections based on the real needs of your target add-in solution. After you select an option, the Yeoman generator will start creating the project files for you. It will take a while (about one or two minutes), depending on the network bandwidth you have, to download the packages and create the full project files. The Yeoman generator will download a bunch of packages and template files from the network to create a project on your environment. In Figure 11-10, you can see the UI of the Yeoman generator within Cmder while creating an Outlook Add-in.

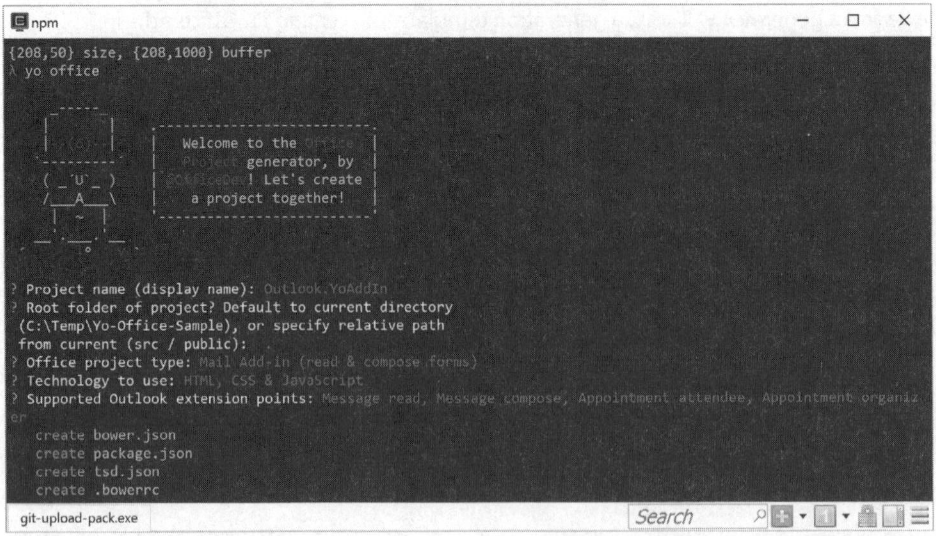

FIGURE 11-10 The Yeoman generator in action within Cmder while creating an Outlook Add-in

Once the Yeoman generator has created the source files, you can start Visual Studio Code against the current project folder by executing the following command:

```
Code .
```

The above command will start Visual Studio Code, directly targeting the current folder, which is the folder of the just-created add-in. In Figure 11-11, you can see the UI of Visual Studio Code, editing an Outlook Add-in project created by using the Yeoman generator.

FIGURE 11-11 A sample Outlook Add-in project created by using the Yeoman generator and edited in Visual Studio Code

The Solution Explorer on the left side of Figure 11-11 shows the outline of the Outlook Add-in project. As you can see, there is the XML manifest file on the root of the project. Under the appread and appcompose folders, there are the HTML, CSS, and JS files that implement the UI of the add-in for both the Message Read and Message Compose use cases. You can change the JavaScript code, like you did in Visual Studio 2015, in this project according to your business needs.

Once you are ready with your code implementation, you can start the project using, for example, Node.js as the target hosting environment. If you installed your development machine properly, as illustrated in Chapter 2, you can just run the following command from the Cmder console:

```
gulp serve-static
```

The *gulp* command will start an HTTPS server listening on *https://localhost:8443/*, and your add-in will be ready to be consumed by Outlook. Start Outlook Web Access, click the Gear icon in the upper-right corner, and select the Mail settings. In the General section, select the Manage Add-ins option, and from there click the + button and the Add From A File option, as you can see in Figure 11-12.

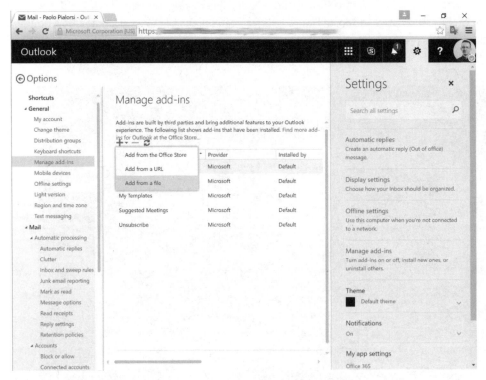

FIGURE 11-12 The Manage Add-ins page of the Outlook Web Access settings

Browse for the XML manifest file of the Outlook Add-in that you want to add and follow the instructions, and your Yeoman-generated add-in will be available in Outlook Web Access for testing purposes.

Once you are ready to release the add-in, you will have to publish it on a public hosting infrastructure, and you will have to update the manifest file to target the public URL of the hosting platform.

Office JavaScript APIs

Aside from the development framework and tools you use, whenever you create an Office Add-in you will leverage the Office JavaScript APIs to interact with the Office client hosting platform.

The Office JavaScript APIs are provided as a library of JavaScript files, which include the main *Office.js* file and some host application–specific .js files (like *Outlook-15.js*, *Excel-15.js*, and so on). These APIs provide a bunch of useful objects and primitives to interact with the hosting platform and to get access to the current context and to the current document, if any.

First, you have to reference the global APIs from a public CDN, like the following:

https://appsforoffice.microsoft.com/lib/1/hosted/Office.js

Furthermore, you always have to implement the *Office.initialize* method, which you saw in the previous section. The *Office.initialize* method represents an initialization event that gets fired when the APIs are fully loaded and the add-in is ready to begin its job.

As you saw in Listing 11-3, the initialization event can rely on third-party JavaScript frameworks like jQuery. In Listing 11-4, you can see a prototype of this kind of method.

LISTING 11-4 Code prototype of the *Office.initialize* event handler for an Office Add-in

```
// The Office initialize function must be run each time a new page is loaded.
Office.initialize = function (reason) {
  $(document).ready(function () {

    // Here goes any code to execute at the very beginning of the Add-in logic flow

  });
};
```

Every page of your add-ins has to provide an implementation of a handler for the *Office.initialize* event because the Office Add-in infrastructure will use it as the entry point for the logic of the add-in.

The most common thing to do within the initialization of an add-in is to get a reference to the current context, which is provided through the *Office.context* object. Through the context object, you can have access to the entire execution context of the add-in. For example, as in Listing 11-3, the property *Office.context.mailbox.item* gives you access to the mailbox item currently selected by the user, if any. Through the *context* object, you can access not only the current *mailbox*, but also the current *document*—if any—in Excel, Word, or PowerPoint.

Moreover, the *context* object provides the entry points for general settings like the *contentLanguage*, the *displayLanguage*, and many other useful pieces of information about the current execution context of the add-in.

To play with the *context* object and figure out what is available through it, you can put a *debugger* statement at the beginning of the *Office.initialize* event handler implementation and inspect the content of the *Office.context* object, or even of the entire *Office* namespace, by using the JavaScript debugger. In Figure 11-13, you can see a hierarchical diagram of the main objects and properties of the *Office* namespace.

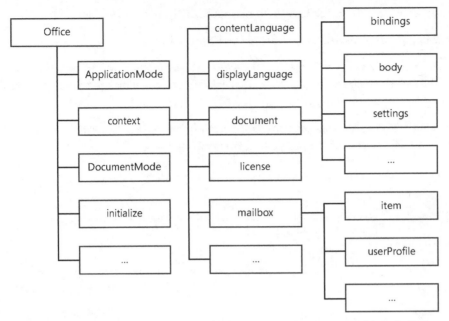

FIGURE 11-13 A hierarchical diagram of the main objects and properties available in the *Office* namespace

In addition to the main *Office.js* file, there are host application–specific .js files that provide functionalities and capabilities related to a specific host. For example, if you are creating an Excel Add-in and you want to access the collection of workbooks, worksheets, cells, and rows of the current sheet, you will need to reference the *Excel-15.js* file, which usually is included in the Scripts/Office folder of the web application that you create for the add-in in Visual Studio 2015.

It is out of the scope of this book to dig into every object or property of the Office JavaScript APIs. Nevertheless, it is important to understand that there is a JavaScript library to interact with the Office client hosting platforms, which is fundamental for creating any Office Add-in.

Creating Content and Task Pane Add-ins

So far, you have seen how to create an Outlook Add-in. However, often you will also need to extend some other client tools like Word, Excel, PowerPoint, or Project. The add-in models available for these kinds of Office client hosts are Content and Task Pane Add-ins. In this section, you will understand the differences of such Office client hosts compared with the Outlook scenario while developing add-ins.

 Note If you would like to see some examples of Office Add-ins, you can refer to the following open source solutions available in the OfficeDev repository on GitHub: 1) the main Office Add-ins repository of PnP: *https://github.com/OfficeDev/PnP-OfficeAddins*; 2) a Word Add-in sample with several real-life examples about how to use Office JavaScript API: *https://github.com/OfficeDev/Word-Add-in-DocumentAssembly*; 3) a sample Excel Add-in to see how to visualize custom content in the document: *https://github.com/OfficeDev/Excel-Add-in-VisualizeExcelData*; 4) a sample PowerPoint Add-in to insert a chart into a presentation: *https://github.com/OfficeDev/PowerPoint-Add-in-Microsoft-Graph-ASPNET-InsertChart*; and 5) a sample solution about how to use the new commands in the UI of Office: *https://github.com/OfficeDev/Office-Add-in-Commands-Samples*.

From an architectural perspective, most of what you learned in the previous sections about Outlook Add-ins is valid for any other kind of add-in. However, depending on the target Office client host, the steps to create an add-in could vary.

For example, if you create a Task Pane Add-in for Word, Excel, PowerPoint, or Project by using Visual Studio, you will have a slightly different manifest file and consequently a different manifest designer. The key difference in the manifest designer, compared with an Outlook Add-in, is that you will not have the Read Form and Compose Form activation rules. Rather, in a Task Pane Add-in you will have a unique Activation tab through which you can specify the activation requirements for the add-in. If the target Office client host does not satisfy the requirements, the add-in will not show up.

These requirements are in terms of API Set minimal required version and explicit application target. You can create a Task Pane Add-in that targets multiple Office client host types at the same time, like a Task Pane that can be used in both Excel and Word, for example.

In Figure 11-14, you can see the Activation tab of the manifest designer for a Task Pane Add-in.

When you define the requirements, Visual Studio will match the supported API Sets against an Office API NuGet package and will determine the versions of Office client hosts that will be able to run the add-in.

The General tab of the manifest designer is also slightly different in a Task Pane Add-in. The permissions that you can declare are:

- Restricted
- Read document
- Read all document
- Write document
- Read write document

Note You can find further details about the available permissions in the document "Permission element," which is available at the following URL: *https://dev.office.com/reference/Add-ins/manifest/permissions*. You can also read the document "Privacy and security for Office Add-ins," which is available at the following URL: *http://dev.office.com/docs/Add-ins/develop/privacy-and-security*.

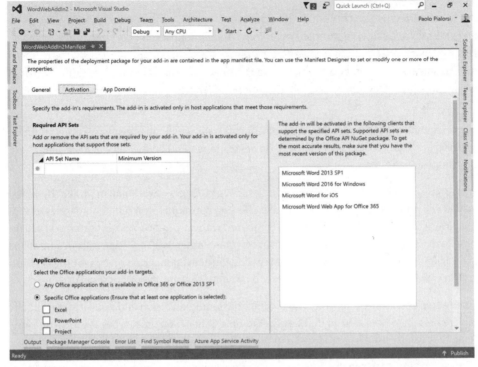

FIGURE 11-14 The Activation tab in the manifest designer of Visual Studio 2015 for a Task Pane Add-in

Moreover, if you create an add-in for Excel by using Visual Studio 2015, there will be a wizard-like tool that will help you define the goal of your add-in. First, the wizard will ask you if you want to Add New Functionalities To Excel, which means adding new commands to the UI of Excel, or if you want to Insert Content Into Excel Spreadsheets, which means creating a Content Add-in that will insert embeddable objects into Excel spreadsheets. In Figure 11-15, you can see the two steps of the wizard. In the top part of the screen, there is the first step; in the bottom part of the screen, there is the second step, which is shown just for Content Add-ins.

From an implementation perspective, all the add-ins will implement the *Office.initialize* event handler and will work with the current document through the *Office.context.document* object that you encountered in the section "Office JavaScript APIs" earlier in this chapter.

FIGURE 11-15 The wizard for creating an Excel Add-in in Visual Studio 2015

In Listing 11-5, you can see an excerpt of the JavaScript code under the cover of a Word Add-in that inserts some content into the current document, which is the default template created by Visual Studio 2015 when you create a new Word Add-in.

LISTING 11-5 Code excerpt of a Word Add-in that inserts some content into the current document

```
// Run a batch operation against the Word object model.
Word.run(function (context) {

    // Create a proxy object for the document body.
    var body = context.document.body;

    // Queue a command to clear the contents of the body.
    body.clear();

    // Queue a command to insert text into the end of the Word document body.
    body.insertText("This is a sample text inserted in the document",
                    Word.InsertLocation.end);

    // Synchronize the document state by executing the queued commands,
```

```
      // and return a promise to indicate task completion.
      return context.sync();
})
.catch(errorHandler);
```

As you can see, the core of the code excerpt is the *Word.run* method invocation, which provides to the Word engine an anonymous function to execute. That function will get a reference to the current context through which the add-in can access the current document. Moreover, the Word JavaScript object model allows you to insert some text in the current document by using the *insertText* method, to get the current user's selection by invoking the *getSelection* method of the *document* object, and so on.

Almost the same approach applies to an Excel Add-in. For example, in Listing 11-6 you can see a code excerpt of an Excel Add-in.

LISTING 11-6 Code excerpt of an Excel Add-in that inserts some random values into a set of cells in the current worksheet

```
var values = [
                [Math.floor(Math.random() * 1000),
                  Math.floor(Math.random() * 1000),
                  Math.floor(Math.random() * 1000)],
                [Math.floor(Math.random() * 1000),
                  Math.floor(Math.random() * 1000),
                  Math.floor(Math.random() * 1000)],
                [Math.floor(Math.random() * 1000),
                  Math.floor(Math.random() * 1000),
                  Math.floor(Math.random() * 1000)]
            ];

// Run a batch operation against the Excel object model
Excel.run(function (ctx) {

    // Create a proxy object for the active sheet
    var sheet = ctx.workbook.worksheets.getActiveWorksheet();

    // Queue a command to write the sample data to the worksheet
    sheet.getRange("B3:D5").values = values;

    // Run the queued-up commands, and return a promise to indicate task completion
    return ctx.sync();
})
.catch(errorHandler);
```

By using the *Excel.run method*, the sample provides to the *Excel* object model a bunch of actions to perform through an anonymous function. Basically, the code selects the current active worksheet and inserts an array of random values into a range of cells.

In such add-ins, you most likely will leverage the Microsoft Graph API and the SharePoint Online sites to load data or look up data related to the current Word or Excel document. To do that, you can use the techniques and tools you saw in the previous pages applied to an Outlook Add-in and based on ADAL.JS and a bunch of REST requests via AJAX.

Summary

In this chapter, you had an overview of the architecture of the Office Add-ins in general, which are based on an HTML, CSS, and JavaScript solution plus an XML manifest file. Moreover, you saw the most common tools to create Office Add-ins and manage their manifest files.

In particular, you learned how to create an Outlook Add-in that can consume the Microsoft Graph API via REST in a secure way by leveraging the ADAL.JS library. Last, you saw a few key differences—compared with Outlook Add-ins—and the challenges of developing Content and Task Pane Add-ins for Word, Excel, PowerPoint, and Project.

## CHAPTER 12

Publishing your applications and add-ins

Once you have created an Office Add-in, a SharePoint Add-in, or a Microsoft Office 365 web application, you most likely will need to make it available to your target users. In this chapter, you will learn how to publish your solution either on a private Corporate Catalog or in the public Office Store.

Options for publishing add-ins and web applications

In this section, you will learn about the options for publishing an application and making it available to the users of your Microsoft Office 365 tenant.

Although the options illustrated in this section target only Office 365 scenarios, you should be aware that the SharePoint Add-ins, Office Add-ins, and Office 365 web applications that you create can also be consumed in on-premises scenarios. In fact, you could have an Office 365 hybrid topology, where you share some services and custom applications across your on-premises infrastructure and the tenant in Office 365. You could also develop a custom solution that targets on-premises only. The development model for Office Add-ins and SharePoint Add-ins is the same for both on-premises and the cloud, aside from the authentication model. In Office 365, you rely on Microsoft Azure Active Directory (Azure AD) and Microsoft Azure Access Control Services (ACS); by default, on-premises you rely on Windows Active Directory. The only exceptions are the Office 365 applications, which by definition are required to be registered on Azure AD and therefore cannot be used in an on-premises only environment. Last but not least, remember that even if you have an on-premises SharePoint environment, you can register Azure ACS as a trusted authority and use the same authentication model that you have in SharePoint Online. This last approach is useful when you are in a hybrid topology.

Private corporate publishing

The first option you have is to publish your custom applications using a Corporate Catalog in SharePoint Online or using Exchange Online if your application is an Outlook Add-in.

This is the most common scenario: you have a custom, tailor-made solution that targets your environment or your company only. If the target is your tenant only, you wouldn't publish such a solution on the public Office Store. In this scenario, the most interesting option is to leverage the Corporate

Catalog site collection of SharePoint Online because out of the box you will have all the capabilities of the store, even if users will not pay for installing your add-ins.

To publish such a solution, you first need to have a Corporate Catalog site in SharePoint Online. As a developer, you shouldn't have to create a Corporate Catalog by yourself, at least not in your production environment. However, you may need to create one in your development environment. If you don't have a Corporate Catalog, open the browser and access the SharePoint Admin Center. Select the Apps menu item on the left, and on the right side of the page, choose the option to access the app catalog. From the app catalog site page, you will be able to create a new app catalog site or provide the URL of an existing site, if any. To create a new app catalog, click the OK button on the lower-right side of the page. You will be prompted with a form to provide some information about the app catalog that will be created. This information includes the site title, the relative URL, the default language, the time zone, the primary site collection administrator, and the server quota resources. After providing this information, click the OK button to create the app catalog. Wait for a while, and your Corporate Catalog will be ready. Keep in mind that the Corporate Catalog in Office 365 is unique for the tenant, so all the add-ins you will publish there will be visible to all of your site collections.

Once you have a Corporate Catalog, browse to its URL. If you have proper permissions, you will be able to add a new Office Add-in by uploading its XML manifest file into the Apps for Office library or a new SharePoint Add-in by uploading the .APP file into the Apps for SharePoint library. For every add-in, you will be able to provide information like the title, the icon, the version, the supported languages, some screenshots, and so on.

> **Note** By default, the app catalog can be read by any member of the group Everyone Except External Users. Moreover, the site collection administrator designated when the site is created will have full control of the site contents. Of course, you can add more users with specific permissions for publishing Office Add-ins or SharePoint Add-ins.

If you are publishing an Office Add-in, you will have to register the app catalog in the Office client applications through the Trust Center of the applications. You can find detailed instructions about how to accomplish this task in the document "Publish task pane and content add-ins to an add-in catalog on SharePoint," which is available at the following URL: *http://dev.office.com/docs/add-ins/publish/publish-task-pane-and-content-add-ins-to-an-add-in-catalog*. If you like, you can also configure the app catalog URLs of the Trust Center in Office client by using a Group Policy in Windows Active Directory.

After you have published an add-in in the Corporate Catalog, you and your tenant users will be able to use it. If you published a SharePoint Add-in, browse to the Site Contents page of the site where you want to install the add-in and select Add An App, choose the add-ins coming From Your Organization, and you will find the SharePoint Add-ins that you published in the app catalog. If you published an Office Add-in, open the target Office client application and select Insert A New Item From The Store. Choose the My Organization tab and search for your tailor-made add-ins.

If you want to update your add-in, you will need to upload an updated version of the file into the target library, increasing the version number, and everything else will be managed by the infrastructure of the add-in.

Office Store

Another option you have is to publish your add-ins or applications to the public marketplace, making them available to everyone through the Office Store.

Before being listed in the Office Store, your add-ins or applications will have to adhere to some strict validation rules.

See Also   *For details about the rules to which your add-ins and applications must adhere, you can read the document "Validation policies for apps and add-ins submitted to the Office Store," which is in version 1.9 at the time of this writing. It is available at the following URL on MSDN: https://msdn.microsoft.com/en-us/library /office/jj220035.aspx.*

To publish a solution on the Office Store, you will have to create an account on the Microsoft Seller Dashboard. More details about this procedure are provided in the following section, "Using the Seller Dashboard."

After you have submitted your solution to the Seller Dashboard and it has been validated and approved by Microsoft, your users will be able to find and install (and possibly buy) your add-ins or applications directly from the Office Store. We say "possibly buy" because you can provide solutions for free and still list them in the public marketplace.

File share publishing

Last but not least, you can publish an Office Add-in through a network file share. This option is not suitable for publishing SharePoint Add-ins or Office 365 applications.

If you want, you can copy the XML manifest file of an Office Add-in into a network share and install it directly from there. You will have to configure the network share as a corporate app catalog in the Trust Center of Office client. You can find detailed instructions about how to accomplish this task in the document "Create a network shared folder catalog for task pane and content add-ins," which is available at the following URL: *http://dev.office.com/docs/add-ins/publish/create-a-network-shared -folder-catalog-for-task-pane-and-content-add-ins*.

This a useful scenario when you want to test your add-ins during the development process without publishing the add-ins in any catalog. It can also be useful in the case of a released add-in that you want to consume with only a small number of Windows desktop clients. For example, if you have a small company, you could avoid creating a Corporate Catalog or registering your add-ins in the Office Store by installing them through a network share.

Using the Seller Dashboard

The most interesting scenario is publishing an add-in or an Office 365 application by using the Office Store. Although the process is straightforward, it's worth the time to explain it in detail, as you will see in this section.

First of all, to publish any kind of solution, you will need a Microsoft account to access the Seller Dashboard, which is available at the following URL: *http://go.microsoft.com/fwlink/?LinkId=248605* (or *https://sellerdashboard.microsoft.com/*). Moreover, you will have to register a Microsoft developer account in the Microsoft DevCenter, if you don't have one yet. You can find further information about how to create a Microsoft developer account at the following URL: *https://developer.microsoft.com /en-us/windows/programs/join*.

Before submitting a solution for approval in the Seller Dashboard, you should double-check the list of requirements Microsoft has defined and made available in the document "Checklist for submitting Office and SharePoint Add-ins and Office 365 web apps to the Seller Dashboard," which is available at the following URL: *https://msdn.microsoft.com/en-us/library/office/dn356576.aspx*.

In Figure 12-1, you can see the home page of the Seller Dashboard, from which every submission process starts.

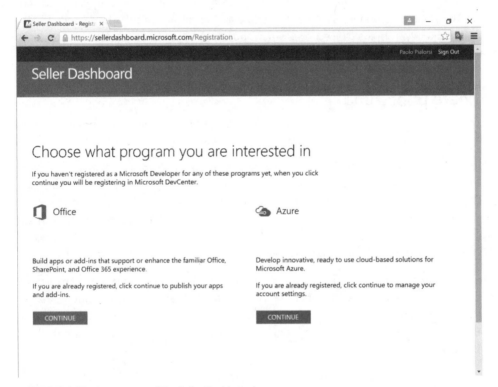

FIGURE 12-1 The home page of the Seller Dashboard

The process can vary, depending on the kind of solution you are going to publish. However, the beginning of the publishing flow is the same, regardless of what kind of application you are going to publish.

Starting from the page illustrated in Figure 12-1, you need to select the red Continue button under the Office column, and you will be prompted with a list of solutions that you have already published in the Office Store or that are in the process of being published. You can click one of the existing apps to update it or complete any draft registration.

To register a new application, select the Add A New App button. You will be prompted with a wizard that will ask you what kind of app you are going to publish. The wizard step will be titled Listing Type, and the available choices, at the time of this writing, are:

- **Office Add-in**   This option allows you to publish an Office Add-in like a Task Pane Add-in or a Content add-in for Word, PowerPoint, or Excel.

- **Outlook Add-in**   This option allows you to publish an Outlook Add-in like a mail app.

- **SharePoint Add-in**   This option allows you to publish a SharePoint Add-in, whether it is a SharePoint-hosted or a provider-hosted solution.

- **Web App Using Azure AD**   This option allows you to publish an Office 365 application registered in Azure AD, as discussed in Chapter 10, "Creating Office 365 applications."

The following paragraphs detail all the provided options.

Publishing Office Add-ins

If you are publishing an Office Add-in, you have to choose one of the first two options in the Listing Type wizard step.

Let's choose the Office Add-in type. The following steps will allow you to provide much more detailed information about the add-in. In the first wizard step, called Overview, you will have to provide the package of the add-in, which will be the XML manifest file, together with some general information about the add-in such as the following:

- **Submission Title**   This is the title of the add-in as it will be shown in the Office Store.

- **Version**   This is the release version of the add-in. It is automatically populated from the manifest file. This field becomes useful when you need to release updates of a published add-in.

- **Release Date (UTC)**   This defines the release date of the add-in in the Office Store. Even if Microsoft approves your add-in before that release date, the add-in will only be available in the Office Store starting from that date. If you are publishing an updated version of the add-in, the currently released version of the add-in will not be available in the Office Store until the new version is approved and released. Of course, customers who already installed your current version of the add-in will be able to continue using it.

- **Category**   You have to provide at least one category for your add-in, and you can provide up to three categories. Those categories will help customers find your add-in while searching the Office Store.

- **Testing Notes**   This is a text field for internal use only between you and the team that will test the add-in before releasing it to the Office Store. Here you can put notes, comments, hyperlinks to resources, or hints that will help the testers do proper testing of your add-in. This information will not be published in the Office Store and will be used only by the testing team.

- You will also have the capability to declare that your app makes calls, supports, contains, or uses cryptography or encryption.

- You must choose if you will make your add-in available in the catalog for iPad. This will imply further testing and compliancy requirements. If you choose to make it available, you will also have to provide your Apple developer ID in the registration form.

- **Logo**   This is the logo that will be used for your add-in in the Office Store. It can be a PNG, JPG, JPEG, or GIF with a size of exactly 96 × 96 pixels and a file size not greater than 250 KB.

- **Support Document Link**   This is the full URL of a document that provides instructions to users who have issues with your add-in.

- **Privacy Document Link**   This is the full URL of a document that provides privacy information to users of your add-in.

- **Video Link**   This is an optional field that can contain the full URL of a video file about your add-in.

- **End User License Agreement**   Through this field, you can provide an optional end user license agreement (EULA). It can be a file in any of the following formats: DOC, DOCX, RTF, TXT, or PDF. If you do not provide an EULA, a default one will be provided on your behalf.

Publishing an Outlook Add-in instead of an Office Add-in will prompt you for the same set of fields.

In the second wizard step, called Details, you can provide additional information about the languages supported by the add-in and all the text messages and images specific to a particular language. The following is a list of fields and settings that you have to provide in this second wizard step:

- **Language**   Allows you to select the current language for which you are providing the detailed settings. By default, every add-in has at least the English language, but there could be many additional languages.

- **App Name**   This is the name of the add-in in the selected language.

- **Short Description**   Defines a short description for your add-in in the currently selected language.

- **Long Description**   Provides a long description for the add-in in the current language.

- **Screenshots**   Allows you to provide up to five sample screenshots of the add-in. At least one screenshot is mandatory; the remaining four are optional.

To add any new language aside from the English language, click the Add A Language button, which is available in the lower side of this wizard step. A pop-up screen allows you to select as many languages as you need. In Figure 12-2, you can see the list of supported languages at the time of this writing.

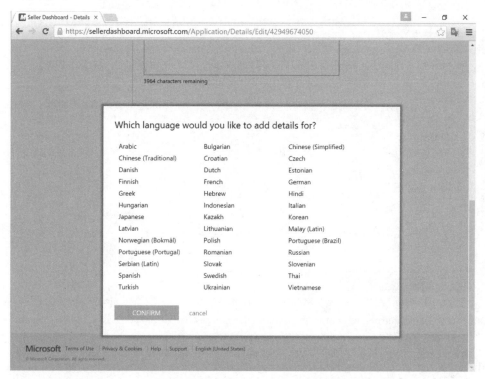

FIGURE 12-2 The screen to add languages to an add-in within the Seller Dashboard

The third wizard step is called Block Access, which allows you to block customers in certain countries or regions from purchasing or even using the add-in. As you can see in Figure 12-3, the list of countries and regions is long and detailed.

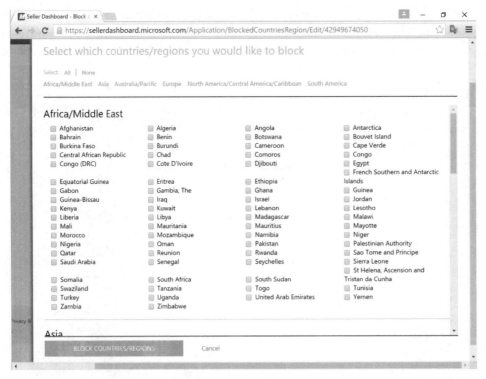

FIGURE 12-3 A list of some of the countries and regions that you can block from purchasing or using the add-in within the Seller Dashboard

The last wizard step is Pricing, which allows you to define the pricing model for your add-in. You have three options from which to choose:

- **This App Is Free** The app is available for free, indeed.

- **This App Is For One-Time Purchase** Customers pay for the app only once.

- **This App Will Be Sold As A Subscription** You want to sell the app according to the Software as a Service (SaaS) model.

If you want to provide the app for free, later you will be able to change the pricing model and convert the app to SaaS or to a one-time purchase mode. If you are not providing the app for free, you will have to choose a pricing model. If you select to sell the add-in using a one-time purchase model, you will later be able to convert the app to the free model, but you cannot convert it to a subscription model. If you select to sell the add-in with a subscription model, you cannot change it to free or one-time purchase model after it has been published.

The price, if any, has to be declared on a per-user basis, through the Price Per User field, and you cannot define whatever price you like. There is a long list of available prices ranging from $1.49 to $999.99, and the available prices are predefined. You can also select a Price Threshold field, which enables you to declare a maximum number of per-user licenses for which you want a single customer to pay. After that number, any further per-user license will have no additional charge. You can select No Threshold or any of the predefined values like 1, 10, 25, ..., up to 1,000.

Here are some example scenarios:

- If you select a per-user price of $9.99 and a price threshold of 10, your customers will pay $9.99 for each user up to 10 users. Starting from the eleventh user, they will not pay any more.

- If you select a per-user price of $9.99 and no price threshold, your customers will pay $9.99 for every user.

- If you select a per-user price of $9.99 and a price threshold of 1, your customers will pay $9.99 just once, and the result will be like a per-site license.

> **Note** To sell an app, you will also have to configure a valid tax account in the Seller Dashboard. Otherwise, you will not be able to publish the add-in in the Office Store because you wouldn't be able to get your money back from Microsoft.

You can also enable trial support for your add-in by enabling the option with label My App Supports A Trial. If you enable a trial, you have to specify the Duration Of Trial, which can assume any of the following values: 15 days, 30 days, 60 days, or Unlimited. One more setting related to the trial of your app is the Number Of Users In Trial option, which can assume any of the following values: 1 user, 5 user(s), 20 user(s), or Unlimited.

Once you have configured all of the settings for the add-in, you can save it as a draft for further editing by clicking the SAVE AS DRAFT button, or you can submit it for publishing by clicking the SUBMIT FOR APPROVAL button.

After submitting an add-in, your solution will go through the validation process and eventually be approved and published in the Office Store, based on the publishing date that you provided.

Publishing SharePoint Add-ins

The process of publishing a SharePoint Add-in is similar to the process of publishing an Office Add-in. However, there are some differences within the fields and settings that you have to provide.

In the Overview first step of the publishing wizard, you will have to provide a package for a SharePoint Add-in, which has an extension of .APP and which is the only supported one at the time of this writing. Moreover, you will have to provide the version number manually instead of having it automatically populated from the XML manifest file, like with the Office Add-ins.

Furthermore, if your add-in needs to act as a service, using server-to-server communication, you will have to declare this need by flagging the field called My App Is A Service And Requires Server To Server Authorization. This option will require you to link the current add-in with a ClientID that you can create using the Seller Dashboard by applying the following procedure.

First of all, to create a new Client ID, you have to select the Client IDs tab in the Seller Dashboard and click the Add A New OAuth Client ID button. You will be prompted with a two-step wizard, as illustrated in Figure 12-4. The first step will ask you to provide details about the app for which you want to register the Client ID.

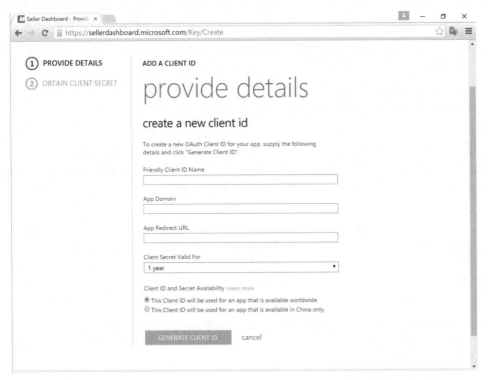

FIGURE 12-4 The UI for creating a new Client ID and Client Secret in the Seller Dashboard

You will have to provide the following information:

- **Friendly Client ID Name**   This is a name to help you recognize the app later.

- **App Domain**   Defines the domain on which your app will run. It has to be a valid domain name, without the http:// or https:// trailer.

- **App Redirect URL**   Declares the URL to which end users will be redirected after accepting the authorization requirements for your app. It has to be a valid URL, including the trailer http:// or https:// protocol.

- **Client Secret Valid For**   Allows you to define how long the Client Secret for the app will last. It can be 1 year, 2 years, or 3 years.

- **Client ID and Secret Availability**   You can choose if you want to make the app available worldwide or in the China market only.

Once you have configured the required fields, click the GENERATE CLIENT ID button and you will be prompted with step two of the wizard, which is called Obtain Client Secret. There, you will find a recap of the previously filled fields and the autogenerated Client Secret. Copy them in a safe place because you will not be able to access the Client Secret after you close the current page.

The page will also provide you the start and end date of validity for the Client Secret, and you should keep track of them to refresh the Client Secret before its expiration.

Once you have created the Client ID and the Client Secret, you can select the Client ID in the SharePoint Add-in registration process, as we saw in previous paragraphs.

Publishing Office 365 web applications

An Office 365 application is slightly different from an Office Add-in or a SharePoint Add-in. As you already saw, to register such an application you will have to select the Web App Using Azure AD option at the beginning of the publishing wizard. Moreover, you will be prompted with requests for some information specific to Azure AD.

You will still have the general information like the title, the release date, the categories, the logo, and so on. However, the version number is a free text field in which you can write the version number instead of a calculated field that is generated from the manifest file of the add-in.

Furthermore, to register an Office 365 application you have to provide some information specific to Azure AD through a section called App Registration, in which you will find the following fields:

- **Azure App ID**   This is the GUID representing the Client ID of the application, which you registered in Azure AD following the procedure illustrated in Chapter 4, "Azure Active Directory and security."

- **Azure Active Directory Instance**   This allows you to choose if the application has been registered in Azure Active Directory Global, which is the more common case, or in Azure Active Directory China, if you are targeting the Chinese market. There are two more options related to Microsoft Account and Microsoft Account + Azure Active Directory Global. However, they are not yet available at the time of this writing.

All of the other steps of the registration procedure are similar to the registration process for an Office Add-in or a SharePoint Add-in. You will go through the Overview, the Details, the Block Access, and the Pricing wizard steps, like you did for Office Add-ins.

Updating or deleting add-ins or Office 365 web applications

Whenever you want to update your published applications, you can just come back to the Seller Dashboard. Select the red Continue button under the Office area of the home page, and you will see the list of published add-ins or Office 365 web applications. Select an item to open a page with all the related details.

Within that page, you can click the Edit Listing button, or you can click the Edit Draft button if your solution has not yet been submitted for approval and thus is not yet published. You will be able to update both the properties and the whole .APP package or the XML manifest file. You cannot update an add-in or application that is pending approval.

Keep in mind that once you update a SharePoint Add-in package or a manifest file, you will have to go through the validation process to see the refreshed solution available in the Office Store. In contrast, from an Office 365 web application perspective, often you will need to update the web application in the hosting environment and will not need to update anything else in the Seller Dashboard.

If you want to update the version number or the pricing model according to the rules and restrictions that you have seen or want to update any other property or image for the Office 365 web application, you will have to go to the Seller Dashboard. Nevertheless, as long as you need to update the UI or the business logic of the Office 365 web application, you are not required to update the Seller Dashboard.

If you want to delete an add-in or an Office 365 web application, you can follow the same procedure that you use for editing it, but you will have to click the Delete button within the Details page.

You can also remove an add-in or an application from the Office Store without deleting it permanently. You just need to click the Unpublish button, which is available only for published solutions. It will take a few days to unpublish the solutions from the Office Store listings.

Licensing model

In the previous section, you saw that whenever you sell add-ins or applications through the Office Store you can choose a pricing model, which is related to a specific licensing model.

You saw that you can provide your solution for free, but you can also sell it by using a per-seat or per-site model or by using a subscription model. Aside from the marketing and sales perspectives, which are out of the scope of this book, it is important to understand how you can programmatically manage and monitor that your customers use your solutions according to the pricing and licensing model that you choose. You will need to verify and enforce that everybody uses your solutions according to the legal use policies that you defined.

In the following paragraphs, you will dig into the techniques for managing and checking licenses from a developer perspective.

Types of licenses

First of all, it's worth explaining in detail the types of licenses available through the Office Store, based on the flavors of solutions that you can publish.

In Table 12-1, you can see a matrix that explains what models are available for what kind of solutions.

TABLE 12-1 Licensing models comparison for the available add-in flavors

Licensing Model	Office Add-in (Task Pane and Content)	Outlook Add-in	SharePoint Add-in
Free	Per-User only	Per-User or Per-Site	Per-User or Per-Site
Paid	Per-User only	Per-User or Per-Site	Per-User or Per-Site
Subscription	Per-User only	Per-User or Per-Site	Per-User or Per-Site

As you can see, Office Add-ins (Task Pane or Content) are available only on a per-user basis, while Outlook Add-ins and SharePoint Add-ins can be purchased on a per-user or a per-site basis. Note that an Outlook Add-in can be purchased on a per-site basis only by an administrator, thereby making it available to all the users of the organization.

All the paid or subscription options can have a trial period, if you want.

Whenever a customer acquires an add-in, whether it is for free, paid, or with a subscription, the Office Store will require the customer to log in with a valid Microsoft account and will generate a license file on the fly, downloading a license token to the purchaser's environment.

For an Office Add-in (Task Pane or Content), the license token will be stored in the user's Office client application. For an Outlook Add-in, the license token will be downloaded and stored in the user's mailbox for a per-user scope or in a system mailbox at the tenant level for a per-site scope. For a SharePoint Add-in, the license token is downloaded and stored in the SharePoint tenant or farm deployment, depending on whether the SharePoint environment is in Office 365 or on-premises.

Furthermore, in the case of SharePoint Add-ins, only site, tenant, or farm administrators can install an add-in. Thus, only those kinds of users can purchase an app, and they can assign the purchased licenses to target users for whom they purchased the licenses.

Whatever your scenario, a license token has an expiration and must be renewed periodically. The only exceptions are the add-ins with a perpetual license type, which have a token that does not expire. The license token expiration model also supports the trial period for add-ins.

When a user launches an Office Add-in (Task Pane or Content), the Office client application checks the license token and renews it if necessary and possible. If the license token is expired and the license model is a trial, the user will not be able to launch the add-in unless she converts the trial into a paid license.

When a user launches Outlook and logs in, the Exchange server infrastructure will check for the license token validity of any Outlook Add-in and will renew it if necessary and possible.

For SharePoint Add-ins, the license token is verified and renewed by the SharePoint App Management services by using a specific timer job. It is also possible to renew license tokens manually, if needed.

Checking license in code

To ensure that only authorized users use your solutions, you will have to enforce license checks within your solutions. License checks require checking a license token file and consuming a service provided by the Office Store. In the following paragraphs, you will learn how to accomplish this task.

License XML schema

First, it is important to understand that an Office Store license token is an XML file that adheres to a specific schema. In Listing 12-1, you can see a sample outline of a license file, with the possible values for the attributes represented.

LISTING 12-1 Sample outline of the XML license file for an Office Add-in

```
<r>
  <t
    aid="{2[A-Z] 8-12[0-9]}"
    pid="{GUID}" | "string"
    cid="{16[0-H]}"
    oid="{GUID}"
    did="{GUID}"
    ts="Integer"
    et="Free" |"Trial" | "Paid"
    sl="true | 1" | "false| 0"
    ad="UTC"
    ed="UTC"
    sd="UTC"
    te="UTC"
    test="true | 1" | "false | 0"
    ss="0" | "1" | "2" | "3" | "4" />
  <d>VNNAnf36IrkyUVZlihQJNdUUZl/YFEfJOeldWBtd3IM=</d>
</r>
```

As you can see, the schema is minimal and provides information about the license type, the pricing model, and so on. In Table 12-2, you can see the list of attributes with their meanings.

TABLE 12-2 Attributes for an Office Store license token XML file

Element/Attribute	Description
r	It is the root element of the license file.
t	It is the token element, and it contains all of the main attributes for the license token.
t/@aid	It is the asset ID assigned by the Office Store to the add-in. It is required.
t/@pid	It is the product ID of the add-in, represented as a GUID, and it is defined in the manifest file of the add-in. It is required.
t/@cid	Represents the purchaser ID when the purchaser is logged in with a Microsoft account. The value is encrypted, and it is optional. If a purchaser is using an organizational account instead of a Microsoft account, this attribute will be empty. See also t/@oid.

Element/Attribute	Description
t/@oid	Represents the purchaser ID when the purchaser is logged in with an organizational account. The value is encrypted, and it is optional. If a purchaser is using a Microsoft account instead of an organizational account, this attribute will be empty. See also t/@cid.
t/@did	For Outlook Add-ins, it represents the deployment ID, as a GUID value, of the target Exchange deployment. For SharePoint Add-ins, it represents the deployment ID, as a GUID value, of the target tenant or farm. For Office Add-ins, it is empty.
t/@ts	It is an integer number that defines the total number of user licenses for a per-user scoped license. If the license is scoped per-site, this attribute will assume a value of 0. It does not apply for Office Add-ins.
t/@et	Defines the type of add-in license. Can assume the values: Free, Trial, or Paid. It is required.
t/@sl	It is a Boolean attribute that defines whether the add-in is scoped per-site or not. It applies only to Outlook Add-ins and SharePoint Add-ins that are scoped per-site, in which case it assumes value True. Otherwise it assumes the value False.
t/@ad	Declares the acquisition date, in UTC format, for the add-in. It is required.
t/@ed	Declares the expiration date, in UTC format, for the add-in license. It is optional and can be used to check for expiration of a trial license.
t/@sd	It is a date time, represented in UTC format, and it represents the initial purchase of the license or the latest manual recovery time, if the purchaser has performed a recovery using his Microsoft account. It is required.
t/@te	Declares the expiration date, in UTC format, for the current license token. It is required.
t/@test	It is a Boolean attribute that defines if the add-in license is in test mode. Add-in licenses in test mode will not be checked by the Office Store license verification service against the expiration or the entitlement. It is optional.

t/@ss	It is an Integer attribute that represents the subscription status, and it can assume any of the following values:
	    - 0 : Not applicable. The add-in license is not for a subscription add-in.
	    - 1 : Active. The add-in license subscription is currently paid for.
	    - 2 : FailedPayment. The automatic monthly payment for a subscription license failed.
	    - 3 : Canceled. The add-in license subscription has been cancelled, and the final monthly billing for which the purchaser paid has expired.
	    - 4 : DelayedCancel. The add-in license subscription has been cancelled, but the subscription is still active because it is within the current monthly billing for which the purchaser paid.
	It is optional, and it applies only to subscription licenses.

d	It is an element that contains the encryption token used by the Office Store license verification service to determine if the license is valid. It is encrypted and required.

In Listing 12-2, you can see a test XML license file for a SharePoint Add-in licensed for 10 seats with a valid subscription active for one year from the date of purchase.

LISTING 12-2 Sample test XML license token for a SharePoint Add-in

```
<r>
  <t
    aid="WA900006056"
    pid="{F49ADBD9-6D1F-4396-B52C-9289ADC6DFF8}"
    cid="32F3E7FC559F4F49"
    did="{9EB13155-D449-430B-A1BC-7DBB95573F01}"
    ts="10"
```

```
      et="Paid"
      test="true"
      ad="2016-06-02T09:15:12Z"
      ed="2017-06-02T09:15:12Z"
      sd="2016-06-02T09:15:12Z"
      te="2016-07-02T09:15:12Z"
      ss="1" />
  <d>VNNAnf36IrkyUVZlihQJNdUUZl/YFEfJOeldWBtd3IM=</d>
</r>
```

In the code sample of Listing 12-2, the encrypted token is fake, but it is a test license token, so the encryption token will not be verified by the license server.

License check in Office Add-ins

Whenever a user launches an Office Add-in from an Office client application, the home page of the add-in will be loaded through an HTTP request, which will receive in the query string an argument called *et* that represents the license token to check.

The *et* argument contains the license token formatted as a base-64 string that has been URL-encoded. Thus, to retrieve the real value of the license token you will have to decode it using the base-64 algorithm and then URL-decode the resulting value. As result, you will have an XML license token according to the schema described in the previous paragraphs.

If your add-in is an Outlook Add-in, the *et* query string argument will be URL-encoded only, and you will have to skip the base-64 decoding phase.

If the user is consuming your add-in anonymously, the *et* token will not be provided to the home page of the add-in, so your add-in will have to be ready for this situation if it allows anonymous access. In general, you should always check for the existence of the *et* query string argument before using it, and you should provide a specific user experience in case the argument is missing.

In Listing 12-3, you can see a code excerpt about how to decode the *et* argument to retrieve its XML value.

LISTING 12-3 Code excerpt to decode the *et* query string parameter of an XML license token

```
String etValue = Request.Params["et"].ToString();

Byte[] decodedBytes = Convert.FromBase64String(etValue);
String decodedToken = Encoding.Unicode.GetString(decodedBytes);
```

Be careful; you should never touch or change anything in the resulting decoded token because the encryption token included in the XML license token is valid only if the XML content has not been tampered with. Thus, you should store the *decodedToken* value without changing or directly processing its content.

To validate the XML license token value, the Office Add-in will have to consume the Office Store license verification service, which is available at the following URL: *https://verificationservice.officeapps. live.com/ova/verificationagent.svc.*

The service is available as a SOAP service and through a REST endpoint. By invoking the above URL, you will get back the WSDL (Web Services Description Language) of the SOAP service. For example, you can add a service reference to your .NET web application that provides the Office Add-in implementation, and you can consume the license verification service with a code syntax like the one illustrated in Listing 12-4.

LISTING 12-4 Code excerpt validating an XML license token through the Office Store license verification service

```
VerificationServiceClient svc = new VerificationServiceClient();

var result = svc.VerifyEntitlementToken(
    new VerifyEntitlementTokenRequest() { EntitlementToken = decodedToken });

if (!result.IsValid) {
    // Handle any license issue here
}
```

As you can see, there is a *VerifyEntitlementToken* operation, which is the only one provided by the service, and which verifies the XML license token. The operation returns an object of type *VerifyEntitlementTokenResponse*, which provides information about the verified license. The most important property of the response object is the *IsValid* Boolean property. If the *IsValid* property has a value of *true*, the license is valid; otherwise, it is not.

Another interesting property of the response object is the *IsTest* Boolean property, which enables you to check if the current license is for testing purposes only. In general, there are a lot of useful properties that you can use—for example, to enable specific features if the license is a paid one. In Table 12-3, you can see the full list of properties of the *VerifyEntitlementTokenResponse* type.

TABLE 12-3 Properties of the *VerifyEntitlementTokenResponse* type.

Property	Description
AssetId	It is the String value of the ID assigned by the Office Store to the add-in or application.
DeploymentId	Represents the deployment ID, of type GUID, for an Outlook Add-in or a SharePoint Add-in.
EntitlementAcquisitionDate	It is a DateTime value that defines when the license has been acquired.
EntitlementExpiryDate	It is a DateTime value that defines when the license expires.
EntitlementType	Represents the type of entitlement. It is a String value and can assume one of the following values: Free, Paid, Trial.
IsEntitlementExpired	It is a Boolean property that declares if the app license is expired.
IsExpired	It is a Boolean property that declares if the license token is expired.
IsSiteLicense	It is a Boolean property that declares if the license is a site license.

Property	Description
IsTest	It is a Boolean property that declares if the license is for testing purposes only.
IsValid	It is a Boolean property that declares if the license is valid.
ProductId	Represents the product ID, of type GUID, for the add-in or application.
Seats	It is an unsigned Integer that defines the total number of seats allowed by the license.
SignInDate	It is a DateTime value that defines the initial purchase of the add-in or application, or the last time a manual license recovery happened.
SubscriptionState	It is a String property that defines any of the possible values for a subscription. The supported values are: NotApplicable, Active, FailedPayment, Canceled, DelayCancel.
TokenExpiryDate	It is a DateTime value that defines when the license token expires and needs to be refreshed.
UserId	It is the String value of the purchaser ID. It is an encrypted value of the Microsoft account, if any, of the user who purchased the add-in or application.

You can play with these properties in your code and implement complex behaviors based on the license status. In Listing 12-5, you can see a full sample about how to handle the main statuses of a license.

LISTING 12-5 Full code sample about how to handle the license verification response

```
if (result == null ||
    result.ProductId != TARGET_PRODUCTID ||
    !result.IsValid) {
    // The license is not valid => redirect user to an "UNLICENSED" message/UI
}
else if (result.IsValid) {
    switch (result.EntitlementType) {
        case "Free":
            // The license is valid and Free => enable Free features
            break;
        case "Paid":
            // The license is valid and Paid => enable Paid features
            break;
        case "Trial":
            // The license is valid but Trial => check Trial period
            if (result.EntitlementExpiryDate < DateTime.Now || result.IsExpired) {
                // The Trial period is expired => redirect user to
                // a "TRIAL EXPIRED" message/UI
            }
            else {
                // The Trial period is valid => enable Trial features, only
            }
            break;
    }
}
#if DEBUG
else if (result.IsTest) {
    // The license is for testing purposes only => behave accordingly
}
```

```
#endif
else {
    // The license is not valid => redirect user to an "UNLICENSED" message/UI
}
```

Notice the check against the test license, which is wrapped in the conditional compilation for a *DEBUG* compilation. Thus, if there is a released version of your code, you will reject any testing license.

As explained earlier, the license verification service is also available as a REST endpoint, which can be invoked through an HTTP GET request against the following URL: *https://verificationservice.officeapps .live.com/ova/verificationagent.svc/rest/verify?token={decodedToken}*

In the previous URL, the token query string argument represents the XML license token encoded by using, for example, the *Uri.EscapeDataString* method of .NET or the *encodeURIComponent()* method of JavaScript.

> **Note** If you are developing an Office Add-in by using Microsoft Visual Studio, you can add an XML license token file to the OfficeAppManifests subfolder of the *bin\debug* or *bin \release* of the project to have a behavior close to the one you have when executing the add-in from the Office client environment through the Office Store. The license token file name has to be the same as the manifest file, but with a .tok file extension.

License check in SharePoint Add-ins

Much of the information shared in the previous section about how to check licenses in an Office Add-in also applies to validating a SharePoint Add-in license. However, in a SharePoint Add-in, the license is not provided through a query string parameter, and you have to query for any available license by using the client-side object model (CSOM).

In Listing 12-6, you can see a code excerpt about how to retrieve licenses for a currently running SharePoint Add-in. The code excerpt also leverages the OfficeDev PnP Core Library extensions that you saw in Chapter 2, "Overview of Office 365 development," to improve the overall availability of the code.

LISTING 12-6 Code excerpt to retrieve an XML license token for a SharePoint Add-in

```
VerifyEntitlementTokenResponse result = null;
VerificationServiceClient svc = new VerificationServiceClient();

AuthenticationManager authManager = new AuthenticationManager();

using (ClientContext context = authManager
    .GetSharePointOnlineAuthenticatedContextTenant(
        targetSiteUrl, userName, password)) {

    var licenses = Utility.GetAppLicenseInformation(context, TARGET_PRODUCT_ID);
```

```
    context.ExecuteQueryRetry();

    foreach (AppLicense license in licenses.Value) {
        var xmlToken = license.RawXMLLicenseToken;

        result = svc.VerifyEntitlementToken(
            new VerifyEntitlementTokenRequest() { EntitlementToken = xmlToken });

        if (result == null ||
            result.ProductId != TARGET_PRODUCTID ||
            !result.IsValid) {
            // The license is not valid => redirect user to an "UNLICENSED" message/UI
        }
        else if (result.IsValid) {
            switch (result.EntitlementType) {
                case "Free":
                    // The license is valid and Free => enable Free features
                    break;
                case "Paid":
                    // The license is valid and Paid => enable Paid features
                    break;
                case "Trial":
                    // The license is valid but Trial => check Trial period
                    if (result.EntitlementExpiryDate < DateTime.Now || result.IsExpired) {
                        // The Trial period is expired => redirect user
                        // to a "TRIAL EXPIRED" message/UI
                    }
                    else {
                        // The Trial period is valid => enable Trial features, only
                    }
                    break;
            }
        }
#if DEBUG
        else if (result.IsTest) {
            // The license is for testing purposes only => behave accordingly
        }
#endif
        else {
            // The license is not valid => redirect user to an "UNLICENSED" message/UI
        }
    }
}
```

The *GetAppLicenseInformation* method of the *Utility* class, which is defined in the *Microsoft.
SharePoint.Client.Utilities* namespace of CSOM, allows you to retrieve all the currently active licenses for
the current user and the current SharePoint Add-in. The result is a collection of licenses that usually is
made of a single item but could be a collection of items. Thus, you should walk through all of them to
seek any useful information. For example, you may have to merge the information of multiple licenses
to determine the real licensed features for the current user related to the current product. The XML
license token is inside the property *RawXMLLicenseToken* of each item of the collection, which is of type
AppLicense.

In the code sample illustrated in Listing 12-6, we iterate through all of the licenses and validate each of them. In a real solution, you probably should do something more sophisticated.

Aside from that, the verification process is almost the same as for an Office Add-in license. The Office Store license verification service does the license verification process, and the response is exactly the one you saw in the previous paragraphs.

For testing purposes, you can load up to 10 test licenses into your environment by using the *ImportAppLicense* method of the *Utility* class.

See Also *You can find further details about the ImportAppLicense method in the document "Utility. ImportAppLicense method," which is available at the following URL: https://msdn.microsoft.com/en-us/library /office/microsoft.sharepoint.client.utilities.utility.importapplicense.aspx.*

Best practices for handling licenses in code

In the previous paragraphs, you learned how to handle licenses and how to check XML license tokens in code. However, it is better to understand when and how to apply license checks than to continuously execute verifications for every request.

Invoking the Office Store license verification service introduces latency in your application logic, and you should avoid checking a license upon every request. It is better to verify the license once, when the user launches your application, and cache the response you get back from the service into a state variable that you can query later if necessary.

For example, you could store the needed information—like the license expiration (if any), the entitlement type, and so on—within a persistent state variable and query that state variable whenever you need to enable a feature or capability that requires a proper license to work.

The state persistence layer can be a trivial session object if few users use the application and you don't need to provide high availability for your solution. However, if you need to run the application on multiple servers or service instances, whether for high availability purposes or for scalability goals, you should rely on a scalable service like the Azure Redis Cache. You can also consider using a session provider that relies on the Azure Redis Cache to keep the implementation simple but still highly available and scalable.

> **Note** You can find further details about Azure Redis Cache by reading the document available at the following URL: *https://azure.microsoft.com/en-us/services/cache/.*

Moreover, you need to consider that the license checks can be done on the server side only. Thus, you cannot plan to perform license checks for an Office Add-in within the JavaScript client code that runs inside the Office client application.

If your application is a SharePoint Add-in, you can run the license checks in the main controller of the ASP.NET web application if the add-in is provider hosted and runs in ASP.NET MVC. Moreover, if the SharePoint Add-in is a SharePoint-hosted add-in, you should rely on an external server to perform the license checks. Any client-side JavaScript license check code could be tampered with by a malicious user.

For example, in the main page of the add-in or in any of the app parts, you can embed an image that loads from an external service and that checks the license on the server side. In case of any failed license validation, you can show an alert image instead of the logo of your add-in. Moreover, you can consider providing a custom REST API that you invoke from the SharePoint-hosted add-in instead of using an embedded image, but you need to be careful because a JavaScript request against a REST service can be tampered with.

It is all about how critical it is to protect your SharePoint Add-in. In general, if you want to protect your solution with a strong licensing model, having a provider-hosted solution instead of a SharePoint-hosted one is the better option. A provider-hosted solution is also better from an architectural and scalability perspective. Thus, any real enterprise-level solution should be implemented as a provider-hosted add-in, not only for license checks but also from an architectural perspective.

Metrics and company profile

Another interesting option you have once you have published an add-in or a web application is to monitor the results in terms of sales and usage of your solution.

Metrics

Within the Seller Dashboard, you can click the Metrics tab after selecting the red Continue button under the Office area, and you will be able to monitor some useful numbers about your solutions. First of all, you have to select a published add-in or application for which you want to see the metrics.

The metrics available through the Seller Dashboard are related to the latest four weeks and include the following insights:

- **Browser hits**   The number of times your solution has been viewed in the Office Store
- **Downloads**   The number of times your solution has been downloaded from the Office Store
- **Trial downloads**   The number of times your solution has been purchased for free from the Office Store
- **Trial conversions**   The number of times a trial has been converted into a paid version of your solution
- **Purchased seats**   The overall number of seats that have been purchased for your solution
- **Purchased site licenses**   The overall number of site licenses that have been purchased for your solution

For SharePoint Add-ins only, you will also have the following metrics related to the time frame of analysis:

- **Installs**   The overall number of install attempts

- **Launches**   The overall number of times the solution has been started

- **Daily unique users**   The sum of daily unique users for your solution

- **Uninstalls**   The overall number of uninstall attempts

- **Failed installs**   The overall number of failed installs, including any retries

- **Runtime errors**   The overall number of errors logged by SharePoint and by the solution within its custom code

- **Failed upgrades**   The overall number of failed upgrades, including any retries

You can also see reports in terms of sales by following the link named View Sales And Tax Data, which will open a specific sales report.

Office Profile

Another set of information that you can manage during the lifetime of your projects is the Office Profile, which can be managed by clicking the Office Profile tab.

Through that page, you will have the capability to update the following data about your company:

- **Logo of the company**   The logo that will be shown in the Office Store for your company

- **Description**   The description of your business, useful in the Office Store

- **Website**   The URL of the website for your business

- **Marketing Contact Email**   The email address of a marketing contact in your company, if any

- **Address**   The physical postal address of your company

- **Phone Number**   The phone number of your company

The Seller Dashboard will use all of these fields to build you company profile in the Office Store.

Summary

In this final chapter, you learned how to publish your SharePoint Add-ins, Office Add-ins, and Office 365 web applications, whether you want to target the Corporate Catalog or the public Office Store. You saw that all of these solutions share the same publishing tool, which is called the Seller Dashboard, if you want to sell them worldwide.

You learned how to create, submit for approval, and publish a new solution and how to update or delete a published one. Furthermore, you saw how to monitor your metrics and sales.

Moreover, you understood the pricing models available through the Office Store and how you can control licenses and subscriptions within your custom developed solutions, working with license files and the Office Store license verification service.

You are now ready to create your real business solutions and eventually to sell them in the Office Store or publish them in the Corporate Catalog. Have fun!

Index

A

Accept HTTP header, used with REST requests, 243–244
access tokens
  accessing resources or services, 121
  accessing SPO, 255
  app-only, 291–292
  Azure AD, 116–118
  claims presented in JWT-formatted OAuth token, 118–120
  consuming Graph API, 334
  consuming SPO, 296–297
  options for getting, 211
  properties, 117
  refreshing, 121
  retrieving from ADAL cache, 134–135
activation rules
  activating Outlook add-ins using Read Form rules, 331–333
  Outlook add-ins, 326
Active Directory Authentication Library. see ADAL (Active Directory Authentication Library)
Active Directory Authentication Library for JavaScript (ADAL.JS). see ADAL.JS (Active Directory Authentication Library for JavaScript)
Active Directory Federation Services (ADFS), 95, 97
AD (Active Directory), Azure. see Azure AD (Azure Active Directory)
ADAL (Active Directory Authentication Library)
  in ASP.NET MVC web application, 123
  authenticating graph client, 212
  installing for .NET, 131–132
  leveraging, 127
  overview of, 123
  retrieving access tokens, 134–135, 211
  supporting multitenancy, 125–127
  supporting single tenancy, 123–125

ADAL.JS (Active Directory Authentication Library for JavaScript)
  consuming Graph API, 336–338
  getting access tokens for consuming Graph API, 334
  referencing in Outlook add-in, 335–336
AddAsync method, adding resources to Graph SDK collections, 221
add-ins
  activating in Outlook, 331–333
  App Domain settings for Outlook add-in, 334–335
  consuming Graph API, 336–338
  creating content and task pane add-ins, 344–346
  creating Excel add-ins, 347–349
  creating Outlook add-ins, 324–325, 328–330
  creating using Visual Studio 2015 templates, 32
  creating with Yeoman generator, 339–342
  interacting by email to quote request, 330
  manifest file, 323–324
  manifest file for Outlook add-in, 325–327
  Office JavaScript APIs and, 342–344
  overview of, 321–322
  publishing by private corporations, 351–353
  publishing Office add-ins, 355–359
  publishing using file shares, 353
  publishing using Office Store, 353
  publishing using Seller Dashboard, 354–355
  referencing ADAL.JS in Outlook add-in, 335–336
  remote client development and, 47–49
  searching for, 15
  SharePoint Add-ins, 43–44
  summary, 349
  tools for creating, 322–323
  types of Office add-ins, 339
  updating or deleting, 361–362
  viewing Outlook add-ins, 338
ADFS (Active Directory Federation Services), 95, 97

B

H

About the Author

PAOLO PIALORSI is a consultant, trainer, conference speaker, and author who specializes in developing Microsoft Office 365 and Microsoft SharePoint–based enterprise solutions. Paolo works in a company of his own (*www.piasys.com*) and has a great deal of experience on Office 365 and SharePoint, and he is a Microsoft Certified Solutions Master – Charter SharePoint, as well as a Microsoft Office Servers and Services MVP.

He is also a regular speaker at international IT conferences. He has spoken at Microsoft TechEd Europe, the European SharePoint Conference, the SharePoint Conference in the United States, and many other IT conferences worldwide.

Paolo is the author of many Microsoft Press books about .NET, Windows 8, SharePoint, and Office 365. His latest books include *Programming Microsoft Office 365*, *Microsoft SharePoint 2013 Developer Reference*, *Build Windows 8 Apps with Microsoft Visual C# and Visual Basic Step by Step*, and *Programming Microsoft LINQ in Microsoft .NET 4.0*. He has also written some Italian-language books about .NET, XML, and Web Services.

In 2014, he was Co-Programme Chair of the European SharePoint Conference. Since January 2015, Paolo has been a proud member of the Office 365 Developers Patterns & Practices Core Team (*http://aka.ms/OfficeDevPnP*).

Now that you've read the book...

Tell us what you think!

Was it useful?
Did it teach you what you wanted to learn?
Was there room for improvement?

Let us know at http://aka.ms/tellpress

Your feedback goes directly to the staff at Microsoft Press,
and we read every one of your responses. Thanks in advance!

 Microsoft